Research Series on the Chinese Dream and China's Development Path

Drawing on a large body of empirical studies done over the last two decades, this Series provides its readers with in-depth analyses of the past and present and forecasts for the future course of China's development. It contains the latest research results made by members of the Chinese Academy of Social Sciences. This series is an invaluable companion to every researcher who is trying to gain a deeper understanding of the development model, path and experience unique to China. Thanks to the adoption of Socialism with Chinese characteristics, and the implementation of comprehensive reform and opening-up, China has made tremendous achievements in areas such as political reform, economic development, and social construction, and is making great strides towards the realization of the Chinese dream of national rejuvenation. In addition to presenting a detailed account of many of these achievements, the authors also discuss what lessons other countries can learn from China's experience.

More information about this series at https://link.springer.com/bookseries/13571

Peilin Li · M. K. Gorshkov
Editors

The Middle Income Group in China and Russia

SSAP

Springer

Editors
Peilin Li
Chinese Academy of Social Sciences
Beijing, China

M. K. Gorshkov
The Institute of Sociology
Russian Academy of Sciences
Moscow, Russia

Published with financial support of the Innovation Program of the Chinese Academy of Social Sciences

ISSN 2363-6866 ISSN 2363-6874 (electronic)
Research Series on the Chinese Dream and China's Development Path
ISBN 978-981-16-1463-7 ISBN 978-981-16-1464-4 (eBook)
https://doi.org/10.1007/978-981-16-1464-4

Jointly published with Social Sciences Academic Press
The print edition is not for sale in China (Mainland). Customers from China (Mainland) please order the print book from: Social Sciences Academic Press.

This Springer imprint is published by the registered company Springer Nature Singapore Pte Ltd.
The registered company address is: 152 Beach Road, #21-01/04 Gateway East, Singapore 189721, Singapore

Series Preface

Since China's reform and opening began in 1978, the country has come a long way on the path of Socialism with Chinese characteristics, under the leadership of the Communist Party of China. Over 30 years of reform, efforts and sustained spectacular economic growth have turned China into the world's second-largest economy, and wrought many profound changes in the Chinese society. These historically significant developments have been garnering increasing attention from scholars, governments, and the general public alike around the world since the 1990s, when the newest wave of China studies began to gather steam. Some of the hottest topics have included the so-called "China miracle", "Chinese phenomenon", "Chinese experience", "Chinese path", and the "Chinese model". Homegrown researchers have soon followed suit. Already hugely productive, this vibrant field is putting out a large number of books each year, with Social Sciences Academic Press alone having published hundreds of titles on a wide range of subjects.

Because most of these books have been written and published in Chinese, however, readership has been limited outside China—even among many who study China—for whom English is still the lingua franca. This language barrier has been an impediment to efforts by academia, business communities, and policy-makers in other countries to form a thorough understanding of contemporary China, of what is distinct about China's past and present may mean not only for her future but also for the future of the world. The need to remove such an impediment is both real and urgent, and the *Research Series on the Chinese Dream and China's Development Path* is my answer to the call.

This series features some of the most notable achievements from the last 20 years by scholars in China in a variety of research topics related to reform and opening. They include both theoretical explorations and empirical studies, and cover economy, society, politics, law, culture, and ecology, the six areas in which reform and opening policies have had the deepest impact and farthest-reaching consequences for the country. Authors for the series have also tried to articulate their visions of the "Chinese Dream" and how the country can realize it in these fields and beyond.

All of the editors and authors for the *Research Series on the Chinese Dream and China's Development Path* are both longtime students of reform and opening and recognized authorities in their respective academic fields. Their credentials and expertise lend credibility to these books, each of which having been subject to a rigorous peer-review process for inclusion in the series. As part of the Reform and Development Program under the State Administration of Press, Publication, Radio, Film, and Television of the People's Republic of China, the series is published by Springer, a Germany-based academic publisher of international repute, and distributed overseas. I am confident that it will help fill a lacuna in studies of China in the era of reform and opening.

Shouguang Xie

The original version of this book was revised. Affiliation of some chapter authors has been updated and author name of chapter 5 has been updated. The correction to this book can be found at https://doi.org/10.1007/978-981-16-1464-4_21

Introduction: China's Path to Overcome the Double Middle-Income Traps

Abstract China is at a crucial stage of overcoming the middle-income trap, while the factors that drive economic growth have undergone significant changes, and domestic consumption plays a more important role in economic growth. Thus, it is necessary to promote mass consumption by expanding the middle-income groups. This paper proposes the proposition of "double middle-income traps", which means that in an economy the per capita output stagnates and the middle-income groups cannot be expanded for a long time. These two factors are mutually related in a very close manner. Based on data from the Chinese Social Survey (CSS)[1] conducted by the Institute of Sociology at the Chinese Academy of Social Sciences, this paper analyzes the scale and development of middle-income groups, the relationship among middle-income groups, middle class and middle-class identity. This paper also analyzes the marginal consumption propensities of middle-income groups. This paper further indicates that the expansion of middle-income groups plays an important role in promoting mass consumption, maintaining continuous and stable economic growth, and overcoming the double middle-income traps.

Keywords Double middle-income traps • Middle-income group • Mass consumption

China's development in the past several decades distinguishes itself from other major nations around the world by setting a long-term goal and making plans to be followed by generations of hard-working people. At the end of the 1970s, when China firstly embraced the Reform and Opening-up policy, it set the goal to build a moderately prosperous society. Entering the twenty-first century, China vows to achieve the goal in a comprehensive way by 2020. To build a moderately prosperous society in a comprehensive way is the dream of the Chinese people for a bright future. One of its main measures is to increase the proportion of the middle-income population,

[1] This paper uses data from Chinese Social Survey (CSS) [2006–2015], which was carried out by the Institute of Sociology, Chinese Academy of Social Sciences (CASS). With the method of multi-stage sampling, the interviewees are above 18 years old in the urban and rural area of 25–28 province/autonomous regions in China. There are a total of 41,685 samples contained in the statistics

narrow the gaps of rural-urban disparity, area differences, and income distribution among industries, and eventually form an olive-shaped distribution structure.

What is the "Double Middle-Income Trap"?

China enters now a new developmental stage when its economic development enters the state of "the new normal", and the society goes through huge transformation. Whether China is able to overcome the "middle-income trap" becomes a critical question. We can in fact add another layer of meaning to the notion of the "middle-income trap", introducing the hypothesis of the "double middle-income trap". On the one hand, it refers to a stage of generally slower growth an economy reaches after becoming a middle-income society. On the other hand, it refers to the inability of a society to curtail the widening of social inequality, or expand the size and proportion of the middle-income population, thus unable to build an olive-shaped society with a dominant middle-income social group. The two problems are intricately related, because most of the countries battling with the "middle-income trap" have to deal with problems of disparities between rich and poor, and such disparities are one of the major causes for the "middle-income trap".

In a 2007 report entitled "An East Asian Renaissance: Ideas for Economic Growth" written by Chief Adviser to the World Bank's East Asia and Pacific Affairs Bureau Indermit Gill and Chief Economist Homi Kharas, the concept of "middle-income trap" was used for the first time (Gill and Kharas, 2007). Later in 2013, the World Bank and the Development Research Center of the State Council jointly released a report entitled "China 2030: Building a Modern, Harmonious, and Creative Society", in which statistics showed that only 13 out of the 101 middle-income economies in 1960 grew into high-income economies in 2008. As many as 87% of the middle-income economies could not overcome the "middle-income trap" in the time span of almost 50 years (World Bank and the Development Research Center of the State Council 2013:13). Yet, the report makes an optimistic estimation that "even China's economic growth slows down by one-third (that is an annual growth rate of 6.6%; for the past three decades, the rate has been 9.9%), China still will make it to the club of high-income economies sometime before the year of 2030, and exceeding the USA to become the largest economy in the world despite the fact the average income per capital remains a fraction of the developed countries". This means China will overcome the "middle-income trap", and in fact transform into a high-income economy from a low-income economy within a time span of merely one and a half generation. To any country who achieves such transformation, this would be a huge achievement, not to mention for such a big country like China (World Bank and the Development Research Center of the State Council 2013:3).

"Middle-income trap" mainly refers to the following situation: in the global economic structure, only a very small minority of the middle-income countries during their transformation can catch up with and eventually join the group of high-income economies. The majority will endure a long-term economic stagnation. They can neither compete with low-income counties over labor cost nor compete with high-income countries over high-end innovation. Accumulated social and economic problems become the bottleneck for further development. They are unable to achieve real social transformation and modernization as their economy remains stalled.

Observing the actual modernization around the world, most of the countries victimized by the "middle-income trap" are from Latin America and the Middle East, such as Brazil, Mexico, and Chile, to name a few typical ones. In Asia, Malaysia can be counted as one. These countries became middle-income countries in the 1970s, similar to that of the "Four Little Dragons" in Asia. Since then, however, the development of these countries seems to have reached the glass ceiling, and they have not made it to the high-income club in the past decades. To those economies trapped in the "middle-income", the threshold of 10,000 GDP per capita seems to be a curse. Those who cross the line are forced to back off eventually.

The oppose case is the successful "East Asian Model", referring primarily to Japan and the "Four Little Dragons". It took them about 10 years to transform from middle-income countries to high-income countries. For example, Japan's GDP rose from 3,000 US dollars in 1972 to 10,000 US dollars in 1984 during a time span of 12 years. South Korea, on the other hand, saw its GDP per capita boosting in eight years from 3,000 US dollars in 1987 to 11,469 US dollars in 1995.

There are extensive literatures on the causes of the "middle-income trap" providing analysis from many perspectives. The list of causes includes deep debts, uncontrollable finance, huge inequality, serious corruption, over urbanization, public service shortage, high-level youth unemployment, social divisions, etc. Nevertheless, all research points out the problem of social inequality and the lack of a sufficiently big middle-income group. In contrast, the countries and regions of the "East Asia Model" such as Japan, South Korea, and Taiwan have relatively low-level income inequality when overcoming the "middle-income trap".

Therefore, we can add another layer of meaning to the "middle-income trap", and introduce the hypothesis of "double middle-income trap". On the one hand, it refers to a developing economy that cannot successfully enter into the high-income stage or achieve modernization because it fails to overcome the middle-income developmental stage; on the other hand, it means the country cannot curtail the widening social inequality, or build an olive-shaped society with a dominant middle-income social group, thus unable to overcome the "middle-income trap". This paper has no intention to provide an overlapping analysis of the relation between the two sides of the trap. The relationship between these two sides may be causal in some cases, or associative in others. There are exceptions, however. Singapore and Hong Kong, practicing also the "East Asia model", entered the high-income club and enjoyed a high-level of international competitiveness. Yet social inequalities in these two regions are high. The two economies nevertheless have their unique characteristics. For example, the population in the two regions both remain under 10 million. They are practically two big cities with a congregation of financial sectors, investments, ports and international headquarters, as well as a large number of international millionaires.

From an economic perspective, an economy, in particularly a relatively big economy, when transforming to a high-income developmental stage, does not depend on large-scale investments or exports. Domestic consumption provides stable support to the long-term sustainable development. Without a growing middle-income group or mass consumption, there will be no strong consumption drives. Under the condition of inequalities between the rich and poor, mass consumption will be stalled. That is, when family consumption decreases as income increases, the minority who has higher consumptive power reaches the level of saturation in terms of their consumption needs. The majority, who desires more consumption, is simply not able to afford it. The percentage of the middle-income group, who practice more flexible consumption, is too small to constitute the core consumption power, thus unable to push forward the coming of the mass consumption era.

From a social perspective, worldwide practices show that an olive-shaped society with a dominant middle-income social group ensures a long-term, stable society for the people to make a good living. Income inequalities and polarization will lead to social divisions and turbulence, thus threatening the stability and security of society and impacting negatively on economic growth.

From a cultural perspective, the middle-income group is the foundation for the formation of social core values. Only a society with a middle-income group can effectively prevent radicalization.

The economists have done many studies on promoting sustained economic growth, aiming to solve the puzzle of the "middle-income trap". In this paper, I will discuss the hypothesis of "double middle-income trap" and focus on analyzing the expansion of the middle-income group.

The Size and Developmental Trend of China's Middle-Income Group

The middle-income group often refers to the group of people who have stable jobs with medium-level income, and live a relatively affluent life. The scholarly discussion on the middle-income group has lasted for over 30 years. In general, the discussion on the middle-income group is related to issues of income and consumption, distribution, poverty, social inequality, and social structure changes. That is, the study of the middle-income group has never been a pure academic topic, but well connected with practical issues. This connection is reflected in two aspects. Firstly, it is connected with the policy-making in relevant areas. To tailor policies of social security, subsidies for low-income families, consumption incentives and employment rate boost, there needs to be definitions for the middle-income group, the low-income group, and the population in poverty. Secondly, it is connected with predicting the global consumption trends. By analyzing the changes of the middle-income groups around the world, it is possible to predict the changing status of the different countries in the global consumption market. Most research on the middle-income group is carried out by the national statistics departments, international organizations (such as the UN, World Bank, OECD), and think tanks.

Until now, unlike the notion of the "international poverty threshold", there is no consensus reached for the definition of the middle-income group. There has been, however, considerable effort carried out to define the absolute standard and the relative standards. In general, the absolute standard is used in international comparative studies and the analysis of the global developmental trend for the middle-income groups, while the relative standards are used in analysis of national income distribution structure and social policies. According to China's National Bureau of Statistics, households with dispensable income between 90,000 RMB and 450,000 RMB are defined as middle-income families, accounting for 24.3% of the total households in 2015. This is the main supporting evidence for the claim frequently appearing in news reportage that the middle-income population exceeds 300 million in China.

Among the numerous international studies on the absolute standard for the middle-income group, three of the studies are frequently referred to in research reports from international organization and research organizations. Firstly, the World Bank economists Brando Milanovic and ShlomoYitzhaki, when analyzing the global income inequalities in 2002, use the annual average income of Brazil as the lower limit, and the annual average income of Italy as the upper limit of the global middle-income group (the middle class). They use the purchasing power calculated by the World Bank in 2000 in parity conversion, and set the daily income per person of 10 US dollars to 50 US dollars (PPP$) as the measurement for the middle-income group (Milanovic and Yitzhaki 2002). The 2007 World Bank Global Development Report adopts this measurement. According to such measurement, the percentage of the middle-income group (the middle class) at a global scale maintains at the level of 8% between 1993 and 2000. Since 2000, however, the percentage increases significantly, and is predicted to reach 16% in 2030 (World Bank 2007). Secondly, Brookings Institute economist Homi Kharas in a 2010 OECD report suggests that if using the measurement of purchasing power parity, the standard for middle-income group (the middle class) should be the daily income per person of 10 US dollars to 100 US dollars (PPP$) (Kharas 2010). The upper limit of the standard is based on the income medium of Luxemburg, the most affluent country among Europe's developed countries. The lower limit of the standard is based on the average poverty threshold in Portugal and Italy, the two countries who adopt the lowest poverty threshold among Europe's developed countries. H. Kharas argues that families within such income range have the highest level of consumption flexibility. He therefore refers to them as the "consumer class". According to Kharas' measurement, the global population of the middle-income group (the middle class) is 1,800 million in 2000, among which 664 million are from Europe, 525 million are from Asia, and 338 million are from North America. China and India have the fastest growing middle-income group. Thirdly, Pew Research Center in a 2015 report uses also the measurement of purchasing power parity, and sets the standard for the middle-income group (the middle class) at a daily income per person of 10 US dollars to 20 US dollars (PPP$). Thus, the proportion of the middle-income group is 13% globally in 2011. The report shows that during the 10 years between 2001 and 2011, the proportion of the middle-income population will increase from 3–18% in China, and 1–3% in India (Pew Research Center 2015a, b).

The studies mentioned above, which provide an absolute standard for the middle-income group, share one common feature. That is, they treat the world as one unified system of income and consumption. They all take a global perspective to explore the changes in income level and the consumption market. They all believe China and India will host the fastest growing middle-income groups in the future. They all set the daily income per person of 10 US dollars (PPP$) as the lower limit to the middle-income group. In most of these studies carried out by economists, the notions of the middle-income group and the middle class share the same meaning. The notion of the middle class, widely known by the public, is more frequently used in these studies. Such measurement bears its strengths. It is easier to be operationalized, and can better reflect the growth of the middle-income group within developing countries. It, however, has some obvious downsides. Firstly, it is applicable to studies of the conditions and changes of the middle-income group in developing economies. In developed countries, however, people who fit the descriptions of the middle-income groups measured by such standards probably fall into the low-income groups, or even populations in poverty. Secondly, using the absolute standard to measure, the middle-income group cannot fully reflect the changes of the income distribution within a country or region. Under the condition of increased average income, even if the degree of inequality remains the same, or intensified, the size and proportion of the middle-income group will increase nevertheless.

Due to the disadvantages of using the absolute standard to measure the middle-income group, the international academia starts to discuss the relative standards for measuring the middle-income group. One simple method is to use the poverty threshold as the baseline, and define the group of people whose income lies between 1.3 times and 3 times of the poverty threshold as the middle-income group. This method is often used to implement policies of social welfare, but the problem is each country, administrative district, or even family type, is measured by different poverty thresholds. Thus, the standards for the middle-income group will be very much fragmented. For example, according to the poverty threshold in 48 neighboring states of the USA, the poverty threshold for one-person households is 11, 490 US dollars, while the threshold for three-person households is 19, 530 US dollars.

The relative standard of the middle-income group widely used by academics is based on the baseline of median or average income distribution, setting the lower and upper limit to a point ranging between 50–75% and 150–250%. M. C. Wolfson, S. P. Jenkins, and Ph. Van Kerm systematically analyze various measures of income inequality and suggest to define the population (family) whose income lies in the range within 75–150% or 60–225% of the median value as "middle-income group" (Wolfson 1994; Jenkins and Van Kerm 2009). Birdsall et al. (2000), economists of the Brookings Institution, propose in a widely received article that the standard of middle class should be set around 50–125% of the median value. The Pew Research Center in the USA issues an annual report on the middle class. The 2015 report sets the standard of US middle-income group in the range of 67–200% of the median value. In another study, Pressman (2015) uses the well-known Luxemburg income survey database, and analyzes the change in the proportion of the middle class in nine developed countries (the USA, Canada, Britain, France, Germany, Italy, Finland, Sweden, and Norway) since the 1970s, defining people's income ranging from 67 to 200% of the median level as the middle class. The study finds that after the global financial crisis in 2008, the proportions of the middle-income group have fallen in almost all developed countries. The results of the study have been used by some media to prove that the rise of populism, exclusivism, and anti-globalization in the general elections in the developed countries is caused by the split and anger of the middle class.

Some Chinese scholars adopt similar standards to analyze middle-income group, but the results often show that the proportion of the middle-income group decreases, instead of increases, when the income gap is widening. Li and Zhang (2008) define the middle-income group as the group of people whose household per capita income is above the average line and below 2.5 times of the average line. The 2006 Chinese Social Survey (CSS) shows that this group accounts for 13% of the total population. By Long Ying's standards (Long 2015), people whose income lies in the range of 75–125% of the median value belongs to the middle-income group. Using the 1988–2010 Chinese Health and Nutrition Survey (CHNS) data, he finds that the proportion of middle-income group decreases from 27.9% in 1988 to 21.1% in 2010. Using income Quantitle tantile value instead of median value, Li and Zhu (2015) argue that the income standard of the middle-income group falls in the middle of the range eliminating the 25% of the lowest and the 5% of the highest. They find that the proportion of the middle-income group is 27%, 28%, 24%, and 25% in 2006, 2008, 2011, and 2013, respectively.

Recently, the Institute of Sociology, Chinese Academy of Social Science (CASS) and the Institute of Sociology, Russian Academy of Sciences is conducting a comparative project on the middle-income group.[2] The study is co-chaired by M. K. Gorshkov, Director of the Sociology Institute from Russia and the author himself. After repeated examination, calculation, and consultation from scholars of both countries, we give up the easy measurement of absolute standard, and adopt the relative standard to measure the position of the income group. People with income below 75% of the median value belong to the low-income group (they can be further divided into the fragile group and the extremely poor group); people with income 76–200% of the median value belong to middle-income group (they can be further divided into the upper-middle and lower-middle- income group); people with income above 201% belong to the high-income group (they can be further divided into rich or extremely rich group). From the comparative view of China and Russia, the percentage of the low-income group in the two countries is more or less the same, but the percentage of people in extreme poverty is more than 10% higher in China than in Russia. Moreover, the percentage of the middle-income group in Russia is 18% higher than

[2] This comparative project on the middle-income group is co-conducted by the Institute of Sociology, Chinese Academy of Social Science (CASS) and the Institute of Sociology, Russian Academy of Sciences. The book named< Middle income Group in China and Russia> will be published soon.

Table 1 Proportion of different income groups in China and Russia

Income group		Income standard (median value percent)	Russia (2015) percent	China (2015) percent
Low-income group	Extremely poor group	25% of median and below	1.43	12.57
	Vulnerable group	26–75% of median	32.53	26.88
Middle-income group	Lower-middle-income group	76–125% of median	34.55	20.22
	Upper-middle-income group	126–200% of median	21.93	18.05
High-income group	Rich group	201–400% of median	8.49	16.37
	Very rich group	401% of median and above	1.08	5.91

Source Russia's data comes from the 3rd National monitoring social survey "Social Transformation Dynamics of Contemporary Russia: Social Economics, Politics, Social Culture and Ethic Religion as Background", finished in Oct. 2015. China's data comes from the Chinese Social Survey (CSS) conducted by the Institute of Sociology, Chinese Academy of Social Sciences

Table 2 Interactive analysis of the middle-income group and the middle class (2015) percent

	Low-income group	Lower-middle-income group	Upper-middle-income group	High-income group
Middle class	9.61	21.59	31.94	47.66
Lower-middle class	90.39	78.41	68.06	52.34
Total	100.00	100.00	100.00	100.00

Source 2015 Chinese Social Survey (CSS)
Notes In this table, the same index as Table 1 is used to define middle-income group. The middle class is defined as the population of non-manual workers, and the lower-middle class is defined as the population of manual workers

China, but the high-income group is 13% lower than China (see Table 1.That is to say, compared with China, the income structure in Russia is more olive-shaped. Russia's Gini coefficient experiences almost the same change with China, which rapidly expanded from 0.289 in 1992 to 0.420 in 2012, and dropped to 0.412 in 2015. Meanwhile, China's Gini coefficient was 0.462 in 2015. (Table 2)

Based on different standards, including both the absolute (adopted by the World Bank and National Bureau of Statistics) and relative standards, we measure the changing proportion of China's middle-income group. Results show that, during the 26 years from 1989 to 2015, calculated by the World Bank standard of income per person per day of $10–$100 (PPP$), the proportion of China's middle-income

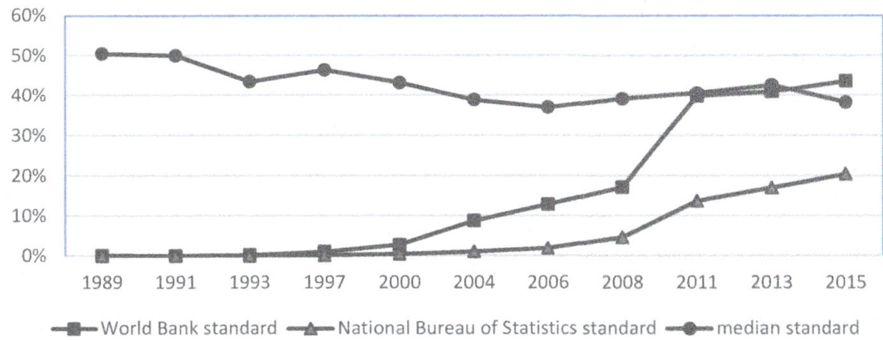

Fig. 1 Trend of China's middle-income group in proportion (1989–2015). *Source* Chinese social survey (CSS) (2006–2015) and Chinese health and nutrition survey (CHNS) (1989–2004)
Notes The standard of World Bank denotes that calculated by purchasing power parity (PPP), the group of people whose per capita income ranges from \$10 to \$100 should be classified as the middle-income group. According to calculations of GDP by ICP (International Comparison Program) in 2011, one US dollar (PPP\$) equals 3.5 RMB. Given the 365 days of a year, the household income per capital that ranges between 12,797 and 127,969 yuan is deemed as the standard of middle-income group. The standard of National Bureau of Statistics refers middle-income group as people with household disposable income of 90,000 to 450,000 yuan. The standard of the median value classifies people whose household income per capital ranges from 75 to 200% of the median value as middle-income group.

group has increased from 0% to 44%; By the standard of China's National Bureau of Statistics, calculating the annual household disposable income ranging from 90,000 RMB to 450,000 RMB as the middle-income group, its proportion has risen from 0% to 20%; If we define the middle-income group as 70–200% of the median value, the proportion of the group lingers around 37–50%, with very slight changes, and almost in line with the trend of income gap. That is, from 1989 to 2006, the proportion of middle-income group has decreased, but starts to increase since 2008, with only a few exceptions (see Fig. 1).

All in all, based on the analysis of the changing trend of the middle-income group, we can conclude that if we use the absolute standard to define the middle-income group, as a country or a nation's economy develops and the income per capita improves, the proportion and size of the middle-income group will increase continuously, just as the population in poverty will continue to decrease, if measured by a fixed standard. However, if the middle-income group is defined in relative standards, as long as the income structure is stable, the middle-income group will also be stable.

The Relation Between the Middle-Income Group, Middle Class, and Middle-Class Identity

Compared with the middle-income group, the definition of the middle class is more diverse within the field of sociology. Criteria such as income, property, occupation, education, power, social status, and even taste in consumption have been used to define and analyze the middle class. The consensus is, however, that the core index of middle class is their occupation, which is quite different from the middle-income group. Among the 400 occupations in the hierarchical scale, the ones in the middle are the middle class. Or in a simpler way, except the categories of farmers, blue-collar workers, the unemployed and the magnates, others are classified as the middle class, with the small and medium business owners being the old middle class and the white-collar class being the new middle class. Others use the three indicators of income, occupation, and education to define the middle class. That is, taking certain income range into consideration, along with a minimum of post-secondary education and while-collar occupations, the middle class is thus determined. Given different weights of the three indicators, it can be further classified into the core, semi-periphery and periphery middle class.

Among China's occupational middle class in 2015, 85% belong to the middle-income or higher-income groups. In the middle-income group (including the lower-middle-income group and higher-income group), there are about 26.47% people who belong to occupational middle class (Among the urban middle-income groups, 35.32% belong to the occupational middle class). Whichever standard is used to define the middle class, the group very much overlaps with middle-income group in analysis of relativity. In 2015, 85% people from middle class belong to the middle-income or upper-middle-income group. However, in the middle-income group (including the lower-middle-income group and higher-income group), 26.47% people belong to the middle class (the percentage is 35.32% in cities). Although "all professions produce masters", as a Chinese saying goes, the reality is that some occupations with higher technological or educational requirements would bring higher income. The rules of human capital are universal. Occupations with better prospects have an obvious competitive edge in income. This is why the expansion of the middle-income group is always accompanied by the upgrading of industrial structure.

In the international comparative studies of the middle-income group, what makes China a unique case is that the self-identification of people with middle social-economic status is generally low. In the social investigation of other big countries, be it developed or developing, usually 60% of the people think their economic and social status lie in the middle level of the society. However, this identification seems to have no logical relation with a country's income distribution. In another word, with stable institutional conditions of a country, most people will identify themselves as belonging to the middle range of the society, even in a county with large income gap. China seems to be the exception of this general rule. According to the comprehensive survey conducted by the Institute of Sociology of CASS, only 37.38% of the Chinese people identify themselves as being the middle group of the society. The percentage

Table 3 Socio-economic identity of various income groups (2015) percent

To which level do you identity your social-economic status?	Low-income group	Lower-middle-income group	Upper-middle-income group	High-income group
Upper level	0.16	0.10	0.29	0.56
Upper-middle level	2.21	3.50	3.57	7.87
Middle level	**29.71**	**35.99**	**40.46**	**49.16**
Lower-middle level	29.23	32.39	34.01	29.14
Lower level	38.69	28.02	21.67	13.27
Total	100.00	100.00	100.00	100.00

Source Using the 2015 Chinese Social Survey, this form shows the self-rated social-economic status of various income groups. If we combine the lower- and upper-middle-income group, 38.1% middle-income group think they belong to the middle group

for upper-middle (3.95%) and upper level (0.27%) is 4.22%, but percentage for lower-middle (30.54%) and lower (27.87%) level is 58.41%. The uniqueness of China's case may be due to three reasons. First, China's society is developing fast in the recent decades, and the social-economic status of its members change dramatically. Deviations between economic status and social status thus emerge. People with high social status may have relatively low economic status. Second, the conspicuous consumption of rich people is over-exaggerated by the media, which easily make people have a high expectation of the life of the middle class. Third, the traditional Chinese culture may explain why some people deliberately hide their wealth. We can see from Table 3 that within the lower-middle-income group, only 35.99% of the people regard themselves as being at the middle level, and 60.41% as belonging to the lower-middle or the lower level. Within the upper-middle-income group, 40.46% of people identify with the middle group and 55.68% with the lower-middle or lower group. Even in the high-income group, only 49.16% identify themselves as being in the middle group and 42.41% as in the lower-middle and lower group. Of course, the proportion of people who identify with the middle group increases from the low-income group to high-income group. However, this does not mean the groups with higher income have higher class identification. The CSS shows that under some special circumstances, class identification is influenced by the directional change of the personal interest curve. For example, migrant workers have low income but relative high class identification. But employees from poorly operated state-owned enterprises tend to have low class identification. Therefore, to maintain social harmony and stability, it's important to pay special attention to the social feelings and emotions of people whose personal interest curve is declining. This downwardly biased social identification would also have immense impact on consumer attitude and behavior.

Marginal Propensity of Consumption (MPC) Among China's Middle-Income Group

According to Keynes's psychological law of consumption, income increases consumption increases but not by as much as the increase in income. In other words, marginal propensity to consume (MPC) is less than one. The fraction of income spent on consumption by the rich families is lower than that of the poor families. In other words, the rich families have a lower MPC as compared to the poor families. If the gap between the rich and the poor is too big, the newly earned income will be concentrated in the hands of the rich who has a lower MPC, resulting in insufficient demand. Then, overproduction occurs. That is the problem from the demand side of consumption. Also, the insufficient demand of consumption can be attributed to problems from the supply side. That is, when the consumption structure of the residents is upgrading, the supply of goods cannot adjust to the changes in consumer demand, leading to dull sale.

Based on the economic research on the general law of consumption, many sociologists focus on introducing the perspective of social stratification into the study of consumption. They assume that the consumption behavior of certain social classes or social groups follow certain rules. For example, Veblen (1994) studies the "conspicuous consumption" or the "squandering" consumption of the leisure class or the upstart, and finds that the higher the price is, the better the product is sold. This phenomenon is called the Veblen effect. Becker (1962) studies the "irrational" consumption behaviors that pursue pleasurable experiences, similar to what people call the "firecrackers effect"; Bourdieu (1984) focuses on the meaning of the "consumption taste" to social stratification, similar to what people call "the identity symbol of consumption" or "consumption attitude". After the Asian Financial Crisis in 1998, we have conducted studies on the consumption trend of different consumption groups, and the impact of consumption on stimulating the economy (Li and Zhang 2001). Li (2011) has done a systematically analysis on the consumption characteristics of the middle class, and Zhang (2016) has studied the consumption tendency from survival consumption to developmental consumption of each social class.

At present, domestic consumption has already become the main driving force of China's economic growth, contributing to 64% of China's economic growth in 2016. However, such a rapid growth is not due to extraordinary changes in domestic consumption, but rather a result of weakened impacts of investment and exports. There is still much potential in China's consumption, and the mass consumption era has not yet come. According to the analysis of CSS 2015, there is a significant decrease in the MPC in China's household consumption. When we divide urban residents into dectile according to household per capita income, the household consumption rates (the proportion of per capita consumption to per capita income in a family) decline with income group (see Fig. 2). The household consumption rate of the lowest 10% families is 85%, while the rate is only 49% among the top 10%

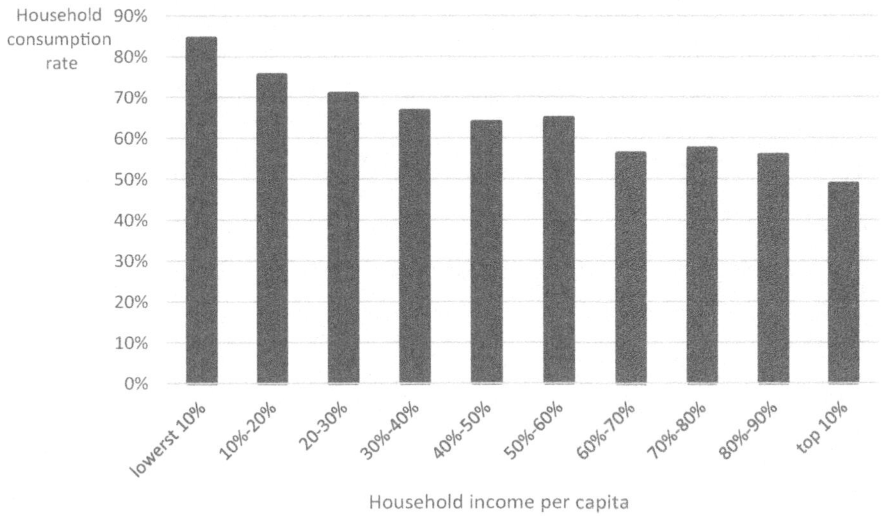

Fig. 2 Marginal propensities of consumption by different income groups of the urban households (2015). *Source* 2015 China Social Survey (CSS)

families. In addition, income of the 20% richest households accounts for 53.3% of total urban household income.

Base on the CSS, the regression model also show that per capita income of the family, place of residence, average schooling years, and family social class all have a significant impact on the survival consumption of the family, such as consumption of food, clothing, water and electricity, housing, medical care, support for the elderly, funeral, and wedding. In terms of the survival consumption, the marginal consumption tendency of the upper-middle-income group is the highest with the regression coefficient of 0.713, much higher than that of the low-income group and high-income group. However, the survival consumption of high-income groups is more likely to be influenced by the place of residence and average educational level. In the analysis of developmental consumption (household consumption in education, tourism, entertainment, home appliances, communications, and transportation), the model shows the similar pattern as survival consumption, and only the impact of place of residence is less significant.

In short, the middle-income group, especially the upper-middle-income group, have a higher MPC either in term of survival or developmental consumption (see Table 4), implying that the hypothesis that promoting mass consumption by expanding the middle-income group can be supported by the law of consumption.

Table 4 Marginal propensity of consumption for different income groups in 2015 (OLS)

Model 1				
Survival consumption	Low-income group	Lower-middle and low-income group	Upper-middle-income group	High-income groups
Constant	5,356***	6,176	6,520	3,050
Household income per capita	0.178**	0.116	0.713***	0.0759***
Place of residence (urban = 1)	1,967***	1,654	3,345**	6,588**
Average years of education in family	129.7**	314.4	553.4***	709.6***
Family social class (middle class = 1)	2,339***	−918.8	−296.3	5,303***
N	3,814	1,954	1,743	2,148
Model 2				
Developmental consumption	Low-income group	Middle-and low-income group	Middle–and high-income group	High-income group
Constant	21.49	−501.5	−1,640	549.0
Household income per capita	0.194	0.233***	0.218***	0.0677***
Place of residence (urban = 1)	2,341*	163.5	−132.3	2,301*
Average years of education in family	114.3	81.92**	170.4***	202.8*
Family social class (middle class = 1)	−467.2	753.6**	1,093***	3,876***
N	3,809	1,953	1,742	2,149

Source China Social Survey 2015 (CSS)
Notes
(1) *** $p < 0.01$, ** $p < 0.05$, * $p < 0.1$
(2) The dependent variable—the survival consumption refers to per capita consumptions on food, clothing, water and electricity, housing, medical care, support for the elderly, funeral and wedding and other expenses; the developmental consumption refers to per capita consumptions on education, tourism, entertainment, home appliances, communications, transportation, and other expenses
(3) For the independent variables of the model, average years of education in family refers to the average years of schooling of family members who are 18 years or older. We measure the family social class according to interviewee's occupation. People with non-manual jobs are defined as the middle class, and people with manual jobs are defined as middle- and low-class

Paths to Overcome the Double "Middle-Income Trap"

To overcome the double "middle-income trap" involves two problems. The first is to solve the problem of stagnation when the per capita GDP reaches a certain level. The other is to solve the long-term stagnation or even decline in the proportion of the middle-income group. Moreover, even if the former has been resolved, the latter may still occur, and may have impact on the former one.

I. Since the reform, China has stepped into the stage of economic take-off and rapid development. GDP per capita has increased from less than $200 in 1978 to more than $800 in 2000. The increase of over $500 in GDP per capital takes more than 20 years. Yet, the increase of more than $7000 in GDP per capita, from more than $800 in 2000 to more than $8000 in 2015, takes only 15 years. During the 37 years from 1978 to 2015, Chinese GDP grows at an annual rate of 9.6%. During such rapid development, the problem of imbalanced development is particularly prominent, especially in terms of the unbalanced development in urban and rural areas and the large income gap between social groups. This becomes the weakness of China's development in global comparison.

China's 13th Five-Year Plan (2016–2020) is crucial for building a moderately prosperous society in a comprehensive way and becoming a high-income country from an upper-middle-income country. According to the 6.5% potential GDP growth rate from now to 2020, China will reach the standard of high-income countries between the year 2022 and 2024. The current GDP per capita standard of high-income country is approximately $12,700. China has a lot of favorable conditions to cross the threshold of the "middle-income trap". For example, China's economic and social structure has a lot of flexibility, especially as the manufacturing innovation capacity continues to improve, and the different regions form a goose-shaped team in their development. In 2015, 10 provinces' GDP per capita reached $10,000. Compared with developed countries, the average educational level has large space for improvement, and the potential of China's human capital growth is still huge. However, we should be careful to claim that there is no risk for China to be caught in the "middle-income trap", as it is rare for a country to become a core country from a periphery one in the past century.

The real difficulty of overcoming the double "middle-income trap" is how to continuously expand the proportion of the middle-income group. Through the analysis of this paper, it can be seen that even under the situation that China's per capita income level grew rapidly and the national income Gini coefficient continued to slightly decline between 2008 and 2015, the proportion of the middle-income group did not significantly increase. The experience of other countries in the world has shown that the income gap can be quickly enlarged, but slowly narrowed. Since the global financial crisis in 2008, the decline in income level of the middle class in some western developed countries, and the rise of social divisionism and populism deserve much attention and reflection. And it is also a new "middle-income trap" in developed countries.

To overcome the double "middle-income trap", China faces many choices and challenges. From the policy-making perspective, China should focus on the following aspects.

Among the determinants of income, the role of human capital is very prominent. The average educational level of China's population over 15 years old in 2015 is more than 9 years, and the gross enrollment rate of higher education is 40%. It is a rapid development. However, there is still a large gap with developed countries, whose average gross enrollment rate of higher education is 70%. In other words, it also means that China has a large potential for development. China should comprehensively improve the quality and income of labor force through implementing the strategy of giving priority to human capital development.

The era of mass consumption is based on the formation of a huge middle-income group, which is closely related to the tax policy promoting mass consumption. China's personal income tax should be deducted or exempted based on the proportion of family's spending on basic living, education, health care, child support, the elderly support, and other aspects in household income.

The success of China's economic transformation and upgrading depends on innovation in the future. A country's innovation often depends on entrepreneurs, scientific and technical personnel, skilled workers, college graduates and professionals, who are usually the main component of the middle-income group. Therefore, China should advance the reform of wage system in educational, medical, and research institutes to reflect the value of professionals' knowledge and human capital and explore new methods of incentives for innovation, such as a better bonus, stock ownership, and stock option package. China's agricultural output has fallen below 10% of the total GDP, yet the proportion of agricultural labor in rural area is still high. Since the vast majority of peasants only have an average of 0.5 hectare of cultivated land, it is difficult for them to live a middle-income-group life by relying solely on farming. China's new-type urbanization should help the majority of peasants to lead a middle-income-group life.

Peilin Li

References

Baudrillard J (2001) The Consumer Society, translated by Liu Chengfu and Quan Zhigang. University of Nanjing Press, Nanjing

Becker Gary S (1987) Analysis of the Family Economy, translated by Peng Songjian. Huaxia Publishing House, Beijing

Birdsall N, Graham C, Stefano P (2000) Stuck in Tunnel: Is Globalization Muddling the Middle Class? Working Paper, No. 14, Brookings Institution, Washington, DC.

Bourdieu P (2015) Distinction: A Social Critique of the Judgement of Taste, translated by Liu Hui. The Commercial Press, Beijing

Davis D, Hanlong L (2001) Consumption culture and consumption revolution [in Chinese]. Sociol Study (5)

Gill I, Kharas H (2007) An East Asian Renaissance: Ideas for Economic Growth. World Bank, Washington, DC

Jenkins SP, Van Kerm P (2009) The measurement of economic inequality. In: Wiermer S, Brian N, Timothy S (eds) The Oxford handbook on economic inequality. Oxford University Press, Oxford

Kharas H (2010) The emerging middle class in developing countries. OECD Development Centre Working Paper, vol 285

Li C (2011) Consumption Level and Style of Middle Class [in Chinese]. Social Sciences in Guangdong (4)

Li P, Zhang Y (2001) Consumption Stratification: Another Perspective to Launch Economy [in Chinese]. Social Sci China (2).

Li P, Zhang Y (2008) The Scope, Identity, and Social Attitudes of the Middle Class in China. Society 28(2)

Peilin L, Di Z (2015) Make efforts to develop an olive-shaped distribution pattern: an analysis based on data from the china social survey for 2006–2013. Soc Sci China (1)

Long Y (2015) Decomposition of Factors that Affect the Proportion Variation of the Middle-income Group from 1988 to 2010: Based on the Evidence of Income Polarization Index [in Chinese]. Stat Res 32(2)

Milanovic B, Yitzhaki S (2002) Decomposing world income distribution: does the world have a middle class? Review of Income and Wealth, International Association for Research in Income and Wealth (1)

Pew Research Center (2015a) Are you in the global middle class? http://www.pewresearch.org/fact-tank/2015/07/16/are-you-in-the-global-middle-class-find-out-with-our-income-calculator/

Pew Research Center (2015b) China's middle class surges, while India's lags behind. http://www.pewresearch.org/fact-tank/2015/07/15/china-india-middle-class/

Pressman S (2015) Defining and measuring the middle class. American Institute for Economic Research (AIER), Working paper (7)

Veblen T (1964) The theory of the leisure class: an economic study of institutions. The Commercial Press, Translated by Cai Shoubai

Wallerstein I (2013) The modern world-system V. 1. Translated by Guo Fang et al The Modern World-System V 1, Social Science Academic Press, Beijing

Wolfson MC (1994) When inequalities diverge. Am Econ Rev 84(2):353–358

World Bank (2007) Global Economic Prospects 2007: Managing the Next Wave of Globalization[M]. World Bank, Washington, DC

World Bank and Development Research Center of the State Council (2013) China 2030: Building Modernized, Harmonized, and Innovative Society. Chinese Financial and Economic Publishing House, Beijing

World Bank (2016) World bank analytical classifications, https://datahelpdesk.worldbank.org/knowledgebase/articles/378834-how-does-the-world-bank-classify-countries

Zhang Y (2016) Consumption Tendencies of Social Classes in Today's China: From Survival Consumption to Developmental Consumption [in Chinese]. Sociol Stud (4).

Introduction: The Middle Class: Issues of Emergence and Research Experiences in Modern Russia

The past decade has been marked by the active collaboration in research between sociologists from the Russian Academy of Sciences (RAS) and the Chinese Academy of Social Sciences (CASS). This refers to more than the fruitful exchange of experience via academic delegations, publications, the sharing of research results, and joint conferences and symposiums. Practical collaborative activities have come to include such crucial staples as comparative research based on secondary analysis of both groups' previous studies and, in recent years, comparative research proper—which is based on mutually approved sociological study methods. This research has been reflected in joint publications that have received highly positive feedback from the Russian and Chinese academic communities,[3] in addition to being made available to Russian audiences through the country's key information platforms.[4]

These effective and scientifically significant forms of collaboration are being developed even further, largely thanks to the input of Chunlin Li, former director of the CASS Institute of Sociology and the current vice president of CASS. He has recently reaffirmed his dedication by initiating the IS RAS-supported research of middle-income groups of the Chinese and Russian populations, which are commonly referred to in Russia as the middle class.

This area of sociological study is more than essential for nations that rank among the top world leaders. If we touch upon Russia's seamless integration into the international community (which should involve not just finding a spot in the global arena, but finding a place worthy of the country's immense intellectual potential and vast natural resources), it becomes evident that rising to this challenge depends on whether

---

[3] See e.g.: *Russia and China: Changes in Social Structure*/Responsible Editors: M. K. Gorshkov, Peilin Li, Z. T. Golenkova. – M.: Novy Khronograf, 2012. – 512 p.; *Russia and China: Youth of the 21st Century* / Responsible Editors: M. K. Gorshkov, Chunlin Li, Z. T. Golenkova, P. M. Kozyreva. — M. Novy Khronograf, 2014. – 424 p.; *The Ideal Society in the Dreams of People in Russia and in China*/Responsible Editors: M. K. Gorshkov, P. M. Kozyreva, Peilin Li, N. E. Tikhonova. – M.: Novy Khronograf, 2016. – 424 p.

[4] Notable examples include the press conference at the Russian TASS Information Agency on November 7, 2016, which featured the results of nationwide comparative studies that had been conducted by researchers from the Institutes of Sociology of RAS and CASS for the first time in their respective countries' histories.

or not the country possesses competitive qualities. The continuous development of these qualities can be identified as a top national priority in the modern world.

The results of many years' worth of nationwide studies carried out by IS RAS[5] allow us to conclude that the mission of ensuring Russia's global competitiveness is intrinsic to the general public's ideas of restoring the nation to its former glory and authority as a world leader. It is also the key to strengthening its people's sense of self-worth and self-respect, and is linked to resolving not only foreign policy issues but also a broad range of key domestic problems. The latter doubtless include a challenge that is among the most fundamental missions, yet one of the least controllable by the state: the challenge of creating a *widespread middle class.* What we refer to here is a social entity that, in countries with a highly developed market economy and democratic political institutions, performs a number of crucial functions: mainly the function of a social safety buffer and the source of new highly qualified labor resources.

Addressing the topic of the middle class in modern society has its own deep historical roots. The philosophers of the Ancient Orient and Ancient Greece already observed the existence of a certain fairly sizeable and rationally thinking middle group between society's highest and lowest points, which could potentially ensure the nation's stability. For instance, in his *Πολιτικά (Politics)*, Aristotle pointed out that moderation and middle ground are the best possible boons, as the middle class's way of life makes it more predisposed towards following the rules of reason, law, and justice than any other class, while the rich and the poor are not inclined to respect these principles.

Two thousand years later, similar ideas were expressed by Niccolò Machiavelli, the notable Renaissance author who believed it ill-advisable to entrust state governance either to the rich or to the poor. Philosophers from an even later period (T. Hobbes, J. Locke, J.-J. Rousseau), in turn, made it abundantly clear that the existence of social classes and strata that were unequal by nature was certain to result in a multitude of cataclysms and problems. And even though that particular epoch lacked a systemic theoretical foundation for reviewing and analyzing these issues, the background for the future theory of class and social stratification was already being formed. The consequences of social stratification and social inequality were analyzed and described by a number of historians, economists, and philosophers of the 18th and early 19th centuries (A. Smith, E. Condillac, C. Saint-Simon, F. Guizot, A. Mignet, and others).

The first written works and discussions of the middle class in a sense close to its modern interpretation date back to the USA of the nineteenth century.[6] A few decades

---

[5] From July 2017, known as the Federal Sociological Research Center of the Russian Academy of Sciences.

[6] S. Blumin, a researcher specializing in the history of the American middle class, believes that the main indication of the emergence of the middle class was the conjunction of common social and economic status, settlement patterns, working culture, self-identification, and worldview among white-collar workers, which was first recorded in the 1830's. For more information, please refer to: Blumin S.M., *The Emergence of the Middle Class:The Social Experience in the American City, 1760–1900.* – NY: Cambridge University Press, 1989.

later, the topic of the middle class began to stir debate among European experts as well. Nevertheless, academic literature far more often links the emergence of the widespread middle class not to the nineteenth century, but rather to the transition to a post-industrial society. This references the formation of a society associated with the disappearance of polar opposition between the rich and the poor, a rise in the number of highly qualified professionals and experts, and the expansion of production facilities. Together with the creation of the first joint-stock companies, this prompted the emergence of a large new category of workers (managers), and contributed to the global changes in social and economic policy that were taking place from the 1930s in the USA and from the 1950s in Western Europe: namely, the shift of priorities from aiding the poor to supporting the middle class.

The generally accepted notion in professional circles is that the most accurate system of singling out social classes, levels, and strata is the concept of multidimensional social stratification, developed by M. Weber, P. A. Sorokin, and other sociologists. The Western European sociological tradition initially defined the middle class based on an individual's general social status score, which depended on their occupation, economic status, and level of education. Later on, taking into account the growing size of the middle class and the need for more detailed analysis of it, the concept of a single unified middle class was replaced by the concept of the "old" middle class (chiefly made out of small business owners) and the "new" middle class (which covered qualified professionals for hire). But, gradually, this model too began to lose its relevance.

Today, the necessity of finding a term for social entities that cannot be classified as either the rich or the poor has prompted Western sociologists to speak not only of the middle class but also of middle-income groups, which, "due to their internal diversity, cannot be viewed as a single social entity". However, in Russia, where the social structure mostly resembles that of Central Europe in the 1970s, the issue of developing our own concept of the middle class is still of immediate relevance. This is reflected by the fact that hardly any other topic has given rise to such keen interest as the middle class problem in Russian stratification research starting from the early 2000s.[7] In addition, more and more emphasis is being placed on the middle class in such activities as the development of an optimal social policy model and the efforts of various government agencies, and Russian President Vladimir Putin has even named the growth of the middle class to up to 60–70% of the population as one of the key milestones for the country's social and economic development by the year 2020. As the government is preparing to tackle this challenge head-on, and the size of the middle class is turning from a topic of theoretical academic debate into a practical policy issue, this imposes a great responsibility upon everyone who studies the subject.

The researchers from IS RAS have been involved in working on this challenge for many years now. Quite notably, they are trying to find answers to the key relevant questions not by speculative deliberation, but by considering the empirical data and sociological facts that have been derived via employing strictly scientific methods.

[7] See the chapter of this book written by N. E. Tikhonova.

The first attempt to grasp the essence of the Russian middle class dates back to the last year of the twentieth century, when Russia was recovering from an acute financial and economic crisis that culminated in the default of 1998. Many people at the time were trying to determine whether or not the newly born, still weak middle class of post-Soviet Russia had been swallowed up by the crisis. The fact that it had, indeed, survived, albeit having grown quite smaller, was demonstratively proved by the research that our work group carried out in the spring of 1999.[8]

We made our second attempt to study the Russian middle class in 2003, during a nationwide survey that involved not only a representational group of respondents from across the country, but also a special subgroup of respondents from the most affluent population strata, thus allowing for a better representation of data on the middle class. The researchers were primarily interested in issues linked to the well-being of the middle class under new political circumstances (during Putin's first presidential term) and the dynamics of its quantitative and qualitative changes in the post-default period.[9]

Yet another study of the Russian middle class was carried out by the IS RAS work group roughly a decade later, in February of 2014. Its **maingoal** was to evaluate the scope, structure, features, social role, and development prospects of the Russian middle class that had been shaped by over 20 years of reform.

This goal determined our research **objectives**, which aimed to find out:

- who could be described as middle class in modern Russia;
- which position the middle class occupied in the labor market;
- which typical jobs the middle class performed and in which specific ways it was evolving;
- which consumption patterns and quality of life were currently typical of the middle class;
- which values and life goals the Russian middle class supported;
- whether there is any mutual support and cooperation between the government and the middle class, and what the latter expects from the former;
- how we could characterize the middle class's position in the structure of post-reform Russian society, and what the specifics of its status identity were.

The empirical base of the research was comprised of the results of a quantitative survey that was conducted both among respondents representing the population as a whole and among an additional group of respondents representing the Russian middle class. These results were entered into the SPSS program and used to form three corpora of empirical data (a nationwide representative corpus, an additional middle class respondent corpus, and a unified middle class corpus, derived by combining responses of middle class representatives from both previous corpora). The statistical

[8] Ref.: *The Middle Class in Modern Russian Society*/Edited by M. K. Gorshkov, N. E. Tikhonova, A. Yu. Chepurenko. M.: ROSSPEN, 1999.

[9] Ref.: *Russia: the New Social Reality.The Rich.The Poor.The Middle Class.*/Edited by M.K. Gorshkov, N.E. Tikhonova. – M.: Nauka, 2004.

analysis of the resulting materials was carried out by means of contingency tables, multi-variant indices, factor analysis, etc.

The study's selection model included two targets:

- the population as a whole, represented by a group of 1600 respondents over 18,
- and an additional group of 300 respondents, selected using a number of criteria that afforded the researchers a very high degree of probability of encountering members of the middle class among them. This was reaffirmed by a subsequent analysis, which showed that 94% of respondents from the additional group had turned out to belong to the middle class we had singled out.

The IS RAS research group had already completed the analysis of the results from February 2014, comparing them to data derived from previous research, when abrupt and unexpected changes in the foreign economic policy and in the political arena (resulting from the return of Crimea and the plummet of oil prices) caused a dire social and economic crisis by late 2014 and early 2015, which did not fail to impact the well-being of various social groups, including the middle class. As a result, we decided to use similar methodology and carry out another nationwide study of the middle class, which we carried out in *October of 2015*. Our chief aim was to determine if there had been any fundamental changes in the typical features that had distinguished the members of various middle class subgroups during the pre-crisis period, and if so, what exactly those changes were.[10]

So, what have we managed to find out? As of Spring 2014 (in other words, before the active phase of the latest crisis), the middle class amounted to 42% of the entire Russian population (and 44% of employed Russians), if we are to use our relatively rigid criteria which will be described in more detail further in this book.

However, just like any other social group, the middle class is not homogenous. It can be split into two subgroups. The first is the *core of the middle class,* which is a relatively stable social entity comprised out of people that display this social group's peculiar characteristics most prominently. The second is the *periphery of the middle class*, where the particulars that are most typical of the people in the core gradually grow less and less evident. Those who belong to the periphery are characterized by qualities and status as members of the middle class that are far less stable.

People raised in urban families with a high level of education form the backbone of the middle class, although even in the core, they amount to barely a half of all middle class members so far. This means that there is currently a significant influx of people to the core positions of the middle class that goes beyond the passing down of middle class status from generation to generation. That said, only one in every five Russians with parents that have not completed the secondary vocational education is part of the middle class (and in 80% of all cases, such Russians find themselves in the outlying segment of the core of the middle class). If one or both parents have finished secondary vocational education, this already ensures that their child makes it to the middle class in 46% of all cases. And if one or both parents have finished

[10] The results of this research are described in: *The Middle Class in Modern Russia. A Summary of Many Years of Research*/Ed. Gorshkov, M. K. and Tikhonova, N.E. M.: Ves Mir, 2016. – 368 p.

higher education, the degree of probability increases to almost 70%. Furthermore, a little over half of respondents with such parents find themselves in the core of the middle class.

Analysis of the derived sociological data has allowed us to conclude that attitudes towards processes in the Russian labor market are quite clearly linked to whether or not the respondents belong to the middle class. If they do, their self-perception is far more optimistic, and if it does differ (in some cases quite dramatically) from the opinions of the nation overall, it is usually for the better.

At the very least, the research data reveals the existence of a certain "social misbalance" in Russia. By this, we mean the discrepancy between the relatively stable (judging by the figures available) condition of the labor market, with its low unemployment rates, and the fear of becoming unemployed in the next 2 or 3 years, which haunts more than 40% of all employed Russians.

Irrational as this fear may seem, it actually has a number of objective and sound reasons behind it, which doubtless include the lack of social protection and low efficiency of the social measures against unemployment taken by the state. At the same time, thanks to more stable and resilient working practices, members of the Russian middle class (especially its core) worry about the prospect of losing their job far less than the rest of the population, believing that, in the short term, this turn of events is either "completely out of the question" or, at the very least, "improbable".

Russia's pattern of employment across industries and, most importantly, across economic sectors, differs substantially from the patterns typical of developed nations (see Table 1).

The differing employment patterns between Russia and the developed nations reflect the fact that Russian society is not going through the same historical development phase as the leading countries of the West; namely, it is still in the late industrial stage. History shows that this particular phase of social development is characterized by an especially rapid emergence of the middle class, which then becomes a dominant social force. And it is during this phase that the structure of the middle class is based on a relatively large share of semi-professionals, clerical workers, office employees, and other similar groups, i.e. white-collar workers with mid-level qualifications, whereas the share of professionals is somewhat lower than in societies dominated by the quaternary economic sector. Both of these trends (the overall increase in the size of the middle class and the surge in the share of white-collar workers with mid-level qualifications within its structure) become evident if we look at the array of jobs typical for the middle class in Russia (see Table 2).

The data provided in Table 2 reveals two main trends. First of all, the foundation of the current core of the middle class is comprised of professionals (whose share has increased of late) as well as managers of all levels and entrepreneurs (whose share, by contrast, keeps noticeably decreasing). Furthermore, the vast majority of top managers and professionals (who were part of the periphery of the middle class in 2003) have now shifted to the core of the middle class, where professionals actually belong due to their status. This has primarily occurred due to the improvement of their financial well-being and the concurrent shaping of their own identity as the middle class. As a result, the core and periphery of the middle class have grown

Table 1 Employment across various industries and economic sectors in Russia, Germany, and the United Kingdom (2012 and 2013, % of the employed population)[11]

Economic sectors	Russia, 2013	Germany, 2012	The UK, 2012
Primary sector	**9**	**3**	**1**
Agriculture and forestry, hunting, fishing and fish husbandry	7	3	1
Mineral extraction	2	0.5	0.4
Secondary sector	**35**	**33**	**23**
Processing and manufacturing (industrial enterprises)	15	23	13
Power, gas, and water production and distribution; construction; transportation and communication	20	10	10
Tertiary sector	**30**	**30**	**38**
Wholesale and retail, service sector (including utilities and other services)	23	22	29
Governance and military security, social services	7	8	9
Quaternary sector	**26**	**36**	**38**
Education, academia, culture, etc.	17	23	26
Financial activity, real estate operations, informational and similar services	9	13	12

far more homogenous in terms of job types than they were in the early 2000s. This process should, without a doubt, be regarded as a positive development, reflecting the general trends signifying the emergence of a widespread post-industrial middle class that are typical of any country at this stage.

Should Russia manage to eliminate the disproportionate wages paid to highly qualified professionals across various sectors, regions, settlement types, etc., and continue to improve its economic policy, an additional 2–3% of the population may join the middle class. Furthermore, the middle class could see another 5–6% increase after certain changes in social policy, being bolstered by retirees with a relatively high level of education, who could be considered part of the middle class even after retiring, due to their previous social status. That is to say, in the most favorable conditions, the maximal expansion of the middle class in the next few years could reach up to 8–10% of the population.

All of the above allows us to surmise that, bearing in mind its current potential, the size of the middle class in the current economic structure is capable of rising to around one half of the Russian population. This, of course, is not exactly the "two-thirds society" (which was typical of the developed Western European nations of the

[11] The data for Germany and the UK has been taken from the ESS (European Social Survey) for 2012. The data for Russia is based on the official statistics for 2013, available on the website of the Federal State Statistics Service (Rosstat).

Table 2 Trends in Jobs Typical for Various Population Groups (2003/2014, % of the employed population)

Professional groups	Middle Class, including				The rest of the population	
	Middle-class core		Middle-class periphery			
	2003	2014	2003	2014	2003	2014
Managers of all levels, business people, and the self-employed	34	20	29	12	1	1
Professional experts whose work requires a higher education	**67**	**80**	24	5	2	1
Other white-collar workers (semi-professionals, clerks, rank-and-file employees in the commerce and consumer services sphere)	0	0	**47**	**83**	8	8
Blue-collar workers	0	0	0	0	**90**	**90**

1960s and 1970s, i.e. at the point of their history when they were at the same stage of development Russia is going through right now), but still fairly sufficient for creating a widespread middle class.

Peilin Li of CASS believes that the key to developing the middle class in China lies in overcoming the so-called middle class two-income trap. In Russia, the situation in this respect is somewhat different, not limited solely to income figures. If we are to discuss the specific features of the status of the Russian middle class via comparisons to the qualitative and quantitative features the middle class currently has in the West, we may find out that the key difference does not lie in qualitative figures at all. The main feature of the Russian situation is the relatively low number of middle-class members involved in the quaternary sector of the economy, unlike in the leading countries of the West, as well as the growing share of social groups that are usually peripheral to the middle class.

As a result, while the evolution of the middle class in the world's most developed countries is moving towards polarization (i.e. the increasing presence of people employed at high-skill and low-skill positions, with mid-level positions shrinking), the Russian middle class, on the contrary, is being bolstered first and foremost by white-collar workers with mid-level qualifications who perform routine non-menial jobs. And in this respect, the emergence of the Russian middle class resembles the processes that occurred in Western European nations such as Germany, the UK, etc., some 40–50 years ago. Russia is going through the same trends that those countries experienced back then; in essence, the middle class keeps growing in size thanks to the influx of clerical workers on the one hand, and the relatively highly educated (secondary vocational training at the very least) rank-and-file employees of the commerce and customer service sector on the other.

These differences follow an established pattern, as the key trend of the Russian middle class's rapid growth by means of absorbing a homogeneous labor force with mid-level qualifications reflects the peculiarities of the Russian economy's current stage of development, in addition to being the result of the economy's rent-seeking nature. The latter leads to the creation of even more mid-skilled and low-skilled jobs, while the addition of new jobs that require highly skilled intellectual labor remains barely significant. Positive trends in export policy, a result of high prices for energy commodities, are the only things that make it possible to keep increasing the average wage across the country. Furthermore, this increase is largely ensured by redistribution rather than by market mechanisms.

The income of the population as a whole, and the middle class in particular, is highly unstable given the current model of its expansion, and any potential crisis-like events in the economy can be expected to result in the shrinking of the country's middle class. The proof lies in the events of 2008 and 2009, when the financial and economic crisis caused the periphery of the middle class to "crumble away" to a very notable extent (in 2009, it shrank by one quarter, from 20% before the crisis to 15% afterwards). A slightly less pronounced but nonetheless similar process occurred in 2014–2015, although it did not actually result in such a dramatic plummet in the size of the Russian middle class. While members of the middle class had to compromise on some of their habitual consumption patterns (meals, clothing, leisure activities, etc.), the qualitative share of this population group remained the same as before the crisis (40–42%).

As for the fundamental expansion of the middle class, its sustained growth will only be possible if Russia completes the late industrial stage of development and starts transitioning to the post-industrial stage, i.e. if the country supports a "knowledge economy" while also diversifying its economic structure overall.

In conclusion, I would like to note that our October (2015) research of middle-income groups in post-reform Russian society employed a set of data points approved by Russian and Chinese sociologists, which served as the basis for the comparative analysis presented in this volume. This is not the first instance of such in-depth mutual research and analysis of the "fabric" of an issue that is so important to both our countries, but I consider it to be fairly substantial. I hope that this experience will bolster further fruitful research collaboration between our teams.

M. K. Gorshkov
Full Member of the Russian Academy of Sciences

Contents

Editors and Contributors

About the Editors

Peilin Li is an Academic Member of Chinese Academy of Social Sciences (CASS). He now serves as Vice-president of CASS. Before the current position, he was director of Institute of Sociology at CASS and served as the President of Chinese Sociological Association. He earned his Ph.D. at University of Paris I (Pantheon-Sorbonne) in 1987. He has published and edited many articles, books, and essay collections, in Chinese, English, and French, on social stratification and mobility (particular Chinese domestic migrant workers) and economic sociology (particular Chinese State Enterprises). He is also hosting several large projects, including "Chinese general social survey", one of largest and earliest national sociological survey since 2006.

M. K. Gorshkov Director of the Federal Center of Theoretical and Applied Sociology of the Russian Academy of Sciences (former Institute of Sociology of the Russian Academy of Sciences), one of the most prominent modern Russian sociologists, renowned for his investigations in social philosophy, sociology of mass consciousness and sociology of public opinion, methodology and methods of sociological research, sociology of youth, sociology of identity, sociology of social inequalities, sociology of Russian everyday life, etc. He earned his Full Doctor degree in Philosophical Sciences in 1989, and was elected Academician (Full Member) of the Russian Academy of Sciences in 2011. Mikhail Gorshkov is the author of over 30 books and 380 articles, essays and reviews, published in Russian, English, German, Chinese, Serbian, Mongolian and other languages. He is also known as a coordinator and leader of more than 150 regional, national and international sociological research projects. He also serves as editor in chief of scientific journals «Sociology and Social Practices» and «Bulletin of the Institute of Sociology».

Contributors

V. A. Anikin HSE University, Institute of Sociology of FCTAS RAS, Moscow, Russia

Yan Cui Institute of Sociology in CASS, Beijing, China

Lei Fan Institute of Sociology, Chinese Academy of Social Sciences (CASS), Beijing, China

Xiaoguang Fan Department of Sociology, School of Public Affairs, Zhejiang University, Hangzhou, China;
Center for Local Governance Studies, Zhejiang University, Hangzhou, China

Yongliang Huang Graduate School of Chinese Academy of Social Sciences, Beijing, Fangshan District, China

A. V. Karavay HSE University, Institute of Sociology of FCTAS RAS, Moscow, Russia

P. M. Kozyreva HSE University, Institute of Sociology of FCTAS RAS, Moscow, Russia;
Institute of Social Policy of the National Research University Higher School of Economics, Moscow, Russia

N. V. Latova Institute of Sociology of FCTAS RAS, Moscow, Russia

Yu. V. Latov Institute of Sociology of FCTAS RAS, Moscow, Russia

Y. P. Lezhnina HSE University, Institute of Sociology of FCTAS RAS, Moscow, Russia

Chunling Li Institute of Sociology of Chinese Academy of Social Sciences (CASS), Beijing, China

Wei Li Institute of Sociology, Chinese Academy of Social Sciences, Chaoyang District, Beijing, China

Peng Lu Tsinghua University, Beijing, China;
Institute of Sociology at Chinese Academy of Social Sciences (CASS), Beijing, China;
Shanghai Academy, Shanghai, China

Svetlana V. Mareeva HSE University, Institute of Sociology of FCTAS RAS, Moscow, Russia

V. V. Petukhov Institute of Sociology of FCTAS RAS, Moscow, Russia

N. N. Sedova Institute of Sociology of FCTAS RAS, Moscow, Russia

A. I. Smirnov Institute of Sociology of FCTAS RAS, Moscow, Russia;
Federal Center of Theoretical and Applied Sociology of the Russian Academy of Sciences, Moscow, Russia

Feng Tian Institute of Sociology, Chinese Academy of Social Sciences (CASS), Beijing, China

N. E. Tikhonova HSE University, Institute of Sociology of FCTAS RAS, Moscow, Russia

Yelin Yao School of Sociology and Political Science, Shanghai University, Shanghai, China

Haidong Zhang School of Sociology and Political Science, Shanghai University, Shanghai, China

Yi Zhang Beijing Association of Sociology, Beijing, China

Di Zhu University of Manchester, Manchester, England

List of Figures

List of Graphs

List of Tables

Chapter 1
Chronological Changes of Middle-Income Group in China

Chunling Li

In 2002, the concept of "middle-income group" was mentioned for the first time in the report "To Build a Moderately Prosperous Society in an All-round way and Open up a New Chapter of Socialist Cause with Chinese Characteristics" issued at the Sixteenth National Congress of CPC by the Chinese government. The report also proposed the development goal of "expanding the proportion of middle-income group". Later public documents stressed repeatedly that "expanding the proportion of the middle-income group" is an important aspect in building a moderately prosperous society in an all-round way which is a target set by the Chinese Communist Party and the government of China to develop and construct an affluent society by 2020. Apparently middle-income group plays an essential role in achieving this target. "A bigger proportion of middle-income group" is a key indicator of whether we can realize the goal of building a moderately prosperous society. Middle-income group should be mainstream of this society. Therefore, "expanding the proportion of middle-income group" has been brought into the "13th Five-year Plan of National Economy and Social Development (2016–2020)" by the Chinese government.

Before the concept was introduced, most Chinese scholars tend to define middle class based on occupation classification. Sociologists and politicians usually follow their western counterparts in providing the definition of middle class, for instance, Charles Wright Mills's notion of middle class, Erik Olin Wright's idea of neo-Marxism middle class (Wright 1979) and the definition of middle class under the new Weber class theory by John Goldthorpe (Goldthorpe 1987). Since the idea of "middle-income group" was put forward and connected with social development goals, Chinese scholars have adopted another significant angle in the study of middle class, i.e. using the index of income to define middle class. The Chinese government introduced the notion of "expanding middle-income group" for two purposes. The

C. Li (✉)
Institute of Sociology of Chinese Academy of Social Sciences (CASS), Beijing, China

P. Li and M. K. Gorshkov (eds.), *The Middle Income Group in China and Russia*, Research Series on the Chinese Dream and China's Development Path,
https://doi.org/10.1007/978-981-16-1464-4_1

first purpose is to improve people's living standard so that more people (middle-income people) can live a moderately prosperous life. The second one is to adjust income distribution to narrow the gap to ensure more people are in middle income level (middle-income people) and eventually form an olive-shaped social structure. Over the past two decades, the changes of middle-income group in terms of size and proportion not only reflected what accomplishments the government has achieved in the two areas mentioned above, but also stood testimony to the comprehensive socioeconomic development of Chinese nation.

1.1 Methodology in Defining Chinese Middle Income Group

Although the government of China aims to expand middle-income group and scholars have had some policy discussions concerning how to do this, there are still no unequivocal statement about the definition, such as who are middle-income people and how to decide the standard of middle income. There are also many disputes in regard to specific classification method. In general, there are mainly two modes used by scholars to define middle-income group, namely, absolute standard mode and relative standard mode.

Absolute standard mode is a method that sets the upper and lower limit of income for middle-income group based on how much earnings needed to maintain a corresponding living standard. In other words, a specific income standard is suggested according to certain living standard or consumption level and then middle-income group is marked off based on this income standard. The poverty line drawn by the World Bank is used as a reference for the income standard of middle-income group around the world. People with per capita income of less than $2 are in the poverty group. Those who earn $2–9 belong to low income group, $10–100 (some say 10–50, 10–60 or 10–80) middle income and above $100 high income group (Chen and Ravallion 2010). In 2002, Blanco Milanovic and Yitzhaki, economists of the World Bank, conducted a study on global income inequality and classified those with an annual salary of $4000 (average annual income in Brazil)-$17,000 (average annual income in Italy) into middle class. The method seems a bit arbitrary, but if we convert based on purchasing power parity(PPP) of 2000 of the World Bank, the equivalent is that those with an average daily income of $10–50 belong to middle class. Based on their calculation, 11% of the world's population are middle class (middle income group), 78% are impoverished and 11% are affluent (Milanovic and Yitzhaki 2002). Later the World Bank issued a global development report called "2007 Global Economy Outlook: Governing the Next Wave of Globalization" and adopted the same standard for the definition of middle class. In this report, it indicated that during the period of 1993–2000, the proportion of middle class among world population hasn't changed (around 8%). However, the figure grew bigger after the year 2000 and is even expected to double and reach 16% by 2030 (World Bank 2007).

Government sectors and researchers proposed the income criterion of Chinese middle-income group by taking the standard of the World Bank as reference and combining reality of China as well as incorporating the index of a moderately prosperous society. Earlier in 1991, the National Bureau of Statistics (NBS) brought up the income standard for a moderately prosperous society. If we convert through PPP, the starting line for average daily per capita income in rural areas is $2.24 and $3.47 in urban areas. Martin Lavaray, economist of the World Bank, believes that China's income standard for moderately prosperous society conforms to the middle income standard set by the World Bank. Based on this standard, he did some calculation using PovcalNet database of the World Bank and came to the conclusion that 500million Chinese were already moderately prosperous back in 2005 (Martin 2009). The research group of City Survey Task Force of the NBS defined those people with an annual family income of 60,000rmb to 500,000rmb as middle-income group in 2005 (research group of City Survey Task Force of the NBS 2005). Economists Li Wei and Wang Shaoguo compared various standards specific to the income distribution in China. They believed the standard proposed by the research group of research institute of NDRC (National Development and Reform Commission) is a better fit to China's reality. By converting through price index, the income criterion for middle class is 21835.2–65,304.5RMB (Wei and Shaoguo 2014).

Relative standard mode is built on the median of income distribution to decide the income standard of middle-income group. The vast majority of scholars who use this approach tend to set 50% or 75% of the income median as the lower limit of middle income and 1.5 or 2 times of that as the upper limit. The income median varies from year to year and as a result, the specific upper and lower limit of the middle income standard also changes.

In 1987, when Lester Thoreau, the American economist, was analyzing income inequality in the US, he adopted the approach of relative standard mode to define middle-income group. He classified those people whose income come between 75 and 125% of the income median as middle-income group (Lester 1987). However, it was Birdsall, Graham and Pettinato, economists of the Brookings Institution, who popularized the approach through an article published in 2000. They pointed out in the article that those whose earnings are between 50 and 125% of the median should be regarded as middle-income group or middle class (Birdsall et al. 2000). After that, the approach soon became popular especially among scholars who study the proportion of American middle income group. In China, there are also some economists that use the median approach to define middle-income group. For instance, Chinese economist Long Ying defined the range of middle income is between 75 and 125% of the median. She calculated the proportion pf middle-income group each year based on Chinese Health and Nutrition Statistics (CHNS) 1988–2010 and discovered that the proportion of middle-income group has dropped continuously from 27.9% in 1988 to 21.1% in 2010 (Ying 2015). However, some scholars found there was a problem with this approach. Due to the existence of a large base of low-income population in China, middle-income group defined based on the method actually contains a large number of low-income people. For instance, Long Ying's study from above shows that the income median of 2010 was 11819RMB while the annual earnings of middle-income group fall between 8864RMB (75% of 11,819) and 14,774 RMB (125% of 11,819). However, such an income level is hardly middle income and it is unlikely for people of such earnings to maintain a decent living standard with the current soaring price level in China. In order to solve this problem, scholars designed some alternatives. Peilin Li and Di Zhu used fractile to replace the median and set the 95th percentile of income distribution as the upper limit of middle income and the 25th percentile as the lower limit. According to this method, the average annual per capital income of middle-income family in 2013 was 28,760–99,540 RMB and 23,211–80,709 in 2011, 16,788–57,080 in 2008 and 13,178–45,252 in 2006. The proportion of middle-income people are 27%, 28%, 24% and 25% respectively for year 2006, 2008, 2011 and 2013 (Li et al. 2015).

The purpose of the two above-mentioned methods varies from each other, so is the scope of application. Absolute standard mode mainly reflects the number of people that reach certain living standard or income level as well as the growth trend of the proportion. It is a method more suitable for developing countries and low and middle-income countries where people's living standard is improving and the population of middle class is on the rise. This mode embodies the growth rate of middle class or middle-income group. Undoubtedly, the method is widely applied in the measurement of global middle class, assessment and predication of world economic development as well as comparison of development level and tendency between different countries. Comparatively, relative standard mode mainly measures the proportional increase or decrease of population whose earnings are in the middle place. It is mainly a reflection of the changing trend of income inequality and is more appropriate for developed countries and high-income countries where middle class is the majority and most people are well off. This mode also reflects the changes of income distribution in terms of whether income inequality is growing (less middle-income people and more high-income and low-income people) or declining (more middle-income people and less high-income and low-income people). The reality is that income inequality is rising for most developing countries in the past two decades. As a result, results of studies using relative method show that the proportion of middle class in most developed countries is going down (Grabka et al. 2016; Pressman 2015). Relative standard mode is not appropriate for developing countries and low-income countries where the income level of middle-income group (people whose earnings are between 75 and 200% of median) is lower and does not conform to the image of middle class or middle-income group in people's mind. In short, absolute standard mode is suitable for growth-type society where the earnings of most people are still low but apparently picking up gradually and more people are becoming affluent while relative mode is a better fit for mature-type society in which the majority are already well-off and they are more focused on social equality and justice.

China got into the list of middle-income countries three years ago and is now striving to become a high-income country. During this period, the Chinese society reveals dual features of both growth-type society and mature-type society. On the one hand, the nation aims to lift more and more people out of poverty. On the other hand, it is pursuing for a fair and reasonable income distribution structure. In this case, the measurement of middle-income group using both approaches is significant and necessary. Absolute standard mode can accurately reflect the number of people who shake off poverty and become prosperous and the growth rate of the proportion while relative standard mode shows the changing trend of income inequality. The proportions of middle-income group defined by both approaches show an evident growth, which demonstrates the progress made by the Chinese government in the pursuit of an "olive-shaped social structure".

1.2 The Changing Trend of Middle-Income Group Defined by Relative Standard Mode

Graph 1.1 shows the changing trend of the proportion of Chinese middle income group from 1988 to 2014 based on relative standard mode. In the graph, the proportion of middle-income families is estimated according to household income per capita of CHNS (Ying 2015) while the proportion of middle-income people is based on personal annual income of CSS. The result of data analysis reveals that the ratio of middle-income group in China continued to drop from 1988 to 2005. During this period of time, despite fast growing economy and improving income, the proportion of middle-income group went down instead of going up. The proportion for 1988 and 1990 was 38.4% and 38.2% respectively. Later the figure went down and reached its lowest point of 28.1% in 2005. Then there was a feeble increase by 1.7%. In 2001, the percentage was 34.2. There was no CSS statistics of the proportion of middle-income

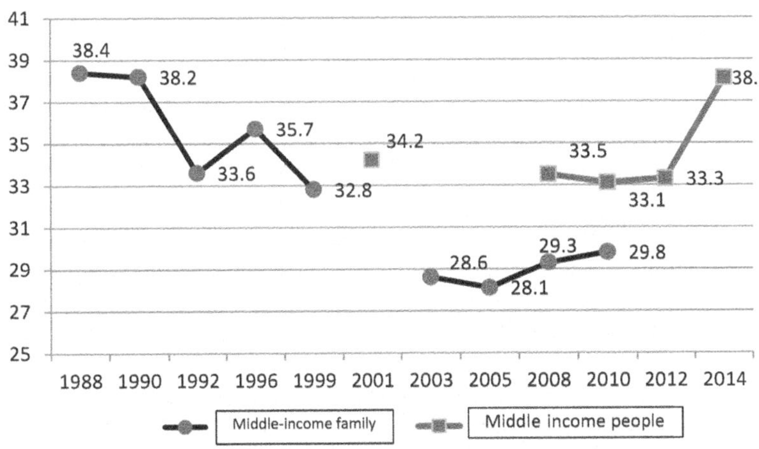

Graph 1.1 Changing trend of the proportion of Chinese middle-income group based on relative standard model (%,1988–2014).[1]

[1] The income standard of middle-income family and middle-income group in Graph 1.1 is between 75%–120% of the median.

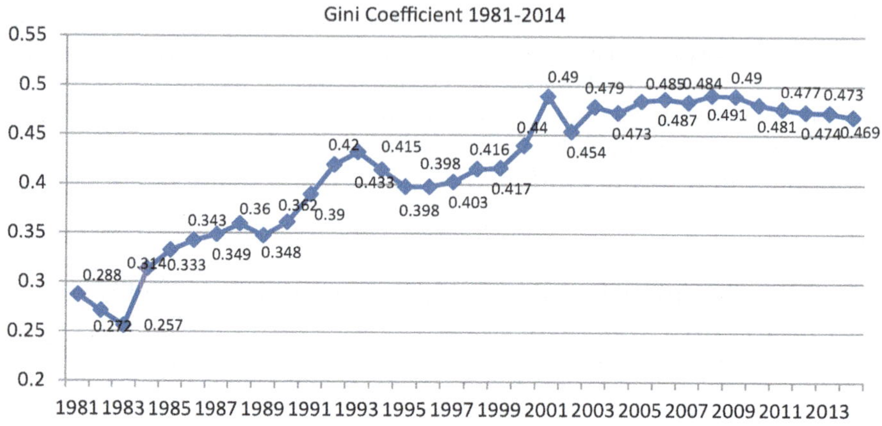

Graph 1.2 The variation trend of income inequality in China (1981–2014)

group from 2002 to 2007. However based on the changes of the proportion projected by CHNS, we speculate the figure was descending in the period of 2001–2005. The change between 2008 and 2012 was not very obvious, but the figure clearly went up in 2014. On the whole, the proportion of Chinese middle class have had a dramatic decline for nearly two decades (from 1988 to 2005) before it went through a stable period of a few years and now began to pick up in recent years. Nevertheless, the size of middle-income group now is still smaller than that in 1988.

The changing trend of the proportion of middle-income group showed in Graph 1.1 accords with the variation tendency of income inequality in China (see Graph1.2). Gini coefficient of China continued to go up from 0.288 in 1981 to 0.491 in 2008, resulting in the fact that the proportion of middle-income group based on relative standard mode dropped continuously. Afterwards there was fluctuation of several years before a slight decline in recent years. Now the proportion of middle income group begins to go up. Apparently, the proportional changes of middle income group defined under relative standard mode are direct reflection of changing trend of income inequality. When income inequality rises, middle-income group shrinks and low and high-income group increases while when income inequality declines, middle-income group grows and low and high-income people become less. However, the proportional change itself is not adequate in reflecting growing economy and improving living standard.

The size of middle-income group defined under relative model fails to increase for a fairly long time due to enlarging income gap, but the income median is going up as the income standard rises. Table 1.2 has listed the average annual income and the median of 2001, 2006, 2008, 2011 and 2015 of CSS survey data. Per capita income grew 5. 6 times bigger from 2001 to 2015 and the median in 2015 was almost 5.8 times up from that of 2001. It means that although the population size of middle class didn't expand in the period of 1988-2015, the income standard went up apparently. In 2001, the annual income of middle class fell in the range between 2700RMB and

7200RMB (75%-200% of the median) and the number went up to the range between 15750RMB and 42000RMB in 2015.

The standard of middle income group increases as the income median goes up. However, for ordinary Chinese people, the income standard set based on relative mode is too low to fit people's impression of middle class. Though China has joined the middle-income countries, but its low-income population is still huge. The fact that there are enormous number of low-income rural people and migrant worker made it more likely to have a low income median. The income standard is thus quite low and those so-called middle class (people in the middle of income distribution map) actually do not make much money. Graph 1.3 shows that the median of annual income of Chinese working-age population in 2015 was 21,000 RMB (50% of annual income is lower than 21,000 RMB while 50% of people makes 21,000 RMB or more). The lower limit of middle income based on relative standard mode is 15750 RMB (75% of the median) while the upper limit is 42000 RMB (200% of the median). That is to say people whose monthly earnings fall between 1313 and 3500 RMB are middle class. Apparently, this definition of middle class can hardly be agreed upon by the public because most of those people may find it difficult to maintain a well-off life. Normally, people consider those who earn 1300–3500 RMB should be classified as low-income group and even if the income is higher than 3500 RMB, it can hardly be called high income. By using relative standard mode to gauge middle class, it can reflect the changing situation of income inequality. However, the definition of middle-income group based on this approach does not conform to the image of middle class or moderately prosperous society in people's mind. In order to expand the middle-income group defined based on this method, we need to narrow down income gap and improve social equality.

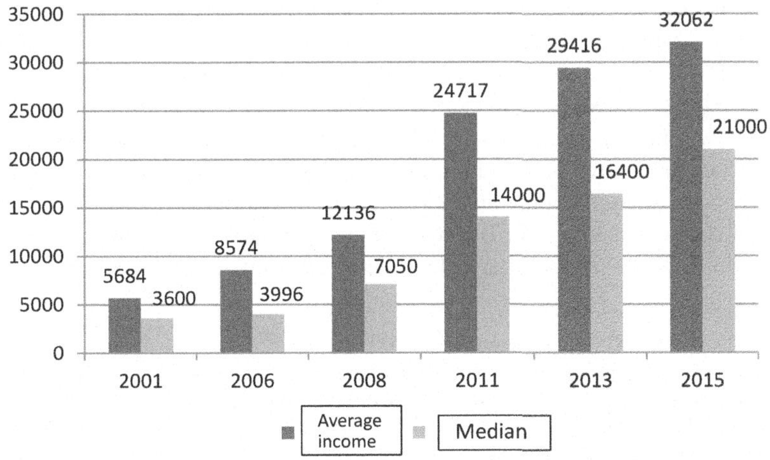

Graph 1.3 The mean value and median of annual income of Chinese working-age population in various years (RMB)

1.3 The Changing Trend of Middle Income Group Defined by Absolute Standard Mode

The changes of middle class population defined by absolute standard mode tend to manifest economic growth and income increase directly. Enlarging middle class over the past twenty years shows that the economy is growing rapidly and people are becoming richer and richer. The absolute standard mode mainly measures the ratio of people who reaches a certain income standard. If the ratio is going up, it means more people are lifted out of poverty and become better off to lead a decent life. This coincides with the development goal of the government of China to build a moderately prosperous society.

One difficulty of this approach is how to select appropriate income standard of middle-income group. It is not easy for both China and around the globe. Worldwide there are developed countries with high income and consumption level alike and low-income developing countries as well as impoverished countries with extremely low income. Sometimes it might be the case that high income of a poor nation is actually below the poverty line of some developed countries. The same is true with China where the gap of income and consumption is huge among different regions. One who is able to lead a moderately prosperous life with the income earned in rural areas and small towns in Midwest China may find it difficult to maintain a basic living standard in tier1 cities with the same amount of money. Scholars in China attempt to solve these problems by proposing numerous complex statistical approaches. They try to strike out a method that fits all situations, including M-curve method of estimation (Long 2012; Wang et al. 2014; Cao et al. 2015), Lorenz curve method (Jian and Yongguang 2007) and method of estimated distribution function (Ji et al. 2009; Zhu 2012), to name a few. Each method has its own merits, but all of them haven't been popularized yet. The most widely adopted approach at present is still to use the most simplified criteria of "daily per capita income of $10–100" proposed by the World Bank as the standard to define middle-income people. The World Bank set the poverty line at daily per capita income of $1.9.[2] People whose earnings are $2–9 belong to low -income group, people who make $10–100 are classified into middle-income group and above $100 is high income. Based on this standard, if we convert daily income to annual income and apply the exchange rate of 6.6 in 2015 between American dollar and Ren Min Bi,[3] we can get a glimpse of the picture of China. In 2015, the Institute of Sociology of Chinese Academy of Social Science revealed

[2] $1.25 is absolute poverty and $2 is relative poverty.

[3] This paper uses market exchange rate of 2015 instead of PPP for conversion. On the one hand, due to evident price increase of day-to-day commodities in China, people's living cost is becoming increasingly higher. On the other hand, Ren Min Bi is now on the way is deflation. However, it seems PPP of the World Bank overrated the real purchasing power of Ren Min Bi, especially purchasing power pf consumer goods related to people's daily lives. According to PPP conversion factor, private consumption (LCU per international $)issued on the website of the World Bank (https://data.worldbank.org/indicator/PA.NUS.PRVT.PP), 1 US$ = 3.82 RMB. Based on this conversion rate, the base line of middle income of daily per capita of $10 translates to 38.2RMB. It is actually very difficult for a person who earns 38.2RMB per day to maintain a basic living standard.

their survey data and showed 18.4% of working-age population in China belonged to lower income group with an annual income lower than 4600RMB, 33.3% are low income (4601–23,999), 47.6% belong to middle-income group (24,000–240,000) and 0.7% are high income group (above 240,000). Annual income between 24,000 and 240,000 is closer to the image of middle-income people in the mind of ordinary citizens. This income level can also provide a moderately prosperous life in most regions of China, except for mega-cities such as Beijing, Shanghai, Guangzhou and Shenzhen where annual income of 24000RMB is too low and should be counted as low income level. A solution to regional differences is to set various middle income standards for various areas, just like what we did with minimum income standard and poverty line. However, this approach is more complex in reality than in theory, for example, how can we decide the specific standard of each region. Furthermore, we need to bear in mind that middle-income group is a national concept rather than a regional idea. It is the same with the concept of global middle class. In the context of economic globalization, even people from developing countries tend to define the term middle class based on the life style of those middle-income people who live in developed countries. With advanced circulation of commodity and information, people who live in small counties are longing for a well-off life that is not confined to local living standard. From the aspect of policy making, it is also more explicit and operable to adopt a unified income standard. Despite that income and consumption level varies from region to region, the standard of middle income should be the same. However, the unified standard should also be able to show regional differences with three categories, high (120,000–240000RMB, equivalent to per capita $50–100/day), medium (60,000–119999RMB, per capita $25–50/day) and low (24,000–59999RMB, per capita $10–25/day) classified. In rural areas, small towns and cities, middle income can ensure a well-off life while one need a medium–high income to enjoy a fairly comfortable life in major cities like Beijing, Shanghai, Guangzhou and Shenzhen. Build on the secondary classification of middle income group, local governments can focus on the expansion of specific categories of middle class according to regional reality while working on realizing the general objective of an enlarging middle-income group.

Based on the middle income standard of 2015, we can convert through price index and obtain the income standard of 2001, 2008, 2011, 2013 and 2015 (see Table 1.1).

Graph 1.4 shows the proportion of middle income group in 2001, 2008, 2011, 2013 and 2015 based on CSS of Chinese Academy of Social Science. The rise of the proportion directly reflects the increase of income, i.e. the number of people with a daily per capita income of over $10 (annual income of 2400RMB) and the increase of its ratio. Meanwhile, the proportion of low-income group dropped sharply from 91.8% in 2001 to 51.7% in 2015. There was a slight increase of high-income people from 0.1% in 2001 to 0.7% in 2015.

The growth of Chinese middle class coincides with economic development and income increases. Graph 1.5 shows that since 2000, China's economy has gained rapid development and people's income level also improved significantly. Consequently, middle income group expanded very fast.

Table 1.1 Middle income standard over the years (RMB). (Based on the standard of the World Bank, below $2 should be classified as poverty. However, China's poverty line is lower than the World Bank's standard. So we put those with a daily per capita income of $2 into low-income group)

	The World Bank (per capita income/day)	2014 (annual income)	2012 (annual income)	2010 (annual income)	2007 (annual income)	2001 (annual income)
Lower-income group	below $2	0–4600	0–4395	0–4065	0–3742	0–3313
Low-income group	$2–9.9	4601–23,999	4396–22,932	4066–21,206	3743–19,521	3314–17,318
Medium-low income group	410–49	24,000–59,999	22,933–57,332	21,207–53,016	19,522–48,805	17,319–43,297
Middle-income group		60,000–119,999	57,333–114,665	53,017–106,033	48,806–97,611	43,298–95,254
Medium-high income group	$50–100	120,000–240,000	114,666–229,331	106,034–212,068	97,612–195,223	95,255–190,509
High-income group	Over $100	Over 240,000	Over 22,933	Over 212,068	Over 195,223	Over 190,509

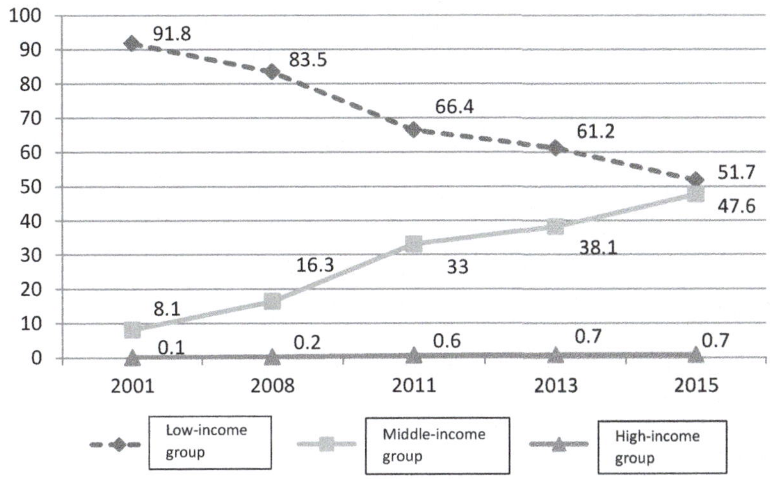

Graph 1.4 The changing trend of middle class proportion based on absolute standard mode (%, 2001–2014)

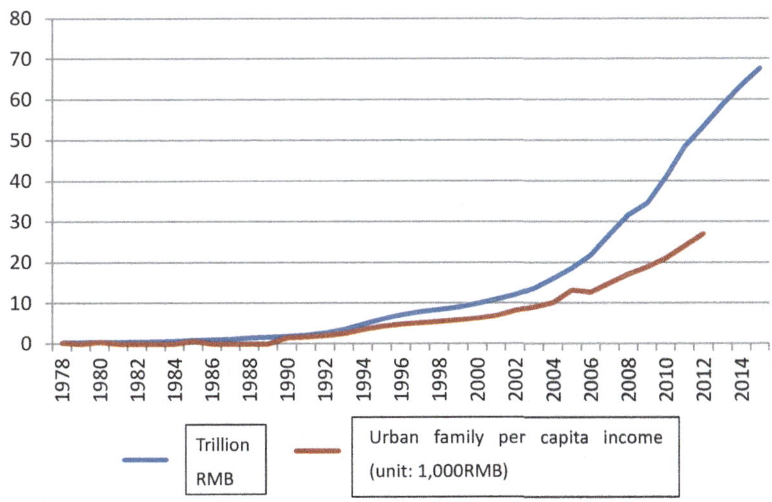

Graph 1.5 China's economic growth and income growth trend

However, while the proportion of middle class was increasing rapidly, its internal structural began to show an irrational picture. Most of the middle-income group are concentrated on medium–low income group. There are few people actually approaching middle income or high income level with a slow growth of the proportion. 86% of middle-income people in 2001 are as a matter of fact at a medium–low income level and this figure went down to 74% by 2015. If we take a look at the growth of various sub-categories of middle-income group, the medium–low income

Table 1.2 2001–2015 growth trend of the proportion of middle income group (%)

	Nationwide					Urban cities	Countryside	Beijing, Shanghai, Guangzhou
	2001	2008	2011	2013	2015	2015	2015	2015
Lower-income group	37.0	30.9	23.1	21.1	18.4	9.1	30.2	8.2
Low-income group	54.8	52.6	43.3	40.1	33.3	26.9	41.4	8.5
Medium–low income group	**7.0**	**13.2**	**26.2**	**30.1**	**35.2**	**45.1**	**22.8**	**42.3**
Middle income group	**0.8**	**2.3**	**5.4**	**6.7**	**9.8**	**14.0**	**4.5**	**28.1**
Medium–high income group	**0.3**	**0.8**	**1.4**	**1.3**	**2.6**	**3.9**	**0.9**	**9.4**
High-income group	0.1	0.2	0.6	0.7	0.7	1.0	0.2	3.5
Total	100	100	100	100	100	100	100	100
Middle class	**8.1**	**16.3**	**33.0**	**38.1**	**47.6**	**63.0**	**28.2**	**79.8**

group has the highest increase. In 2001, the proportion was 7% and it went up to 35.2% by 28% in 2015. The medium layer comes second with a growth rate of 9% while medium–high income group only increased by 2% (see table 1.2). Based on the data of 2015, the internal hierarchy of middle class comes in a classic inverted T-shape with three-quarter of the people at the bottom, 5% on top and 20% in the middle.

There are big regional differences in regard to the proportion and hierarchy of the middle class. In rural areas where the ratio of middle-income group is low, the majority (71.6%) are lower and low-income groups while in urban cities, the proportion of middle-income group reaches 63%, but most of the people are in medium–low income level and only a very few enter into medium–high income group. Moreover, over one third urban population is still at lower and low-income level. In major cities like Beijing, Shanghai and Guangzhou, most people are already middle class but still the majority of them are at the lower end of middle income. In those super big cities, people with low income level may find it difficult to sustain a so-call middle class life or well-off life with rocketing housing prices and other living cost. In this sense, a lot of middle-income people may not be counted as real middle class.

1.4 Conclusion

Russia made it to the ranking of high-income countries in 2012 while China only became a middle-income country in 2010. Needless to say, the two nations have different social structures and social-economic development level. Russia's social structure is more similar to that of most developed countries where the expanding or withering of middle class defined by relative standard mode is an excellent index to reflect the changes of social composition. Whereas in China the economy and society are developing more rapidly than ever, there are more impoverished people and a large quantity of low-income rural population and migrant workers. As a result it is necessary to combine both relative standard mode and absolute standard mode for the definition of middle-income group to fully embody the changes of social structure of China, in particular the changes of income structure.

Over the past twenty years, while China gained rapid economic growth and income increases, its income gap also enlarged in 1990s and early this century. The size of middle-income group defined based on relative standard mode decreased rather than increased. In recent years, as income gap shrank, middle income group began to expand. However, the size still hasn't recovered to what it was back in 1980s. In order to develop middle-income group defined based on the relative standard mode, it is necessary for the government to take further measures to adjust income distribution, narrow income gap and facilitate social justice.

The proportion of middle-income group defined by absolute standard mode increased rapidly in the past two decades. From 2001 to 2015, the number went up from 8.1% to 47.6% with an average yearly growth rate of nearly 3%. This coincided with the trend of China's social-economic development and adequately reflected the phenomenon that personal income was growing and an increasing number of people have cast off poverty and become prosperous.

However, in spite of a growing proportion, the majority of middle-income group merely crossed the base line of middle income and were still at the bottom of the pyramid of middle income. Few people reached the middle or the top. The internal structure of middle-income group is still quite unreasonable.

In conclusion, it is necessary to give both priority to economic development and income distribution adjustment. The former is to increase people's income level and the latter is to promote social equity. More importantly, the olive-shaped social structure where middle-income people are the majority must be formed. Not only do we need to expand middle class, but also to adjust and optimize its internal structure. While striving for a higher proportion of middle-income people, it is also a significant task ahead of us to facilitate middle-income group to evolve from current inverted T-shape to pyramid shape and eventually form the most ideal spindle shape.

References

Changcun Z (2012) Measurement and decomposition of urban middle income group----based on income distribution methodology of non-parametric estimation. College J Yunnan Finance Econ Univ (12)

Chen S, Ravallion M (2010) The developing world Is Poorer than we thought, but no less successful in the fight against poverty. Policy Research Working Paper (4703), World Bank

Foster JE, Wolfson MC (2010) Polarization and the decline of the middle class: Canada and the US. J Econ Inequality (2)

Goldthorpe JH (1987) Social mobility and class structure in modern Britain. Clarendon Press, Oxford

Grabka MM, Goebel J (2016) Carsten Schröder and Jürgen Schupp. Shrinking Share of Middle-Income Group in Germany and the US. DIW Econ Bull (18)

Hong J, Yun C (2009) Research on the proportion of Chinese middle Income People and its variation measurement. Econ Perspec (6)

Jian Z, Yongguang Z (2007) Analyzing the correlation between Gini coefficient and the proportion of middle income group. J Quant Scientific Econ 2007

Jinglin C, Lingnan T (2015) Demographics and variation measurement of China's middle Income Group from the perspective of consumption. College J Guang Dong Finance Econ Univ (6)

Lester T (1987) A surge in inequality. Scientific Amer (256)

Milanovic B, Yitzhaki S (2002) Decomposing world income distribution: does the world have a middle class? Review of Income and Wealth, International Association for Research in Income and Wealth (1)

Mills C (1951) Wright. The American Middle Classes, Oxford University Press, White Collar

Nancy B, Graham C, Pettinato S (2000) Stuck in tunnel: is Globalization muddling the middle class?. Working Paper (14), Brookings Institution, Washington, DC

Peilin L, Di Z (2015) Striving for an olive-shaped distribution structure---analysis based on 2006–2013 survey data on China's social Condition. Soc Sci China (1)

Pressman S (2015) Defining and measuring the middle class. American Institute for Economic Research (AIER), Working paper (7)

Ravallion M (2009) The seveloping World's bulging (but Vulnerable) 'Middle Class'. Policy Research Working Paper (4816), World Bank, Washington, DC

Research Group of City Survey Task Force of National Bureau of Statistics, "60,000–500,000: Study on Chinese Urban Middle Income Group". Data, 2005 (6)

Research Group of Social Development Research Institute of National Development and Reform Commission, "Empirical Analysis and Policy Suggestion on How to Expand the Proportion of Middle Income people". Economic Perspective, 2012(5)

Wei L, Shaoguo W (2014) The impact of income increase and income distribution on the proportional changes of middle income people. Statist Study (3)

World Bank (2007) Global Economic Prospects 2007: Managing the Next Wave of Globalization[M]. World Bank, Washington, DC

Wright EO (1979) Class structure and income determination. Academic Press, New York

Yanming W, Qifa X, Jinju X (2014) New method to measure the size of middle income group and Tts application". Statist Study (10)

Ying L (2012) Dynamic changes of population size of chinese middle income group and polarized income: statiscal description and measurement. Finance Trade Res (2)

Ying L (2015) Decomposing factors of proportional changes of middle income group---empirical evidence based on income polarization index. Statis Study (2)

Chunling Li is a Research Fellow of Institute of Sociology of Chinese Academy of Social Sciences (CASS), and director of the Department of Youth Studies and Social Problems in the Institute. She is also a professor of Department of Sociology of CASS. Her primary research interests are social stratification, sociology of education and youth studies. Books she published include *Attitudes, Experiences and Social Transformation: A sociological study of 'Post-1980' Youth*; *Rising Middle Classes in China*; *Gender Stratification and Labor Market*; *Formation of Middle Class in Comparative Perspective: Process, Influence, and Socioeconomic Consequences*; *Theories of Social Stratification*; *Cleavage or Fragment: A Empirical Analysis on the Social Stratification of the Contemporary China*; *Social Mobility in Urban China*; *Youth and Social Change: A Comparative Study Between China and Russia.*

Chapter 2
Trajectories of the Middle Class's Evolution in Modern Russia

N. E. Tikhonova and A. V. Karavay

The issues of middle class in Russian society are covered in many research papers by Russian and even foreign scholars.[1] And that is quite natural, as on the one hand, the middle class performs a number of very important social functions (such as sustaining social and economic stability, providing the economy with highly skilled workforce, creating demand for highly innovative goods and services, etc.), and on the other hand, it undergoes highly dynamic development compared to other social entities, having emerged across the world fairly recently in humankind's history. In Russia in particular, calling a certain social stratum the middle class became possible only late last century.

The emergence of mass middle class worldwide is generally linked to the transition to the late industrial development stage. This transition resulted in a significant rise in the number of people who could not be classified neither as the rich nor the poor. Increasingly intensive, sophisticated, and large-scale production called for greater numbers of highly skilled workers, primarily engineers and managers. The development of education and healthcare systems boosted the number of doctors, teachers, etc. The development of the service sector, with many services requiring the providers to have specialized high skills, also contributed to the expansion of the middle class, along with the growth of the state machine. It was this aggregate of objective processes (and not just the general improvement of material well-being) that resulted in the rise of the middle class in the post-war Europe and North America,

[1] See e.g.: Kivinen (2004), Avraamova (2008), Belyaeva (2007), Srednie classy v Rossii: ekonomicheskie i sotsialnye strategii [Middle Classes in Russia: Economic and Social Strategies]/Ed. *Maleva T.M.* Moscow: Gandalf Publishers, 2003; Tikhonova (2009), Avraamova (2014), Belanovsky and Dmitriev (2010), Sredniy klass v sovremennoy Rossii. Opyt mnogoletnikh issledovaniy [Middle Class in Modern Russia. Summary of Many Years' Worth of Research]/Ed. *Gorshkov, M.K. and Tikhonova, N.E.* Moscow: Ves Mir, 2016; et al.

N. E. Tikhonova (✉) · A. V. Karavay
HSE University, Institute of Sociology of FCTAS RAS, Moscow, Russia

P. Li and M. K. Gorshkov (eds.), *The Middle Income Group in China and Russia*, Research Series on the Chinese Dream and China's Development Path,
https://doi.org/10.1007/978-981-16-1464-4_2

where its size first rivaled that of the working class and then, driven by the continuous structural economic overhaul, even outstripped it. Similar trends emerged in the Soviet Union and later in Russia. At the same time, since Russia was generally falling behind the world's most developed nations, this, quite naturally, affected both the growth rate of the middle class and the specific features of its structure.

Quite possibly, the relatively short history of the middle class and its high diversity in different countries are precisely the reasons why experts do not yet have a universally shared opinion on what the middle class actually is. Russian sociologists first became engaged in active discussions on whether or not to consider certain individuals or households as the middle class 10 years ago, and the debate still goes on. Foreign scholars have been discussing this for around a century; we may single out four main approaches that are used in today's sociology to determine the nature of the middle class.[2]

The **first** approach views the middle class studies as an immensely significant political matter. Consequently, when setting the criteria for the middle class within this approach, the key focus is given to individual's social identification and psychological characteristics, as these are the factors that have the most influence to on people's social self-perception and social and political behavior. In other words, this approach usually defines the middle class based on people's self-identification as members of the middle class or mid-tier population groups. As a result, this approach may be called *subjective.* Widespread as it is, the subjective approach has significant heuristic limitations, as subjective self-evaluation is highly dependent on the economic and political environment, which is prone to rapid changes. Nevertheless, we will occasionally use the "subjective" concept of the middle class in this book when appropriate.

The **second** approach is based on the specific features of the volume, type, and structure of resources that a given individual has at his disposal and derives income from. According to this approach, these features define different people's positions in society, which allows us to refer to it as *resource-based.* The resource-based approach, without a doubt, has a number of advantages, but when applied in practice, it gives rise to a major methodological issue. This approach makes the middle class "dissolve": it disappears as an integrated and holistic research object, splitting into a number of subgroups based on the specific resources its members have. Furthermore, while in the first half of the twentieth century, researchers divided the middle class into "old" (small business owners) and "new" (owners of high-quality human capital), during a later period, the "new" middle class also underwent further subdivision—into professionals and semi-professionals, i.e. people with different human capital quality. Afterwards, a distinction was made between creative workers and other types of "white collars". It is also highly important to note that this definition of the middle class does not account for the return on investment, which means that the middle class can include even the poorest people, as it happened, for instance, in

[2] The history of studying the middle class, as well as Western authors' points of view on the issue are described in detail in the following paper: N.E. Tikhonova, S.V. Mareeva Sredniy klass: teorii i realnost [The Middle Class: Theories and Reality]. Moscow, IS RAS, 2009.

Russia in the 1990s with many people on government-paid jobs, as they had high-quality human capital and drastically low income. Such inconsistent results speak of serious limitations imposed on the overall heuristic capabilities of the resource-based approach, which is why we shall not use it in our book.

The **third** approach to defining the middle class is based on this class's perception as a large social group that is characterized primarily by a high consumption level. In this case, defining the middle class is based on such criteria as per capita income and/or owning a certain set of expensive items. This approach, which might be referred to as *economic,* is mostly typical of economists or scholar specializing in economic sociology. Suffice to say, this is the strategy used for defining the middle class in the analytical reviews of the World Bank that describe the developing nations, including Russia. Its specially developed methodology assumes that the standard per capita income is $10 per day, with the purchasing power parity (PPP) calculated in 2005 prices.[3] Many foreign researchers also use the same criterion for defining the middle class.[4] At the same time, other Western scholars, while also basing their middle class definition on minimal income thresholds, use different figures, which fluctuate from $2 based on the purchasing power parity[5] up to the $10 suggested by the World Bank.

Almost all researchers who rely on this approach to the middle class (which, similarly to the absolute approach to defining the poor, may also be characterized as absolute, as it relies on certain absolute, predetermined figures)[6] focus their work on developing or post-socialist nations. There are certain exceptions in this area, which[7] include the works of a number of authors that focus their attention on analyzing the global middle class or the middle class's place in the income stratification system in different countries; that said, most of these countries are still developing. Yet another important research pattern typical of the authors that use the absolute approach to defining the "economic" middle class is their tendency to split the middle class into a number of subgroups rather than view it as a single entity. In most cases, there are

[3] Russia Economic Report. World Bank. Russian Office. March 2014, Issue 31.

[4] Birdsal et al. (2000), Cárdenas et al. (2011), Kharas (2010), López-Calva and Ortiz-Juarez (2014), Meyer and Sanchez-Paramo (2014), Meyer and Sanchez-Paramo (2014). World Bank. Russia Economic Report. No 31; Pew Research Center. (2015). *The American Middle Class Is Losing Ground: No longer the majority and falling behind financially*. Washington, D.C.: December. (at https://www.pewsocialtrends.org/files/2015/12/2015-12-09_middle-class_FINAL-report.pdf), Vakis, R., Jamele, R. & Lucchetti, L. (2015). *Overview: Left Behind: Chronic Poverty in Latin America and the Caribbean*. Washington, DC: World Bank. License: Creative Commons Attribution CC BY 3.0 et al.).

[5] Ravallion (2010), Ravallion et al. (2009).

[6] To learn more about the scholars that work within the absolute approach to defining the middle class, see *Anikin V., Lezhnina Y., Mareeva S., Slobodenyuk E., Tikhonova N.* Income Stratification: Key Approaches and Their Application to Russia. NRU HSE. Series WP BRP/PSP "Public and Social Policy". 2016. Issue. WP BRP 02/PSP/2016.

[7] Milanovic and Yitzhaki (2002), Kharas (2010), Pew Research Center. (2015). *The American Middle Class Is Losing Ground: No longer the majority and falling behind financially*. Washington, D.C.: December. (at https://www.pewsocialtrends.org/files/2015/12/2015-12-09_middle-class_FINAL-report.pdf), et al.

two subgroups, which, following the logic of vertical income stratification, represent the lower and the upper strata of the middle class. Sometimes, however, the middle class can be divided into three subgroups, which may be referred to with different terms by different authors.

Apart from the absolute approach, there is also a different way of defining the middle class based on income. Namely, the relative approach, which also uses income level to define the middle class; in this case, however, the middle class income thresholds are derived from the specific features of income distribution in this particular country. In some cases, the definition of the middle class according to this interpretation is based on quintiles (for instance, the middle class may be viewed as three middle quintiles of income stratification[8]) or deciles (e.g. 3–9 deciles[9]). Furthermore, some authors base their definition of the middle class on subsistence level (poverty line), applying a special multiplier to it. For example, S. Rose, who singles out three subgroups of the middle class, uses the following thresholds: subsistence level × 1.5 for the lower middle class, subsistence level × 2.5 for the middle class proper, and subsistence level × 5 for the upper middle class.[10]

However, most often within the relative approach to middle class the median of the nationwide income distribution is used. It is worth noting that different researchers may have different points of view as to where exactly lies the middle class thresholds in relation to the median; that said, the lower threshold of the middle class is usually placed at around median income × 0.6 up to median income × 0.75. The division between the lower and upper tiers of the middle class is generally made at approximately median income × 1.25 up to median income × 1.5. When the figures exceed median income × 2, all researchers unanimously[11] state that this is where the high-income level begins.[12] It is this median-based version of the relative approach that we have opted for as we attempt to identify the middle class in Russia and China within this book. We have placed the upper threshold of the middle class at median income × 2; whereas the lower threshold, taking into account the relatively low level of median and middle income in Russia and in China (Table 2.2), is set at median income × 0.75.

The diversity of viewpoints and theoretical and methodological approaches to defining the middle class, which we have demonstrated above, is hardly surprising: the patterns of inequality in different societies, along with the specific features of

[8] Barro (2000), Easterly (2001).

[9] Solimano, A. (2008). *The Middle Class and The Development Process: International Evidence.* Santiago, Chile: Economic Commission for Latin America and the Caribbean. Mimeographed document.

[10] Rose, S. (2016). *The Growing Size and Incomes of the Upper Middle Class.* Urban institute. Research report June 2016. (at https://www.urban.org/sites/default/files/alfresco/publication-pdfs/2000819-The-Growing-Size-and-Incomes-of-the-Upper-Middle-Class.pdf).

[11] Atkinson and Brandolini (2013), Grabka and Frick (2008).

[12] To learn more about the key authors specializing on the relative approach to the middle class, see *Anikin V., Lezhnina Y., Mareeva S., Slobodenyuk E., Tikhonova N.* Income Stratification: Key Approaches and Their Application to Russia. NRU HSE. Series WP BRP/PSP "Public and Social Policy". 2016. Issue. WP BRP 02/PSP/2016.

Table 2.1 Some Statistics on the Social, Economic, and Demographic Environment in Russia and in China (The World Bank. World Development Indicators, URL: https://databank.worldbank.org/data/reports.aspx?source=world-development-indicators# (accessed on 04/29/2017))

Per capita GDP based on PPP, USD						
Country	1980	1990	2000	2005	2010	2015
Russia	–	8,013	6,825	11,822	20,498	25,186
China	–	987	2,933	5,093	9,333	14,451
Share of urban population, %						
Country	1980	1990	2000	2005	2010	2015
Russia	69.75	73.39	73.35	73.46	73.69	74.01
China	19.36	26.44	35.88	42.52	49.23	55.61
Employment in the agrarian sector, %						
Country	1980	1990	2000	2005	2010	2015
Russia	–	13.87	14.49	10.17	7.92	6.71
China	68.75	60.10	50.00	44.80	36.70	28.30
Population growth, in % compared to the previous year						
Country	1980	1990	2000	2005	2010	2015
Russia	0.71	0.39	−0.42	−0.38	0.04	0.19
China	1.25	1.47	0.79	0.59	0.48	0.51

these societies' typical models of income distribution, are largely depend on the type of society in a given country, as well as on the progress this country has made up the path towards industrialization and urbanization, along with the country's civilization type. As a result, these patterns and models can differ dramatically from society to society.[13] Consequently, as we set the income thresholds for the middle class, it is important to understand what development stage this particular society is now undergoing. Table 2.1 contains some characteristic features of Russia and China that may allow us to answer this question, at least in a rough approximation.

As we see from Table 2.1, despite falling a long way behind at first, China has made a colossal leap forward over the past 25 years in terms of all basic figures that describe society overall, growing much closer to Russia in most aspects. Nevertheless, the income stratification models in Russia and in China continue to diverge in some respects, mostly because the latter country tends to suffer from rural poverty of the pre-industrial type,[14] and also due to the sheer difference in the numbers of rural

[13] Anikin and Tikhonova (2016), Tikhonova (2017).

[14] Pre-industrial poverty is the oldest type of poverty that humanity ever faced. It has two main varieties: mass rural poverty and poverty in marginalized urban communities at the times of intense urbanization. Pre-industrial rural poverty stems from the low efficiency of natural or semi-natural agricultural production. In turn, the classic version of pre-industrial poverty in marginalized urban communities, which goes back to the history of developed European countries in the eighteenth and nineteenth century, is caused by uncontrollable mass migration to cities from overpopulated rural

Table 2.2 Characteristic Features of Income Distribution in Russia and in China, 2012. (To calculate the household income levels based on the ISSP-2012 body of data, we used the following indices: PPP conversion factor, private consumption (LCU per international $) (The World bank. PPP conversion factor, private consumption (LCU per international $) (https://databank.worldbank.org/data/reports.aspx?source=2&series=PA.NUS.PRVT.PP&country =) (accessed on 15.08.2016). To demonstrate the country's general development level by characterizing the per capita GDP while accounting for PPP, we used the GDP per capita and PPP figures (current international $) (The World Bank. GDP per capita, PPP (current international $) (https://data.worldbank.org/indicator/NY.GDP.PCAP.PP.CD) (accessed on 17.03.2017).)

	Russia	China
Monthly Household Income, $, based on PPP [a]	***565.0***	***300.3***
Average monthly per capita income in households, $, based on PPP	650.2	523.3
Ratio between the median and average income	0.87	0.57
Ratio between the nationwide median and the average Russian income median	1	0.53
The ratio between the income or consumption of the richest and poorest 10%[b]	14.0	15.0
Gini[c]	41.6	42.2
For reference: Per capita GDP, based on PPP	***25,316.6***	***11,351.1***

[a]From this point onward, all the figures in the table shall be calculated based on ISSP-2012, unless explicitly stated otherwise
[b]Basis of the calculations: The World bank. World Development Indicators: Distribution of income or consumption (https://wdi.worldbank.org/table/2.9) (accessed on 17.03.2017).
[c]The World bank. GINI index (World Bank estimate) (https://data.worldbank.org/indicator/SI.POV.GINI?locations) (accessed on 17.03.2017).

population traditionally have lower income than urban population in developing countries.

When speaking of the key development dynamics in these countries, we must mention the changes that have occurred in income differentiation over the past 25–30 years. Many international organizations, such as the World Bank, OECD, the UN, etc., have been evaluating these changes for a lengthy period of time. The relevant data is aggregated from many sources by one of the research divisions of the United Nations University (UNU), thus comprising the international Gini coefficient database. Some of this database's information on certain countries dates back to the beginning of last century.[15] It shows that over the past few decades, most countries, including Russia and China, have been experiencing a rise in income inequality. For instance, in Russia the Gini reached[16] 31.2% in 1991 and as much as 41.6% in 2012. In China, the figures rose from 27.4% in 1991 to 33.9% in 2012. By comparison,

areas at the dawn of industrialization and urbanization (for more on the subject, see: Tikhonova and Anikin (2014).

[15] UNU-WIDER, World Income Inequality Database (WIID3.4)', URL: https://www.wider.unu.edu/database/world-income-inequality-database-wiid34 (accessed on: 25.03.2017).

[16] As UNU-RIDER shows Gini data from a number of sources, there are several different annual figures; thus, we calculated the average for every given year.

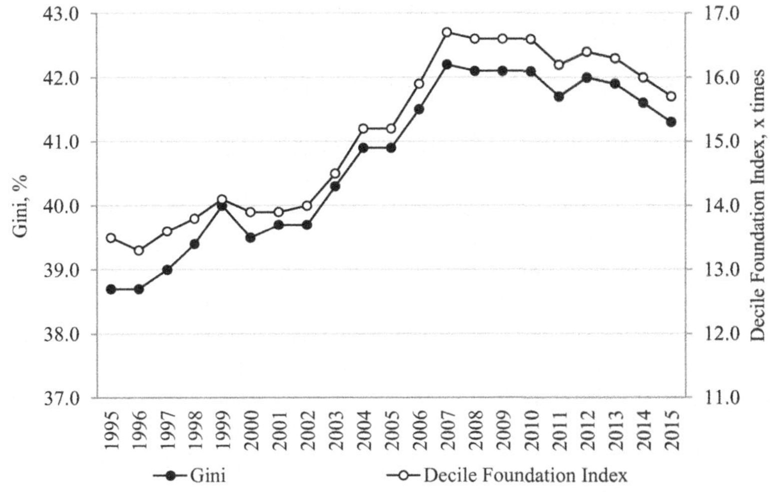

Fig. 2.1 Income Distribution Figures, FSSS, 1995–2015

in the USA, the increase was from 38.2% to 43.3% during the same period of time. Against the background of the general trend towards a rising Gini coefficient, the Scandinavian nations are a notable exception: in Norway, for one, the same period saw a fall in the Gini figures from 29.7% to 24.2%; although a steady decrease started only in 2004 (from the initial point of 31.5%).

Russian statistical reporting offices, primarily the Russian Federal State Statistics Service (FSSS), also conduct annual monitoring of income inequality nationwide and within separate regions. FSSS data[17] (see Fig. 2.1) shows that from 1995 to 2007, Russia experienced a notable rise in income inequality, and the trend was somewhat mitigated only during the last 10 years. Nevertheless, as recently as in 2015 the first income decile still surpassed the income of the poorest 10% by 15.7 times, while in 1995, the gap was substantially smaller (13.5 times). Moreover, the Gini coefficient exceeded the mid-1990s figures by 2.6%—which is quite striking, bearing in mind that the key liberal reforms in Russia had been implemented by 1995.

Despite the remaining differences between Russia and China, the changes that occurred in the general social environment during the last decade, including income stratification specifics in both countries, have brought them closer together in terms of both the main features and the key indicators of income inequality (Table 2.2) among the mass social groups (who usually participate in sociological surveys). These similarities allow us to rely on the relative version of the income approach when comparing the "economic" middle class in Russia and China. The absolute approach, however, has turned out to be inapplicable to defining and analyzing the Russian and Chinese middle class, as, if we take into account the data of the International

[17] Russian Federal State Statistics Service. "Distribution of the General Volume of the Money Income and Characteristics of the Differentiation of the Money Income of the Population". URL: https://www.gks.ru/free_doc/new_site/population/bednost/tabl/1-2-2.doc (accessed on: 25.03.2017).

Social Survey Programme (ISSP) (which covers 50 countries, including Russia and China),[18] it turns out that the middle class (as defined by the absolute approach)[19] already encompassed 85.9% of the population in Russia and 50.6% of the population in China back in 2012.[20] By 2016, the figures increased even more in both countries, reaching as high as 90% in Russia.[21] Such colossal size of the middle class contradicts the notion that Russians have of it in their public conscience, while in terms of theory, it blurs the specific features of this group, as compared to other population strata, and makes the analysis of the middle class pointless a priori. The situation in China is also developing in a similar direction.

At the same time, as we apply the median-based version of the relative approach to comparing the Russian and Chinese middle class, it bears remembering that the two middle classes will be characterized not only by diverging quality of living but also by different professional, settlement, etc. composition, as the two countries are still quite different in terms of the general social and economic development level. As we evaluate Russia's "economic" middle class, we must also keep in mind that the income inequality in Russia, just as in China, is characterized by salient differences in inequality depending on the region (Fig. 2.2). For instance, in December 2015, the Gini coefficient across Russian regions fluctuated from[22] 33.9% in Tver Oblast to 42.9% in Tyumen Oblast; moreover, in 72 regions out of 83, the Gini figures were lower than the nationwide coefficient, and in half of the regions the figures did not even exceed 37.5%. Out of densely populated regions, only Moscow stood far apart from the others, with its Gini figures for December of 2015 reaching 43.2% (according to FSSS) against the national average of 41.2%. These differences need to be accounted for if we use the nationwide median as the basis for our calculations, as high Gini figures speak of a relatively poorer status of the middle class, first and foremost (whereas the decile coefficient reflects the specific features of inequality concerning poorest population group). Consequently, even if the income of the middle class appears to be similar in different regions, this superficial similarity may conceal significant differences in the actual well-being and social and economic positions of the middle class.

That said, Russian regions differ dramatically not only in terms of income inequality distribution, but also in terms of absolute income figures, including, in particular, median income, subsistence level (poverty line), and many other parameters that are directly linked to income stratification. Consequently, the inner regional

---

[18] To learn more about the study, go to its official websites: https://www.issp.org and https://www.gesis.org/en/issp/home.

[19] It is worth bearing in mind that this approach sets the lowest threshold of the middle class at 10 US dollars (based on PPP).

[20] Anikin (2016).

[21] *Tikhonova, N.E.* Stratifikatsiya po dokhodu v Rossii: spetsifika modeli i vektor izmeneniy [Income Stratification in Russia: Specific Features of the Model and Direction of Changes] // Obshchestvennye nauki i sovremennost [Social Sciences and Contemporary Age]. 2017. Issue 2. P. ….

[22] FSSS, Central Statistic Database, Gini (Income Concentration), URL: https://cbsd.gks.ru/ (accessed on: 17.03.2017).

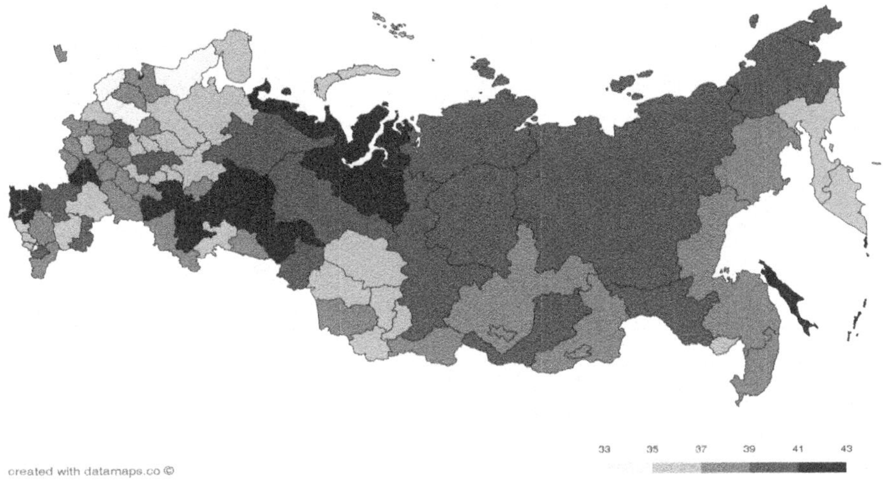

Fig. 2.2 Gini Figures in Different Russian Regions, FSSS (Drawn with reference to: FSSS, Central Statistic Database, Gini (Income Concentration), URL: https://cbsd.gks.ru/ (accessed on: 17.03.2017).), 2015, %

specifics of income inequality overlap with inter-regional differences in the population's income level. This complex parameter system is what shapes the real models of income stratification in each Russian region. These models also have a substantial impact on the specific features of the local middle class. In this book, however, we shall not focus too closely on the regional specifics of the mid-income tier, considering only the general state of the middle class in Russia.[23] We shall limit ourselves merely to pointing out the regional differentiation and diversity of the Russian middle class to the reader.

We shall now, once again, turn to the matter of defining the "economic" middle class among the rest of the population. *We are setting the thresholds of the middle class at per capita monthly income median × 0.75 (lower threshold) and × 2 (upper threshold).*[24] *This has allowed us, based on the data of the Monitoring Survey*

[23] If you wish to compare the overall picture to the results of data aggregation in specific regions (with the median in mind), please consider these sources: *Anikin V., Lezhnina Y., Mareeva S., Slobodenyuk E., Tikhonova N.* Income Stratification: Key Approaches and Their Application to Russia. NRU HSE. Series WP BRP/PSP "Public and Social Policy". 2016. Issue. WP BRP 02/PSP/2016 and N.E. Tikhonova. Income Stratification in Russia: Specific Features of the Model and Direction of Changes. In: *Social Sciences and Contemporary Age.* 2017. Issue 2. P. 23–35.

[24] The chapters written by the Russian contributors to this book are based on different corpora of empiric data, which are described in the Appendix. This particular chapter relies on the data bodies of the RAS Institute of Sociology surveys dating back to different years. The methodology used for compiling the selection was similar for all surveys, which allowed us to place the bodies of data along a unified time scale, following the data compatibility principle.

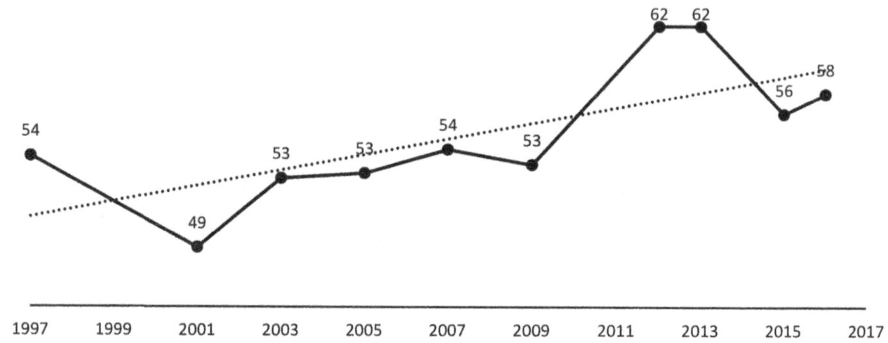

Fig. 2.3 Size Dynamics of the "Economic" Middle Class and the Trend of Changes from 1997 to 2016, in % of the Overall Population

conducted by the RAS Institute of Sociology in the fall of 2016, to define a social structure model where the low-income groups amount to a 35% of the overall Russian population, the mid-income groups amount to 58%, and the high-income groups amount to 7%.

Turning to the size dynamics of the middle class, which has been defined based on the income-based approach, we see that the figures have fluctuated notably throughout the past 20 years. To be more precise, each economic crisis caused the middle class to shrink temporarily, with the most adverse impact being delivered by the crisis of 1998–1999. During the periods of stability, by contrast, the middle class experienced continuous growth; and the overall trend in the change of its size over the past 20 years has been positive (Fig. 2.3).

Bearing in mind the almost threefold (from × 0.75 to × 2 income distribution medians) income differentiation of the middle class, we have opted for following the international tradition and divide the middle class into two subgroups for further analysis. One of these subgroups, with per capita income ranging from median × 0.75 to median × 1.25, may be referred to as the lower middle class, which demostrates a quality of life typical of the country as a whole. The second subgroup, with income ranging from median × 1.25 to median × 2, may be regarded as the part of the "economic" middle class that is quite wealthy compared to most of the population and sets the standard of living that the majority of Russians aspire to. Quite notably, the former subgroup has continuously been dominant within the Russian middle class for at least the past two decades (Fig. 2.4).

However, the dynamics of the middle class, as defined with accordance to median per capita income levels, cannot be reviewed separately from the changes undergone by the median itself, especially since the analysis of Russians' average per capita income over the past 20 years shows that the changes were quite significant: the nominal median income increased 35 times from 1997 to 2015 (from 400 to 14,000 rubles, respectively). If we look at real income and take into account the accumulated

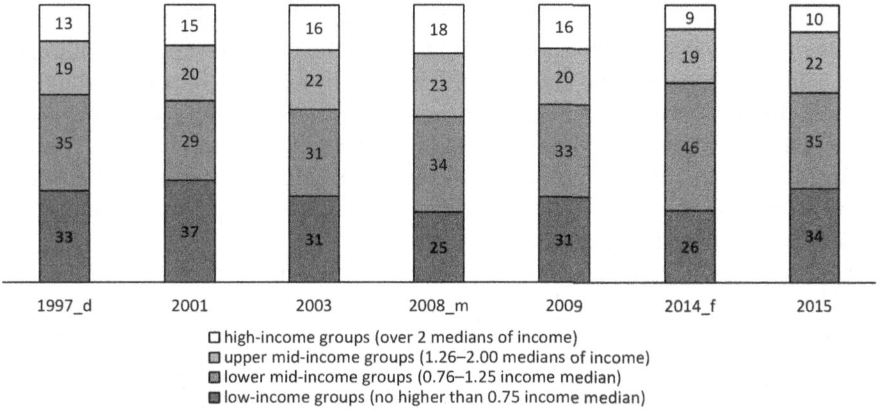

Fig. 2.4 The Size Dynamics of Different Population Groups in Russia from 1997 to 2016, IS RAS, %

inflation level, we may see that the actual increase of the median per capita income was, albeit slightly smaller, still fairly substantial, by more than 3 times (from 400 to 1244 rubles in the 1997 prices[25]).

All of the above means that *over the past two decades, Russia has been going through two parallel processes, which have had a direct influence on the country's social structure. On the one hand, there were changes, and rapid ones at that, in the income level of all population groups, including the mid-income tier. This, quite naturally, impacted the middle class's consumption standards.* On the other hand, *the ratio between different social groups within the overall model of Russian's social structure also underwent transformation, which involved shifts in the proportions of different groups and the "historic background" of their members. The relevant risks of social position change were different for people belonging to different groups and strata.* For instance, over the past few years, high-income groups have been facing the highest risk of losing their privileges, as the number of people in these groups, which had reached its peak before the 2008–2009 crisis (18%), dropped to 7% by 2016 (among people taking part in mass surveys)[26] (Fig. 2.4).

As for the middle class, data of Institute of Sociology RAS reveals that its size fluctuated within the range between 49 and 65%, depending on the economic conditions[27] (Fig. 2.4). It is quite notable that the expansion of the middle class over the past 10 years has been occurring mostly due to people with high income "sliding down"

[25] We have based our calculations of actual average per capita income with the use of FSSS data on indices of consumer prices for goods and services, URL: https://www.gks.ru/wps/wcm/connect/rosstat_main/rosstat/ru/statistics/tariffs/# (accessed on: 23.03.2017).

[26] The figures may be slightly different in other data corpora, but regardless, they also show a decrease in the number of people with high income. The Russian Longitudinal Monitoring Survey, in particular, shows that, since the time before the 2008–2009 crisis, the size of the high-income groups has shrunk from 15 to 9% (see Chap. 6).

[27] The Monitoring data also confirms this patterns (see data in Chap. 6).

the income scale, whereas before the 2008 crisis this expansion used to be ensured mostly by people from the lower middle class transitioning to the upper middle class level, while the lower middle class, in turn, was fed by an influx of people from low-income groups. During the 2014–2016 crisis, the high-income groups' tendency to partially transition to the upper middle class was complemented by the latter's inclination to partially "slide down" into the lower middle class. This means that the well-being of the most well-off groups of the Russian population has suffered somewhat over the past 8–10 years.

However, this does not mean that all was well among Russians with relatively low income: rather than steadily "sliding down", they suffered from a chronic lack of stability. This was most typical of groups with income at 26–35% within the overall income scale (Fig. 2.4). These groups kept drifting between different income strata depending on the state of the economy, forced to switch back and forth between[28] the low- and mid-income lifestyle.

Having characterized the subjective and resource-based approaches to defining the middle class, we have dwelled in detail on the economic approach, which is the main approach used in this book. We have also given an overview of some results of analyzing the evolution paths of the middle class in Russia over the past 20 years. However, sociology also offers a fourth approach to defining the middle class. This **fourth** approach is based on applying the definition criteria that are typical of the so-called multidimensional stratification (i.e. the certain features of the social and professional status, education, and income and property, with self-identification sometimes added to the mix). This approach, which matches the traditions of the neo-Weberian school of sociology and may be referred to as the *multi-criteria* approach, is quite widespread among researchers of the middle class both worldwide and in Russia. However, researchers do not share a uniform opinion on exactly what type of professional occupation or what education level may serve as the defining criterion of the middle class, especially today.[29] Nevertheless, bearing in mind the popularity of this approach and its heuristic potential, we were unable to pass it by in our study, and this book will, in fact, occasionally use it.

The methodology of defining the middle class within this approach is based on the following criteria and threshold parameters:

- *education* (no lower than secondary specialized education/vocational college);
- *professional status*, implying the non-manual labor;

[28] Like the size of the middle class, the size of low-income groups is characterized by a clear correlation to the country's economic environment: it grows after each economic crisis and shrinks during the period between crises.

[29] For more information, please refer to: N.E. Tikhonova, S.V. Mareeva. Sredniy klass: teorii i realnost [The Middle Class: Theories and Reality]. Moscow, IS RAS, 2009; N.E. Tikhonova. Sotsialnaya struktura Rossii: teorii i realnost [Russia's Social Structure: Theories and Reality]. – Moscow. Moscow, Novy Khronograf: Institute of Sociology RAS, 2014.

Fig. 2.5 Size Dynamics of the Middle Class, as Defined within the Multi-Criteria Approach, and the Pattern of Changes that It Underwent from 2003 to 2015, in % of the Overall Population

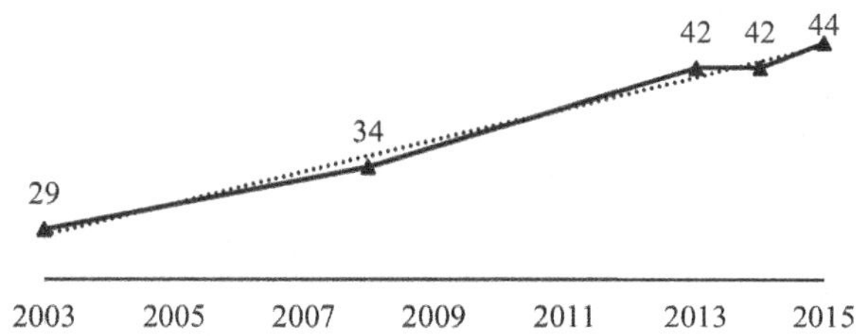

- *material well-being* (the average monthly per capita income should not be lower than the median for the type of settlement, or the number of durable goods owned by the person should not be lower than the overall median for the entire population);
- *self-identification* (the integral self-evaluation of the person's social status should be 4 out of 10 or higher).

We should note that, while the employed population needed to "pass" all 4 criteria to be ranked as the middle class, in the case of the unemployed population the middle class status was determined depending on three out of four aforementioned criteria, with professional status not being taken into account. Additional examination has shown that the vast majority of unemployed members of the middle class classified as above is still linked to the structural professional positions typical of the middle class: they either used to hold these positions earlier (retirees with higher education) or will occupy them in the future (college and university students).

As revealed by sociological data, middle class in this definition also underwent considerable expansion in Russia from 2000 to 2010. However, the most intensive growth of the middle class (from 29 to 42%) occurred before 2013; later on, the middle class stabilized, amounting to a little more than 40% of the overall population (Fig. 2.5). And even though the economic crisis of 2014–2016 hit the lifestyle of the Russian middle class quite hard, this did not reduce the share of population belonging to the middle class.[30]

As we see in Figs. 2.3 and 2.5, the size of the middle class in Russia has undeniably grown over the past 15 years, regardless of how the middle class is interpreted; nevertheless, the economic and neo-Weberian middle classes differ in size quite substantially. The consequences of economic crises also seem to affect the two middle classes in different ways. Their professional composition is also different: for instance, a large share (around one third) of the income-based middle class is comprised out of blue-collar laborers, who are excluded from the middle class by the multi-criteria approach. The latter approach also disregards many routine employees of the trade sector, who are also part of the mid-income population group. On the

[30] To learn more about the economic crisis's impact on the Russian middle class and to see why it did not cause the middle class to shrink, despite the deteriorating standard of living, consult the following: Sredniy klass v sovremennoy Rossii. Opyt mnogoletnikh issledovaniy [Middle Class in Modern Russia. Summary of Many Years' Worth of Research]/Ed. *Gorshkov, M.K. and Tikhonova, N.E.* Moscow: Ves Mir, 2016.

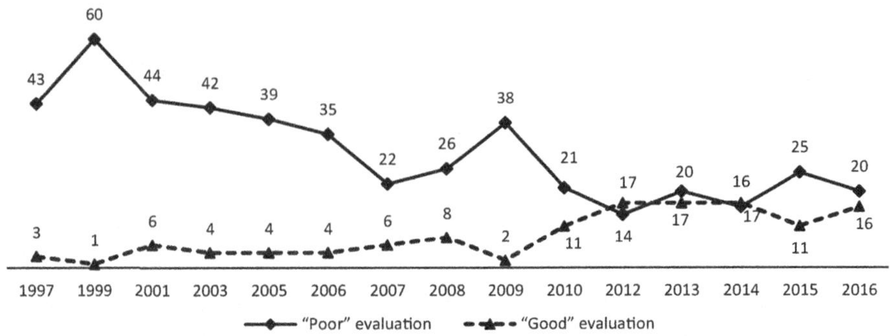

Fig. 2.6 The Dynamics of Evaluating Material Well-Being as "Poor" or "Good" among the Lower Mid-Income Groups from 1997 to 2016, RAS IS, %

other hand, the average per capita household income of certain individual members of the "multi-criteria" middle class may prompt to classify these individuals as part of the low-income groups, despite them owning a relatively large selection of property. It should be acknowledged that we are dealing with overlapping sets, and if we look at the ratio between the representatives of the Russian middle classes in their various definitions, we can conclude that in the fall of 2015, 30% of all Russians could be described as the middle class from both definitions, while 26% did not belong to it in any case, 6% had higher income than the upper threshold of median income × 2, and the remaining 38% could be defined as either the "economic" or the "multi-criteria" middle class.

As we mentioned before, taking into account the formidable size of the latter group, it would seem rational to use both approaches to the middle class as we analyze a number of issues, primarily those related to the employment and identity of the middle class. However, as the use of the terms "middle class" in two different contexts lead to confusion, we have decided to use two different terms in our analysis: the first is "mid-income groups" (MIG), which describes people that are defined as middle class under the economic approach; and the second is "middle class", defined according to the multi-criteria approach. The lower strata of the "economic" middle class, in turn, have been named "lower mid-income groups" (occasionally abbreviated as LMIG), while the upper strata are to be referred to as "upper mid-income groups" (UMIG).[31]

In light of studying the issue of the "economic" middle class's development path, it is also important to bear in mind that, over the course of the past two decades, the consumption standards of the upper and lower mid-income groups have changed as much as their income, although the differences between the two are still evident (Fig. 2.6). But even though the past 20 years have brought significant change in

[31] It should be noted that the upper mid-income groups are characterized by a larger "overlap zone" with the "multi-criteria" middle class: by the end of 2015, 64% of people from these groups could be described as the middle class under the above approach. By contrast, in the lower mid-income groups, the "overlap zone" reached only 46%.

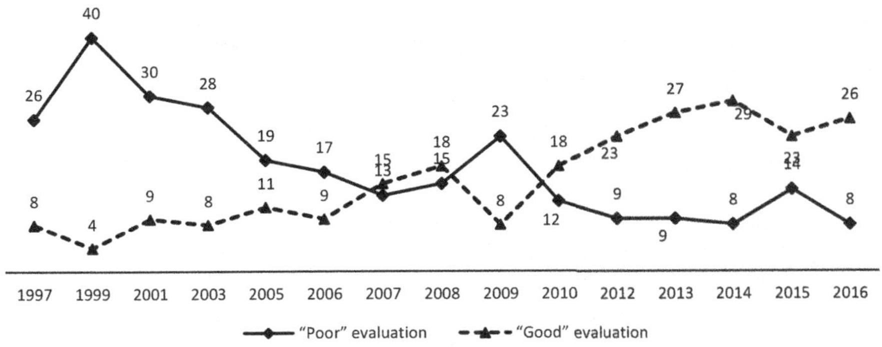

Fig. 2.7 The Dynamics of Evaluating Material Well-Being as "Poor" or "Good" among the Upper Mid-Income Groups from 1997 to 2016, RAS IS, %

the living standards of both subgroups of the Russian mid-income population level, their respective crucial milestones were different. The lower mid-income groups, having responded painfully to the crises of 1998–1999 and 2008–2009, finally started exhibiting at least some satisfaction with their material well-being only in the 2010s. At any rate, it was at that time that the share of favorable and unfavorable responses regarding material well-being started evening out (Fig. 2.6). This relative stability did not last, however, and the new crisis at the end of 2014 once again caused a surge of negative evaluations. However, the two curves once again drew closer in 2016 (Fig. 2.6), and that allows to hope that the trend towards improved material well-being of the lower mid-income groups, which was typical of the 2010s, may occur again in the nearest future.

In the case of upper mid-income groups, after their material well-being suffered dramatically during the 1998–1999 crisis, the situation started gradually improving, and by the mid-2000s, the groups' favorable evaluation of their material position started dominating over unfavorable evaluation. The crisis of 2008–2009 rekindled the dominance of negative responses, but after it was over, the positive trend quickly emerged again. The 2014–2016 crisis, in turn, despite having a temporary negative impact on the ratio of the upper mid-income groups' favorable and unfavorable responses regarding their material well-being, did not jeopardize the dominance of the overall satisfaction with their current material position (Fig. 2.7).

The vastly different experience that characterize two subgroups of the Russian "economic" middle class gets reflected in the way they view their future prospects. As shown in Table 2.3, after peaking in 2014, the share of positive opinions of future prospects remained at around 30% for the upper mid-income groups and 20% for the lower mid-income groups for two years in a row. As for skeptical opinions on the future, the figures were far less constant, displaying a notable improvement trend in 2016 (Table 2.3).

Quite plausibly, it might be the relatively high degree of certainty in the future, together with the general satisfaction with their material well-being, that allows

Table 2.3 The Difference Between Negative and Positive Opinions on the Future Dynamics of Material Well-Being among the Mid-Income Population Groups in 2001–2016 (The figures are given in percentage points and represent the difference between the number of positive and negative responses on the future prospect dynamics.), RAS IS, percentage points

Year	The difference between the negative and positive evaluations of personal status improvement prospects			For reference: the same figures for the low and high-income population groups	
	Upper mid-income group	Lower mid-income group	Mid-income groups overall	Low-income	High-income
2001	19	1	***8***	−3	46
2006	24	−5	***7***	−15	47
2008[a]	35	14	***27***	14	49
2009	−29	−47	***−40***	−46	−2
2010	31	13	***21***	7	45
2013	27	19	***21***	10	22
2014	33	23	***26***	6	50
2015	−5	−18	***−13***	−24	10
2016	6	−8	***−3***	−16	13

[a]The data for 2008 was obtained in April, i.e. before the 2008–2009 crisis began

people from both subgroups of the mid-income strata, despite all the differences between them, to identify as members of the "subjective" middle class: as many as three quarters of them state that in different degree they can say "that's us" about the middle class, in one respect or another. Furthermore, the overwhelming majority of them place themselves in the middle of the social scale when completing the graphic self-identification test. However, consistent self-identification as the middle class is typical only of one in every five people from mid-income groups; the same number of people consistently identifies themselves as the working class.[32] However, considering that blue-collar workers amount to over one third of the mid-income groups, this is hardly surprising.

Let us summarize

The distinction of various income groups is the traditional research subject that interests economists, sociologists, and statisticians alike. This issue is especially relevant for Russia, where the income stratification model has gone through dramatic changes at least twice from the beginning of the 1990s, which is clearly demonstrated by the dynamics of Gini, the decile coefficient, the average and median income, etc. It is especially important to note that during this period, the income of all the Russian population first plummeted in the 1990s, and then increased manifold in the 2000s

[32] To learn more about the way mid-income groups and specific subgroups identify themselves, go to Chap. 7.

and 2010s (even in real terms). Due to these developments, Russians' standard of living transitioned into a completely new quality, and that had an impact on members of mid-income groups as well.

Regardless of the salient differences in income stratification models across Russia's different regions, use of figures that characterize Russia as a whole is preferred when drawing international comparisons. The optimal indicator, in terms of heuristic potential for making international comparisons and drawing timelines, is the median income. Foreign sociology's traditional definition of the middle class, whereupon it is set to comprise people with income ranging in between median × 0.75 and median × 2 and subsequently gets divided into 2 or 3 subgroups, is also applicable to Russia, thus it is the method we have opted for in this book.

When defined in accordance to this approach, the Russian middle class constitutes a massive social entity: as of the end of 2016, it included 57% of the country's adult population. This was noticeably less than in the early 2014, before the 2014–2016 crisis, when the middle class had amounted to almost two thirds of the population, but still quite substantial. Nevertheless, bearing in mind the methodology we have selected for defining the "economic" middle class, these dynamics show that almost 10% of Russians who used to afford the typical average nationwide lifestyle have now "sunk" to a completely new level, affected by the latest crisis, which has forced them to not only start cutting their expenses but also to change their lifestyle. But by the end of 2016, the situation had already begun to show signs of improvement. This gives us reason to hope that the past two decades' tendency towards the sustainable (albeit disrupted by an occasional economic crisis) growth of the middle class will soon pick up again.

The comparison between the "economic" middle class and the middle class as seen by other approaches shows that, regardless of how it is defined, the Russian middle class is a large and consistently increasing social entity, even though the middle classes described by different theories do not coincide completely on the micro-level. For instance, if we look at the "multi-criteria" middle class defined according to the neo-Weberian tradition and compare it to the "economic" middle class, the former will turn out far narrower than the latter (in the fall of 2016, only 44% of Russians could be described as part of this middle class, against the 57% that were part of mid-income groups). These two entities are overlapping rather than inclusive (their "overlap zone" covers 30% of all Russians).

In turn, the ratio between the "economic" and "subjective" middle class is far from clear-cut. This stems from the fact that a large share of Russia's mid-income population groups (around 35%) is comprised out of blue-collar workers and, consequently, people belonging to these groups are characterized by ambiguous class identification. Furthermore, the very concept of the middle class is relatively new for Russia, as most groups belonging to the middle class used to be described as "intelligentsia" (creative workers, the academia, engineering graduates, etc.). This is the main reason why consistent verbal self-identification as the middle class is not a strong trend in Russia. However, in a graphic test where preople were asked to define their social status, members of mid-income population groups were overwhelmingly prone to placing themselves in the middle.

All of the above reaffirms that the process of the middle class's formation as an independent large-scale social entity within Russia's social structure is progressing relatively smoothly, although it is far from being completed. This means that every point of view on this entity is valid. The "economic" middle class in particular, considering the functions performed by its representatives in the goods, finance, and other markets, and its role in stabilizing the country's social and political environment, doubtlessly deserves special and careful consideration. It is this consideration, including detailed analysis that focuses on the specific features of the middle class's status, behavior, and mindset, that will be covered in the following chapters of this book.

References

Anikin V, Lezhnina Y, Mareeva S, Slobodenyuk E, Tikhonova N (2016) Income Stratification: Key Approaches and Their Application to Russia. NRU HSE. Series WP BRP/PSP "Public and Social Policy". 2016. Issue. WP BRP 02/PSP/2016

Anikin VA, Tikhonova NE (2016) Poverty and inequality in the BRICS nations: the specific case of Russia. In: Society and economy 1:78–114

Atkinson A, Brandolini A (2013) On the identification of the middle class. In Gornick J, Jäntti M (Eds), Income inequality: economic disparities and the middle class in affluent countries. Stanford, California: Stanford University Press, pp 77–100

Avraamova EM (2008) Sredniy klass epokhi Putina [The Middle Class in the Putin Era].—Obshchestvennye nauki i sovremennost [Social Sciences and Contemporary Age] (1)

Avraamova EM, Maleva TM (2014) Evoliutsiia rossiyskogo srednego klassa: missii i metodologiya [The Evolution of the Russian Middle Class: Missions and Methodology]. Obshchestvennye nauki i sovremennost [Social Sciences and Contemporary Age] (4):5–17

Barro R (2000) Inequality and growth in a panel of Countries. J Econ Growth 5:5–32

Belanovsky SA, Dmitriev ME, Misikhina SG (2010) Sredniy klass v rentoorientirovannoy ekonomike: pochemu Moskva perestala byt Rossiey? [Middle Class in a Rent-Oriented Economy: Why Did Moscow Stop Being Russia?]—SPERO, Issue 13, fall-winter of 2010. pp 69–86

Belyaeva LA (2007) I vnov o srednem klasse Rossii [And Again on the Russian Middle Class]. Sotsiologicheskie issledovaniya [Sociological Research]. (5)

Birdsall N, Graham C, Pettinato S (2000) Stuck in tunnel: Is globalization muddling the middle? Center Soc Econ Dyn Working Paper 1

Cárdenas M, Kharas H, Henao C (2011) Latin America's global middle class. Working Paper, Global Economy and Development at Brookings, Washington, DC

Easterly W (2001) The middle class consensus and economic development. J Econ Growth 6(4):317–335

Grabka M, Frick J (2008) The Shrinking German middle class—signs of long-term polarization in disposable income? DIW Berlin Weekly Report 4(4):21–27

Kharas H (2010) The emerging middle class in developing countries. OECD Development Centre Working Paper, vol 285

Kivinen M (2004) Sredniy klass v sovremennoy Rossii [Middle Class in Modern Russia]. Mir Rossii. Sotsiologiya. Etnologiya [World of Russia. Sociology. Ethnology] (4):143–169

López-Calva L, Ortiz-Juarez E (2014) A vulnerability approach to the definition of the middle class. J Econ Inequality 12:23–47

Meyer M, Sanchez-Paramo C (2014) In Focus: economic mobility and middle-class formation. In: Confidence crisis exposes economic weakness. World Bank. Russia Economic Report. No 31

Meyer M, Sanchez-Paramo C (2014) In focus: economic mobility and middle-class formation. In: Confidence crisis exposes economic weakness

Milanovic B, Yitzhaki S (2002) Decomposing world income distribution: Does the world have a middle class? Rev Income Wealth 48(2):155–178

Ravallion M (2010) The developing world's bulging (but vulnerable) middle class. World Dev 38(4):445–454

Ravallion M, Chen S, Sangraula P (2009) Dollar a day revisited. World Bank Econ Rev 23:163–184

Tikhonova NE (2017) Income stratification in Russia as compared to other nations. In: Social sciences and contemporary age 3:26–41

Tikhonova NE, Anikin VA (2014) Bednost' v Rossii na fone drugikh stran [Poverty in Russia Compared to Other Countries] // Mir Rossii: Sotsiologiya. Etnologiya [World of Russia: Sociology, Ethnology] 23(4):59–95

Tikhonova NE, Mareeva SV (2009) Srednie klassy v sovremennoy Rossii [Middle Classes in Modern Russia]. Moscow. Alfa-M

N. E. Tikhonova Doctor of Sociology, Professor at the National Research University Higher School of Economics and Chief Researcher the Federal Center of Theoretical and Applied Sociology of the Russian Academy of Sciences (former Institute of Sociology, Russian Academy of Sciences). She is a recognized specialist in cultural dynamics, social stratification and social policy. Author of about 400 scientific works, 3 individual monographs and 4 monographs in co-authorship, including 3 monographs published in Great Britain in 2000-2009. Her main publications include: in English—"Work and Welfare in the New Russia» (London, 2000, in co-authorship), "Poverty and Social Exclusion in the New Russia" (London, 2004, in co-authorship), "Health and Health Care in the New Russia" (London, 2008, in co-authorship). In Russian—"Middle class: Theory and Reality" (2009, in co-authorship), "The Social Structure of Russia: Theory and Reality", 2014.

A. V. Karavay Senior Researcher at the Institute of the Social Analysis and Forecasting of RANEPA, Researcher at the Federal Center of Theoretical and Applied Sociology of the Russian Academy of Sciences (former Institute of Sociology, Russian Academy of Sciences). Holds Ph.D. in Sociology from Institute of Sociology (2015). Main areas of interests include workers (working class) as the special social and professional group, the human capital of different professional groups, social structure, processes of social and economic adaptation. Author of over 20 articles and chapters in scientific monographs. Her recent publications in English include articles "The Attitude of Russian Workers to Managing Their Resources: Finances, Health and Spare Time". Zhurnal Issledovanii Sotsial'noi Politiki. 2016. Vol. 14. No. 2; "Participation of Russian Workers in Continuing Professional Education". Educational Studies (Moscow). 2016. No. 4.

Chapter 3
Analysis of Employment Structure of Middle Income Group: 2006–2015

Lei Fan

Since the reform and opening up, we have seen rapid development of economy and society and the expansion of the middle income group. It is our consensus to form the olive-shaped social structure for consumption update by growing domestic demand, keep a medium–high speed of growth and maintain a stable and harmonious society. Employment plays a significant role in consolidation and expansion of the middle income group. On one hand, labor remuneration is the major income source of middle income group. Employment related salary income and operation income account a quite high percent of the per capita income. If calculated according to the data from China Statistical Yearbook 2015, of all the per capita disposable income, 56.7% was salary income, 18% was operation income, 7.9% was property income and 17.4% was transfer income. Even it was written in Report to the Seventeenth National Congress of the Communist Party of China that "to enable more people to enjoy their property income", and it was also mentioned in Report to the Eighteenth National Congress of the Communist Party of China that "grow people's income in multiple channels". For most households, employment related salary income and operation income in earning over quite a long time. On the other hand, the economic structure and growth along with other factors also shape the structure and feature of the middle income group in typical time and regions. In the United States in eighteenth century, an agricultural society with the main body of the middle income group, which were comprised of farmers, small proprietor owners, small traders, etc., was formed. With the advancing of industrialization and education, the white-collar group that includes the enterprise executives, technicians, etc. who mainly depended salary, rose as the main body of the middle income group. Whereas in the post-industrial time, the gap between the white and blue collar was narrowed, partly because some blue collars received higher salary and was ranked as the lower middle income group. So, the

L. Fan (✉)
Institute of Sociology, Chinese Academy of Social Sciences (CASS), Beijing 100732, China

P. Li and M. K. Gorshkov (eds.), *The Middle Income Group in China and Russia*, Research Series on the Chinese Dream and China's Development Path,
https://doi.org/10.1007/978-981-16-1464-4_3

analysis of employment on the structure of middle income group helps understand the group's phase characteristics during its development and change.

The so-called employment structure means how the workforce is divided up in the main employment sectors and the percentages in the overall population. It indicates the labor resource allocation or the variation characteristics. As employment structure directly correlates with personal income (not the household income per capita), with the interviewees' personal income as the relative index (those whose personal income below 0.75 times of the median are defined as the low income group, whose income between 0.75 times and 2 times (included) of the median are defined as the middle income group, and those whose values above 2 times of the median are the high income group.), based on the statistics in the China Social Survey (CSS) 2006–2016 by Institute of Sociology, Chinese Academy of Social Sciences (CASS), the paper depicts and analyzes the current middle income group in China from the perspective of the employment structure. The relative standard is used for better understanding the middle income group on the income perspective (Li and Zhu 2015), and this provides better analyses of influence on social strata from the change of income and distribution structure.

The following characteristics in our social structure change are shown from the perspective of employment structure.

3.1 Preliminary Formation of Modern Social Stratification with the Transformation of Economic Structure in China

Since the reform and opening up in 1980s, the society has transformed from an agricultural society into an industrial one within a very short time with re-structured of economy. In recent years, the rapid growth of tertiary industry contributed a lot in improving economic structure, maintaining medium–high speed economic development, keeping employment and raising livelihood. According to the statistics, the percentages of our main employment sectors were changed from 70.5:17.3:12.2 in 1978 to 28.3:29.3:42.4 by the end of 2015, realizing the transformation from a traditional agricultural society to a modern one (see Fig. 3.1).

Petty-Clark theorem was developed based on the moving out of labor force from the primary, the secondary, to the tertiary sector. Currently, the percentage of the tertiary industry is well over 60% in the developed countries. Since the reform and opening up in China, the tertiary industry gained quick growth, and the employment percentage in this industry kept increasing. This did not only lay a solid foundation for high-speed and sustained economic development, alleviate the job pressure, but also helped form the modern social structure in China. In recent years, there began the differentiation within this industry. In addition to the sustained growth of the labor-intensive sub industries such as commerce, trading and catering, capital-intensive sub industries such as finance, insurance, real property, and technology-intensive

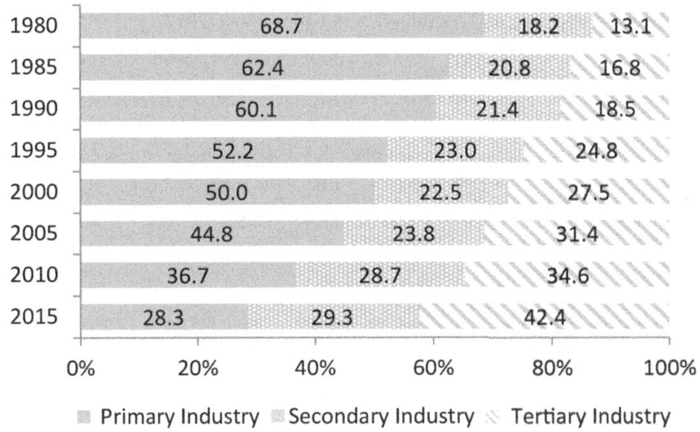

Fig. 3.1 Employment structure in three sectors in China 1980–2015. Primary industry, Secondary industry, Tertiary industry. *Source* China Statistical Yearbook 2016, China Statistics Press, 2016

sub industries all gained fast development. Those powered the expansion of the middle income group. Especially the Mass Entrepreneurship and Innovation Policy, which was mainly for the technology intensive tertiary industry during the transition of high to medium–high growth rate of economic development in China, has greatly propelled the expansion and consolidation of the tertiary industry. According to the statistics, the number of new registered enterprises in China was 5.528 million in 2016, with a 24.5% year-on-year growth rate; VCs raised $53.69 billion, with a year-on-year growth rate of 79.3%; the amount of technology transfer contracts, for the first time reached 1 trillion, with a year-on-year growth of 15.97%. With the constantly increasing employment percentage of both capital intensive and technology intensive sub industries, the economic structure shall be further optimized and the modern social stratification in China shall be solidified and optimized.

In terms of the occupation structure, the statistics from National Bureau of Statistics and years of CSS show that remarkable changes of occupation structure and social strata have taken place since 1990. The percentages of people who worked in the farming, forestry, animal husbandry, fishery and water conservation sectors were dropping all the time, from 70.69% in 1990 to 34.4% in 2015; the percentage of people who worked in the governmental and public department, technicians, clerks and related staff, manufacture and transportation workers and related staff were on the slight rise; the added percentage of people who worked in the commerce, trading and service sector was the highest, from 5.41% in 1990 to 21.9% in 2015 (see Table 3.1). This showcased the preliminary formation and the on-going evolvement toward reasonable of the modern social stratification in China.

However, the transformation of social structure is agging behind to some extent when compared with its fast transformation of economic structure. Mr. Lu Xueyi (renowned sociologist, honorary member of Academic Committee, CASS), once used the "profound change that has never happened for the whole history in China"

Table 3.1 Occupation structure and social strata in China 1990–2015

	1990	2000	2005	2006	2008	2011	2013	2015
People in charge in governmental and public departments	1.75	1.69	0.5*	2.4	2.7	4.2	3.1	3.4
Technicians	5.32	5.67	7.60	6.0	3.6	8.8	6.8	8.5
Clerks and related staff	1.74	3.08	3.68	5.7	6.4	8.6	7.7	8.7
Business sector workers	5.41	9.22	12.17	10.6	10.7	12.3	11.7	12.1
Service staff				7.1	8.0	9.0	9.1	9.8
Working staff in the farming, forestry, animal husbandry, fishery and water conservation sectors	70.69	64.38	56.95	50.2	49.5	37.1	35.6	34.4
Manufacture and transportation workers and related staff	15.03	15.89	17.85	17.2	18.8	18.9	25.4	22.2
Police and people in the uniforms	–	–	–	0.4	0.2	0.5	0.3	0.2
Others	0.05	0.07	0.23	0.3	0.1	0.8	0.4	0.6
Total	100.0	100.0	100.0	100.0	100.0	100.0	100.0	100.0

*Data of 1990–2005: 2000–2005: Occupation structure and social strata in China, Statistical Research, Feb. 2008; data for 2006–2015 are from CCS. Data of people in charge in governmental and public departments in 2005 are missing

to depict such change of social structure in China after the reform and opening up. He believed that the real historical change to Chinese social structure happened after the reform and opening up, and the structure went through the transformation of agricultural to industrial, rural to urban and traditional to modern society, and reached the preliminary stage of a modern society. However, the social structure is about 15 years behind the current economic structure (Lu 2010). Currently, the lagging behind situations exist in the following areas: First, as the agricultural population is still the biggest, it is critical to raise the proportion of middle income group therein to expand the whole middle income group in China. Compared to its general output value, too many people are working in the primary sector and too low is the labor productivity. Combined with the slowdown economic growth and lagging behind development of 3 and 4-tier cities in China, the growth rate of migrant workers is going down. This would bring the hidden rural unemployment issue on to the table, further slowing down the income growth of the rural residents. This shall hinder the further optimization of employment structure and social stratification and slow down the step from a traditional to a modern, and an agricultural to an industrial society. Secondly, the moving tendency of labor from the primary, secondary to tertiary industry along with the raise of economic level seemed to be shared by the industry evolvement of all developed country and regions. Whereas, the moving of labors in China since the reform and opening up was not that obvious: when labor flow from the primary to the secondary industry had not fully unfolded, the quick flow from primary to the tertiary industry already began. They happened somehow simultaneously. According to the statistics from CSS, the percentages of migrant workers of all the manufacture workers and people who worked in the commerce, trading and service sector, were separately 57.7% and 45.2% in 2006, 66.2% and 48.1% in 2008, 74.5% and 62.9% in 2011, 82.9% and 70.8% in 2013, and 81.4% and 68.3% in 2015. This to some extent has affected the full development of the secondary industry, and would bring the labor cost advantage to an earlier end. This in long term shall be adverse for the sustained growth of middle income group among the rural population and the further expansion of all the middle income group in this country.

3.2 Analysis of the Multi Sources of Current Employment Structure of Middle Income Group in China

With the further deepening of reform and opening up, the stratification in China is becoming evident with a preliminary scale of middle income group. Using the annual personal income as a relative standard, 45.8% of the employed labors belong to low income group, 30.1% middle income group and 24.1% high income group (see Table 3.2).

From the employment structure, various percentages of people who worked in different sectors all found their own paths into the middle-income or high-income group. With the comparison of the Chinese and western middle-class development,

Table 3.2 Occupation structure by income-group (%)

	Total	Income group (%)			
		Low income group	Middle income group (%)	High income group (%)	Total
White collar	20.5	9.1	34.3	56.6	100.0
Gray collar	3.6	6.7	31.5	61.8	100.0
Blue collar in the commerce sector	11.6	17.1	38.9	44.0	100.0
Blue collar in the service sector	8.6	22.8	44.0	33.1	100.0
Blue collar in the manufacture and construction sector	19.4	17.4	48.1	34.5	100.0
Farmer	34.4	77.0	18.5	4.5	100.0
Senior citizen re-employment	2.0	35.0	40.8	24.2	100.0
Total	100.0	45.8	30.1	24.1	100.0

Jianping Wang holds that: the modernization of China was brought by external factors, and the social transformation was quite abrupt. So, the being, developing, structure and characteristics in China were all different from those developed countries. The entire change route was highly impacted into the route of the pre-industrial—industrial—post-industrial society. So, new and old middle-income class occupations co-exist in the change of social employment structure (Wang 2007). Yi Zhang believes that the advancing of the middle class has been combined with the on-going post-industrialization and networked process. He thinks the social development in China is "compacted leaping modernization", that is, the convergence of middle classification, post-industrialization and homogeneous networked social development (Zhang 2016). There are other scholars who have incorporated the interior transformation factor in China to highlight the complexity of current society. Wanli Zhang believes that the drastic transformation against the systematic division and regional division have caused multiple diversion of the new middle income group. Zhang (2007) In all, the scholars make a combination analysis of the birth and evolvement of the middle income group, the transformation from an agricultural, an industrial to a post-industrial society, as well as the incorporation of urbanization, networked situation and the institutional transition. It is shown that the rules of being and evolvement of middle income group changed quickly in a very short term, with quite special and complex features. So, the fast transformation of economic structure and social stratification provide development opportunities for all occupation groups. Development paths to become the middle income group have been formed, which represents the multi sources of the employment structure of middle income group in China currently.

The white-collar class which are made up of staffs working in the governmental and public department, technicians, trading staff and clerks embodies the production from industrialization and modernization, representing the middle-income group or middle class in a general sense. Proper educational attainment, relatively high and stable salary income, and good occupation reputation have turned those people into the desired objects and consumption symbols in the business marketing campaigns. As for our country's white-collar class, in addition to those advantage above, the "in-system" character is also worth mentioning. CSS shows that 56.9% of the white collars are working in the governmental department, state owned enterprises and public institutions, 34.5% of them are working in the private enterprises and the rest are working for the overseas invested enterprises, non-governmental public institutions. So, it can be put that the current white-collar class are not completely shaped by the market transformation or the modernization process, but made out of the well secured "in-system" elite.

A quite high proportion of on-site manufacture workers, highly skilled workers in the service sector and those gray collar workers who have managerial expertise become the middle or high income group. Although there is still no consensus on the definition of gray collars, the integration of low-end white-collar and blue-collar technician is a reality with the requirement from the technology advancing and management improvement in the post-industrialized period. Some researchers think that the gray-collar class earn relatively low in terms of market positioning, which is caused by the wide spread traditional conception of preference for higher educational attainment. However, the supply that falls behind the demand shall send the income and social status of those gray collars up (Chen 2008). In the domestic labor market, the lagging behind development of the vocational education, especially the higher vocational education, has led to a long-term shortage of highly skilled technicians, which is a structural problem. So, the scarcity of gray class in the post-industry time shall make them middle or high income group currently.

80% of the blue workers in the commerce, service, industry and construction sectors there are the middle-income or high income group (see Table 3.2). The labor cost is going up fast in China in recent years. According to the data released by International Labor Organization (ILO), the average salary income since 2016 in China has grown more than 1 time, which stood at 685 US dollars in China's mainland in 2014; and according to the *2016 Global Manufacturing Competitiveness Index* jointly published by ChinaInfo100 and Deloitte Global, the labor cost has quintupled in a decade since 2005. From the data of CSS, the growths of the annual average income in the commerce, service, industry and construction blue collars from 2007 to 2014 were separately 2.3 times, 1.5 times and 3.8 times, reaching separately ¥49,302, ¥35,112 and ¥36,197. For the first time, the labor-age population since 2012 saw a decreased number. The total number of migrant workers continued declining since 2011. Added with the increasing urban living cost, the blue worker in commerce, service, industry and construction sectors, whose main body are the migrant workers enjoyed general income growth.

Of all the groups, the percentage of the farming people that belong to the middle or high income group are the lowest, whereas 77% of the farmers are still retained in the low-income category (see Table 3.2). For those who make their living on planting, they are ranked as the middle or high income group mainly because the scale operation realized by land transfer. CSS 2015 showed that the average household farming acreages of those middle and high income group were separately 12.5 mu and 13 mu, and 7.1 mu for those low-income households. Meanwhile, compared with the statistics in 2013, there was a significant expansion of real operation scale for the agricultural households that were the middle or high income group in 2015.

The employment of age group 60–69 elderly is made as a separate item to highlight the new phenomenon on the job market against the aging trend of population. Since 1990s, the employment rate of the above 60 elderly in cities and towns has been going through a downward process. From all the demographic censuses, the employment rate of the elderly in the cities and towns in 1990, 2000 and 2010 were separately 17%, 10.1% and 6.7%. But in recent years, the rate was picking up. Years of statistics in the CSS show that the employment rate of the 60–69 elderly in cities and towns were respectively 9.5%, 10.4%, 8.9%, 18.8% and 17.5% in 2006, 2008, 2011, 2013 and 2015. With the downward pressure of economic growth rate, decrease of basic pension replacement rate and weakened intergenerational provision for the aged—and the elderly devouring children, the fading employment took a fundamental turn in the elder in cities and towns, leading to the rise of both their employment will and rate. The re-employment of those groups indicates both the consolidation of their individual income status as well as the promotion of the household income status.

For those employed age group of 60–69 in cities and towns in 2015, the average annual pension for unemployed was ¥24,061, while the re-employed had an annual ¥34,192 extra income, which averagely equaled to 42.1% of all their pensions.

The multi sources of occupations are the characteristics of the middle and high income group currently as described above, that is, each person in their occupation get ranked middle or high income group following their own logical route, such as the "in-system" factors for the white collars, the scarcity of the gray collars in the post-industrialization, the labor shortage of blue collars in the industrialization, the scaling up operation of the farmers and the pension compensation factor of the elder employed population. Therefore, the multi-source occupations for the middle and high income group under the quick change of economic structure have largely determined the heterogeneity of the middle income group in China currently.

In terms of the industry structure of the employment, the monopoly of an industry, the ownership and technology all have their impact on the scale of the middle-income group for those in those sectors. Of all the income discrepancy, the regional, urban–rural and inter-industry income gaps are quite evident. The studies of inter-industry income gaps show the significant influence from the monopoly factor. The so called industrial monopoly is the policy-based access and exit with production and operation of proprietary monopoly. Since 1996, the gaps only got wider between the monopolized and non-monopolized industries, with a yearly expansion rate of 43%. The first few high income industry monopolies are airlines, banks, tobacco, oil and natural gas production. While the last few non-monopolies in terms of income are expectedly textile industry, catering services, farming, forestry, animal husbandry and fishery. The average salary in the monopolies are 5–10 times that of the national average salary (Cui 2015). According to the statistics of the CSS, above 50% of the employed in the monopolies are in the high income group while less than 10% are in the low-income group. High share of high income group leaves people in this sector with a relatively low share of the middle income group. Of which, as high as 67.4% of those employed in the financial sector enjoy their high-end income (see Table 3.3).

The factor of ownership is mainly reflected in the public welfare sector. This sector includes departments, enterprises and facilities that directly or indirectly provide services for the economic, social and individual activities. In the long last central planning economy, this sector was mainly established and operated by national investment. Deepened as the reform goes, the sector is open to the private investment along with its restructuring. However, as the government investment is still high, the sector shows strong trace of "in-system". Affected by the ownership, a large group of the people are the high income group, as 50% are high-end group, above 10% are the low income group and 30%-40% are middle income group (see Table 3.3).

In terms of the technology factor of the industry, those who work in the scientific research, geological prospecting, information transmission, computer service and software and the financial sector enjoy higher percentage of high income group, which is around 70%; those who work in such fields see low percentage of low income group, which is around 10%. Their percentage of middle income group is around 20% (see Table 3.3).

Table 3.3 Industrial structure by income-group (%)

Industry monopoly	Industry	Income group (%)			
		Low income group	Middle income group (%)	High income group (%)	Total
Monopoly	Electricity, natural gas, water sector	7.4	38.1	54.6	100.0
	Transportation, warehousing and mail services	10.1	29.1	60.7	100.0
	Financial industry	9.0	23.6	67.4	100.0
Non-monopoly	Farming, forestry, animal husbandry and fishery sector	42.7	39.0	18.3	100.0
	Mining sector	8.9	31.1	60.0	100.0
	Manufacture sector	21.3	37.0	41.7	100.0
	Construction sector	21.4	41.9	36.7	100.0
	Information transmission, computer service and software sector	10.9	20.2	68.9	100.0
	Wholesale and retail sector	17.6	39.1	43.3	100.0
	Accommodation and catering sector	17.7	38.5	43.8	100.0
	Real estate sector	15.0	43.5	41.4	100.0
	Leasing, commerce and service sector	15.8	21.2	63.1	100.0
	Water conservation, environment and public facilities sector	0.0	0.0	0.0	0.0
	Resident service and other services	17.4	42.5	40.2	100.0
Public welfare sector	Scientific research, technology service and geological prospecting sector	9.5	18.3	72.2	100.0
	Education sector	11.0	32.0	57.0	100.0
	Health, social security and social welfare sector	17.0	32.6	50.4	100.0

(continued)

Table 3.3 (continued)

Industry monopoly	Industry	Income group (%)			
		Low income group	Middle income group (%)	High income group (%)	Total
	Culture, sports and recreation sector	8.3	33.6	58.1	100.0
	Public management and social organization sector	13.2	39.8	47.0	100.0
Others		19.6	35.7	44.8	100.0

Therefore, each person in their industry get ranked middle or high income group following their own reasonable path, that is, those who are employed in the monopolies, public ownership dominated sectors or the sector that require high technology have better chance to get themselves ranked as the middle or high income group. For the workers who are in the non-monopolized industries, private industries and industries that require low technology, such as real estate, resident service and other services, and construction sector see a higher percentage of middle-income group peers. From the perspective of the development tendency, the income large gap shall be cut down gradually. In the procedure, the administrative monopoly in the monopolized industries shall be eliminated, and the reform and the introduction of social capital shall be furthered. Those shall cut down the percentage of those worker in the high income group and expand the middle income group.

3.3 Future Uncertainty and Vulnerability of the Middle Income Group in China

Despite the preliminary formation of modern social structure in China and the scale of the middle income group, there are still uncertainty and vulnerability of the future development. The concerns are as follows:

First, the blue collars of the middle income group shall be under much pressure against the economic structure upgrade and transformation. On one hand, the construction sector workers take a very high share in the blue-collar workers in China. According to the CSS, there is a sustained growing percentage of the construction workers in the blue collars along with the development of the real estate market and the scaling up of the infrastructure. The shares were separately 14.5% in 2008, 19.9% in 2001, 22.4% in 2013 and 24.3% in 2015. Currently, the regulatory policies upon the hot spot cities' real estate markets and the high inventory pressure of the 3 to 4-tire city housing all indicate the growth rate of real estate investment shall go down in the future, which shall affect the demand for labor in the construction sector later. On the other hand, the raised labor cost in the manufacture sector accelerates the wide application of industrial robots. China is now the country using most industrial robots. Wide application of industrial robot shall remarkably cut down the labor demand of those industrial blue collars. According to the data provided by Dongguan City of Guangdong Province, the special project of replacing labor with robotics had cut down 80,000 human labors by September 2016. As for commercial robots, year 2016 saw its launching and year 2017 is seeing its acceleration. In the commerce and service sectors such as catering, hotels and supermarkets, the application of robotics shall further replace the repetitive work, which certainly shall minimize the labor demand for blue collar workers in the commerce and service sector.

Second, with the supply side reform of agriculture, the farmer group structure may change greatly and new professional farmers shall see their number growing. Currently, low efficiency and high cost, unbalanced farm products demand and supply, steep resource and environmental issues, insufficient innovation, aging of the labors, etc., are all strictly confining the development of agriculture in our country. For such, the central government is making a big push on the agricultural supply side reform so as to raise the comprehensive efficiency and improve the products' international competitiveness. In addition to the efforts made in the institutional aspect to improve the agricultural productivity, such as accelerating the land system, pricing mechanism and household registration, the enlarged, intensified and professional operation and innovation of scale operation, critical measures also include the cultivation of quality agricultural operators. According to the Ministry of Agricultural, by the end of the twelfth five-year plan, there would be 12.72 million new professional farmers, 55% more than that in 2010. And the number shall be well over 20 million by the year 2020. It is expected that the farmer group structure may take great changes and new professional farmers shall see their number growing.

Third, the expansion of white-collar workers in the non-public sector shall be critical to the growing of the middle income group in China. As the pretty high share of "in-system" white collars, the expansion of the white-collar group shall be determined by the "out-of-system" white collars' scale. However, the increased downward pressure of our economic growth and the tendency of focus shifted from the real to the virtual economy, the real economy suffers much restriction on development as the private investment growth sharply declines. The data from National Bureau of Statistics showed that the private investment dropped heavily in 2016, with 3.1% growth between January and November, a year-on-year fall back of 7.1%. This was first time of decrease since the private investment policy was launched in 2012. To safeguard the private economy, *Opinions of the Central Committee of the Communist Party of China and the State Council on Improving the Property Right Protection System and Providing Law-based Protection to Property Rights* was published by the end of 2016, in which the protection of property rights of private enterprises was raised. The media considered it as a huge boost of the private enterprises, as it conveyed the sailing of the private business and economy. But the real implementation still depends on the transformation of government functions, reform of financial and taxation system and state-owned enterprises and other serial reforms. The issues lasted for ages must be addressed too.

Forth, the current employment quality of middle income group needs to be further improved. Stable positions and open promotion channels are the basic expectation people have on the characteristics of the middle income group' jobs. In reality, the position quality of the group is not that reasonable, such as unstable position, high rate of informal employment and lacking of chance of promotion. The research shows that, in terms of job stability, 75% of the high income group express that they shall remained employed in the next 6 months, the rate for the middle income group stands at 61.9%, and for the low income group, 50.9%; in terms of occupation structure, the shares who believe to be employed for the next 6 months are separately 81% for the white collars, 67.3% for the gray collars, 66.8% for the commerce blue collars, 61.2% for the service blue collars and 51.4% for the manufacture and construction blue collars. It can be seen that all other groups but the high income group and white collars showed much concern over the stability of their employment in the future. In terms of the employment forms, as the middle income group show high informal employment, their rights and interests as labors can be difficult to be safeguarded. The research indicates that, the share of the informal employment for all workers in 2015 were as follows: 16.2% for the white collars, 37.3% for the gray collars, 52.2% for the commerce blue collars, 58.2% for the service blue collars and 63.4% for the manufacture and construction blue collars. And 46.3% of the middle income group have informal jobs. Compared with the formal employment, informal employed workers tend to show issues of social security, labor protection and employment quality, such as lower payment of social security, less signature of labor contracts and long extra working hours. In terms of promotion opportunities, this is where the middle income group show the lowest satisfaction rate. In the research, we ask the interviewees to grade their satisfaction of their non-agricultural sector employment. With 10 as the full mark, the results show that the middle income group have the satisfaction for their interpersonal relationship above 7 points, for working place security, working environment and exertion of competence above 6 points, for remuneration above 5 points and promotion opportunities below 5 points. So, for the middle income group and part of the high income group, the employment is more about the income than about the upward flow along the social ladder.

So, the general situation for the current middle income group, the decreased demand for blue collar workers, the slow development of the "out-of-system" white collars, smaller professional farmers and the occupation quality of the middle income group, has largely added up to the uncertainty and vulnerability of the growth of the middle income group in China. On the other hand, the vulnerability of the future that is currently covered by the high speed economic development and the rise of the income could be revealed when the economic growth is slowed down. In fact, even in those developed countries, as the middle income group are considered as the backbone of the society, concerns over the vulnerability of them are also stated by people. Likewise, uncertainty of the future of the current new emerging middle income group in China exists.

Measures shall be taken to first address the issues in the rural areas given the current middle income group. The population in the rural area takes a large portion of all the population. They have high share of low-end income group. And the migrant workers from the rural area are the main body of the blue collars. So, to expand the percentage of middle income group in the rural population could be of significant meaning to grow all the middle income group in China. When enhancing the agricultural scale operation, the secondary and tertiary industry shall also be promoted to effectively raise the income of the rural residents; the advance of urbanization shall be carried out along with the citizenization. Secondly, the labor market shall be improved to promote the employment. The rights and interests of the labors shall be safeguarded and the job quality shall be enhanced to bring more sense of security and stability. Besides, more human capital shall be invested and the educational equality shall be promoted; vocational education and adult education shall be improved to help raise the labor quality for their adaptation of the further industrialization and the development of high-tech industries. And the path for middle income group that is based on professional development and boasts the ordered social mobility mechanism shall be thus formed. Meanwhile, the austere reality of our aging society calls for both the improvement of the old-age security and the promulgation of the re-employment of the elderly to consolidate the scale growth of the middle income group.

References

Chen Q (2008) Gray collar class research based on Max Webber's theory of social stratification. J Nanjing Audit Univ No. 4

Cui Y (2015) Elimination of administrative monopoly is the call of narrowing the income gaps among industries. NetEase News, November 9, 2015, https://news.163.com/15/1109/18/B80H9P3N00014AED.html

Lu X (Ed) (2010) Social structure of contemporary China. Social Sciences Academic Press, Beijing

Peilin L, Di Z (2015) Make efforts to develop an olive-shaped distribution pattern: an analysis based on data from the China social survey for 2006–2013. Soc Sci China, No. 1

Wang J (2007) The inner anxiety and apprehension of the middle class in China. Modern China Studies, No. 1

Zhang Y (2016) The great transition as in the networked Chinese social strata and governance. Ifeng News, Dec 26, 2016, https://news.ifeng.com/a/20161226/50475656_0.shtml

Zhang W (2007) The power repulsion to the new middle class by the elite alliance. People's Tribune, No.9, https://politics.people.com.cn/GB/8198/5714217.html

Lei Fan associate professor of the Institute of Sociology in CASS, Ph.D, specialized in social development research and social research method. Major publication includes The Labor Division in Chinese Current Labor Market During the Process of Urbanization, The Political Attitude of the Post-80s Generation.

Chapter 4
Employment and Work of Middle Income Groups

V. A. Anikin

The present chapter explores the middle income groups regarding their employment status and place in industrial relations. According to the prior literature, once we get the evidence that certain middle income groups hold advantaged positions in the labor market—for example, more stable employment and more influential negotiation position with employers or lower unemployment risks, or they represent a group of skilled labor professions and are able to find a more interesting and promising job where human capital is in demand, we will be entitled to speak about class-based nature of the middle income groups in Russia.[1]

What can we say about **employment and unemployment** in these groups? First of all, it is worth noting that the income of most representatives of the middle income groups is of a work nature, i.e. based on paid employment. This is due to poor diversification of income sources of the Russian population, which is the case even with affluent Russians. Income received at the usual place of work is the main source of income for most Russians. Any additional sources of income in the form of rental payments, leased real estate, and interest on deposits are relevant to no more than

[1] In Western literature, all listed attributes are typical for middle class. For example, J. Goldthorpe highlights the fact that employment relations characterized by a written employment contract, a high degree of autonomy at the workplace, and accompanying additional social benefits testify to one's belonging to the middle class (Goldthorpe J.H. Rent, Class Conflict, and Class Structure: A Commentary on Sorensen. The American Journal of Sociology, 2000, Vol. 105, No. 6, pp. 1572–1582). E. Wright notes that middle class jobs are somewhat contradictory because they are occupied by highly skilled employees performing various complex types of work, which increases their influence on the organization; however, they remain suffering from exploitation (see in detail Wright E.O. Classes. Verso Book, 1997).

[2] Here and further in this section, data from the IS RAS Monitoring Study of October 2015 are provided.

V. A. Anikin (✉)
HSE University, Institute of Sociology of FCTAS RAS, Moscow, Russia

P. Li and M. K. Gorshkov (eds.), *The Middle Income Group in China and Russia*, Research Series on the Chinese Dream and China's Development Path,
https://doi.org/10.1007/978-981-16-1464-4_4

Table 4.1 Level and Type of Employment in Different Income Groups of Russians, IS RAS, 2015, % (The category of Russians on maternity leave or child-care leave is excluded from the analysis due to the small sub-sample size (under 1%))

	Low-Income Groups	MIG		High-Income Groups
		LMIG	UMIG	
Currently employed (total)	*63*	*62*	***79***[a]	***88***
Including				
Permanent employees (hired under an order or open-end contract)	45	49	**62**	**70**
Employed under a temporary written agreement	9	8	11	**13**
Employed under an oral arrangement	**9**	5	6	5
Currently unemployed (total)	***37***	***38***	*21*	*12*
Including				
Pensioners (including disabled pensioners)	**23**	**24**	10	5
Students of higher education institutions and secondary specialized education institutions	4	8	8	5
Unemployed	**10**	6	3	2

[a]Here and further in this section, any statistically significant relationships ($\alpha < 0.05$) are put in bold. The income groups with a statistically insignificant difference in proportions in terms of the analyzed attribute at $p < 0.05$ are put in gray (Bonferroni correction)

3% of Russians.[2] Despite this, it is still unclear where to draw the line after which employment becomes the typical feature of any income group.

According to our estimates, paid employment is an integral component of the economic middle class, in particular, its upper subgroups whose income is at least 1.25 times the Russian median value (Table 4.1).[3] Thus, the share of Russians who are currently employed is 79% of the upper subgroup and 62% of the lower subgroup of the middle income population groups. Since the median value of 1.25 is a kind of counterpoint defining these groups, *the dividing line of life chances of Russians related to their employment status passes through the middle income group as if splitting it into two, but not beyond its boundaries.*

This discrepancy is mainly due to differences in the level and type of employment of the lower and upper subgroups of the middle income groups, on the one hand, and differences in the structure of unemployed representatives of these groups, on the other hand. Thus, less than half of the lower subgroup of the middle income

[3] 31% of Russians receive such income.

population groups are permanent employees, i.e. they are hired under an order or open-end contract. The share of such Russians belonging to the upper subgroup of the middle income population groups is considerably higher and is 62% (which is more typical of high-income groups, with the share of permanent employees reaching 70%, regarded as the maximum amount in Russia). As seen in Table 4.1, the significantly larger share of permanent employees hired under an order or open-end contract is an essential feature that differentiates the lower and the upper subgroups of the middle income population groups. In other words, *any official permanent employment is associated with the more privileged position of Russians in the production sphere, which guarantees under other equal conditions a higher income and, as a result, a higher probability of belonging to the economic middle class.*

Other forms of employment relations do not have such a feature. It is relevant to both official temporary employment and unofficial employment, which is statistically lower among the middle income population groups than among the low-income ones. Despite the fact that unofficial employment can be associated with additional financial rewards in the labor market (for example, for certain categories of self-employed Russians),[4] on average employment based on an oral arrangement results from discrimination and exploitation, which becomes especially salient during the crisis. Consequently, unofficial employment in many cases is involuntary and low paying.

As for official temporary employment, in industrialized Western countries this form of employer-employee relationship at the primary place of employment can also be associated with increased risks for an employee in the production sphere.[5] However, in contemporary Russia, temporary employment is of a more complicated nature and may not be related to low income.[6] Apparently, this is because temporary contracts are sometimes considered a high-risk insurance against unemployment for certain categories of employees. Table 4.1 demonstrates that employment in the usual place of work under a temporary written agreement is associated with high-income population groups. Thus, the share of temporary contract employees is statistically higher among Russians whose income exceeds two national median values (13% vs. 9% on average in Russia).

In the case of the high-income population groups' representatives, their relatively high salaries can be regarded as a bonus for risks involving temporary employment that are covered by an employer due to the employees' skills. However, this is more the exception than the rule. The average temporary contractual employment in Russia of 80% is typical of employees in the commercial and service sectors and manual workers, i.e. those categories of hired labor that hold less qualifications and bargaining power with an employer.

Thus, the lower and the upper subgroups of the middle income population groups are described by opposing situations in the employment spheres. Despite the fact that both of these subgroups are referred to as the economic middle class, they are

[4] Lehmann and Zaiceva (2015).

[5] For example, see works by Forrier and Sels (2003), Giesecke and Groß (2003).

[6] Gimpelson and Kapelyushnikov (2007).

so different that they can be regarded as a single social group in terms of their employment status only in exceptional and very rare cases.

A similar situation is typical of unemployment, the nature of which in the lower and upper subgroups of the middle income population groups is also opposite. Thus, the relative share of the unemployed included in the lower subgroup of the middle income population groups is 1.5 times less than in the upper subgroup thereof (38% and 21%, respectively) and by 2.7 times less than among the high-income groups (12%). The profile of unemployed representatives of the lower subgroup of the middle income population groups is determined by citizens living on pensions and welfare as well as economically active but unemployed Russians. The share of unemployed pensioners and students within this subgroup of the middle income population groups is 24% and 8% (i.e. 63% and 21% of the unemployed representatives of the lower subgroup of the middle income population groups), respectively. In general, almost half of the representatives of the lower subgroup of the middle income population groups, both employed and unemployed, live on money transfers (pensions, allowances, alimony, assistance provided by state and public organizations, etc.). While on average in Russia transfers are one of the main sources of income for 38% of the population, in the low-income population groups as well as the lower subgroup of the middle income population groups, the share of such citizens is 46% and 45%, respectively.

The share of currently unemployed but economically active Russians included in the lower and upper subgroups of the middle income population groups are strikingly different. Table 4.1 shows that unemployment among the representatives of the upper subgroup of the middle income population groups is half as common as in the lower subgroup thereof, which sits at the national level (6%). However, in general, unemployment of economically active Russians is a phenomenon mainly associated with income that is 75% below the national median value. Thus, the share of the unemployed among the low-income groups is statistically higher than on average across the country and stands at 10%. This relationship demonstrates the extreme degree of ineffectiveness of the social support measures currently implemented in Russia. *It means that in case of a job loss, a person is actually condemned to live below the poverty line.*[7] *The real risk of mass withdrawal of Russian citizens from the middle income population groups upon retirement is increasing.*

Thus, *for most Russians even a low paying job is not only the main source of income but also a guarantee of maintaining their social position, achieved class affiliation and the amount of resources and opportunities associated with it.* In light of this, there is an important question—where do the middle income population groups' representatives work? When considering the middle income population groups as the economic basis of the middle class, one can suppose that employment of the middle income population groups will be localized in any tertiary and quaternary sectors of the economy. However, according to the research results, employment of the middle income population groups by economic sector corresponds to the average Russian

[7] As will be shown in the following chapters, any income not exceeding 0.75 times the median value is most likely to mean income that is lower than the regional minimum subsistence level, taking into account the household composition.

level and there is no statistically significant link between employment in certain sectors of the economy and income groups. The only exception is represented by Russians with income less than 75% of the average Russian median value, among whom there are twice as many employees in the primary sector of the economy as in the country as a whole (10 vs. 5%) who are employed in the agricultural production sphere. For the middle income population groups as well as for the high-income ones, employment in the primary sector of the economy is an extremely rare and atypical phenomenon (at the level of 1–4%). In other words, the middle income population groups are evenly distributed across all sectors of the economy (except for the primary sector, where they are practically not represented), and the sectoral type of employment is not so important from the viewpoint of a person's inclusion in the economic middle class.

Russian citizens do not enjoy any obvious advantages from employment with state enterprises. The type of enterprise ownership amid the 2015 crisis did not produce any statistically significant impact upon distribution of Russians among the income groups, except that employment with state enterprises under otherwise equal conditions guaranteed them an income that was not lower than 0.75 times the national median value while employment with private companies, in contrast, reduced this guarantee. Thus, a quarter of employed representatives of the low-income population groups were employed with newly established commercial structures, while among the upper middle income population groups this share was just 17% (despite the fact that the average national employment rate at this type of enterprise covered no more than 20% of the then-employed population). Thus, *the state as an employer more frequently guarantees income standards no lower than certain minimum values while maintaining a broad range of wages, while the policy of private companies usually means keeping wages at extremely low levels. However, opportunities for high earnings for a certain portion of their employees are maintained (though they will not exceed similar opportunities at state-owned enterprises). This is another factor in the polarization of hired workers.*

Among all population groups in Russian society, low-income citizens are in the least protected position regarding their employment. Thus, about 27% of the employed representatives of this group confirmed that they had employment issues during the year. If compared with the low-income population groups, the middle income groups are in a relatively more privileged position. Thus, the specified negative phenomena in the employment sphere of the middle income population groups are at the average Russian level (25%). In other words, *the position of the economic middle class in the employment sphere is not characterized by anything special, it is rather "no worse than the others". The frequency and volume of additional social benefits at the workplace provided by an employer which were reduced during the crisis seem to be perceived by the middle income population groups as the best of a bad situation amid actual violations of the labor rights of Russian citizens, which became widespread in the crisis, affecting even budgetary organizations.*

Table 4.2 Occupational Structure of Different Income Groups of Russians, IS RAS, 2015, % of employed

Occupations	Low-Income Groups	MIG		High-Income Groups
		LMIG	UMIG	
Managers of all levels, entrepreneurs and the self-employed	5	7	**12**	**15**
Professionals whose work involves using higher education	15	26	**35**	**39**
Semi-professionals, office employees, administrators, and clerks	**17**	15	11	13
Other non-manual workers (service workers and shop and market sales workers)	**17**	13	10	10
Manual workers	**46**	38	32	23

Speaking of the **structure of employment** of the economic middle class representatives, the data from IS RAS show that their middle position is mainly ensured by the specifics of the jobs they hold. In addition to the abovementioned employment parameters, the key cross-section allowing to us to gain a comprehensive picture of the employment specifics is a cross-section of the occupational structure. This cross-section becomes especially relevant today when sectoral and industrial differences do not provide such a clear picture of the middle income population groups' localization as they did 10 years ago. In spite of the fact that social scientists have been using the occupational structure as the main cross-section of the social and economic life of a society for a long run,[8] Russian economists have just realized its critical importance.[9]

The impact of the occupational structure upon income stratification is quite obvious. Table 4.2 shows that: (a) the employed representatives of the middle income population groups hold jobs mainly in the sphere of non-manual labor (62% of the lower subgroup, and 68% of the upper subgroup of the middle income population groups), (b) there is a considerable difference in the nature and quality of jobs held by the lower and upper middle income population groups as well as by their presumed skill level. Thus, 47% of employed representatives of the upper subgroup of the

[8] In this regard, we should point out works not only by foreign authors but also by Russian sociologists, including O. Shkaratan, V. Mansurov, G. Yastrebov, A. Bessudny, V. Anikin, etc.

[9] Above all, we mean the recent analytical report of the group of authors led by R. Kapelyushnikov and V. Gimpelson published as the brochure "Professional Structure in the Russian Labor Market" (Chief editor: N.T. Vishnevskaya. Publishing House of National Research University Higher School of Economics, 2017). The appearance of a Russian-language monograph edited by economists, which focuses on economic structure but not on separate occupational groups, can be seen as a significant step forward in relation to previous research attempts to analyze the social origins of economic processes (e.g. work by Sabirianova et al. (2002)).

Fig. 4.1 Distribution of Manual Workers by Different Income Groups, IS RAS, 2015, %

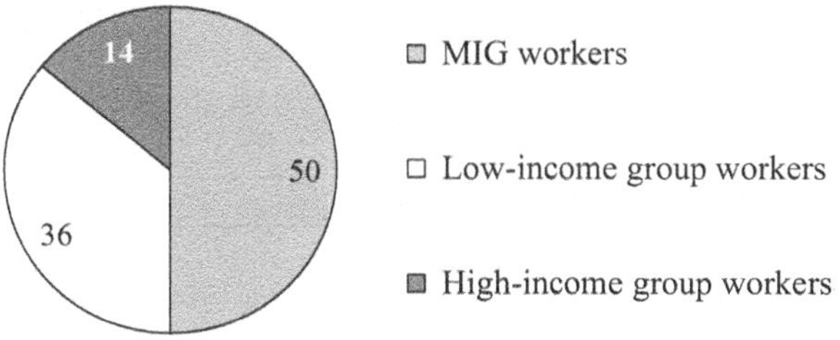

middle income population groups occupy positions as managers and professionals, while the related share of these managers and professional among the working population of the lower subgroup of the middle income population group is just one-third.

Another important feature of the employment structure of the middle income population groups is that workers and employees engaged with routine manual labor are quite widely represented in it, which is usually atypical for the middle class.[10] Thus, manual workers make up 38% of the employed representatives of the lower subgroup and 32% of the upper subgroup of the middle income population groups while rank-and-file employees of the commerce and consumer services sphere make up 13% and 10%, respectively. *Considering that the typical income of Russian workers and rank-and-file employees of the tertiary sector is less than the mean and median values for Russia, the inclusion of some employees in the middle income population groups can result from their higher qualifications, the particular nature of their work, and more developed human capital.*

Let us test these hypotheses and consider how Russian workers fall into the economic middle class. Is the "embourgeoisement"[11] of some of the Russian manual workers the result of their higher education level and developed skills or is their inclusion in the middle income population groups determined by other reasons not related to their knowledge and skills? To answer this question, let us consider manual laborers belonging to the middle income population groups in more detail. As seen in Fig. 4.1, the middle income population groups include half of all Russian workers (which is 18% of all the employed in the country). The other half of Russian workers mainly belong to the low-income population groups, and only an insignificant portion of them belong to high-income population groups (5% of employed Russians). It is important to note that the basic formal characteristics of workers' education level among those belonging to the middle income and low-income population groups are approximately at the same level. Thus, 68% and 61% of these workers have secondary specialized and/or incomplete higher education, respectively; 24% and 28% have secondary general education; 4% and 7% have incomplete secondary

[10] Mills (2002). Please see information on the social and professional make-up of the middle class according to the Neo-Weberian approach below.

[11] British sociologists J. Goldthorpe and D. Lockwood were the first to talk about the phenomenon of embourgeoisement in industrial developed society: Goldthorpe and Lockwood (1971).

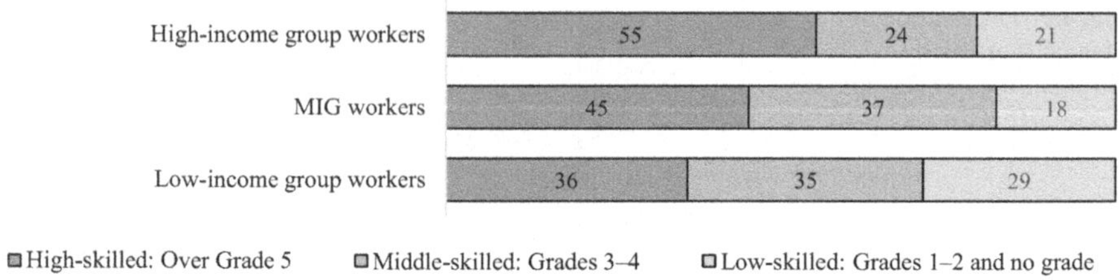

Fig. 4.2 Qualification Level of Workers in Different Income Groups, IS RAS, 2015, %

Table 4.3 Pairwise Comparison of Distribution of Wages of Workers with Different Qualification Levels, IS RAS, 2015

Compared subsamples of workers	Test statistics	Significance
Low-skilled—high-skilled[a]	94.499	0.000
Middle-skilled—high-skilled	14.615	0.000
Low-skilled—middle-skilled	40.373	0.000

[a]Each line tests the null hypothesis that the distribution of wages within the above sample groups does not differ. All the tested hypotheses are reflected with an error probability of less than 0.01%

general education; and 3% and 3% have higher education, respectively. In other words, the inclusion of manual workers in the middle income population groups is determined by factors other than formal indicators of their education level.

At the same time, the differences between the acquired skills of workers belonging to different income groups are more significant. Figure 4.2 shows that the share of workers with high skills (5th grade workers and higher) in the group of workers belonging to the middle income population groups is considerably higher than among workers from the low-income population groups (45% and 36%, respectively). In this case, they make up the majority (55%) of those manual workers included in high-income population groups.

Therefore, *inclusion of workers into the economic middle class is related not only to formal differences in the education level but also to differences in their skill level, i.e. higher skilled workers under otherwise equal conditions will have the highest wages*. Thus, the median wages of high-skilled workers (5th grade and higher) in 2015 was 25,000 rubles per month, middle-skilled workers (3rd and 4th grade)—20,000 rubles, and low-skilled workers (1st and 2nd grade and no grade) –15,000 rubles per month. These differences are statistically significant, which is confirmed by the data in Table 4.3, demonstrating the results of pairwise comparison of the wage distributions of workers holding different qualification levels.

Despite the fact that recent research in this field argues that the labor of skilled workers is paid unfairly low[12] (which is also partially confirmed by our research), it is worth noting that the *high skill level of workers is obviously sought after by the real sector, which is reflected in their wages*. This means that it is the skill and not

[12] For example, see works by Karavai (2016).

the formal education level that acts as the key characteristic of their human capital, which is an essential addition to those conclusions drawn by a number of Russian researchers when assessing the return on human capital based on formal education indicators, not taking into account the difference in employee skill levels or extracting them from occupational structure.[13]

This finding allows us to reassess the problem of human capital development of manual workers in contemporary Russia. If one speaks about the policies contributing to an increase in wages and the level of well-being of Russian workers, the regulators should more actively develop the workers' practical skills, including their competencies in the ICT field, which are especially important in the formation of a high-tech economy. It must be said that these skills are already being compensated by Russian employers with an increased return, thus providing Russians integrated in the ICT sphere with higher chances of belonging to the upper subgroup of the economic middle class[14]; however, this has yet to apply to manual workers.

Thus, the relative share of Russians who use computer skills every day is 42% of the upper middle income population groups and only 34% of the lower ones (in the lower-income groups whose income does not exceed 0.75 times the median value, their share is just 25%). However, additional income for using computer skills at work is mainly enjoyed by skilled non-manual workers. Most manual workers (88%) either lack any computer skills or hold jobs that do not involve use of these skills, even if they have them. Even among highly skilled workers, the share of people integrated into the ICT sphere is rather small, i.e. just about 6% of high-skilled workers use computer skills within their professional activities on a daily basis. In general, the share of workers using a personal computer at work among manual workers does not exceed 12%. All this speaks to the *low quality of jobs occupied by high-skilled workers, even those included in the economic middle class, which is a serious institutional barrier on the path to a new economy.* Successful technological modernization of jobs in the real sector will allow engagement of a rarely used or unused ICT capacity of almost 70% of high-skilled workers already integrated into the ICT technologies but not using the relevant skills within their work yet.

In spite of this, the development of computer skills by Russian workers is a necessary measure as the presence of these skills is associated with developed human capital. Thus, if the share of people lacking computer skills among high-skilled workers is just 25%, among middle-skilled workers this figure is 30%, and among low-skilled workers it reaches 46%. This means that the *creation of new-generation jobs for Russian workers must be associated with an extensive advanced training campaign for manual workers that should include not only development of specialized competencies but also skills in computerized equipment operation. This will make it possible to increase the potential for successful integration of the real sector of the Russian economy into the international economic system as well as maintain high*

[13] Lukyanova (2010).

[14] It completely corresponds to foreign experience. See Peng and Eunni (2011), DiNardo and Pischke (1997).

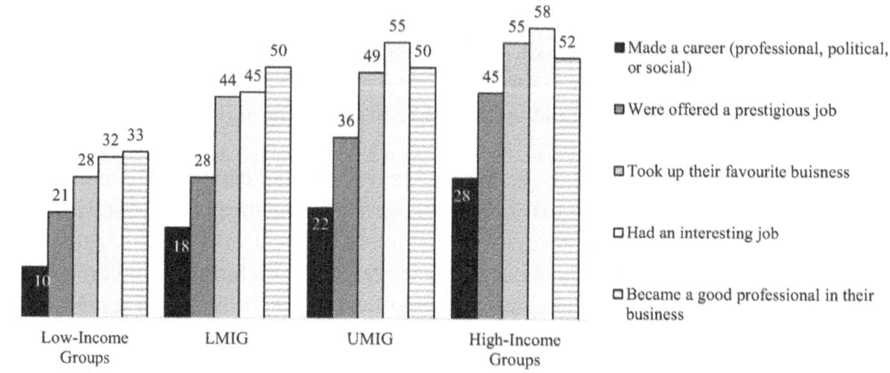

Fig. 4.3 Implemented Achievements in the Professional Sphere (Self-Assessment), IS RAS, 2015, % of employed

levels of employment of manual workers amid automation and robotization of most jobs, which will affect the real sector of the Russian economy in the next 7–10 years.

The above data mainly concern the employment situation if applied to middle income population groups and separate occupational subgroups included in it. Let us consider the differences between the upper and lower subgroups of the middle income population groups formed in relation to their occupational achievements. Because inclusion into the upper middle income groups is more likely for those Russians employed in management positions and in the sphere of intellectual labor, the work of the upper subgroups' representatives turns out to be more interesting and respected than that of the lower subgroup of the middle income population groups. For example, among the upper subgroup of the middle income population groups, the share of Russians who, according to their self-esteem, managed to find a prestigious or interesting job was 37% and 55% in 2015, while the same indicators for the lower subgroup of the middle income population groups were considerably lower, at the level of 28% and 45%, respectively.

The same can be said about the sphere of Russians' career achievements in the upper and lower subgroups of the economic middle class. However, the data in Fig. 4.3 provide reasons to state that the difference between the occupied jobs of the upper and lower subgroups of the middle income population groups is quite significant, but still not so critical as to seriously affect the perception by the economic middle class of its life chances in the production sphere. Those Russians included in the middle income population groups confirm that they do not experience limitations in their professional growth, and also consider themselves to be 'good professionals' in their field. This means that a *more positive perception of one's professional level and advantages of one's job is a distinctive feature of middle income Russians when compared to other social groups, in particular, low-income groups.*

What can we say about the self-rated employment situation declared by the working representatives of the middle income groups? The share of their employed representatives assessing the employment situation as good is at least three times the respective share of those who have a negative perception thereof. Thus, a positive self-rated employment situation is typical of 34% and 37% of representatives of the lower and upper subgroups of the middle income population groups, while a negative perception is expressed by just 11% and 7%, respectively. In other words, in spite of the fact that jobs of the lower and upper subgroups of the middle income population groups considerably differ in favor of the upper subgroup, the representatives of both subgroups are quite unanimous when self-rating the situation at their job. This is ensured under the conditions of differences with respect to the jobs they hold due to the fact that the lower and upper subgroups of the middle income population groups emphasize different parameters of employment and the workplace. It is relevant not just for real experience in increasing one's professional level, which is different in these subgroups. While the lower subgroup of the middle income population groups, due to the specifics of the positions held by its representatives, values 'good relations at work' and 'the amount of payoffs', the upper subgroup of the middle income population groups emphasize the demand for their human capital, the content of their labor, and opportunities for professional self-fulfillment with an adequate level of compensation for their efforts.[15]

This corresponds to the empiric verifications of the human capital theory,[16] according to which any income is determined not only by "bad" job positions but also by poor human capital.[17] To what extent a membership in the middle income population groups, in particular, in their upper subgroup, is related to the developed human capital of their representatives? According to classic sociological research, the middle class differs from other social groups by the fact that its representatives' education is sought after by the market so they can receive income from returns to their human capital[18]; this tends to determine this group's specifics.

The level of human capital accumulation among the lower-subgroup members of the middle income population groups is characterized by the national average indicators, due to which one can state that these Russians' job positions are not related to their high level of education. Thus, the share of employed citizens with higher education does not exceed 35% of the representatives of the lower subgroup of the middle income population groups (while the share of their representatives with secondary specialized and incomplete higher education is 50%). At the same time, the shares of employed Russians with higher education among the upper subgroup of the middle income population groups are 45% and 43%, respectively. Therefore, *while secondary specialized and incomplete higher education is the most typical education level of the lower subgroup of the economic middle class, for the upper subgroup thereof, it is the third stage of vocational education, almost half of which*

[15] Anikin (2013).

[16] According to the classic interpretation, human capital means the knowledge and skills (including non-cognitive ones) accumulated by individuals that can lead to higher earnings in a competitive social system based on meritocratic principles.

[17] Becker (1993).

[18] If compared, the main source of the working class's income is its ability to work, and for the highest class it is economic capital.

is represented in this group by university graduates holding a degree in technologies and the natural sciences, which is likely to ensure human capital of a better quality in contemporary Russia. The fact that university graduates with technical degree belongs to the upper middle income groups speaks to the higher demand for this type of education in Russian today and the readiness of the economy to pay for this education.

Despite the fact that the educational profiles typical of the middle income population groups are different for the lower and upper subgroups thereof, both these groups actively invest in their human capital, and this is very important when **assessing the employment prospects** of the middle income groups. Thus, the real practices of accumulation and upgrading of human capital of the working representatives of the middle income population groups are encountered more often than in the low-income groups and are close to the high-income ones. For example, from 2013 to 2015, the education and/or qualification levels of 17% of the lower subgroup and 15% of the upper subgroup of the middle income population groups increased. When compared, in the same period only 11% of the representatives of the low-income population groups were able to make investments in their human capital, while the share of such people among the high-income population groups was nearly twice this figure, amounting to 19%.

Nevertheless, the prospects for accumulation of human capital during the 2015 crisis in these subgroups were different. Thus, in 2015 one-third of the representatives of the upper subgroup and 27% of the lower subgroup of the middle income population groups self-rated their opportunities for receiving the required education and knowledge as good. The same can be said about their opportunities in the field of professional development. Though about half of the employed representatives of the middle income population groups consider themselves established professionals, the self-rated assessment of further prospects for professional development in the lower and upper subgroups of the middle income population groups differs considerably. Representatives of the upper subgroup of the middle income population groups acknowledge that they have greater opportunities for professional self-fulfillment (40%) when compared to their lower subgroup (31%).

Despite the fact that the prospects for human capital accumulation in the lower and upper subgroups of the middle income population groups are considerably different, the professional mobility indicators in them are very similar and actually mirror the national level. Thus, the relative share of the working economic middle class who managed to get a promotion or find a new, more suitable job was 15% and 16% in the lower and upper middle income groups in 2015, respectively. If compared, this share among the low-income groups of Russian society was 10% and among the high-income groups was 26%. This data confirms the results of recent research, according to which the intensity of upward professional mobility is severely limited for most employed Russians.[19] The only exception is made by professionals moving into managerial positions; this is associated with an increase in status and income and is reflected in the corresponding statistics of the high-income population groups.

[19] Yastrebov (2016a, b).

Table 4.4 Influence of Different Income Groups, % of employed

Influence at work	Low-Income Groups	MIG		High-Income Groups
		LMIG	UMIG	
Able to influence decision-making within the entire enterprise	8	8	7	**14**
Able to influence decision-making within one's department	24	34	**42**	**46**
Their opinion does not affect any work decisions	**68**	**58**	51	40

The self-rated assessment of the employment prospects and mobility of the working population of the middle income groups is affected by economic crisis phenomena. Like most Russians, the employed representatives of the middle income population groups believed in 2015 that for the first crisis year the unemployment situation got worse and professional opportunities decreased. The risks of unemployment are only uncommon for the high-income groups. This reflects the fact that well-to-do Russians have greater opportunities than other social groups.

Influence as a resource at work also considerably differs in different income groups. For example, Table 4.4 shows that the upper middle income population groups possess much higher decision-making power at work than the lower subgroup thereof. However, this resource of theirs is usually limited by the size of their department (decision-making power within the entire enterprise is much more typical of the high-income groups). As performed work becomes more complex and management functions increase, influence at the workplace and the degree of autonomy also increase. The results of analysis of variance show that the average number of work aspects that an employee makes independent decisions about is statistically higher in the upper middle income and high-income groups.

In conclusion, we can say that the situation at the usual work in the lower subgroup of the middle income groups corresponds to the national level. This is quite logical considering their median position. At the same time, in the upper subgroup of the middle income population groups this situation is typically better than the national level (Table 4.5) and close to the high-income groups' indicators in all key aspects.

Therefore, despite the similarity between the lower and upper subgroups of the middle income groups in the sphere of employment in various sectors of the economy, upward mobility, human capital investments, etc., *we still cannot argue that the lower and upper middle income groups are within the single space of life chances in the production sphere. This raises the question of consistency of the middle income groups and testifies to the need to check the concept of the so-called sociological middle class identified within the New-Weberian theory based on several criteria* described in Chap. 1. Based on the set of attributes characterizing their employment, the economic basis of the multi-criteria middle class in its New-Weberian tradition is formed by the Russians whose income starts from 1.25 times the median value,

Table 4.5 Map of Differences Between Upper and Lower Subgroups of the Middle income Groups regarding their Fundamental Economic Characteristics, as of 2015

Characteristics	LMIG	UMIG
Employment characteristics		
Presence of full-time employment	National level	+
Unemployment	National level	–
Employment as managers and professionals	National level	+
Employment in manual labor positions	National level	National level
Employment in tertiary and quaternary sectors of the economy	National level	National level
Work characteristics		
Good situation at work (self-rated assessment)	National level	+
Can influence decision-making within the department	National level	+
Human capital characteristics		
Higher education and above	National level	+
Experience in human capital investments	National level	National level
Daily use of computer skills	National level	+
Characteristics of the main life chances		
Opportunities to become a good professional in one's occupation	+	+
Good opportunities for professional self-fulfillment (self-rated assessment)	National level	+
Crisis worsened the situation with employment and professional opportunities	National level	National level
Access to high-quality education	National level	+
Professional development prospects (self-rated assessment)	National level	+
Upward occupational mobility	National level	National level

Note "National level" is indicated adjusted for employed Russians (where necessary). "+" means a statistically significant relationship between this indicator and the subgroup. "–" means the attribute is practically not represented in this subgroup of the middle income population groups

i.e. the upper subgroup of the middle income population groups and high-income Russians. In fact, the "overlapping" area of the sociological and economic middle class is the working population of the upper subgroup of the middle income groups, which is mostly formed of managers and professionals (Table 4.6).

Let us summarize

Understanding the prospects for Russian middle class development depends on its interpretation. Identification of the middle class, even based on just one criterion (income), allows us to specify the middle income groups that possess a set of specific attributes, which enables us to interpret them as the basis for forming the middle class from the sociological point of view.

Table 4.6 Professional Composition of Economic and Sociological Middle Classes, IS RAS, 2015, % of employed

Professional statuses	Economic middle class (MIG)			Sociological middle class, MG
	LMIG	UMIG	MIG as a whole	
Managers of all levels, entrepreneurs and the self-employed	7	**12**	9	***16***
Professionals whose work involves using higher education	26	**35**	***30***	***49***
Semi-professionals, office employees, administrators, and clerks	15	11	*13*	***20***
Other non-manual workers (service workers and shop and market sales workers)	13	10	*12*	***15***
Manual workers	38	32	*35*	*0*

Nevertheless, the studied characteristics of employment and work of the middle income groups in contemporary Russia makes it possible to conclude that they are very heterogeneous regarding their structure. The lower subgroup represents the average situation in Russia. As the general situation in Russia is characterized by mass employment in positions not requiring valuable human capital, high qualifications and complex work, the lower subgroup of the middle income population groups inherits the same features with all the subsequent consequences. The upper subgroup of the middle income population groups represents the labor force possessing lower unemployment risks and more developed human capital. As a result, those jobs held by its representatives are associated with greater influence at their workplace and better career prospects.

The differences in human capital (education and skill levels) are most important when characterizing the heterogeneity of the economic middle class, regarded as more significant features differentiating the two subgroups of the middle income groups as compared, for example, to a sector of the economy an individual is working in. Post-crisis negative stabilization can lead to further internal polarization of the middle income groups in the production sphere.

Therefore, the Russian middle class interpreted from the economic viewpoint is a complex, heterogeneous phenomenon as if "bringing together" two different epochs of economic development possessing different requirements for the labor force and different qualification standards. In case of further deterioration of the employment and work situation, the lower subgroup of the middle income population groups may be included in the high-risk zone, which can lead to proletarization of a considerable part of Russian society and set Russia back many years. Therefore, the government, playing the central role in the key social and economic changes in Russian society, must create conditions for bridging the gap between the middle income subgroups, in particular, by modernizing workplaces and developing the competencies of ICT employees because amid the current challenges faced by Russia, it is the middle class that will have to become the main subject of social and economic development.

References

Anikin VA (2013) Motivation to work in Russia: the case of protracted transition from non-competitive to competitive system. J Comparat Econ Stud 8:35–60

Becker GS (1993) Nobel lecture: The economic way of looking at behavior. J Political Econ 101(3):385–409

DiNardo JE, Pischke, J-S (1997) The returns to computer use revisited: have pencils changed the wage structure too?. Quart J Econ 112(1):291–303

Forrier A, Sels L (2003) Temporary employment and employability: training opportunities and efforts of temporary and permanent employees in Belgium. Work, Empl Soc 17(4):641–666

Giesecke J, Groß M (2003) Temporary employment: chance or risk?. Europ Sociol Rev 19(2):161–177

Gimpelson VE, Kapelyushnikov RI (2007) Wages in Russia: evolution and differentiation. Moscow: Publishing House of the State University—Higher School of Economics

Goldthorpe J, Lockwood D (1971) The Affluent worker: political attitudes and behaviour. Cambridge University Press, Cambridge

Karavai AV (2016) Human capital of Russian workers: condition and factors. Inst Sociol Bullet 17:91–112

Lehmann H, Zaiceva A (2015) Redefining informality and measuring its determinants: evidence from the Russian labour market. J Int Dev 27:464–488

Lukyanova AL (2010) Return on education: meta-analysis Results. Higher School Econ Econ Magaz 14(3)

Mills C (2002) White collar: the American middle classes. Oxford University Press

Peng G, Eunni RV (2011) Computer skills, non-routine tasks, and wage premium: a longitudinal study. J Strategic Inform Syst 20(4):449–460

Sabirianova Z et al (2002) The great human capital reallocation: a study of occupational mobility in transitional Russia. J Comparat Econ 30:191–217

Yastrebov GA (2016a) Social mobility in soviet and post-soviet Russia: new quantitative assessment based on the representative survey materials of 1994, 2002, 2006, and 2013. Part I. World Russia: Sociol Ethnol 24(1):7–36

Yastrebov GA (2016b). Social mobility in soviet and post-soviet Russia: new quantitative assessment based on the representative survey materials of 1994, 2002, 2006, and 2013. Part I. World Russia: Sociol Ethnol 24(2):6–36

V. A. Anikin Senior Researcher at the Federal Centre of Theoretical and Applied Sociology of the Russian Academy of Sciences (former Institute of Sociology, Russian Academy of Sciences), Assistant Professor and Senior Research Fellow at the National Research University Higher School of Economics. He holds Ph.D. in Population Economics and Demographics from Institute for Socio-Economic Studies of Population, Russian Academy of Sciences (2011) and Ph.D. in Sociology from Essex University (2017). His main areas of interest include social structure and social stratification, development studies, and advanced statistics. He has published over 60 articles and chapters in scientific monographs. His recent publications in English include a paper "Occupational Propensity for Training in a Late Industrial Society: Evidence from

Russia" published in International Journal of Training and Development (2017); "Russia in Post-Transition: New Frontiers". The Journal of Comparative Economic Studies. 2017. Vol. 12; "Poverty and Inequality in BRICS Countries". Sociological Research. 2016. Vol. 55. No. 5 (co-authored with Tikhonova N.E.).

Chapter 5
Variations in the Income and Education of the Middle Income Group in China

Feng Tian

With the high-speed economic growth in last three decades, the living conditions of Chinese people have gradually improved along with the larger disparity of wealth in all the social classes. And the trend is only getting more and more significant when we look at the demographic characteristics, social mentality and political engagement of different income groups. Despite of plenty of experience from the western developed countries that the expansion of middle income group could stabilize society and promote economic growth, generally speaking, almost all developing countries encountered the "middle income trap" on their journey to a more developed society. To successfully overcome the trap and get ranked later as a developed country has been rare. So, whether China could avoid this trap is still to be seen. Typically, whether the middle income group in China can serve as the social stabilizer just like what their counterpart group does in the western society, when experiencing so remarkable transformation and ever enlarged wealth gap, is still a question. And what are their numbers and proportion in China? What is the social status structure within the group? What transformation did they go through in the last decade? What is the difference between them and other groups? All those basic questions remain unanswered in China. This paper tries to begin with defining the concept of the middle income group, analyze its scale, character in social structure and changing trends, and based on which, we can analyze and predict the future tendency of the society in China.

The original version of this chapter was revised: Correct chapter author for this Chapter has been updated as "Feng Tian" instead of "Peng Lu and Xiaoguang Fan". The correction to this chapter is available at https://doi.org/10.1007/978-981-16-1464-4_21

F. Tian (✉)
Institute of Sociology, Chinese Academy of Social Sciences (CASS), Beijing, China
e-mail: gaoj@ssap.cn

P. Li and M. K. Gorshkov (eds.), *The Middle Income Group in China and Russia*, Research Series on the Chinese Dream and China's Development Path,
https://doi.org/10.1007/978-981-16-1464-4_5

5.1 Background

As the statistics by World Bank, China has been advancing rapidly from a low-income country to a middle income one since its reform and opening up, almost 4 decades ago. In 1998, China was ranked a lower middle income country for the first time. In 2010, it became a upper middle income country for the first time. As indicated by the data published by National Bureau of Statistics of PRC, its GNI per capita was above $7500 in 2015, approaching the average limits of upper middle income countries ($4036 to $12,475). Calculated from the growth trend of Chinese economy over the last three decades, the historical leap of the income is expected to happen around year 2025 and China by then shall be one of the high-income countries, as long as China could avoid the so called "middle-income trap". However, the global financial crisis and its aftershocks in 2008 has brought dramatic decline to the economy in China with the falling of both the growth rate of GDP and GDP per capita (refer to Graph 5.1). "New Normal" began to take over, of which remarkable transformation of economic structure and economic engines happened whereas the growth rate got slowed down from the high to medium–high speed.

As China's economy has entered the new phase of "New Normal", the income distribution must be adjusted with the transformation of economic growth model. However, whether the "middle-income group", as emerged and grew with the high-speed economic growth, shall sustain series of new changes as what happen to the income restructure is still a question. To answer this, the analyses shall start from the characteristics of trends for the groups in the fast-developing decade. Further discussion on the coming tendency can be continued only based on the following full analysis of the income and education distribution in China.

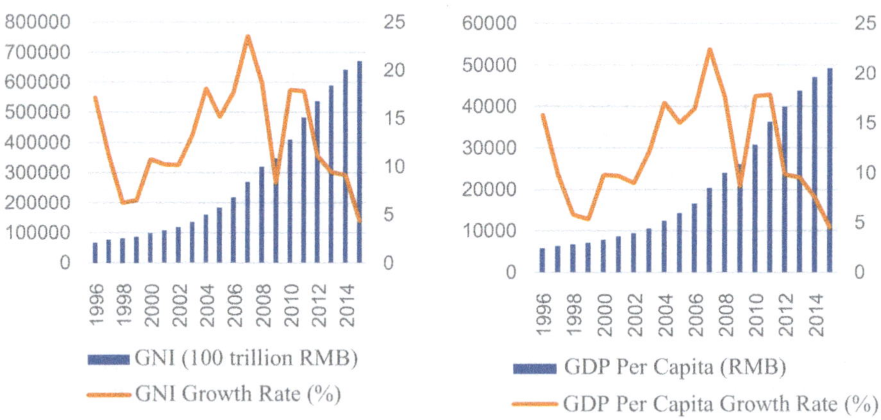

Graph 5.1 China GNI and GDP per capita 1996–2015

5.2 Income Level and Distribution Over the Last Decade

According to the statistics of five rounds of GSSs carried out between 2006 and 2015, the growth of household income in the last decade was very quick, and averaged number grew from below ¥20,000 in 2006 to approximately ¥65,000 in 2015. And the gross median household income rose from a little above ¥10,000 in 2006 to over ¥40,000 in 2015. Both indicators show the general fast increase of family earnings levels. Along with income increase, the middle income group changed rapidly, as it is a group mainly divided by income. Social groups that have enjoyed advantage in the income distribution are more likely to gain benefits from the above increase while the underprivileged tiers are prone to fall down the ladder of economic status (Graph 5.2).

The distribution in China has greatly shifted as the incomes keep growing. From the Graph 5.3, the negatively skewed household incomes in 2005 mainly fell in the interval of below ¥50,000. Then the distribution started its expansion to the evenly spread interval of above ¥50,000 with significantly increased intensity. Actually, the generally uniform distribution within the $100,000 interval means there is no obvious bipolarization occurred with the added average income and median income. It is showcased in the following incomes quintiles.

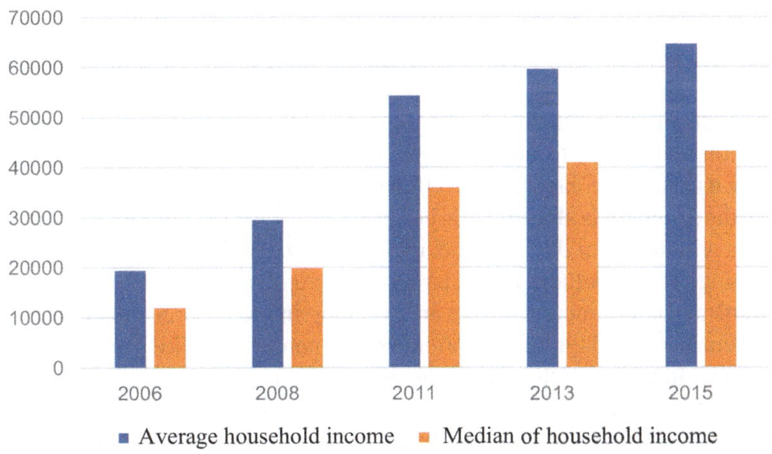

Graph 5.2 Chinese average household incomes and median of household incomes between 2006 and 2015

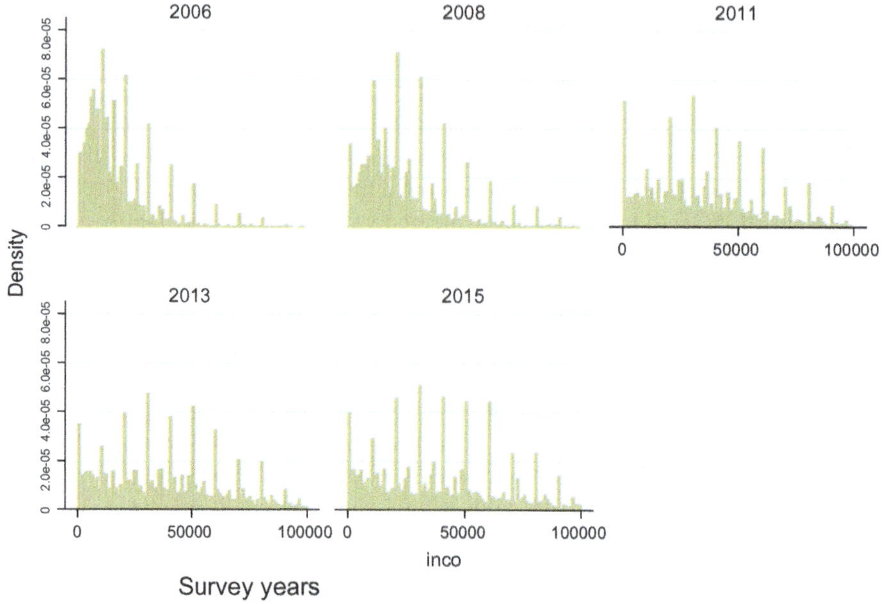

Graph 5.3 Income distribution 2006–2015

In the decade of 2006 to 2015, by the shares in the income quintiles, there was a slight fall for the 20% people in the top tier from 49.28 to 44.43%. And there was an increase for higher-middle, middle, lower-middle income tiers, separately from 22.39, 14.06 and 9.20% to 26.51, 14.82 and 10.85%. Meanwhile, the low income group saw its share decreased, from 5.08 to 3.39%. As the general income level rose in China, the groups at both ends showed shrinking shares in their gross income. Only the groups with upper middle income, middle income and lower middle income had more earning. This concludes that in terms of both income and wealth, the possession proportions of middle income group are going up in the general social wealth. This could in return affect their consumption, social mentality, political engagement and other aspects. In addition, the change of shares was not drastic, as the shares of each group remained relatively stable. There is still the wide income gulf between groups who earn the most and the least. This is alluded to the little optimization of income distribution structure in China. Such mechanism conductive to the building up of the middle income group is yet to improve (Graph 5.4).

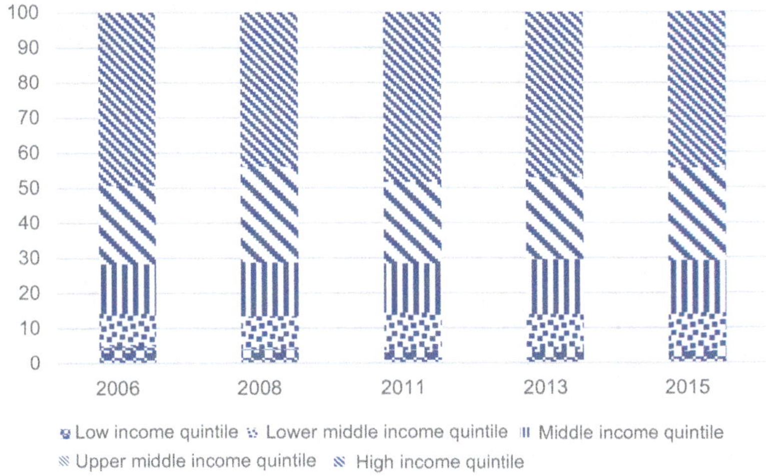

Graph 5.4 Change of share for incomes quintiles 2006–2015

5.3 Educational Attainment and Distribution Over the Last Decade

An unprecedented higher education expansion started from 1990s, for which the opportunities to get enrolled in colleges soared, and therefore the overall population's educational attainment in China has been significantly improved. However, the improvement of educational attainment after such expansion is based on a large number of the population and in a relatively short time, the role the result plays is quite limited. From the statistics herein, the population enjoyed higher education (junior colleges graduates, undergraduates and graduates) were respectively 8.51% in 2006, 10.41% in 2008 and 13.27% in 2015. In the same term, the share of those who received junior middle school education or below fell from 73.60% in 2006 to 68.79% in 2015, with 5% less. This means that a general moving up along the education distribution for the whole society was achieved by the production tens of millions of higher educated graduates in the last decade. It was an overall improvement of the population for the educational attainment. But the low education receivers still take a large part of the existing population. But the education of the aged population shall not be improved by the expansion of higher education. To foster middle-income class, drive stable and sustained socio-economic development and continually raise the education level of those less educated, introducing more life-time vocational learning shall be greatly relied upon (Graph 5.5).

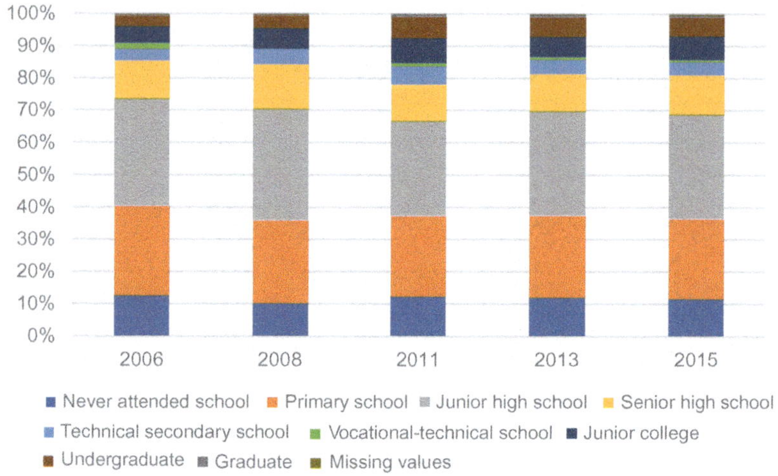

Graph 5.5 Different educational attainment shares 2006–2015

The changes of education levels are different among different age groups in China under the influence of expanding higher education enrollment. According to statistics, the average years of education of the population stood at 8.11 in 2006 and 8.63 in 2015, with 0.52 years added; population of young people aged 35 or younger received 10.16 years of education averagely in 2008 and 11.49 in 2015, with 1.33 more years. The above indicates that, with the general raised education background, when enter the job market, the young people under 35 years old benefited more. Their years of education showed evident increment, their acquired more knowledge and skills from such learning and they should probably become the main body of the future middle-income tiers (Graph 5.6).

Traditional sociologists have different ideas on education: some believe that education is a servant to industrialization, as its development requires technicians and experts. The role of higher education system is to provide professionals for industrialized society. Others believe that modern education system has stimulated the rise of the new intellectual class, or so called intellectual bourgeois. The new class shall in the end topple the social existence including industrial society and capital privileges with its cultural discourses. Although with the unbalanced development across regions in China, socio-economic process cannot be simply labeled as "industrialization", but well-educated youth shall still have their great influence on the existing social structure in no doubt. Their knowledge and skills shall pave their road to the middle income group. Also, previous research has already verified the high correlation between income and education. This relation shall secure higher

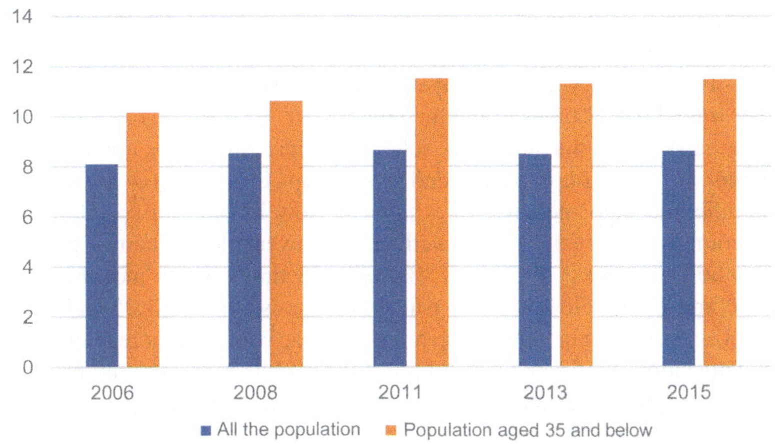

Graph 5.6 Mean years of schooling of all and young people aged 35 and below 2006–2015

professional positions and income for the young people and raise the possibility for them to enter the middle income group.

5.4 Definition of the Middle Income Group and Their Trends

Different from the concept of middle class or intermediate stratum, the middle income group is defined basically by one measurement and standard: their income. Actually, when compared with the middle class or the intermediate stratum concept, there is less rich connotation in this concept, or it could be deemed as a secondary concept to the middle-income countries. After all, it only makes sense for the middle income group in middle income countries that share similar socioeconomic status. Or gaps between countries would make it difficult to make such comparisons. This is the drawback when the concept of the middle income group sticks to only one standard.

There are two common international standard models for the middle income group, the absolute standard model and relative one. According to Chunling's study (2016), the two measurement models serve different objects and apply to different scopes. The absolute standard model mainly reflects the population and their percentage of growth trends whose living standards are beyond certain threshold, that is, people from the developing countries and lower middle income countries. While the relative standard model measures increase and decrease of the percentage of those whose incomes are in the median level, or, the inequality trend of incomes. The widely used absolute standard model is based on the poverty gap line as set by the World Bank (at $1.90 a day). Those whose income fall in the interval of $10–15 or $10–100 belong to the middle income group. The relative standard model determines the income standard of the middle-income tiers based on the median of the income distribution, for which the lower limit is set as 50 or 75% of the median and the higher limit 1.5 or 2 times of the median.

For the purpose of this study, the relative standard model is applied here, and the different income groups are divided into groups of low, lower middle, middle, upper middle and high incomes, of which, the low income group refers to those whose income is below 75% of the median, the lower-middle-income group refers to those whose income is between 75% and 1.25 times of the median, the upper middle income group refers to those whose income is between 1.25 and 2 times of the median, and the high income group refers to those who earn more than 2 times the median. The adoption of relative standard of the middle income could bring certain difficulty for horizontal and vertical comparison research, but it fits the nation reality of China as a member of the upper middle income countries. This model shall provide more accurate definition among groups and ease the systematic analysis of variables beyond income.

Limited by the definition of the middle income group, the only standard for telling the middle income group apart is income. According to the middle income group defined in the context, annual statistics are used to make such partitioning and to calculate the proportion they take in the whole population. From the Graph 5.7, if the groups are divided annually, the percentage of the middle income group is quite stable. The data over the years are: 37.43% (lower middle income people and upper middle income people included) in 2006, 39.49% in 2008, 38.46% in 2011, 40.56% in 2013 and 37.33% in 2015. According to the relative standard, the middle income group remains in the interval of 37–41%. Actually, the division made based on one single factor, income, makes it difficult to see the changes of the group's income over the years, as the median shifted all the time and the standard for such group is

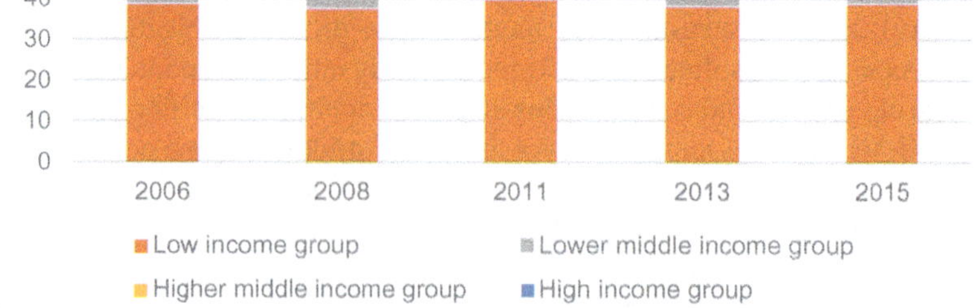

Graph 5.7 Income stratification based on absolute income standard 2006–2015

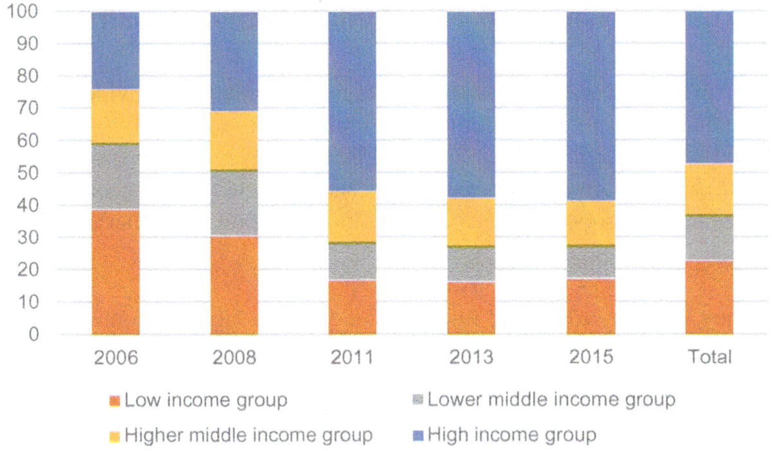

Graph 5.8 Social stratification based on relative income standard 2006–2015

changed accordingly. There is no point in making vertical comparison of the trends for group with relative stable percentage in the overall population.

As the vertical comparison is impossible using the relative standard, the study tries to depict trends with the fixed standard, for which the income in 2006 is used as the base line for analyzing the change over the last decade. From the Graph 5.8, with the middle income group's income in 2006 as the standard to define groups, the percentage of middle income group was 37.43% in 2006, 38.56% in 2008, 37.96% in 2011, 25.28% in 2013 and 24.51% in 2015. While over the same period, the percent of the high income population is gaining quickly, 23.69% in 2006, 30.55% in 2008, 55.26% in 2011, 57.37% in 2013 and 58.20% in 2015. Here we can see the drawback of the fixed standard: there are more high income people according to this standard, while many of them still belong to the middle income group in reality. Especially in developing countries like China, the fixed standard of the middle income group may fail in only one decade because of its rapid economic development and surging income growth.

From the above analysis of the absolute and relative standards, this article argues that the definition of the middle income group is rather stable. With such quick income growth in China, application of the fixed standard tends to lead to exaggerated change of the middle income group, and the results shall be skewed. The concept of middle income group fits more to such cycle when the social and economic level reaches a plateau, while the relative standard suits groups in a quick developing society. Therefore, the following analyses are based on data from annual survey, using "independent" reference of middle-income group definition to determine the change of their income structure and educational attainment.

5.5 Structured Analysis of the Middle Income Group

Based on the relative income standard, the annual population is divided into groups of low income, lower middle income, upper middle income and high income. After that, the different characteristics of the middle income group (lower middle income and upper middle income groups included), such as household registration (hukou) types, income structures and education backgrounds shall be further analyzed.

(1) Discrepancy of hukou types

Discrepancy between urban and rural income leads to higher income of those who hold non-agricultural hukou over those with agricultural hukou. It can be deduced that, in the regards of hukou, the percentage of the agricultural hukou is higher in the low-income group and the percentage of the non-agricultural background shows larger share in the high-income group. This speculation can find its root from the five rounds of GSSs. In addition, the percentage of agricultural hukou in the middle income group[1] is a bit lowered than its share in the survey. In 2006, the proportion with agricultural hukou was 60.23% among the total surveyed people and 58.20% among the middle income group, with a gap of 2.03%. In 2008, the numbers were 56.52 and 54.05%, with a gap of 2.47%. In 2013, they were 71.65 and 70.63%, with a gap of 1.02%. And in 2015, the numbers became 72.36 and 71.56%, with a gap standing at 0.80%. From the above data, hukou structure of the middle income group has a similar structure shared by the average level of all the population. That indicates that the gradually opened up hukou system has enabled more migrant workers with agricultural hukou to work in the urban area and they have close income with those lower-income urban people. This can also be verified by their occupational distribution. They constitute a large share in both the blue-collar jobs and self-employed services. Meanwhile, they tend to keep their agricultural identity to gain benefits from the added value of rural and homestead land due to Chinese urbanization.

(2) Income structure

In the regards of the income structure, income from salary, operation and property have all shown great changes. In 2006, the income from salary took 35.02% in low income group, 53.73% in lower middle income group, 62.97% in upper middle income group and 61.97% in high income group. Salary income is short in the low income group, while it played a more decisive part than others elements for income. When it came to 2015, the percentages of salary income of the above groups were

[1] The agricultural household registration includes both the holders living in the rural and urban area. Therefore, the proportion of these holders is higher.

respectively 57.67, 69.60, 71.71 and 57.85%. The data showed certain increases of salary income in all groups but high income group compared to 2006, which means that the decisive role of salary was going down while the operation income was going up in the high income group. The statistics show that the operation income accounted for 23.79% of the high-income group's total income, far more than that of the upper middle income group, which was 14.86%. It should be noted that, this operation income is different from the traditional rural operation income. Even the rural operation income registered a high percentage of 30.86% in the low-income group, their poverty-stricken reality remained.

In addition, the property income share has gained a lot. In 2015, it took up to 7.41% of the incomes for the high income group with non-agricultural hukou, much higher than the numbers for the upper middle income and lower middle income group in the same time, separately being 1.18 and 1.25%, and higher than the number of its self in 2006, which was 3.93%. It is obvious that the polarization among the high, middle and low income groups became evident, and property income plays an important role in telling apart income groups.

From the vertical and horizontal comparison made among different groups over the last decade, the increase in salary income became the main power of driving up income for the whole society. Even for the low-income population who hold agricultural identity, their salary could take up more than 50% of the total income. The number for the upper middle income group even went beyond 70%. It was also found that the decisive difference between the middle and high income group is the operation and property income. Therefore, the rise of labor remuneration in GDP is critical in expanding the middle income group. Meanwhile, the property income is a double-edge blade as it could both boost the general income level and cause intensified bipolarization between income groups, bringing larger income gaps (Graph 5.9).

(3) Educational structure

Since the new century, both the income and education levels are rising. The statistics help point out that the average income level shows positive correlation with years of education in different groups of income levels. Higher income tends to be brought by higher average years of education. In 2006, the averaged years of education were 6.43 years, 7.79 years, 8.92 years and 10.55 years separately for the groups of low, lower middle, upper middle and high incomes. The numbers rose to respectively 6.82, 8.20, 9.48 and 11.30 years. When compared vertically, the averaged years of education for the low-income group rose by no more than 0.4 years while that of the high income group rose by 0.75 years. That indicated those who received higher education enjoyed better opportunity of being ranked in the middle or high-income group. This was typical true since the enrollment expansion of higher education in

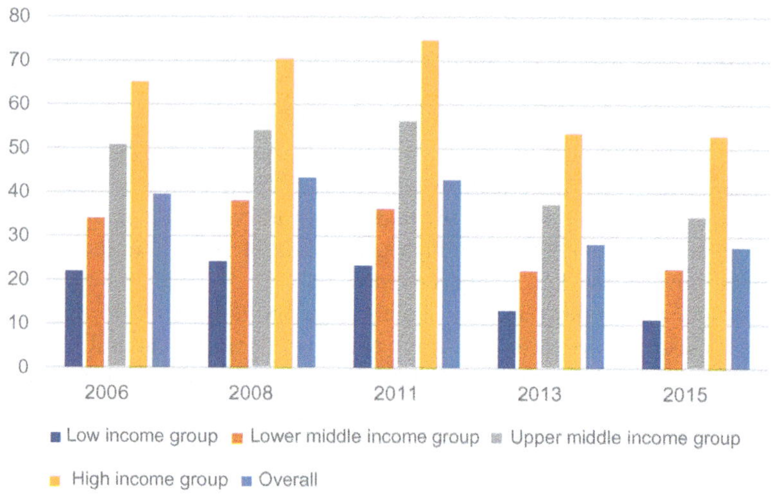

Graph 5.9 Proportional change of salary among different groups

China. This ever-expanding group have the best chance to get included in the groups of wealthier groups. Therefore, proportions of higher education receivers in different groups need to be analyzed.

It is found that the proportions of those who receive higher education in the low income, lower middle income, upper middle income and high income group were respectively 2.22, 3.97, 9.29 and 23.56% in 2006. Those numbers were then 4.69, 7.66, 15.29 and 33.06% in 2015. The proportion of the well-educated people grew most in the high income group, then in the upper middle income group, lower middle income group, and least in the low income group. If the high income group is divided into two parts, the traditional middle income subgroups and the emerging middle income subgroups, it is certain that the properly educated youth shall be the main part of such new emerging subgroups. According to the experience from the western developed countries, the traditional subgroup could show a shrinking proportion in the middle income group as the new added youth shall become the main strength in forming the olive-shaped society with their knowledge and skills (Graph 5.10).

(4) Age structure

When taking the close relation between income and education into consideration, the possibility for well-educated youth to get integrated into the middle and high income groups are higher. For example, according to the survey result in 2015, those who were born in the 40, 50 and 60 s of last century accounted for more than 2/3 of the

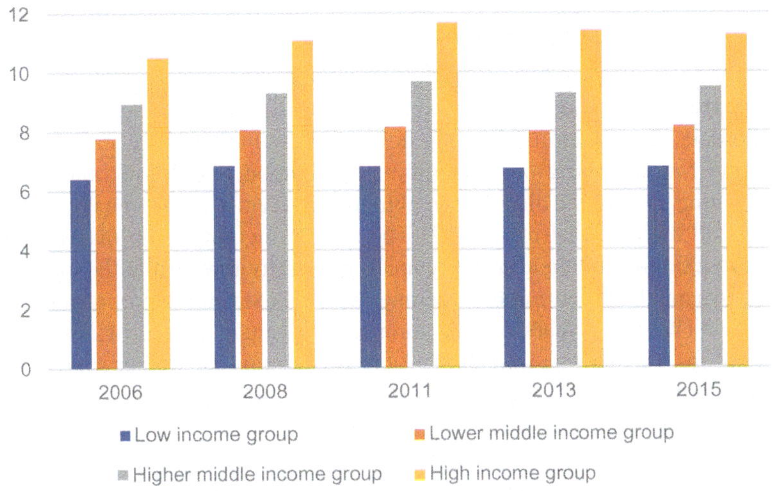

Graph 5.10 Mean years of schooling in different groups 2006–2015

total low-income people and more than 1/2 of the total lower middle income people. As for the upper middle income group, the share of 40, 50 and 60 s generation is 49.14%, and that of the late 70, 80 and 90 s generations 50.86%. The pair of numbers became 44.64 and 55.36% as in the high-income group. It can be concluded that, when the groups are divided according to the single income standard, the averagely well-educated youth enjoy certain advantage, as they show higher proportions in the upper middle income and high income groups. Still, the standard of living and social status are not only decided by the matter of income in reality.

Given the concept of the middle income group is defined by the single income standard, the revealing intergenerational inequality from the above analysis may be covered by the concept itself. In recent years, the intergenerational inequality and other social issues have emerged: On one hand, the educated youth who know new knowledge and skills may be on the high-end of the salary spectrum, but they also shoulder heavy loan from both living and purchasing homes with little accumulated wealth. It has been not very long since they began to receive high salaries. This is typically true for 80 and 90s generations who have jobs in metropolis and use quite a portion of their salaries paying their rents. Therefore, they could have worse living quality than those aged people who have the same or even less income. From the observation of Taiwan and Hong Kong, although the youth are more likely to enter the middle income group, they are the most unstable people in society and more prone to be incited.

(5) Summary

Here are the features of middle income group after the comprehensive analysis: (1) as high and upper middle income group are mainly constituted of those non-agricultural hukou holders, the agricultural hukou holders show higher share in lower middle income and low income groups. Combining the upper middle income and lower middle income groups, the distribution of household registration type is quite similar to the overall national distribution. (2) The middle income group mainly relies on their salary income, and their property income is pretty low. While the high-income group enjoys much higher property income, with ever shrinking proportion of salary income. (3) The mean years of education for the upper middle income and high income groups are growing quickly, and the two groups see higher share of higher educated people. The average years of education for the lower middle income group are slightly lower than that of the overall level. (4) There is a large possibility that those late 70, 80 and 90s generations could enter upper middle income or high income group, with certain intergenerational inequality. Portrayed by the structures of household registration types, incomes, educational attainment and ages, the profile of the middle income group is more likely to be "the average man" of the society. However, as much higher proportion of youth will be included in the middle income group by this dividing standard, and their social conditions are more likely to show unstable characteristic, whether the middle income group shall play the role of social stabilizer remains to be seen.

5.6 Policy Suggestion

After getting ranked as a middle income country, China shall go through its corresponding social structure change correlated to its economic development. This in return may possibly be shown in the expansion of its middle income group, in regard of income groups. As from the experience from the international community, stable socio-economic development is required to overcome the middle-income trap, during which time the middle income group can play a key role. However, nowadays the definition and structured analysis of such group remains respectively insufficient. Therefore, this article puts forward some policy suggestions as for defining and growing such middle income group.

(1) Be cautious in the definition of the middle income group

Whether the concept of middle income group is defined by fixed standard or relative standard, it has certain flaws, in the quick development of both economy and income. Current analysis proves that the very group shows features close to "the average man". The definition should reflect loyally the social reality and become an important index that represents the dominant trending at the same time, which should be stable and reliable when carrying out vertical and horizontal comparisons. Thus, the definition of the middle income group should be improved according to multiple sources in order to avoid its misuse or abuse.

(2) Labor remuneration proportion in the income of the middle income group should be raised to expand the middle income group

Different from the high income group who enjoy high operational and property incomes, the middle income group relies mainly on their salary income, that is, the labor remuneration. Since 1980s, the labor remuneration share in GDP has dropped severely, which affected the social instability. According to the survey by All-China Federation of Trade Union, over 60% of the employees believe that the most unfairness lies in low remuneration (Weiguo 2010). Therefore, it is not only a precondition of expanding the middle income group, but also an important condition of maintaining social equality to raise the proportion of compensation in GPD.

(3) Importance should be attached to human capital when expanding the middle income group

The advent of post-industrial society means the income effect brought by knowledge economy has becomes more evident. Human capital represented by educational attainment can never be overlooked in raising incomes. Analyses show that higher incomes tend to correlates to higher education backgrounds. In China, there is a significantly higher educated proportion in the upper middle income and high income groups. Besides, education enables one to go up the social ladder. So, improving education equity, maintaining higher education enrollment scale properly and further enhancing the quality of higher education are all requirements of strengthening the middle income group.

(4) Deepened reform and elimination of institutional barriers are required when expanding the middle income group

Hukou system has long been the representative system of social inequity. Research shows that while the hukou type distribution almost fits the overall registration type distribution, the non-agricultural types has significantly higher proportion in the upper middle income and high income groups than that in the lower middle income group. Although the household registration policy tends to loosen these years, the historical urban and rural discrepancy cannot be eliminated within a short term. Besides, there are gender discrimination, regional discrimination and other institutional barriers on the labor market too. Only through deepened reform and removal of such hindrance would labors play full role of their initiative and thus enhance the middle income group (Table 5.1).

(5) New inequity should be prevented when expanding the middle income group

Technology and social development brings both advantages for people and plights for those aging people with relatively low education background as they may suffer from declining or capped income. Higher proportion of young and educated people in middle income group could indicate a possible scenario that the less educated and aging people are moving towards the low income or lower middle income group. It is necessary to prevent the less educated people, especially the aging people with agricultural hukou, from sliding into a group called "working poor".

Table 5.1 Household registration statistics of different income groups

Years	2006		2008		2011		2013		2015	
Hukou type	Non-agr.	Agr.	Non-agr.	Agr.	Non-agr.	Agr.	Non-agr.	Agr.	Non-agr.	Agr.
Low income group	22.20	77.80	24.41	75.59	23.52	76.48	13.23	86.77	11.33	88.67
Lower middle income group	34.26	65.74	38.28	61.72	36.49	63.51	22.35	77.65	22.75	77.25
Upper middle income group	50.79	49.21	54.00	46.00	56.13	43.87	37.30	62.70	34.43	65.57
High income group	65.43	34.57	70.79	29.21	75.02	24.98	53.81	46.19	53.18	46.82
All	39.77	60.23	43.48	56.52	43.02	56.98	28.35	71.65	27.64	72.36

References

Chunling L (2016) Accurate defining of the middle income group is required. People's Daily, December 7, 2016
Li, C (2016) The sense of insecurity and anxieties. Beijing Cult Rev (4)
Weiguo Y (2010) Low labor remuneration is the biggest inequity. Workers' Daily, May 18, 2010

Chapter 6
Middle Income Groups: The Correlation Between Education and Material Well-Being

P. M. Kozyreva and A. I. Smirnov

The specific features of the way mid-level income groups are formed are largely determined by the solutions for the country's education issues, mainly those of accessibility and quality of education. This, in many respects, may be explained by the special role education plays as a mechanism of socialization and social and cultural integration, an upward mobility channel, and a means of producing and accumulating human and social capital.

Modern sociological research views education inequality as combined inequality of social circumstances that impact education opportunities and inequality of education outcome.[1] It bears noting that research conducted in different countries demonstrates an overall positive link between the differentiation of the population's education level and income.[2] Empirical data makes it obvious that the improvement of education level is the main factor of increasing income and combating poverty, while higher income, in turn, serves as one of the key prerequisite for a rise in education level and the accessibility of high-quality professional education.[3] The status of material well-being tends to be viewed as one of the objective indices of education and career success or lack thereof.[4] Another point being highlighted is the importance of income security for all workers, regardless of age and professional group,

[1] Breen and Jonsson (2005).

[2] Latov (2014).

[3] Income and Social Services: Inequality, Vulnerability, Poverty. Moscow: Higher School of Economics National Research University Publishing House, 2005. pp. 168–182.

[4] Konstantinovsky et al. (2011).

[5] Gorshkov and Sherega (2015).

P. M. Kozyreva (✉)
HSE University, Institute of Sociology of FCTAS RAS, Moscow, Russia

A. I. Smirnov
Institute of Sociology of FCTAS RAS, Moscow, Russia

P. Li and M. K. Gorshkov (eds.), *The Middle Income Group in China and Russia*, Research Series on the Chinese Dream and China's Development Path,
https://doi.org/10.1007/978-981-16-1464-4_6

as they name income as the primary motivational factor that prompts them to work and invest in their education.[5]

In this context, we would also like to draw attention to another important fact: namely, that the numerous sociological papers on the issues of the middle class in modern Russia view education as one of the key criteria of belonging to the middle class, alongside with social and professional status, a certain level of material well-being, and an individual's subjective evaluation of their position in society. As access to education evens out and the quality of professional education increases, this prompts an expansion of the mid-income population tier, which is a major factor of harmonizing the entire range of social and economic interests and a powerful force that helps keep the current social and political institutions stable.

As market relations keep developing and social and economic inequality keeps growing, the correlation between income and education in Russia has become even more prominent and transitioned to a new state, which is chiefly linked to the rapid development of the education services market.

The large-scale transformations taking place in the education sector during the post-Soviet period were complemented by the active involvement of additional funds from various sources and a greater diversity of legal entities that provided education. There was a massive emergence of non-state education institutions, as well as various divisions, correspondence departments, courses, etc. that were affiliated with state institutions and provided education services for a fee. The active encouragement of private investments into broadening the scope of fee-based education services not only made the differentiation of education programs more profound, but also helped increase their flexibility and better adapt the education process to the constantly changing demands of the labor market.

As private education, with its diversity and flexibility, adapts to changes in the labor market and the social sphere quicker and with greater ease,[6] fee-based professional education services became especially widespread in post-Soviet Russia, with the population increasingly regarding such services as a something normal or inevitable. This became evident, first and foremost, as the number of private professional higher education institutions started rising, along with the number of students at such institutions. These processes also affected higher education funded out of the state budget, albeit to a lesser extent.

The expansion of fee-based options in the Russian education sector was accompanied by changes in the education network's structure. For instance, back in the early 2000s, the pool of students of professional education institutions was dominated by those receiving higher education, and difficulties with building up material and technical resources forced non-state institutions to focus mostly on training experts in the humanities. At the same time, it bears mentioning that in the latest time period, training mid-tier professionals has notably started getting more attention. In 2015, the Russian government announced its new plans to restore a robust mid-tier professional education system. The upgrade of this system is set to include the development and broad implementation of structural and technological innovation, the development

[6] Gorshkov and Klyucharev (2011).

of modern standards and the overhaul of the entire professional training system's structure, based on these standards.[7] The development directions of mid-tier professional education are to be adjusted depending on the demands of the labor market, allowing to do away with the surplus of graduates in some sectors and the lack of professionals in others (Table 6.1).

The rapid, often haphazard and uncontrollable increase in the number of higher education institutions in the later 1990 and early 2000s contributed to the differentiation in quality. Consequently, many graduates started expressing their dissatisfaction with the low quality of (mostly fee-based) education services. More and more graduates started admitting that investing their money in education had been a poor decision, as after completing their training, they could not find work in the relevant field and were often forced to perform jobs that had no direct link to their qualifications. At the same time, the government started pursuing a more active policy aimed at supporting state education institutions. This boosted competition in the education services market. As a result, the most underperforming private higher education institutions failed to survive the intensifying race and began to shut down. But it is still too soon to claim that the competitive mechanisms in today's education are more or less efficient. The constant lack of education funding hinders the improvement of the faculty pool and education service quality and does not make higher education any more accessible, which has a negative impact on both the development of domestic competition and the competitiveness of Russian colleges abroad.

Today, the people receiving education for a fee come from a very varied range of financial backgrounds, but the best benefits are enjoyed by those who possess enough resources to receive high-quality education, which will later allow them to take up a higher or more advantageous social position. Furthermore, research shows that families with a high and secure social and economic status find human capital investments to be more accessible and alluring, while people from poor and disenfranchised families do not concern themselves with increasing their education level nearly as often, and are more likely to contribute to expanding the pool of unskilled and low-skilled workers.[8] But at the same time, education services are in high demand among those members of groups with few resources who do not shy away from tackling challenges and strive to achieve their full potential; they expect the highest return on investment into education. And more often than not, it turns out that they made the right choice.

While remarking on the necessity to improve the quality of both free and fee-based education services, today's students are using these services far more intensively. This is reaffirmed, for instance, by the rising share of university students who treat their education in a more responsible and diligent manner, increasingly viewing it as the foundation for materializing their life strategies and plans and achieving the goals they have set. Among other examples, the survey carried out by the Russian Public

[7] Decree no. 497 of the Government of the Russian Federation on the Federal Targeted Education Program for 2016–2000, dated May 23, 2015. https://dokipedia.ru/document/5221854 (accessed 9 April 2017).

[8] Petrakov (2011).

Table 6.1 Professional higher education organizations and organizations training mid-tier professionals, 1993–2016 (as of the start of the academic year) (Russia in figures. 2016: Statistics Overview. Federal State Statistics Service. Moscow, 2016. pp. 144–148. https://www.gks.ru/free_doc/doc_2016/rusfig/rus16.pdf, accessed 20 March 2017)

	Academic year								
	1993/94	2000/01	2005/06	2010/11	2011/12	2012/13	2013/14	2014/15	2015/16
Higher education organizations									
Overall number of education organizations	626	965	1068	1115	1080	1046	969	950	896
Including									
State and municipal	548	607	655	653	634	609	578	548	530
Private	78	358	413	462	446	437	391	402	366
Overall number of students, in thousands	2613	4741	7064	7050	6490	6075	5647	5209	4766
Including students of education organizations									
State and municipal[a]	2543	4271	5985	5849	5454	5145	4762	4406	4061
Private[a]	70	470	1079	1201	1036	930	885	804	705
Organizations training mid-tier professionals									
Overall number of professional education organizations	2607	2703	2905	2850	2925	2981	2709	2909	2891
Including									
State and municipal	2607	2589	2688	2586	2665	2725	2494	2665	2645

(continued)

Table 6.1 (continued)

	Academic year								
	1993/94	2000/01	2005/06	2010/11	2011/12	2012/13	2013/14	2014/15	2015/16
Private	–	114	217	264	260	256	215	244	246
Overall number of students, in thousands[b]	1994	2361	2591	2126	2082	2087	1984	2103	2180
Including students of education organizations									
State and municipal[a]	1994	2309	2473	2017	1984	1984	1858	1963	2031
Private[a]	–	52	118	99	98	103	126	140	149

[a]Until the 2013/2014 academic year, the figures included external degrees

[b]The figures describing the number of students include both those taking mid-tier professional training courses at professional education organizations and those receiving higher education

Table 6.2 Completed levels of education across income groups, 2006–2016, %

Education level	Income groups							
	High-income groups		Upper mid-income groups		Lower mid-income groups		Low-income groups	
	2006	2016	2006	2016	2006	2016	2006	2016
Primary general education or no completed primary education	1.0	0.6	3.2	1.8	6.5	2.8	9.4	2.1
Basic general education	12.0	7.1	15.6	11.9	20.6	16.6	28.2	24.8
Secondary general education	26.3	19.7	31.2	26.0	32.4	28.7	35.1	37.4
Secondary professional education	22.8	24.1	26.2	26.0	23.9	27.5	18.4	23.3
Higher education	37.9	48.5	23.8	34.3	16.6	24.4	8.9	12.4

Opinion Research Center (VCIOM) in early 2017 showed that the share of Russians believing that students had notably improved their attitude to studies increased from 19% in 2013 to 37% in 2017. The figures even reach as high as 47% among people whose family members were students.[9]

This chapter mainly focuses on the studies of correlation between the professional education level and professional training, on the one hand, and the material well-being of middle income groups, on the other hand; as well as on the specific features of the way these groups formulate and put into effect their education strategies while the Russian education services market continues to emerge and develop. The analysis is based on the data from RLMS-HSE.[10]

The monitoring data has, once again, reaffirmed the close connection between Russians' education level and material well-being. As evidenced by Table 6.2, all of the income groups singled out for the purposes of this study are experiencing growth of the human capital accumulated within the basic formal education system; however,

[9] Student-2017: Eagerness to Learn and Career Prospects VCIOM press-release No. 3292. https://wciom.ru/index.php?id=236&uid=116041 (accessed 2 April 2017).

[10] «Russia Longitudinal Monitoring survey, RLMS-HSE», conducted by National Research University "Higher School of Economics" and OOO "Demoscope" together with Carolina Population Center, University of North Carolina at Chapel Hill and the Institute of Sociology RAS (RLMS-HSE websites: https://www.hse.ru/rlms, https://www.cpc.unc.edu/projects/rlms).

Table 6.3 Average number of years spent on education by respondents from different income groups, 2006–2016, %

Year	Income groups			
	High-income groups	Upper mid-income groups	Lower mid-income groups	Low-income groups
2006	13.1	12.1	11.2	10.0
2007	13.2	12.2	11.1	10.1
2008	13.3	12.4	11.4	10.2
2009	13.4	12.2	11.4	10.3
2010	14.0	12.9	12.0	11.4
2011	14.2	12.9	12.1	11.7
2012	14.0	12.9	12.1	11.5
2013	14.2	13.0	12.2	11.5
2014	14.2	13.0	12.2	11.5
2015	14.2	13.1	12.2	11.6
2016	14.2	13.0	12.4	11.7

in absolute terms, this growth has proven to be far greater in groups of respondents with high income than those with low income. For instance, from 2006 to 2016, the share of respondents with higher education among the most disenfranchised Russians increased by as little as 3.5% points; while among Russians from lower mid-income groups, the figures increased by 7.8% points; among Russians from upper mid-income groups, by 10.5% points; and among the wealthiest Russians, by 10.6% points. At the same time, the share of respondents with only primary education, basic general education, and general secondary education shrank in all income groups. Quite notably, *throughout the entire research period, groups with mid-level income ranked in the middle in terms of not only material well-being but also the education stage they had fully completed before the survey.* In the end of 2016, the share of people with higher and secondary professional education reached 60.3% among people from upper mid-income groups and 51.9% among people from lower mid-income groups.

A higher education level means that studying at various education institutions will take longer. This is clearly illustrated by the data provided in Table 6.3. For instance, this data shows that the growth of human capital across income groups from 2006 to 2016, which we remarked on above, was accompanied by the prolongation of the average education period required for building up this human capital. Moreover, the average time spent at education institutions was greater in groups comprised out of the wealthiest respondents with more substantial human capital that in groups comprised out of respondents with low income.

A typical feature was the domination of women over men in each group in terms of education level. This ratio was preserved due to the comparable education improvement rate in cohorts where various genders were represented together. All groups being analyzed exhibit a very clear trend that demonstrates that the respondents' education level keeps rising in correlation with the status of the area where they reside. *The most striking differences in the urban and rural population's education level may be observed in lower mid-income groups, while the most insignificant differences are typical of upper mid-income groups.*

By applying the age-based criteria to the Monitoring data, we have discovered that *the highest level of education across all income groups is typical of respondents aged 30 to 45, i.e. people who are active and capable of working and have reached an age that corresponds to the peak of income earning in Russia.* As the respondents' age increases, their education level starts decreasing gradually in both lower and upper mid-income groups, while remaining mostly unchanged in the low- and high-income group. When it comes to foreign language mastery or computer literacy, the most impressive figures are typical of the youngest Russians (under 29), regardless of material well-being. For instance, in late 2016, the share of people who knew at least one foreign language fluctuated between 27.1% (among young people from low-income groups) and 61.0% (among young people from high-income groups). In the youth cohorts from lower and upper mid-income groups, the share of such respondents amounted to 41.4 and 52.1% respectively. The differences in the share of young people who had used a PC within the past 12 months were less significant: 81.6% of young people from low-income groups and 96.9% of young people from high-income groups. In spite of the above, *the largest shares of people belonging to high-income and upper mid-income groups, i.e. people from the topmost tier of material well-being, were found among respondents aged from 45 to 59, with higher or secondary professional education* (Table 6.4).

When speaking of the strengthening link between education level and material well-being, it is important to highlight that, even though education does help increase individual and household income, it does not guarantee full protection against financial vulnerability and poverty. In today's Russia, there is a great number of households that include adult family members with higher education and still suffer from significant financial challenges that render them unable to buy essential items such as food, clothing, etc. In this context, it is important to note that, according to RLMS-HSE data, in 2016 12.4% Russians with higher education belonged to groups of people with low income. Furthermore, over the past ten years, their share grew by more than a half, largely due to the downward shift of people with higher education from mid-income to low-income groups.

The peculiarities noted above have had a significant influence on the way the professional make-up of various income groups is structured, as demonstrated by data in Table 6.5. For instance, this table clearly shows that *the rise in the numbers of people with higher education is linked to the increasing share of highly skilled experts in all income groups.* That said, this upward trend is mostly typical of high-income groups, where the share of topmost experts rose from 26.2 to 32.6% (i.e. by 6.4% points) between 2006 and 2016, whereas in all the other cohorts, the increase was never >0.8–1.2% points. The key contributing factor was the increasing number of women with higher education. At the same time, the share of mid-tier experts dropped from 22.8 to 20.3% in high-income groups, while rising significantly in all other cohorts. In the lower mid-income groups in particular, the share of such

Table 6.4 Distribution of respondents across income groups depending on their age and professional education level, 2016, %

Income groups	Age groups							
	14–29 years old		30–34 years old		45–59 years old		60 years or older	
	Higher education	Secondary professional education	Higher education	Secondary professional education	Higher education	Secondary professional education	Higher education	Secondary professional education
High-income groups	15.6	9.6	14.7	6.0	24.2	10.6	16.0	7.5
Upper mid-income groups	32.3	21.1	27.0	17.7	33.9	25.9	29.6	23.3
Middle mid-income groups	34.8	39.4	36.8	34.7	32.2	39.1	44.6	49.7
Low-income groups	17.3	29.9	21.4	41.6	9.7	24.4	9.8	19.5

Table 6.5 Professional make-up of income groups, 2006–2016, %

Professional group	Income groups							
	High-income groups		Upper mid-income groups		Lower mid-income groups		Low-income groups	
	2006	2016	2006	2016	2006	2016	2006	2016
Heads of state authorities and management bodies of all levels, including heads of organizations and enterprises	11.3	11.2	6.3	6.8	3.5	4.9	2.6	2.6
Experts with topmost skill level	26.2	32.6	19.4	20.2	14.1	15.0	10.6	11.8
Experts with middle skill level	22.8	20.3	15.7	20.7	16.3	19.2	11.8	15.1
Personnel involved in preparing information, document management, record-keeping, and client handling	4.1	5.4	6.1	6.0	5.5	5.5	5.1	5.2
Personnel involved in the service, utilities, or commerce sector	10.9	9.9	16.9	16.2	18.8	19.7	20.0	22.4

(continued)

Table 6.5 (continued)

Professional group	Income groups							
	High-income groups		Upper mid-income groups		Lower mid-income groups		Low-income groups	
	2006	2016	2006	2016	2006	2016	2006	2016
Skilled workers involved in agriculture, forestry, or hunting	0.3	0.0	0.3	0.1	0.8	0.1	0.6	0.1
Skilled workers employed at industrial enterprises or construction, transport, or communication firms	10.4	8.3	14.3	12.1	16.4	15.1	17.2	14.6
Operators, equipment control workers, installation and machine operators, and maintenance fitters	11.3	9.2	14.5	11.8	16.8	13.2	17.6	16.9
Unskilled workers	2.7	3.1	6.5	6.1	7.8	7.3	14.5	11.3

experts rose from 16.3 to 19.2%, whereas in the upper mid-income groups, the figures shifted from 15.7 to 20.7%. Another notable phenomenon is the marked decrease of the overall percentage of blue-collar workers in all the income groups that we have singled out.

As we have revealed a correlation between the accumulation of education resources and income increase, this, once again, brings into focus the need for a systemic and more active encouragement of human capital investments. In the Soviet era, there was little return on human capital investments, or it came too late; in the current circumstances, on the other hand, a higher level and quality of education has turned into a major factor that boosts income, grants competitive advantages in the labor market, and allows people to find jobs that bring them more satisfaction. This is the reason why large numbers of Russians, coming from vastly different income, age, etc. cohorts, have started investing into their human capital more actively. And even if some Russians do opt for not following this strategy, despite realizing the importance of building up education resources, this is merely due to how challenging this choice is. A decision to get education, unlike a decision to find or change a job, is, in many respects, an investment choice, as one must take into account not only the obvious advantages and benefits but also various expenditures and other types of material and non-material loss. Moreover, any investment decision is further complicated by the fact that potential losses may be incurred sooner than the investor can reap the promised benefits. And the longer one waits for these benefits, the less value they generate.

One of the noticeable trends that became apparent during the so-called recovery growth period was a larger number of families that built their adaptation strategies while believing that education expenses were inevitable. These expenses gained more weight in the overall family budget structure, as well as in the make-up of expenditures ensuring that the Russian households met the goals that drove their decision to start saving money. It is typical of people from lower income groups to spend less on their studies, often receiving cheap education of lower quality than that available to people with higher income. But even so, they suffer far more from carrying the burden of education expenses, which is especially apparent in the case of higher education.

Furthermore, *during the crisis, the investment capacity of many Russian families significantly declined, which still has a negative impact on their human capital accumulation plans.* Table 6.6 shows that from 2006 to 2016, the share of state-sponsored transfers (which, as we all know, amount to very little) in the overall household income structure increased significantly. The better the household's material well-being, the more these figures grew. At the same time, there was a decrease in the share of wage income and monetary and in-kind income from home produce and informal jobs.

The most crucial demand of the modern life, which sets the conditions for putting Russia's modernization plans into effect, is a more up-to-date process of building up and renewing the human capital, which, on the one hand, makes it necessary to raise awareness of issues arising out of the creation and development a life-long education system and, on the other hand, encourages people to constantly improve their education level and increases the demand for education services. Nevertheless,

Table 6.6 Structure of overall household income across various income groups, 2006–2016, %

Income source	Income groups							
	High-income groups		Upper mid-income groups		Lower mid-income groups		Low-income groups	
	2006	2016	2006	2016	2006	2016	2006	2016
State-sponsored money transfers (retirement payments, unemployment benefits, scholarships, etc.)	12.3	22.8	23.2	38.1	41.8	50.1	41.8	42.2
Monetary income from home produce and informal jobs	4.0	2.2	4.8	1.5	4.3	1.7	8.5	3.6
In-kind income from home produce and informal jobs	1.3	0.6	2.1	1.1	3.4	1.5	7.3	1.9
Income from selling personal property	0.3	0.7	0.1	0.1	0.1	0.1	0.3	0.2
Income from renting out personal property	0.7	1.3	0.4	0.5	0.3	0.2	0.2	0.1
Dividend profits	0.9	0.6	0.1	0.3	0.2	0.2	0.0	0.0
Financial aid from family members and charities	10.2	5.8	7.3	5.6	6.8	5.0	8.0	9.1
Overall wage income, including:	70.2	66.0	61.9	52.8	43.0	41.2	33.5	42.9
– income from working at state-owned enterprises	28.1	30.5	30.2	22.8	22.8	18.1	20.3	21.1

(continued)

Table 6.6 (continued)

Income source	Income groups							
	High-income groups		Upper mid-income groups		Lower mid-income groups		Low-income groups	
	2006	2016	2006	2016	2006	2016	2006	2016
– income from working at privately owned enterprises	37.2	31.6	26.0	26.8	16.2	20.7	10.7	19.2
– income from working at public–private enterprises	4.9	3.9	5.7	3.2	4.0	2.4	2.5	2.6

this desire to get educated has begun to wane over the past few years, which may be attributed both to the challenges of the crisis period, which made the matter of sheer survival more urgent for the increasingly poor population, and exacerbated a number of issues linked both to the human capital and the population's improved education level. Some other hurdles in this case also include the slow development of innovative industries and high-tech economy sectors, as well as the greater shortage of high-paid jobs, which weakens the stimuli for accumulating and renewing the human capital.

The data provided in Table 6.7 shows that *many experts with higher education cannot apply their knowledge in practice or convert it into a suitable level of material well-being or social status.* For instance, 11.0% of experts with higher education and the most positive subjective evaluation of their professional skills have to perform jobs with the lowest wages, while 31.6% more have jobs that are barely enough for them to fit into the lower mid-income groups. *If the situation persists long enough, this may turn into an urgent issue that will lower the prestige of higher education and cut the share of high-qualified workforce.* It is a well-known fact that in the long term, the supply of experts with higher education in the labor market may increase or decrease depending on the size of the corresponding wage bonus. If a high education level does not guarantee employment and a comfortable lifestyle, this inevitably degrades the value of human capital.

As evidenced by Table 6.8, between 2011 and 2016, the share of working-age (14–60) Russians who intended to continue their education, by attending various professional courses, colleges, universities, post-graduate schools, or doctoral programs within the next three years, shrank by more than one third—from 15.1 to 9.5%. *Furthermore, we can note a significant decrease of mid-income respondents' willingness to invest in their human capital.* For instance, our research has revealed that workers from mid-income groups have started to express a desire to continue their university or college studies (including studies on Masters programs, post-graduate

Table 6.7 Distribution of respondents with higher education and various subjective estimates of their professional skill across income groups, 2016, %

Income groups	Professional skill levels (where the first level is novice and the ninth level is top-tier professional)								
	Lowest level	2nd level	3rd level	4th level	5th level	6th level	7th level	8th level	Highest level
Low-income groups	30.8	24.3	14.7	21.1	18.8	18.1	14.7	9.8	11.0
Lower mid-income groups	38.5	40.5	45.3	39.5	37.2	38.5	37.8	39.4	31.6
Upper mid-income groups	19.2	24.3	25.3	25.7	29.5	26.6	30.2	33.9	31.9
High-income groups	11.5	10.8	14.7	13.8	14.6	16.7	17.3	16.9	25.6

Table 6.8 Willingness to Continue Education Across Income Groups, 2011–2016, in % of Employed Population Aged 14–60 (The term "employed population" includes all people who are currently (at the time of the survey) involved in work activities, as well as all workers who are currently on paid or unpaid leave, including parental leaves directly before and after childbirth and for caring for children under three)

	Total		Including across groups							
			High-income groups		Upper mid-income groups		Lower mid-income groups		Low-income groups	
	2011	2016	2011	2016	2011	2016	2011	2016	2011	2016
Intend to continue studies by attending training courses, colleges, universities, post-graduate schools, or doctorate programs in the next three years	***15.1***	***9.5***	21.7	17.6	16.2	10.7	12.8	8.1	12.1	6.3
Members of these groups that intend to study										
At professional courses	***37.9***	***50.8***	41.9	66.7	35.7	44.5	32.5	45.5	41.7	49.9
At a technical college	***7.6***	***9.3***	2.9	6.1	5.4	3.1	10.5	14.0	12.4	15.4
At a university, post-graduate school, or on a doctorate program	***61.8***	***45.9***	64.6	40.0	66.7	57.6	62.2	43.8	52.4	37.5

schools, or doctoral programs) not nearly as often. The share of such respondents among workers from the lower mid-income groups exhibiting an intention to keep studying for the next three months decreased almost as much as by one third, from 62.2 to 43.8%; whereas in the higher mid-income groups, the drop was less steep, from 66.7 to 57.6%. This downward trend occurred mostly due to the increasing share of people who wanted to continue their education by attending professional courses.

The intention to keep on learning, improve one's professional qualifications, expand one's knowledge area, enrich one's professional background, and hone one's skills is, in many respects, determined by the nature of one's occupation. Table 6.9 reveals that this intention is expressed most firmly by experts with top-level skills, which is hardly surprising. Research shows that it is professionals' ability to undergo further training that is in most demand in today's economy, allowing workers from this category to feel sufficiently confident in the labor market as they look for work.[11] It is quite notable that *professionals from mid-income groups express a wish to continue their education far less often than professionals from both more and less wealthy income groups,* as they consider their status to be secure and are satisfied with their material well-being.

The least willingness to invest into human capital is typical of workers engaged in low-skilled and unskilled labor. That said, low-skilled workers from upper mid-income groups do express a wish to invest into human capital more often than representatives of other income groups. Many of them would prefer to advance to a higher level in the employment structure and a more respected position in society, but feel that their education is insufficient for putting these plans into fruition.

The most essential element of life-long learning is additional training, aimed at comprehensively meeting all of the individual's needs to improve their knowledge, moral compass, physical form, and/or professional skills, without transitioning to the next education level.[12] But, as evidenced by our analysis, *the annual number of adult Russians who avail themselves of additional training services, for the purpose of meeting their education and professional needs, achieving professional development, and ensuring that their skill level matches the constantly changing professional and social environment, has been shrinking continuously over the past few years.* While in 2006, the overall share of respondents who stated that within the last 12 months, they had attended professional courses, further training courses, or any other courses, including those dedicated to studying foreign languages or workplace training, reached 4.4%, by 2016 the figures had dropped to 3.1%. Nevertheless, it must be noted that the figures did rise by a small amount among employed respondents, from 7.1% to 7.6% respectively. As for the lower and upper mid-income groups, throughout the same period, the share of respondents from these two groups that had been involved in various forms and practices of additional professional

[11] Golenkova (2015).

[12] Federal Law "On Education in the Russian Federation" No. 273-FZ, dated December 29, 2012. https://www.consultant.ru/document/cons_doc_LAW_140174/ (accessed 4 April 2017).

Table 6.9 Correlation between the intention to continue education and professional occupation among members of various income groups, 2016, % of the working population aged 14–60, distributed into groups

Professional group[a]	Intend to continue studies by attending training courses, colleges, universities, post-graduate schools, or doctorate programs in the next three years			
	Including across income groups			
	High-income groups	Upper mid-income groups	Lower mid-income groups	Low-income groups
Heads of state authorities and management bodies of all levels, including heads of organizations and enterprises	21.4	9.5	13.3	10.3
Experts with topmost skill level	22.9	12.9	13.2	16.7
Experts with middle skill level	18.1	12.3	8.0	10.4
Personnel involved in preparing information, document management, record-keeping, and client handling	13.8	4.1	8.3	7.8
Personnel involved in the service, utilities, or commerce sector	12.0	13.2	7.9	5.1
Skilled workers employed at industrial enterprises or construction, transport, or communication firms	4.4	10.7	5.8	3.3
Operators, equipment control workers, installation and machine operators, and maintenance fitters	3.9	6.1	4.8	2.4
Unskilled workers	5.1	6.0	4.8	1.5

[a]The group of skilled workers involved in agriculture, forestry, or hunting has been excluded from the analysis due to its small size

Table 6.10 Sources of funding for attending fee-based professional courses, 2016, %

Sources of funding	Overall	Including across income groups			
		High-income groups	Upper mid-income groups	Lower mid-income groups	Low-income groups
Enterprise sponsorship	***59.0***	67.9	61.2	52.8	56.4
Personal funds	***31.3***	24.6	31.1	38.2	27.3
Other	***9.7***	7.5	7.7	9.0	16.3

training within the past 12 months decreased from 3.5% to 2.4% and from 5.3% to 4.9% respectively (among employed respondents, the figures decreased from 6.1% to 4.3% and from 7.1% to 6.6% respectively).

An indicative trend is that *people who already have high-level education use additional training services more actively.* For instance, in 2016, the shares of people with higher and secondary professional education among people from the lower mid-income groups who attended various professional training sessions and workplace courses reached 44.1% and 30.1% respectively, while among respondents from the upper mid-income groups, the shares of such people were 48.6% and 24.3% respectively. But people with the highest income and education level use the above services even more actively (74.1% and 14.8% respectively). Furthermore, around one third of them is comprised of people over 50.

Many of such respondents continue their education not only in order to improve their skills or obtain additional skills and advance at work, increase their income, or find a better-suited job, but also in order to try out a completely new type of professional activity and master a new job. It is hardly an accident that in 2016, almost one in every three people who used additional training services did so in an area that different completely than the job they had at the moment of enrolling at the courses. The share of such respondents in the lower and upper mid-income groups reached 32.3% and 31.3% respectively, much less than the 40.7% of low-income respondents but more than the 22.6% of high-income respondents. Approximately one in every three such respondents, regardless of income level, was a young person aged 20–29, while one in every five was aged 30–39.

Further analysis allowed us to conclude that most trainees who improve or overhaul their work skills at various professional courses and other types of training sessions are sponsored by the enterprises they work for (Table 6.10). However, the share of people who study at their own cost is also quite substantial. Higher education serves as a factor that stimulates the consumption of fee-based education services of this type, while the lack of higher education curbs consumption activity.

Those members of mid-income groups who demonstrate a high capacity and readiness for planning and putting into effect long-term life strategies stipulating the need for investing their personal funds into education are more likely to opt for paying for professional courses out of pocket. One half of them tries to invest their income and savings into improving their professional skills and refreshing their professional knowledge, while the other half intends to master a new profession altogether. Expenses in this area are considered a high risk for a household or an individual, because not everyone achieves positive return on investment, and the economic benefits tend to be quite modest. As shown by the analysis of the Monitoring data, appealing to various forms and practices of additional professional training often turns out to be an inefficient means of increasing individual income. Education only helps obtain statistically negligible income, i.e. it can only make an additional contribution in this respect.[13]

To conclude, we would like to point out that education largely determines mid-income groups' willingness and ability to climb the social ladder and helps them put into effect their social and economic behavior strategies so that they can stay attuned to the demands of the current market environment. But at the same time, our study has revealed a number of contradicting trends that characterize mid-income groups' human capital accumulation activity. Against the background of the clearly obvious build-up of mid-income groups' human capital, which usually occurs at institutions and organizations that belong to the basic formal education system, we can note the decrease of the overall share of mid-income respondents who use additional and informal education services. The upper mid-income groups, with more resources at their disposal, express a greater practical interest towards renewing and accumulating their human capital, and thus are more active in their consumption of fee-based education services than the lower mid-income groups, which have fewer resources. In spite of that, both groups being researched are characterized by a significant ebb of willingness to invest into their human capital in the nearest future.

We have also discovered that the number of people who use fee-based professional education services has risen, especially among the upper mid-income respondents. The volume of expenditure on professional education has risen substantially, together with the share of such expenditure in household budgets. But at the same time, respondents from mid-level income groups have started expressing more concern over the issue of having to pay for education and the increasing commoditization of professional education and higher education in particular. Respondents from mid-income groups, while having solid education resources, cannot implement them in practice, and the time, effort, and money spent on improving or increasing one's education level often yields a return on investment that does not cover all costs.

Our analysis has, once again, reaffirmed the increasing relevance of promptly resolving the issue of bringing the current education system into compliance with today's demand for upgrading the Russian economy and developing the Russian society, the key factor of which is the greater role of education as a means of improving the population's standard and quality of living. Education must be turned into one of the most efficacious drivers of Russian families' income and purchasing power, as well as the engine of economic growth. For this reason, it is especially important to put the life-long learning principle into practice and to make high-quality professional training more accessible.

[13] Didenko and Dorofeeva (2016).

References

Breen R, Jonsson JO (2005) Inequality of opportunity in comparative perspective: recent research on educational attainment and social mobility. Ann Rev Sociol 223–243

Didenko DV, Dorofeeva ZE (2016) Additional professional education in Russia: the dynamics of scale and economic efficiency (2000–2013). Mir Rossii (4):87–110

Golenkova ZT (ed) (2015) Hired worker in modern Russia. Novy Khronograf, Moscow, p 156

Gorshkov MK, Klyucharev GA (2011) Life-long education in the modernization context. IS RAS, Federal State Research Institution "Center for Social Research", Moscow, p 100

Gorshkov MK, Sherega FE (ed) (2010) The modernization of Russian education: issues and prospects. TsSPiM (Center of Social Forecasting and Marketing), Moscow, pp 35–36; The facets of Russian education. Center for Social Research, Moscow (2015), p 312

Konstantinovsky DL, Voznesenskaya ED, Cherednichenko GA, Khokhlushkina FA (2011) The education and lifestyle paths of the youth: 1998–2008. TsSPiM (Center of Social Forecasting and Marketing), Moscow, pp 94–98

Latov YV (ed) (2014) Lifelong education as a stimulus for personal development and social and economic inequality factor. TsSPiM (Center of Social Forecasting and Marketing), Moscow, p 257

Petrakov NY (ed) (2011) The modernization of Russia: social and humanitarian aspects. Nestor-Istoriya, Moscow and St. Petersburg, p 141

P. M. Kozyreva Doctor of Sociology, is First Deputy Director of the Federal Center of Theoretical and Applied Sociology of the Russian Academy of Sciences (former Institute of Sociology, Russian Academy of Sciences). She also serves as Director of the Center for Longitudinal Studies at the Institute of Social Policy of the National Research University Higher School of Economics. She is the Editor-in-Chief of the journal "Sotsiologicheskiy Zhurnal". P. Kozyreva directs one of the largest longitudinal surveys in Russia—"The Russia Longitudinal Monitoring Survey of HSE" (RLMS-HSE), which has been conducted since 1994. Selected publications in English: Ethnicity and Trust: Evidence from Russia//American Political Science Review, 2005 (in co-authorship with D. Bahry, M. Kosolapov and R. Wilson); "Consumption and Lifestyle in Russia" in Handbook on Social Stratification in the BRIC Countries. Change and Perspective/Editors: Peilin Li (Chinese Academy of Social Sciences, China), M.K. Gorshkov (Russian Academy of Sciences, Russia), Celi Scalon (Brazilian Sociological Society, Brazil), K.L. Sharma (Jaipur National University, India)//World Scientific Publishing Co. Pte. Ltd. 2013 (in co-authorship with A. Smirnov and A. Nizamova); Economic Change in Russia: Twenty Years of the Russian Longitudinal Monitoring Survey//Economics of Transition. 2015. Vol. 23. No. 2. (in co-authorship with Klara Sabirianova Peter); Data Resource Profile: The Russia Longitudinal Monitoring Survey—Higher School of Economics (RLMS-HSE) Phase II: Monitoring the Economic and Health Situation in Russia, 1994–2013//International Journal of Epidemiology. 2016. Vol. 45(2) (in co-authorship with Kosolapov M., Popkin B).

A. I. Smirnov Doctor of Sociology, Senior Researcher at the Federal Center of Theoretical and Applied Sociology of the Russian Academy of Sciences (former Institute of Sociology, Russian Academy of Sciences). His major interests include political sociology, social factors of Russian society consolidation (including institutional changes in army, family, etc.), dynamics of socio-economic conditions of Russian population. His publications are wide range, for example , "Factors forming Trust in Russian Army"//Sociological Studies. 2009, Issue 2, "Labyrinths of Development of Democracy in Russia", 2007 (in co-authorship with Kozyreva P.), "Consumption and Lifestyle in Russia" in Handbook on Social Stratification in the BRIC Countries. Change and Perspective/Editors: Peilin Li (Chinese Academy of Social Sciences, China), M. K. Gorshkov (Russian Academy of Sciences, Russia), Celi Scalon (Brazilian Sociological Society, Brazil), K. L. Sharma (Jaipur National University, India)//World Scientific Publishing Co. Pte. Ltd. 2013 (in co-authorship with P. Kozyreva and A. Nizamova).

Chapter 7
Consumption and Lifestyle of the Middle Income Group

Di Zhu

Currently, consumption is playing an increasingly prominent role in growing economy in China. As the total retail sales of consumer goods maintain a two-digit growth, the final consumption expenditure contributed to 64.6% of the total economic growth in 2016, which was 4.9% higher than that in 2015.[1] It was pointed out in the Report on the Work of the Government 2017 that "China's domestic demand potential is huge, and must and may be further expanded. The key is to know the proper place to begin with." As the middle income group is a strong force in expanding consumption, its expansion and development becomes the key to economic and social transformation. The 13th Conference of Leading Group for Financial and Economic Affairs (an inner group of the Central Committee of the Communist Party of China) which was held in 2016 discussed the implementation of the supply-side structure reform and expanding the middle income group. In which the Secretary General (and President of China) Xi Jinping stressed that "the expansion of the middle income group is relevant to the full realization of a moderately well-off society. And it is also an inevitable requirement for transforming the economic growth pattern and restructuring the economy".[2]

The middle income group refers to the group of people with stead jobs, relatively affluent material life and medium income level. Compared to the high income group whose consumption is saturated, the middle income group tends to have higher elasticity in its consumption, including some rigid demands and pursuit of higher level development and enjoyment; compared with the low-income group, the middle income group shows higher purchasing power and stronger purchasing desire. General growth of family income and accumulation of household wealth brings about

[1] www.sina.com, https://news.sina.com.cn/o/2017-02-21/doc-ifyarref6334427.shtml.

[2] https://news.xinhuanet.com/finance/2016-05/17/c_128988752.htm.

D. Zhu (✉)
University of Manchester, Manchester, England

P. Li and M. K. Gorshkov (eds.), *The Middle Income Group in China and Russia*, Research Series on the Chinese Dream and China's Development Path,
https://doi.org/10.1007/978-981-16-1464-4_7

increased consumption power. Therefore, mass consumption with the middle income group as the main strength has become an important engine for expanding domestic demand and transforming economic growth pattern.

This chapter uses data from China Society Survey (CSS) 2006–2015, and focuses on the consumption trends of the middle income group, mainly its household expenditures, expenditure structure and consumption of durable goods. It tries to reveal the consumption features of the group and explore its consumption potential and related factors. Based on the research findings, this chapter will also make a few policy suggestions for expanding consumer demands.

7.1 Main Characteristics of the Middle Income Group in China

The middle class and middle income group generally owns higher economic capital and cultural capital and is proved to be the main strength in expanding consumption by many empirical studies. According to the research group of Social Survey and Data Center of Shanghai Academy (2016), the middle income group in Shanghai has stronger financial power and consumption desire and shows rich and diversified lifestyles. They frequently participate in culture, entertainment and leisure consumption and would invest on children's education, high-end events, leisure and travel and tourism as well as eco-friendly goods consumption. With the data from Yi (2016) found that farmers, working class and aged middle class generally show higher marginal propensity to consume for survival, while the new middle class shows higher marginal propensity to consume for development. However, there is a gap between the production provision and the sophisticated tastes of the new middle class. Linjiang and Weihua (2016) argues that the middle class requires more personalized, quality, distinguished and refined goods and services, and emphasizes on the experience of the services; therefore, supported by the remarkably huge consumption transformation of the class, there is vast space for the imagination economy that offers good consumption experience.

However, the middle class and middle income group have currently encountered hindrance to upward mobility, life quality, social security and class identity, which prevent expansion of the middle income group and improvement of social structure. Policy suggestions on enhancing the middle class and middle income group covering income, employment, supply, consumption and other aspects are made (Peilin and Di 2015; Di 2016; the research group of Social Survey and Data Center of Shanghai Academy 2016). In terms of income, the structure of income distribution should be improved for a straightened arrangement and an olive-shaped social structure; in terms of employment, the employment system of modern service sector should be built with gathered speed, so as to promote the employment and business startups of college graduates and migrant workers of the new generation and explore improved and humanized human resource management system; in terms of supply, industry should be upgraded and products should be innovated; in terms of consumption, the social security system should be improved, commodity and housing prices should be stabilized, and market supervision and consumer environment should be enhanced. Yi (2016) specially stressed that the essence of expanding consumption was to advance people's livelihood—benefits from the consumption stimulus policies should be evaluated farily amongst all social classes, so that the fruits of reform and opening up could be shared by all the people.

As for the definition of the middle income group, the absolute standard and the relative standard are mainly used. The absolute index is to define the middle income people based on the development level. Economist Homi Kharas (Kharas 2010) set the definition that those whose daily household spending stands between USD 10–100 (with PPP, purchasing power parity) falls in the category of middle income group. With this standard, of all the middle income groups in 2009, 18% were from those in North America, 36% from Europe 36 and 28% from Asia–Pacific Region.

Credit Suisse Research Institute (CSRI 2015) defines that group who keeps a wealth of USD 50,000–500,000 (by PPP, purchasing power parity) belongs to the middle class. According to CSRI, the middle class in China accounted for 10% of all the adults in 2015, and the middle class and above accounted for 11.3% of all the adults when the most influent class were integrated therein; the proportion of the middle and above class in USA stood at 50%, in India 3.2%, and in Russia 4.6%. Figure 7.1 shows the change in number of middle class in some countries between 2000 and 2015. The middle class and above saw a growth of 43.30 million people in China, and the growth number was 22.00 million in the States, 7.70 million in India and −0.6 million in Russia; the economic crisis between 2007and 2008 affected middle class in all countries mentioned above (Table 7.1 and Fig. 7.2).

Scholars in Russia generally believe that the survey by CSRI has underestimated the middle income group and middle class in Russia (Vercueil 2016). By the income standard as set by the World Bank, those whose daily income stands between USD 10–50 (by PPP) are the middle income group, in which those who earn USD 10–25 are the lower middle income group, those who earn USD 25–50 are the upper middle income group. PPP is calculated with each country's GDP index, which is relative. This measurement used by the World Bank is named as "Weak Relative Strength Index (RSI)" (Anikin et al. 2016). With data from Russia Longitudinal Monitoring Survey (RLMS-HSE) and the measurement of the World Bank, the lower middle income group in Russia took 54.6% of all Russian people in 2014, and that of the upper middle income group was 27.3%. The values then became 56.3 and 27% separately in 2015 (Anikin et al. 2016).

The relative index depicts the middle income people from the perspective of the income structure, that is, the share of the middle income people is determined not only by the general improvement of income level, but also the change of the income structure. There are two kinds of relative indexes used by the academia and the government: The poverty thresholds and the statistics of income (SOI, such as median and percentile) are used as two reference standards. Relevant studies include using income percentile values to define those whose income ranging from 25th percentile to 95th percentile are the middle income groups (Peilin and Di 2015).

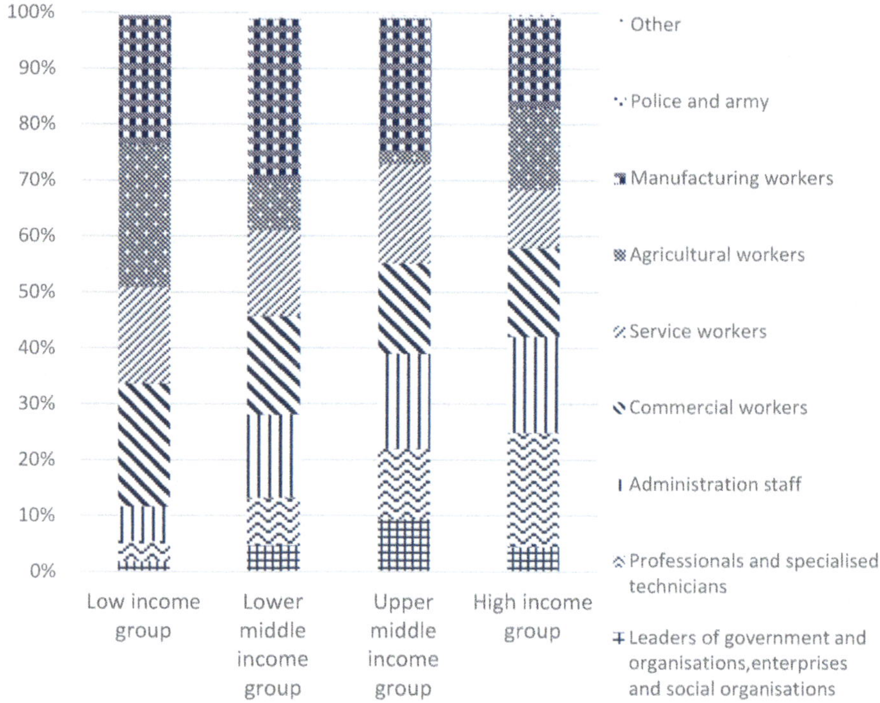

Fig. 7.1 Occupations of different income groups in the urban areas (economically active population)

Table 7.1 Number of adult population of middle class and above, 2000–2015 (in Million)

	2000	2000–2007	2007–2008	2008–2015	2015	2000–2015
China	71.8	102.0	−67.3	8.5	115.1	43.3
USA	99.7	11.9	−6.8	17.0	121.7	22.0
India	17.8	12.5	−5.5	0.7	25.5	7.7
Russia	5.6	11.1	−2.5	−9.2	5.0	−0.6

Source Credit Suisse Research Institute (2015). Zurich: Credit Suisse AG

Although the absolute index enables comparisons between countries and time, it is hard to reflect the complexity of the middle income group's development mechanism—influence from factors such as economic development, income distribution system and income disparity. Whereas the relative index reflects both the development level and the change of the income structure. In this chapter, with the relative index used, and the income median value as the reference, people whose income below 0.75 times of the median are defined as the low income group, whose income between 0.75 times and 1.25 times (included) of the median are defined as the lower middle income group, whose income between 1.25 times and 2 times of the median

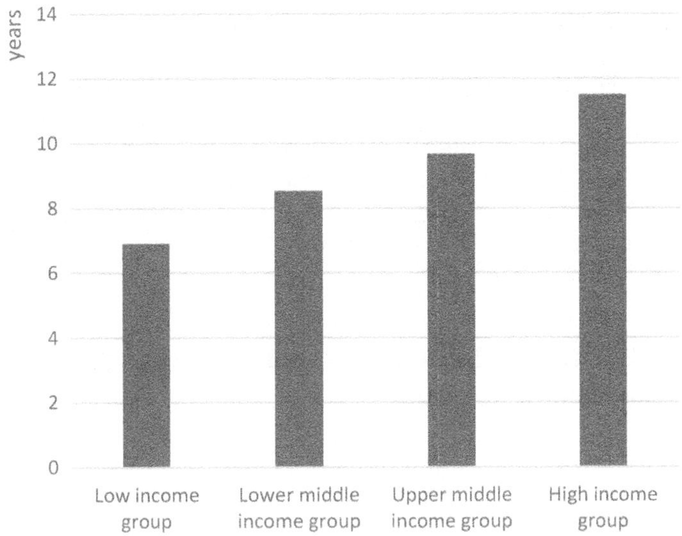

Fig. 7.2 Years of education for different income groups

are defined as the upper middle income group, and those whose values above 2 times of the median are defined as the high income group.

This chapter uses data from China Society Survey 2006–2015, which was carried out by the Institute of Sociology, Chinese Academy of Social Sciences (CASS). With the method of multi-stage sampling, the survey population are those above 18 years old in the urban and rural area of 25–28 province/autonomous regions in China. There are a total of 41,685 samples contained in the statistics.

The middle income group mainly reside in the urban areas. For instance, in 2015, 62% of the middle income group lived in the urban areas, and only 38% lived in the rural area. Typically, 82% of the high income group lived in the urban areas; only 32% of the low income group lived in the urban areas, whereas 68% of them lived in the rural area. So, the distribution of income groups also reflects the great urban and rural development discrepancy.

As for the occupations, those of the middle income group mainly work in the service sector and the manufacture sector. This is even evident in the urban areas. As shown in Fig. 7.1, 26% of the lower middle income group and 24% of the upper middle income group working in the manufacture sector. They account for the highest share of all the middle income group, who are the technicians or skilled workers with higher income than general workers. 14% of the lower middle income group and 17% of the upper middle income group are administration staff; 16% of both the lower and upper middle income group are working in the commercial sector; 14% of the lower middle income group and 18% of the upper middle income group are the service workers. The three sectors mentioned above hired the second largest number of middle income people only next to the employment number in the manufacture sector. Employees hired in the three above sectors may be earning limited salary, but they are relatively young (with average age 31–43, younger than the average age of the low income group who work in the same sectors) and better educated. Therefore, they registered certain characteristics both in their consumption and lifestyles.

The average years of education for the lower middle income group was 9 years, approximately junior school graduates, and the average years for the upper middle income group was 10, approximately high school graduates, which is much better than the low income group whose average years of education was 7.

7.2 Main Trends of Household Expenditures of the Middle Income Group in China

From the above analysis, most of the middle income group live in the urban areas and mainly work in the service sector or they are the technicians. They possess certain amount of economic and cultural capital. The consumption trend of the middle income group will be discussed from the perspective of consumption expansion. The analysis focuses on the spending and the possession of durable goods. In addition, their consumption potential and impact factors will be explored.

The annual household expenditures for the lower middle income and upper middle income group were RMB 54,137 and RMB 66,817 in 2015. Please refer to Fig. 7.3 for expenditure details. Food and beverages account a large proportion for all groups, as the spending of the lower and higher income-groups were respectively RMB 13,858 and RMB 16,813. The high income group paid RMB 22,932. High income group actually paid extraordinarily more money on every category, medical care excluded, especially on food and beverages, downpayment and mortgages and durables. Low income group paid most for their medical care, as much as RMB 7,478 annually, next to which were RMB 7068 and RMB 6770 separately for the lower and upper

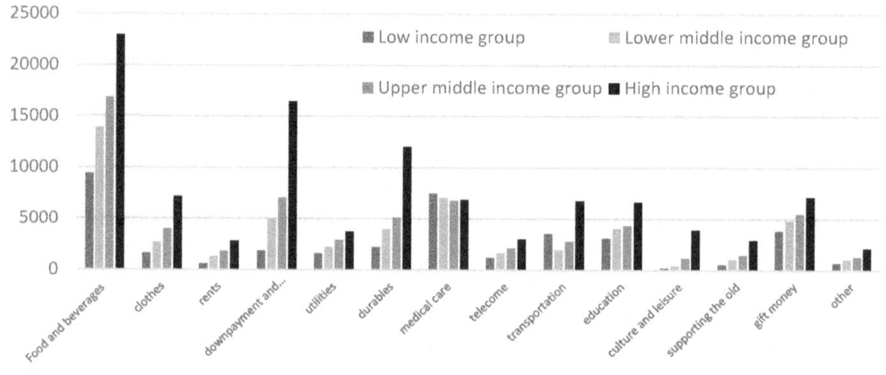

Fig. 7.3 Annual household expenditures of different income groups 2015

middle income group annually. The high income group, however, spent least on their medical care, and that was RMB 6,883 annually.

The expenditure structure reveals more about life quality discrepancy of different groups, as shown in Fig. 7.4. Higher spending on food and beverages by high-income groups turned out to be a very low share of 21% of the total household expenditures. And the figures for the lower and upper middle income groups separately reached 26 and 25%. Compared with the high income group, the middle income group spent higher share of expenditures on food and beverages, rents, education and gift money (social favor returning); compared with the low income group, the middle income group paid more share of expenditure on food and beverages, downpayment and mortgages and durables.

According to the household expenditures 2006–2015, the high income group basically paid more on every category, especially on rents, food and beverages and culture and leisure. Since 2011, the surging spending of downpayment and mortgages has been seen across all groups, and high-income groups showed the highest increase on such spending, from less than RMB 5000 in 2008 to RMB 11,505 in 2011 and RMB 16,451 in 2015. Since 2013, the spending on durables by the high income group has been gaining quickly, from RMB 7553 in 2011 to the more than the doubled number, RMB 16,190 in 2013; however, the growth of expenditures on durables for the middle and low-income groups have been slow. The upper middle income group

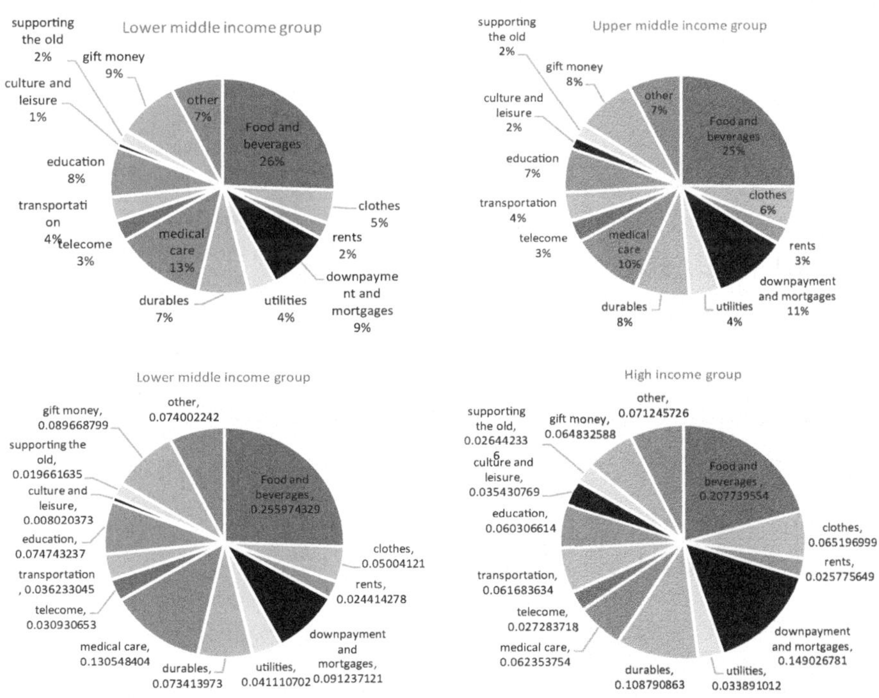

Fig. 7.4 Annual household expenditures structure of different groups 2015

spent RMB 2416 in 2011, RMB 4843 in 2013 and RMB 5121 in 2015, with a low growing amount. The middle and low income groups, however, paid pretty much slow for their medical care, and the trend became more evident in 2015.

From the expenditures structure (Fig. 7.5), the middle income groups had higher share on food and beverages and education while the consumption trends for the high income groups were highlighted by the gained momentum of housing spending since 2011, which reflected much improved life quality. However, as refrained by the medical care and gift money, the low income group even did not show much improvement in 2015.

From the above analysis, the middle income group show their certain uniqueness for their food and beverages consumption and social security related collective consumption. The characteristics of the spending on the two categories by the

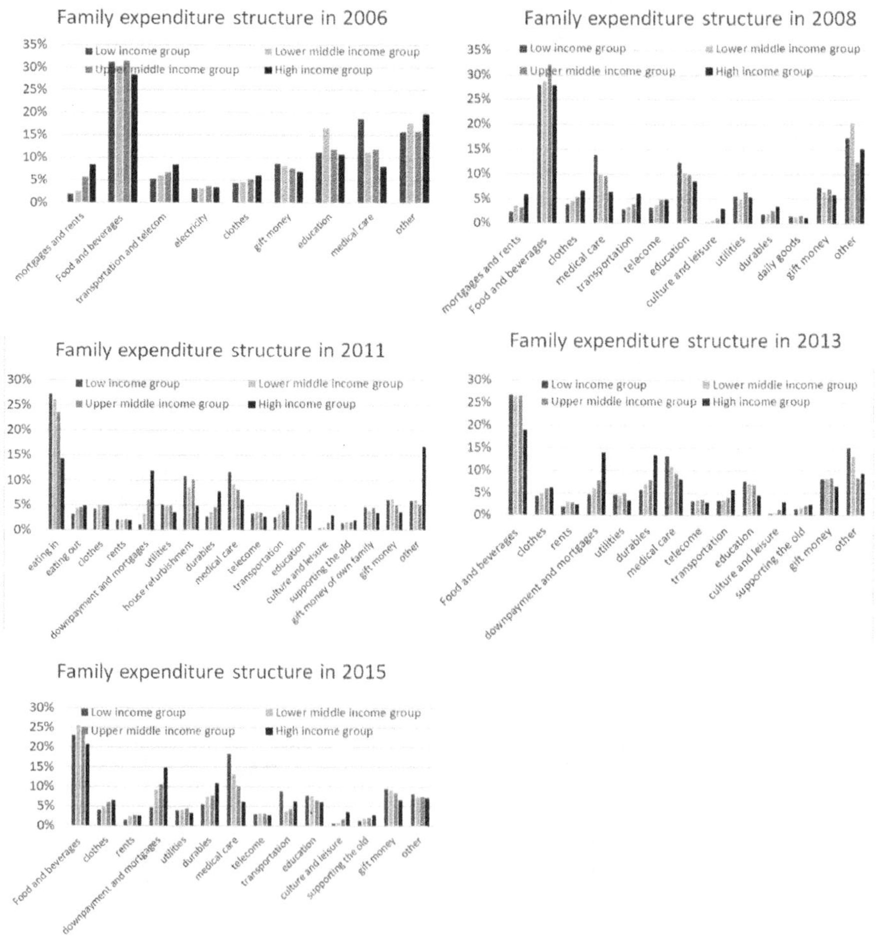

Fig. 7.5 Annual household expenditure structures of different income groups 2006–2015

middle income group will be discussed later in this chapter. From Fig. 7.6, the share of spending on food and beverages had been going down against the middle income group's household expenditures, from 30% of total expenditure in 2011 to 25% in 2015. But the percentage of food and beverages among the middle income group was higher than that of both the low and high income groups. This even higher percentage than that of the high income group indicated the middle income group's restraints on living, while the higher percentage than the low income group reflected their consumption need for quality food and beverages and related catering industry services. Data in 2011 distinguishes the eating in and eating out consumptions, which more significantly reflect the above characteristics of the middle income group. It is noteworthy as the middle income group had such a high spending on eating out: the lower and upper middle income group paid 4 and 5% of their total household expenditures separately for their eating out, and even the high income group spent only 5% of their total expenditure on eating out. From the perspective of consumption expansion, the middle income group did show their potential in convenient and quality food and beverages spending.

From the above, we understand that the expenditure amount as well as share of durables goods and culture and leisure, which are for self cultivation and life quality improvement, were both relatively low among the middle income group. The main reason is the imperfect collective consumption that had confined these expenditures. Collective consumption is a concept that refers to the goods and services that are provided by collectivity such as countries, cities and communities and consumed on an allocation mechanism, such as public housing, infrastructures, education and health care (Castells 1977: 459–462; Warde 1990; Ning 2014). The imperfect social security system in China made the residents include the items of education, medical care and old-age care into their own bills. Both the present spending and the expected pensions, children's education and medical care have frozen their money,

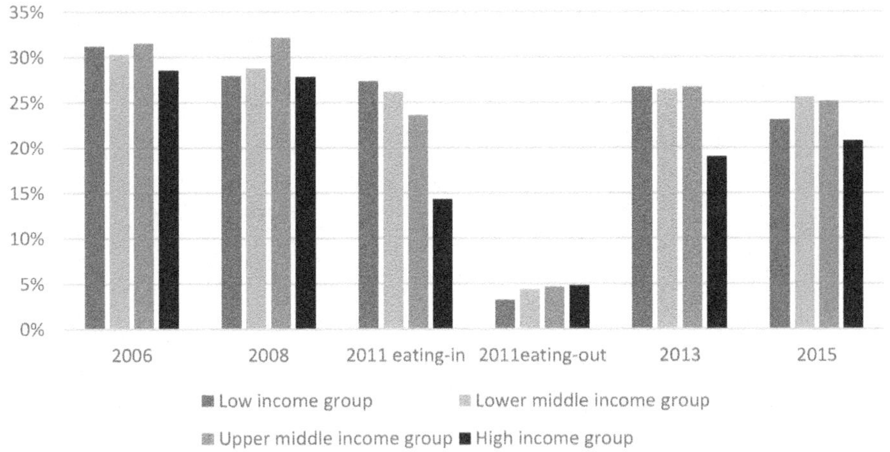

Fig. 7.6 Expenditure percentage on food and beverages of the middle income group 2006–2015

thus refraining the middle income group's purchasing power. Figure 7.7 is an explicit description of this dilemma, in which for the lower and upper middle income groups, the medical care spending accounted for more than 8% of the household expenditures. The spending percentages of the lower and upper middle income group surged to 13% and 10% respectively in 2015. Secondly, the downpayment and mortgage cost the households a lot, especially for the upper middle income group. It was 11% in 2015, surpassing the share of medical care insurance. On the other hand, spending on durables remained steady between 2013 to 2015, and for the lower and higher income groups, the numbers were 7 and 8% separately.

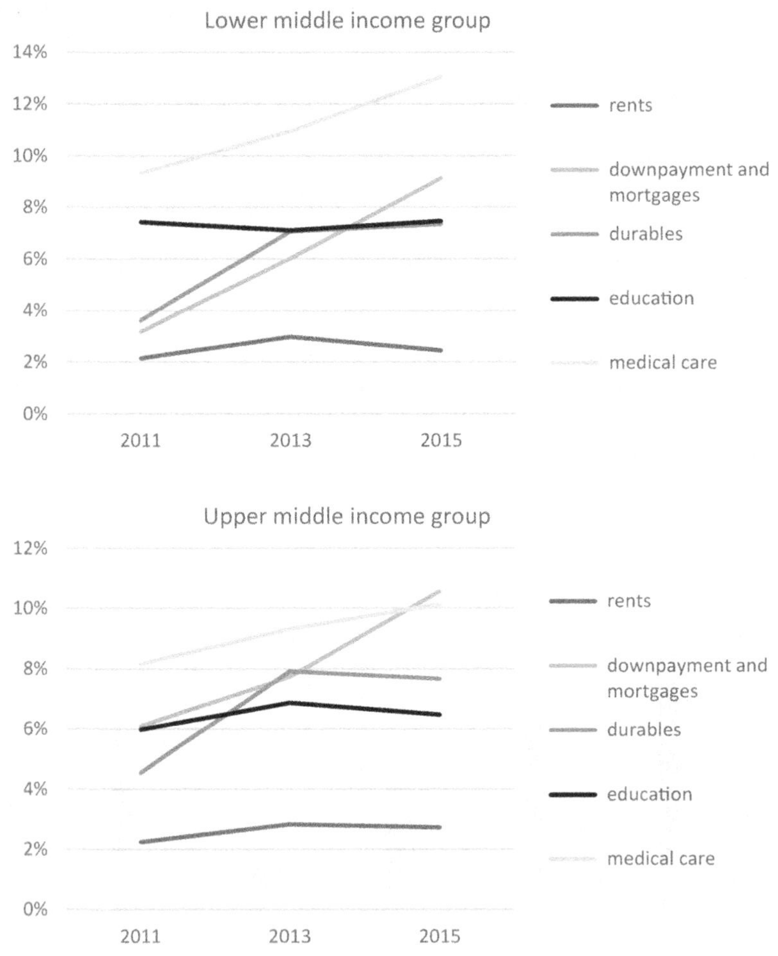

Fig. 7.7 Expenditure share on housing, durable goods, education and medicare by the middle income group: 2011–2015

7.3 Main Characteristics of the Middle Income Group's Consumption on Durables

Following is the analysis of durables consumption in 2008–2016, as in Table 7.2. The upgrading of durables can be the first thing to be notice. Technology revolution has swept the home appliances and digital goods in recent years, such as LED televisions, smart phones, tablet computers, saw the traditional durables stepping down the historical stage, CRT televisions, ordinary mobile phones, just to name a few; technology innovation helps bring down the cost and prices and promotes the democratization of durables. Durables that had been for the high-end consumers in the past were being brought into all families, such as air conditioners, microwave ovens and other kitchen appliances, and vehicles. Smart mobile phones typically represented the quick spread of new technology among the public. They were owned by 93% of the high-income people, 83% of the middle income people and 66% of the low-income people in 2015.

Secondly, the consumption preferences varied between all income groups. The high income group showed their strong purchasing power and vigorous consumption desire, and especially dominated the market of expensive durable goods, such as vehicles, with the higher growth rate than any other income group. The percentage of vehicles owned by the high income group went up to 44% in 2015, while the figures for the lower and upper middle income people were respectively 18 and 26%.

However, higher consumption orientation was also manifested in certain household durables for the middle income group and some people from the low income group. Although the ownership of TV and washing machine probably reached saturation for every groups, or began going down, the owning percentage of refrigerators kept growing, because of more environment-friendly and practical advance productions with rich options all enhanced by technology. The ownership percentage grew relatively fast in the low income group. For the high-grade home appliances, the high income group owned more, however, the low and middle income group bought them home at a gathering speed with more spending. For instance, for the kitchen appliance such as microwaves and ovens, the ownership percentage grew from 59% in 2008 to 75% in 2015, and the percentages for the low and middle income groups, although based on small percentage, roared separately from 7 and 17% in 2008 to 46 and 55% in 2015.

Factors that influence the residents as for their ownership of high-grade durable goods will be examined in this part, so as to assess the consumption desire of different income groups and the factors that hold the residents back from consumption upgrading. Generally, as purchase of digital products depends largely on the age and personal interest, and owning a motorcycle means certain technical knowledge and much more money than ordinary household durables, the two categories are excluded from the high-grade durable list. The analysis of CSS 2015 data focuses on the relatively high-end home appliances, including LED/PDP televisions, microwaves and ovens/food processors/BBQ ovens/bread machines and other kitchen appliances, dishwashers, air conditioners and vacuum cleaners. The five variables are added

Table 7.2 Ownership percentages of household durable goods for all income groups

		Low income group			Lower middle income group			Upper middle income group			High income group		
		2008 (%)	2011 (%)	2015 (%)	2008 (%)	2011 (%)	2015 (%)	2008 (%)	2011 (%)	2015 (%)	2008 (%)	2011 (%)	2015 (%)
Ordinary home appliances	CRTTVs	88	89	79	96	90	74	98	84	67	99	73	59
	Refrigerators	32	56	77	56	76	87	72	86	92	88	93	95
	Washing machines	49	58	73	65	77	84	77	84	90	89	87	95
High-grade home appliances	LED TVs	–	6	31	–	13	46	–	24	58	–	39	74
	Microwave ovens	7	–	46	17	–	55	31	–	65	59	–	75
	Dishwashers	–	–	1	–	–	1	–	–	1	–	–	3
	Air conditioners	–	14	28	–	31	47	–	50	62	–	67	76
	Vacuum cleaners	–	–	2	–	–	5	–	–	10	–	–	23
Digital products	PCs	5	17	27	17	40	47	32	67	63	61	89	80
	Cameras	1	2	5	1	5	11	4	11	22	13	21	45
	Dumb phones	68	84	–	85	95	–	89	96	–	95	94	–
	Smart phones	–	–	66	–	–	82	–	–	87	–	–	93

(continued)

Table 7.2 (continued)

		Low income group			Lower middle income group			Upper middle income group			High income group		
		2008 (%)	2011 (%)	2015 (%)	2008 (%)	2011 (%)	2015 (%)	2008 (%)	2011 (%)	2015 (%)	2008 (%)	2011 (%)	2015 (%)
	Tablet computers	–	–	8	–	–	18	–	–	30	–	–	50
Vehicles	Motorcycles	–	–	72	–	–	76	–	–	71	–	–	68
	Domestic brand vehicles	2	3	10	4	6	18	5	10	26	17	14	44
	Joint venture brand vehicles	–	1	–	–	2	–	–	4	–	–	11	-
	Foreign brand vehicles	–	0	1	–	1	2	–	1	4	–	5	10

to get the high-grade home appliance ownership index, which ranges from 0 to 5. Higher scores indicate more high-grade appliances owned. The average index for all residents is 1.6. The other variable in the statistics, "Whether any expensive durable goods such as automotive or furniture have been purchased since 2012?", measures the consumption orientation of high-grade durable goods to some extent. About 14% residents gave the answer of "Yes".

According to the research purposes, the income groups variable is a key factor that affects the ownership of the high-grade home appliances by the residents. In addition to the objective measurement of income, we would also like to explore the impact of subjective class identity on owning high-grade home appliances, that is, whether the family members shall have stronger desire of owning those luxuries if they identify themselves as middle-class families. In addition, as we make the assumption that the life situations of the residents also affect their purchasing desire of such, we added the variables on improvement of financial situations since 2012 and family pressure into the model to measure life situations. Family pressure index is gained from a group of variables on the respondents' life pressure, including poor living condition/home unaffordability, children's high education expenditures, poor family relation, high medical cost, affected life quality due to prices on the rise, touch living from low family income, family members who have unstable employment or are out of employment, heavy burden of caring for aging parents, high spending on social favor returning and victims of such as fraud, theft and robbery. The family pressure index measures the pressure the respondent family suffer, ranging from 0 to 10. Higher scores indicate higher pressure. The average index for all the residents was 2.7.

The living area and the ownership of the currently living house are integrated into the model as control variables. The assumption indicated is that the ownership of high-grade home appliances is affected by the differences in economic development in both the urban and rural areas and that those who live in their own house tend to purchase high-grade home appliances. Please refer to Table 7.3 for descriptive statistics of the dependent variables and independent variables.

First, we use the family life pressure index to construct the model of ownership of high-grade home appliances to measure the influence from family life pressure. Table 7.4 shows the model of high-grade home appliance ownership index, which can explain 28% of the variance. The variables of the subjective and objective aspects, such as income groups, financial situations improvement and family pressure index are all significant. High-grade home appliance ownership index for the lower middle income group, upper middle income group and high income group are respectively 0.316 points, 0.592 points and 1.075 points higher than that of the low income group; the high income group own remarkably more household appliances, while the gap between the high and the upper middle income group, 0.483, is smaller than the gap between the upper middle income group and low income group, 0.592. Families which have improved their financial situations since 2012 and self-identify as middle-class households or those families with less family pressure have seen their evidently higher high-grade home appliance ownership index. In the control

Table 7.3 Descriptive statistics of the dependent variables and independent variables in regression model

Variable	Sample	Mean	Standard deviation	Min	Max
High-grade home appliance ownership index	10,238	1.644266	1.208482	0	5
Whether any expensive durable goods such as vehicles or furniture have been purchased since 2012	9997	0.138942	0.345903	0	1
Income groups	9680	2.216426	1.16398	1	4
Whether the financial situation has been improved since 2012	9996	0.367047	0.482024	0	1
Family life pressure index	10,243	2.68642	2.051494	0	10
Whether there is pressure from high children-rearing expenditures	10,243	0.213902	0.410079	0	1
Whether there is pressure from medical care spending	102,43	0.362199	0.480659	0	1
Whether there is pressure from the unemployment or unstable employment of family members	10,243	0.312409	0.463498	0	1
Whether there is pressure from caring aging parents	10,243	0.109148	0.31184	0	1
Whether identify one's family as a middle class one	6501	1.679742	0.466612	1	2
Living in urban or rural area	10,243	1.45514	0.498008	1	2
Whether own the house currently live in	10,105	0.871846	0.334278	0	1

variables, the high-grade home appliance ownership index is much higher for those families who live in the urban areas and own the houses they live in.

Tables 7.5 shows the model using the classified family pressure variable to replace the family pressure index, measuring detailed life burdens that restrict consumption upgrade. This model can explain 27% of the variance. As shown in Table 7.5, the variables of income groups were still evident. The highest restriction effect of family pressure comes from the pressure of medical spending, families with this pressure got 0.139 less points on their high-grade home appliance ownership index; very next to them were those households with family member had unstable or no jobs, who got 0.0627 points less. Much spending on high children education and caring the aging parents had little influence on owning high-grade home appliances, which can be explained by the family's endeavor in meeting their children's education demand anyway. Therefore, high education tuition was not a problem for having high-grade appliances; the economic, or possibly the mental burden as for caring aging parents could have little to do with buying such high-grade appliances. The analysis stresses

Table 7.4 Linear regression model of high-grade home appliances in urban and rural areas (family pressure index)

Independent variable	Coefficient	Standard error
Income groups (with the low income group as reference)		
Lower middle income group	0.316***	0.0364
Upper middle income group	0.592***	0.0389
High income group	1.075***	0.0398
Financial situation improvement (with the unimproved situation as reference)	0.113***	0.0269
Family pressure index	0.0506***	0.00674
Identify as middle class family (with those do not identify them as such as reference)	0.196***	0.0289
Living in urban area (with those living in rural area as reference)	0.558***	0.0298
Own the house one is living (with those living in the rent house as reference)	0.471***	0.0409
Constant	0.567***	0.0545
Sample size	6066	

***$p < 0.01$, **$p < 0.05$, *$p < 0.1$

that the life situations, especially the medical security and job security, play a key role in consumption upgrading.

We also constructed a logit regression model on whether buying or not the valuables. The variables of income groups are still significant. The middle and high income groups have higher possibility in purchasing valuables. In addition, financial situation improvement also plays a key role. Since 2012, households who enjoyed financial improvement are 1.8 times more likely to add valuables to their belongings. Self identification of middle class households significantly led to higher possibility of purchase of valuables.

The ownership index of high-grade home appliances indicates the quantity possessed, which is in a large sense affected by financial conditions and material security; however, the mechanism of buying vehicles, furniture and other valuables is even more complicated. The above mentioned purchase are possibly related to important life events and phases of life, such as moving to a new place (thus have to buy furniture) and sending kids to schools (thus have to buy a car), in addition to economic status and lifestyles. So, buying expensive durables can be "a must" when big moments come, with differences in grades though, which is relatively independent of the factor of life security. The model indicates that buying valuables can be also independent of whether living in the urban or rural area or whether living in the owned house. Insignificant differences between rural and urban areas reveal the vigorous consumption demand from the rural areas—despite their low consumption level, their elasticity of consumption is greater as income grows. The possibility of purchasing new valuables such as furniture and vehicles among rural families insignificantly differentiates with that for urban families.

Table 7.5 Linear regression model of high-grade home appliances in urban and rural areas (family pressure classification variable)

Independent variable	Coefficient	Standard error
Income groups (with the low income group as reference)		
Lower middle income group	0.314***	0.0365
Upper middle income group	0.606***	0.0390
High income group	1.096***	0.0398
Financial situation improvement (with the unimproved situation as reference)	0.118***	0.0270
Whether there is pressure from high children education expenditures (with those have no such burden as reference)	0.0171	0.0331
Whether there is pressure from medical spending (with those have no such burden as reference)	−0.139***	0.0288
Whether there is pressure from the unemployment or unstable employment of family members (with those have no such burden as reference)	−0.0627**	0.0300
Whether there is pressure from caring aging parents (with those have no such burden as reference)	−0.0553	0.0433
Identify as middle-class family (with those do not identify them as such as reference)	0.206***	0.0289
Living in the urban area (with those living in the rural area as reference)	0.561***	0.0299
Own the house one is living (with those living in the rent house as reference)	0.490***	0.0409
Constant	0.473***	0.0517
Sample size	6066	

***$p < 0.01$, **$p < 0.05$, *$p < 0.1$

7.4 Conclusion and Policy Implications

With the data of CSS 2006–2015, this chapter reveals the consumption characteristics and trends of the middle income group. First, the middle income group showed its certain consumption potential. The food and beverages spending share of the middle income group was generally going down. However, the expenditure share of food and beverages among the middle income group was higher than both the low and high-income groups; the middle income group was significant on eating-out consumption, showing their potential on convenient and quality food and beverages consumption. The middle income group showed their strong consumption preference on some high-grade household durables, mainly the refrigerators and kitchen appliances manufactured with new technology. It grew fast in the recent years.

However, the middle income group spent less and low share of their household expenditures on culture and leisure and those items for self-improvement. Although there was some increase on the owning percentage of household durable goods, the spending and the expenditure share were still low. Imperfect collective consumption, especially the health care, laid constrains on such spending. The middle and low income group spent high on medical care, which become more evident in 2015. Fast increasing mortgage was another restraining factor. According to the model analysis, social security factors had significant influence on the quantity of high-grade home appliances owned of both the urban and rural areas. The pressure from medical spending was the biggest, and the second factor next to it was the pressure from the unemployment of family members.

With the consumption plights and the reasons behind of the middle income group, this chapter highlights the main policy suggestions of improving the livelihood based on increasing income. Policy suggestions are made on the aspects of entrepreneurship innovation upgrading and comprehensive arrangement of rural markets from the perspective of supply.

Here are the policy suggestions:

1. **Deepen reforms of the income distribution system, increase residents' income and expand the middle income group**. It is predicated that the slow-down of economic speed may not significantly put off China from being ranked as a high-income country. Therefore, we can press ahead with our economic development with economic development restructuring and distribution system reform deepening. The per capita disposable income for the urban, despite the constant growing, when deducted the price factor, showed limited growth. The in-depth reason is the low labor remuneration in GDP. Besides, the imperfect redistribution system engraves the residents' income level and the equity of the income distribution. As for the primary distribution, employment of both university graduates and migrant works should be attached great importance to. The upward mobility of the low and lower middle income group should be enhanced and the middle income group shall be enlarged.
2. **Improve the social security system, stabilize the commodity and housing prices and expand consumption based on livelihood improvement**. Consumption enlarged based on improved livelihood (as the core purpose) shall be effective and sustainable. The government should actively improve the social security system that includes housing, education, medical and supporting for the aged. The investment management of social security funds should be properly regulated. The trust and confidence from the public on this should be enhanced. The measures for high livelihood and therefore the expanded domestic consumption should be more practical. The commodity and housing prices should be stabilized. Speculations on housing should be combated. Multi investment channels should be expanded and improved to allow proper consumption and investment of the middle income group.
3. **Promote the production innovation and develop the middle-end to better satisfy the consumption upgrade**. Currently, the middle-end goods provision is insufficient. Goods available are either for the high-end demand from the affluent class or roughly and poorly made products. The demand for delicate designs, reliable quality and reasonable prices from the middle income group

cannot be met currently. Most of them began turning for overseas shopping. The enterprises should focus on developing the middle-end market, renewing their design and improving the quality to meet the middle income group's demand. Meanwhile, research and development of products should be advanced to cut down costs and encourage families to use new generation products to enjoy quality life.

4. **Expite the development of service consumption, promote the level of the service sector and improve the consumption environment**. Although demands for quality goods can be met by overseas purchase, demands for better services can only be satisfied locally. Currently, the supply of services range from catering, tourism, leisure to house purchase and finance and all need improvement. Better services are only about the quality and attitude of services but also about food safety, property safety and personal security. Low service level would refrain the growth of consumption. The opportunities of growing demand for services should be availed to improve the traditional services and promote the development on cultural innovation, medical and health care combination, information consumption and other emerging services. The 'Internet+' practices and sharing economy for products research & development and service mode innovation should be encouraged. The integration of resources should be promoted to benefit more people. The government should vigorously rectify the market order and regulate the market, such as addressing food safety issues, telecommunications frauds and counterfeiting. The corporates and the government should work jointly in improving supply of products and services as well as the consumption environment. This can better satisfy the general consumption upgrade in China.
5. **Activate the consumption demand of the rural middle income group by seizing the opportunities in the rural markets**. Recent years, quick rural income increase has brought about growing demand on household durables. Although the general rural consumption is relatively low now, there tends to be good consumption flexibility with the increased rural income. So, the demand from the rural middle income group should be highlighted. The links such as production, sales and logistics with the rural consumers should be well connected by both the government and corporates. The e-commerce and express service should reach rural communities so as to meet the rural residents' demand for improving their quality of life.

References

Anikin VA., Lezhnina YP, Mareeva SV, Slobodenyuk ED, Tikhonova NN (2016) Income stratification: key approaches and application to Russia. NRU Higher School of Economics. WP BRP Series: Public and Social Policy.

Castells M (1977) The urban question: a marxist approach. The MIT Press, Cambridge, MA

Credit Suisse Research Institute (2015) Global Wealth Report 2015. Credit Suisse AG, Zurich

Di Z (2016) Development and plights of the middle class in BRICS countries. Cult Rev (8)
Kharas H (2010) The emerging middle class in developing countries. OECD Development Centre Working Paper No. 285
Linjiang Z, Weihua Z (2016) The expansion of middle-class, increase of domestic demand and economic transformation. Chinese Cadres Tribune (9)
Ning W (2014) Local consumerism, urban comforts and industry structure optimization—a perspective of sociology of consumption on industry upgrading. Soc Study 4
Peilin L, Di Z (2015) Make efforts to develop an olive-shaped distribution pattern: an analysis based on data from the china social survey for 2006–2013. Soc Sci China (1)
Research Group of Social Survey and Data Center of Shanghai Academy (2016). Expand the middle income group and use the consumption to drive the economy—a research on the middle income group in Shanghai. Jiangsu Soc Sci (5)
Vercueil J (2016) Income inequalities, productive structure and macroeconomic dynamics. A regional approach to the russian case. Presented at sustainable development and middle class in metropolitan cities of the BRICS nations, Shanghai
Warde A (1990) Introduction to the sociology of consumption. Sociology 24(1):1–4
Yi Z (2016) Current consumption tendency for all social strata in China—from consumption for survival to consumption for self-cultivation. Soc Study (4)

Di Zhu is an Associate Professor in Chinese Academy of Social Sciences. She is also the Secretary General of the Research Committee of Sociology of Consumption of the Chinese Sociological Association.She got her Ph.D. and Msc degrees from the University of Manchester, and B.A. degree from Fudan University. Her research interests include: sociology of consumption, sustainable consumption, social stratification, and consumer culture of youths. Her main publications include 'Taste and Material Aspiration: Consumption Patterns of the Middle Class in Contemporary China' (book) in 2013, 'Make Efforts to Develop an Olive-shaped Distribution Pattern: An Analysis Based on Data from the Chinese Social Survey for 2006–2013' (2015).

Chapter 8
Consumption and Lifestyle of the Middle Class

Svetlana V. Mareeva

There are several advantages to defining middle class via "economic" approach based on income level. These include both an opportunity to draw global comparisons, and the correct application of this approach to reviewing issues that are linked to the economic aspect of population life—first and foremost, consumption patterns. By analyzing the specific features of consumption and the arising lifestyles of two middle-class subgroups, we will gain answers to several questions that are crucial to understanding the current condition of the Russian society as a whole. This will allow us, firstly, to determine which standard of living is currently typical of the Russian population (in this context, it bears reminding that the median income level, determined according to the methodology we use to define the middle class, is typical of the lower mid-income population group, which is the group comprising Russians with income around the nationwide median, lower than it or exceeding it by no more than a quarter. Consequently, this group may be viewed as the "median group", which displays the lifestyle and consumption patterns that are typical in the country at this economic development stage). Secondly, we will have a chance to understand which standard of living the majority of Russians would like to aspire to, as it is the middle-class standard of living that is generally reviewed by the majority as a desired social norm (in this particular case, the bar will be set by the consumption capabilities of the upper mid-income group). Lastly, another question that we will attempt to answer in this chapter is linked to the transformation of Russian society overall: namely, whether the past 15 years have lead to any significant changes in Russians' standards and quality of living and whether the changes have been distributed evenly among different population groups.

As we begin our analysis of the middle class consumption patterns, we shall first look at the way respondents from the middle class evaluate the **various aspects** of their lives that, in one way or another, **are linked to consumption** (Table 8.1). Our

S. V. Mareeva (✉)
HSE University, Institute of Sociology of FCTAS RAS, Moscow, Russia

P. Li and M. K. Gorshkov (eds.), *The Middle Income Group in China and Russia*, Research Series on the Chinese Dream and China's Development Path,
https://doi.org/10.1007/978-981-16-1464-4_8

Table 8.1 Self-assessment of various lifestyle aspects linked to consumption across income groups, Fall of 2016, in % (The options that gained more than 50% of responses are highlighted in bold the acceptable responses also included "satisfactory", which is not shown in the table)

Evaluation of various lifestyle aspects	Low-income	Lower mid-income	Upper mid-income	High-income	Overall population
Food					
Good	26	39	**53**	**63**	39
Poor	9	5	1	3	5
Clothing					
Good	16	25	44	**57**	29
Poor	18	9	2	3	10
Housing					
Good	32	41	44	**54**	39
Poor	13	9	5	4	9
Leisure options					
Good	18	30	37	**51**	29
Poor	27	17	8	8	18
Vacation opportunities					
Good	9	17	29	43	19
Poor	40	23	12	8	25

data shows that mid-income population groups are generally rather cautious in the evaluation of their material well-being: only 16% of respondents from the lower mid-income group and 26% of respondents from the upper mid-income group consider their material position to be good, and in the first group, the share of those who consider their material status to be poor even exceeds the share of those who find it good (20%). This considered, it is hardly surprising that the mid-income groups review other lifestyle aspects that are linked to material status and consumption capabilities with a grain of salt as well. The evaluation made by Russians from the upper mid-income group is more favorable than that made by Russians from the lower mid-income group, but the breadth of the gap depends on the lifestyle aspect: for instance, the two groups' evaluation of their housing does not differ as much as their attitudes towards their clothing, meals, or vacation opportunities.

On the other hand, the share of positive responses regarding every aspect (excluding the lower mid-income group's view on vacation opportunities) does exceed the share of negative responses in the case of both groups, whereas the low-income groups' situation is completely opposite (excluding the evaluation of housing). By contrast, the vast majority of respondents from high-income groups provide a positive evaluation of the various aspects of their life that are linked to consumption. All of this signifies that the different income groups in Russian society

Table 8.2 Self-assessment of various lifestyle aspects linked to consumption in mid-income groups, 2003–2016, in % (The highest number of positive or negative responses is highlighted in bold; the acceptable responses also included "satisfactory", which is not shown in the table)

Evaluation of various lifestyle aspects	Lower mid-income			Upper mid-income		
	2003	Spring of 2014	Fall of 2016	2003	Spring of 2014	Fall of 2016
Food						
Good	**16**	**42**	**39**	**28**	**50**	**53**
Poor	15	5	5	9	2	1
Clothing						
Good	7	**29**	**25**	**17**	**41**	**44**
Poor	**30**	7	9	16	3	2
Housing						
Good	**25**	**36**	**41**	**26**	**41**	**44**
Poor	17	10	9	19	5	5
Leisure options						
Good	12	**32**	**30**	18	**44**	**37**
Poor	**38**	11	17	**29**	8	8
Vacation opportunities						
Good	11	**26**	17	13	**39**	**29**
Poor	**56**	19	**23**	**39**	10	12

are characterized not only by the vastly different standard and quality of living, but also by different levels of satisfaction with their lifestyle, and the average standard across all population groups is relatively low, as affirmed by the lower mid-income population group, which reflect the lifestyles typical of Russians overall.

The way Russians view the consumption-linked aspects of their lifestyle depends on the economic development stage that the country is passing through. Consequently, it is immensely interesting to look at the long-term dynamics of their evaluations, as well as at the changes they have gone through as a result of the latest economic crisis of 2014–2016. We can evaluate these trends based on our research data (Table 8.2).

The first conclusion that may be derived from the data above is the significant change in the material status of mid-income population groups during an economic upturn. During the decade following 2003, members of the lower mid-income group, which reflects the typical lifestyle of the entire population, have experienced a significant rise in the share of positive responses and a drop in the share of negative responses in terms of evaluating such lifestyle aspects as food, housing, and vacation opportunities. And if we look at such lifestyle aspects as clothing and leisure options, we shall see that, even bearing in mind the impact of the latest crisis, the situation in the lower mid-income group has changed dramatically: while in 2003 the share of negative responses far exceeded the share of positive responses, by 2016 this ratio has transformed to the opposite. Based on seen dynamics, respondents from low mid-income groups could also have evaluated their vacation opportunities in the same way, if it were not for the latest crisis—but the past two years have turned the tide of positive dynamics. But even after a prolonged period of decreasing actual income and the corresponding changes in consumption, which we shall review in more detail below, the lower mid-income group's evaluation of various lifestyle aspects linked to consumption reveals significant improvement in the consumption standards compared to the early 2000s.

Turning to the status of the upper mid-income group, we see that it has noticeably improved as well. In the spring of 2014, the number of instances when members of this group reviewed all the consumption-linked aspects of their lifestyle positively exceeded the reverse manifold. The crisis did not prompt any significant changes in this respect, but it did have a quantitative impact, primarily on vacation opportunities, the positive evaluation of which experienced a rather dramatic drop.

Consequently, *the impact of different economic crisis phases over the past few years has affected not only the size of mid-income groups, but also their standard and quality of living. Their consumption capabilities have grown significantly; however, the lower mid-income group is characterized not only by a more modest living standard, but also by greater vulnerability, which results in qualitative changes in their consumption when crises strike. The status of the upper mid-income group is more favorable and stable. The crisis does, without a doubt, influence this group's consumption capabilities, but does not affect its basic needs, only being reflected in the lifestyle aspects that concern stylized consumption and the opportunities to form and diversify one's lifestyle, such as by going on vacation.*

Housing is an important aspect of integral quality of living. As revealed by the data above, Russians are generally more satisfied with their housing than otherwise, although average (satisfactory) level of assessment statistically dominates. This is also typical of mid-income groups. But if we consider objective figures that describe the housing quality, we shall see that as income increases, both the availability of living space per family member and the availability of utilities increases as well. The average amount of living space per family member is 19 m^2 in low-income groups, 21 m^2 in the lower mid-income subgroup, 22 m^2 in the upper mid-income subgroup, and 26 m^2 in high-income groups. The complete set of utilities is enjoyed by 67% of Russians from low-income groups, 85% of Russians from the lower mid-income subgroup, 86% of Russians from the upper mid-income subgroup, and 93% of Russians from high-income groups. As we can see, both subgroups of mid-income population groups are relatively close to one another in this respect. On the other hand, there is a certain noticeable differentiation within the mid-income population groups, based on the type of settlement: as we move from large cities to smaller populated areas, the share of people who do not have at least some utilities at their home starts to rise (reaching 42% of the lower mid-income subgroup and 30% of the upper mid-income subgroup in rural settlements). By contrast, the amount of free living space is minimal in metropolitan areas and starts increasing as we move to smaller towns and villages.

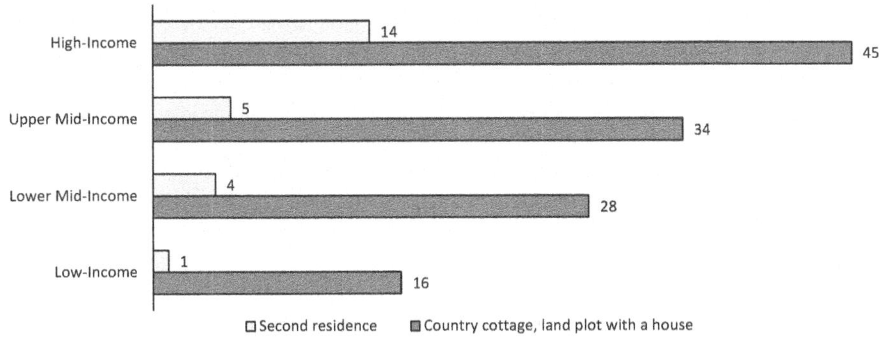

Fig. 8.1 Ownership of additional real estate across various population groups, Fall of 2015, %

Ownership of main living premises (an apartment or a house) is a parameter that barely reveals any differentiation between population groups—from 86 to 92% of respondents from each group own either an apartment or a house. What marks a far more substantial difference is ownership of additional premises—a country cottage or a second residence (Fig. 8.1). The safety cushion provided by these extra premises, along with additional consumption opportunities (such as going on vacation in the country), is where the various groups differ substantially, and in this respect, mid-income groups occupy the middle position. The lower mid-income group, once again, reflects a trend that is common for Russians overall: owning a country house is typical of <30% of this group's members (the figures are highest in large cities, amounting to almost one half), while owning a second apartment is typical of <5%, and is more widespread among people residing in the regional and district centers or in small towns.

Another aspect of an integral standard of living is ownership of **durable goods** which also make a significant contribution to consumption standards and determine consumption patterns. So what are the characteristic features of the material possessions owned by mid-income groups? Our data shows that sets of durable goods available in households with different income levels differ quite substantially (Table 8.3).

The "standard" set of goods that is owned by more than a half of the entire Russian population includes an automatic washing machine, a cell phone, a number of kitchen appliances, a computer or laptop, and color TV. There are some differences in the ownership of certain items from this set in certain income groups, but they are not too dramatic. The same set is also a common standard in the lower mid-income group, which, as mentioned above, reflects the typical nationwide standard of living. However, with respect to owning durable goods, this groups comes closer to Russians with low income, although the overall share of people who own most of the durable goods listed above is still higher in the lower mid-income group. In the upper mid-income group, on the other hand, the standard set of durable goods is extended by digital devices (video camera or cell phone), smartphones, and foreign cars, which brings it closer to Russians with high income (although in the upper mid-income group, the number of people who own certain durable goods still tends

Table 8.3 Availability of durable goods across income groups, Fall of 2015, in % (Classified according to the overall availability of durable goods. Names of durable goods that are owned by more than 50% of the income group are highlighted in bold)

Durable goods	Low-income	Lower mid-income	Upper mid-income	High-income	Overall population
TV set, including	**99**	**99**	**99**	**99**	**99**
Regular	**76**	**70**	**69**	**56**	**70**
LCD or plasma	**59**	**68**	**80**	**90**	**69**
Refrigerator	**99**	**98**	**99**	**97**	**98**
Vacuum cleaner	**91**	**93**	**93**	**92**	**92**
Automatic washing machine	**81**	**90**	**95**	**96**	**88**
Cell phone	**86**	**86**	**82**	**86**	**85**
Microwave oven, food processor, or any other kitchen appliance	**72**	**81**	**87**	**94**	**81**
Computer (laptops included)	**66**	**69**	**80**	**89**	**72**
Car, including	**52**	**57**	**73**	**85**	**62**
Foreign model	21	31	**51**	**71**	36
Russian model	36	33	32	29	34
Video or digital camera	33	46	**60**	**73**	47
Smartphone (iPhones included)	34	42	**55**	**70**	45
Tablet (iPads included)	31	39	49	**67**	41
Satellite dish	30	32	36	48	33
Air conditioner	14	13	18	38	17
Dishwasher	7	10	17	39	

Table 8.4 Dynamics of owning certain types of durable goods across mid-income groups, Spring of 2014—Fall of 2015, in %

Durable goods	Lower mid-income		Upper mid-income	
	Spring of 2014	Fall of 2015	Spring of 2014	Fall of 2015
Smartphone (iPhones included)	27	42	36	55
Foreign car	26	31	43	51
Tablet (iPads included)	22	39	38	49
Satellite dish	20	32	26	36
Air conditioner	13	13	15	18
Dishwasher	5	10	12	17

to be lower). *It is the ability to buy additional durable goods that go beyond the basic set that reveals the specifics of stylized consumption typical of the upper mid-income subgroup but so far absent in the lower mid-income subgroup.* It is worth highlighting that the differences in the sets of durable goods demonstrate not only the gap in the material well-being of various income groups but also the difference in life opportunities of people from these groups, as durable goods open vastly different possibilities when it comes to engaging in leisure activities, self-teaching, mastering digital technology (which may later be used in the workplace), and more.

As we attempt to predict the future changes in the durable goods set owned by the low-income group, we may expect greater proliferation of innovative and complex technology, which is already well integrated into the households of the upper mid-income group. This conclusion is reaffirmed by the tendency to upgrade the set of durable goods, common in various income groups even against the background of an economic recession—even though such renewal was not too active during the crisis, the mid-income groups' standard sets of durable goods have expanded notably over the past two years, in particular thanks to purchases of relatively complex and innovative appliances (Table 8.4). In this respect, both subgroups of the mid-income strata show great willingness to familiarize themselves with new technology. They may be expected to gradually prompt the category of these goods to change from innovations to elements of an expanded set of durables for the whole population. Foreign cars are also beginning this transition to the expanded set category, as they are currently owned by over a half of the upper mid-income group and more than 70% of the high-income group.

In this context, it is hardly surprising that the use of computer technology in everyday life is typical of both the lower and upper mid-income group. For instance, our data for 2014 shows that 41 and 51% of respondents from each group respectively used the computer every day, and an additional 21% and 22% respectively used it several times a week. What is more, 38% of respondents from the lower mid-income group and 45% of respondents from the upper mid-income group used the Internet every day, and 23% and 26% respectively used it several times a week. 31% of respondents from the lower mid-income group and 20% of respondents from the upper mid-income group did not use the computer (for various reasons, including the lack of necessary skills), whereas 33% and 21% respectively did not use the Internet. High-income groups that are not part of the middle class are even more active as computer users (58% of them use the computer on a daily basis, while 52% use the Internet every day); low-income groups, however, are involved in digital consumption far less frequently than both subgroups of the mid-income strata (using the computer and the Internet is typical only of 34 and 31% of all respondents from this group, respectively). In other words, inequality in digital consumption overlaps with income inequality, exacerbating the vulnerability of lower-income groups, as different levels of access to ICT impacts not only the range of available leisure activities, but also the access to information, education options, labor opportunities, and even cheaper goods.

If we look at the dynamics of durables accessibility in the longer term, our data will also reveal that the mid-income groups' standard of living has improved significantly, if compared to 2003. For instance, the standard set of durable goods began to include cell phones and computers, and in the case of the upper mid-income group—even various digital devices and a car, whereas in 2003, these categories of durables were owned by less than a half of households in the respective groups. Furthermore, the share of people who own domestically made cars in the upper mid-income group keeps falling, while the share of those who own foreign cars keeps rising. The 2003–2015 period also saw a rise in the share of people with mid-level income whose households own rare goods or goods that are considered prestigious in Russia as a whole, such as satellite dishes, air conditioners, or dishwashers. This goes to show that over the past decade and a half, durables consumption opportunities of the middle class have expanded significantly, which reflects changes in the consumption standards of the overall Russian population (Table 8.5).

All the same, mid-income groups' positive consumption dynamics from 2003 to 2014 were limited mostly to the rise in positive subjective evaluations of the key consumption-related lifestyle aspects and the upgrade of the goods set. The level of more notable achievements in this area remained practically unchanged, and even dropped due to the crisis. For example, only 17% of respondents from the lower mid-income group managed to notably improve their material well-being over the course of three years preceding the survey, both in 2003 and 2014; the crisis made this figure decrease to 12%. The share of such respondents was higher in the upper mid-income group—30% in 2003 and 26% in 2014, but during the first crisis year, this share dropped to 20%. Costly purchases were available to 11–13% of respondents from the lower mid-income group and 14–18% of respondents from the upper mid-income group. In turn, the opportunity to travel abroad was used by an increasing number of respondents in both subgroups of the mid-income strata in 2003–2014, but then the figures shrank (see Fig. 8.2).

The probability of significant and costly consumption activities also differs within the mid-income strata: members of the lower mid-income group, once again, find themselves closer to the low-income level, though they do outstrip people with low income in terms of positive dynamics; whereas Russians from the upper mid-income

Table 8.5 Dynamics of owning certain types of durable goods across mid-income groups, 2003–2015, in % (Names of durable goods that are owned by more than 50% of the income group are highlighted in bold)

Durable goods	Lower mid-income			Upper mid-income		
	2003	2015	Growth, in %	2003	2015	Growth, in %
Cell phone	12	**86**	74	26	**82**	56
Computer (laptops included)	13	**69**	56	25	**80**	55
Microwave oven, food processor, or any other kitchen appliance	31	**81**	50	**51**	**87**	36
Video or digital camera	4	46	42	9	**60**	51
Satellite dish	1	32	31	1	36	35
Foreign car	2	31	29	7	**51**	44
Air conditioner	1	13	12	2	18	16
Dishwasher	0	10	10	1	17	16
Vacuum cleaner	**85**	**93**	8	**93**	**93**	0
Russian car	26	33	7	36	32	−4
Automatic washing machine	**85**	**90**	5	**88**	**95**	7
Refrigerator	**99**	**98**	−1	**99**	**99**	0
Color TV, regular	**94**	**70**	−24	**98**	**69**	−29

group are closer to those with high income, though they do not quite achieve the figures typical of the latter. To illustrate: according to 2015 data, only 9% of Russians with low income and 12% of Russians with low mid-income managed to improve their material well-being, in contrast with 19% of Russians with upper mid-income and 22% of Russians with high income. Various high-cost purchases were made by 7%, 11%, 18%, and 26% respectively, while trips abroad were made by 5%, 8%, 16%, and 26% respectively.

Specific consumption patterns of different groups are also revealed by their **use of paid services**. In this respect, respondents from mid-income groups also occupy a middle position between high-income and low-income Russians. The most widely used paid service is paid healthcare: over the course of the three years preceding the survey, paid healthcare was acquired by almost a half of Russians with middle

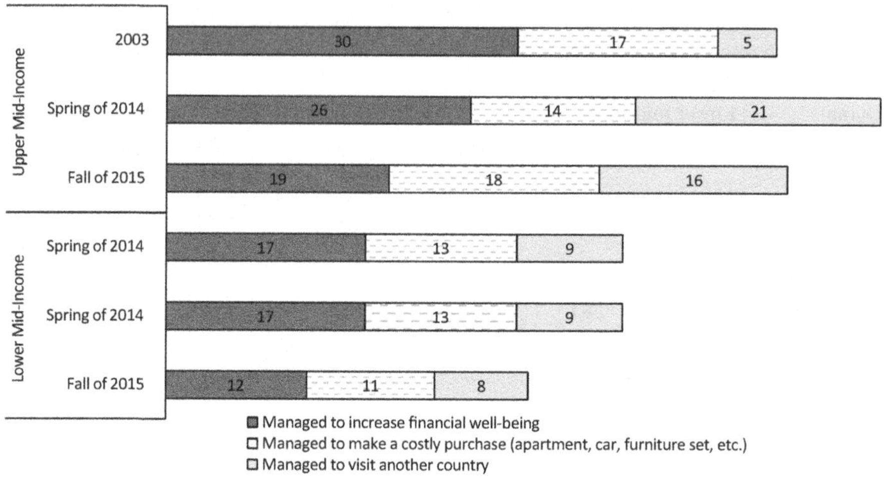

Fig. 8.2 Consumption achievements of mid-income groups during the three years preceding the survey, 2003–2015, in %

income level. Paid education services for adults are not nearly as popular: they were acquired only by 15% of Russians from mid-strata groups. Payment for services for children are more widespread, with the shares of such respondents being higher in the lower mid-income group than in the higher mid-income group: for instance, paid healthcare services for children were used by 38% and 33% of respondents respectively, and paid education services were used by 37% and 28%, respectively (Table 8.6). However, when giving the reason for availing themselves of paid services, mid-income respondents cite the lack or inaccessibility of free counterparts far more often than the search for better-quality services, i.e. they are, to an extent, forced to resort to using paid services; this opinion is expressed by two thirds (64%) of Russians with middle income who have used such services over the past three years.

The mid-income groups do not follow a single shared pattern in terms of using a particular type of paid social services; one of the criteria behind the differentiation of consumption patterns is the consumers' age. Even though all age groups use paid services for adults in roughly equal shares (53–57% of overall mid-income respondents), travel and education services are somewhat apart from the rest, in that using them is more typical of young people (these services were used by 16% of respondents under 35, 12% of mid-income respondents aged from 36 to 55, and 4% of respondents over 55). Services for children are used most actively by mid-income respondents aged from 36 to 55 (57% among respondents with children).

As for changes in the use of paid services compared to 2003, in the lower mid-income group there had not been any notable shifts in how often respondents acquired various types of paid services. Certain particular types of services experienced multi-directional fluctuations. In the upper mid-income group, negative trends prevailed: fewer respondents continued using paid healthcare services, education and health improvement services for children, or education services for adults. The only type

Table 8.6 Use of paid services across income groups during the three years preceding the survey, Fall of 2015, in % (Data on paid services for children is only provided for households with minors)

Used paid services during the three years preceding the survey	Low-income	Lower mid-income	Upper mid-income	High-income	Overall population
Paid healthcare services for adults	43	49	49	57	48
Paid healthcare services for children	31	38	33	33	33
Paid education services for children	27	37	28	43	31
Paid education services for adults	11	14	16	19	14
Paid health improvement services for adults	7	12	16	25	12
Paid health improvement services for children	8	16	10	19	12
Educational or leisure tours abroad	3	7	17	29	10

of service undergoing a positive trend was travel: the share of respondents going on leisure or education tours abroad increased from 5% in 2003 to 17% in 2015, even in the crisis reality of that period's economy (Table 8.7). Taking into account the aforementioned data above on the availability of durable goods and consumption opportunities in terms of food, clothing, and leisure, we can arrive at the conclusion that *people from the upper mid-income group invested most of their free funds into consumption, while investments into human capital shrank. As a result, the lower mid-income group even began to outstrip the upper mid-income group when it came to use of a number of paid services, most notably education and health improvement services for children.*

Another important issue that may help improve our understanding of mid-income groups' consumption patterns is the **strategy of using free funds**. First of all, we must mention that today, mid-income groups still do not have much freedom for stylized consumption: around a half of the upper subgroup and 43% of the lower

Table 8.7 Use of paid services across income groups during the three years preceding the survey, Fall of 2015, in % (Data on paid services for children is only provided for households with minors)

Used out-of-pocket services during the three years preceding the survey	Lower mid-income			Upper mid-income		
	2003	2010	2015	2003	2010	2015
Paid healthcare services for adults or children	55	48	53	67	62	54
Paid education services for children	33	28	37	39	36	28
Paid health improvement services for children	16	20	16	20	28	10
Paid education services for adults	18	13	14	30	21	16
Paid health improvement services for adults	9	11	12	16	16	16
Educational or leisure tours abroad	3	6	7	5	11	17

subgroup state that they never have any free funds (by comparison, in the low-income group, this figure reaches 63%, while in the high-income group, it is a mere 22%). Among those respondents who do have the opportunity to manage free funds, at least once in a while, the leading strategies include saving money "for a rainy day" or depositing it in a bank, as well as such consumption expenses as buying durable goods and entertainment (Table 8.8). Investment strategies—investing in real estate, land, stock, or even commercial banks—are rather rare among people with a middle income. Their management of free funds boils down to a single choice between consuming goods or entertainment here and now, or saving a little something for later.

As we continue to discuss the peculiarities of the middle class's spending patterns, we should also consider the issue of **savings and debts**. In terms of the ratio between people who have savings or any type of debt commitments, mid-income groups differ substantially from people with low income: the share of people with savings is comparable to the share of those with debts (in the lower group) or even exceeds it (in the upper group), while the situation in the low-income groups is exactly opposite. That said, the safety cushion provided by savings is rather small: only 6% of respondents from the lower mid-income group and 12% of respondents from the upper mid-income group have enough savings to last for at least a year. Debt obligations, in turn, are equally common for mid-income and high-income groups. The most prevalent among different types of indebtedness are bank loans, which are typical of a quarter of respondents from both the lower and upper mid-income subgroup. Another 12% have an assortment of smaller debts (Table 8.9).

Table 8.8 Free funds management strategies across income groups, Spring of 2014, in % (The table reflects only those options that have received no <10% of responses in at least one group)

Free funds management strategies	Low-income	Lower mid-income	Upper mid-income	High-income	Overall population
No free funds	63	50	43	22	50
Saving "for a rainy day"	19	21	17	13	19
Depositing to a savings account	10	14	17	26	15
Buying costly durable goods	8	13	12	28	13
Spending on entertainment	5	12	18	34	13
Material help to family and friends	6	10	14	17	10

Table 8.9 Loans and savings across income groups, Fall of 2015, in %

Savings and loans	Low-income	Lower mid-income	Upper mid-income	High-income	Overall population
Savings of any amount	21	36	43	56	34
Including savings that are enough to last for over a year	*4*	*6*	*12*	*25*	*8*
Any types of debt commitments	46	35	34	33	38
Have both savings and debt commitments	4	8	7	10	7
Do not have any of the above	38	37	31	22	34

Compared to the point of time before the latest economic crisis, the financial behavior of mid-income groups has changed very little: the share of people with debts has grown somewhat (as of the spring of 2014, 35% of respondents from the lower and 30% from the upper mid-income subgroup had debts of any given kind), but the share of people with savings has increased even more (30 and 36% in the spring of 2014, respectively)—quite unlike the low-income groups, where the share of savings dropped during the crisis, from 26 to 21%. That said, the increase in figures pertaining to mid-income groups was caused by a rising amount of smaller savings, which people tended to put away "just in case", influenced by the new economic conditions and expecting the economy to grow unstable, whereas the share of people with enough savings for a proper safety cushion remained unchanged.

But if we, once again, draw a comparison with 2003, the status of mid-income groups' financial strategies will change more drastically: i.e. back then, only 3% of the lower mid-income group and 7% of the upper mid-income group had savings that could last for a long period of time, and only 20% of the former and 29% of the latter had savings of any kind. On the other hand, debt obligations were not as wide-spread either: the share of respondents with any type of debt commitments amounted to 28% of the lower mid-income group and 26% of the upper mid-income group.

Overall, throughout the past decade, mid-income groups have started exhibiting more financial activity: in 2003, over a half of the lower subgroup (55%, against 37% in 2015) and almost a half of the upper subgroup (48%, against 31% in 2015) did not have any savings or debts whatsoever. Today, such financial passiveness is mostly typical of two polar age groups of the mid-income strata: the youth and the seniors.

Important lifestyle aspects linked to consumption also include **leisure options**. In this respect it is very indicative that, first and foremost, a very sizeable share of people with middle income suffer from a lack of time for resting or enjoying leisure activities. The figures exceed one third (35% of the lower subgroup and 39% of the upper subgroup). However, in their case, the situation is somewhat better than in the case of respondents with high income, who claim that they do not have enough time for leisure in 43% of cases.

All types of leisure activities may be grouped into several major categories: simple leisure (basic household and country house chores, watching TV or video, listening to music, "lounging about"), traditional leisure (reading books and periodicals, using the computer and the Internet, engaging in various hobbies without leaving home, meeting friends, spending time outdoors, going to church) and, finally, active leisure (clubbing; dancing at discos; enrolling at a gym and training for sports; going to theaters, concerts, movies, museums and exhibitions, cafes and restaurants; joining hobby clubs or getting additional education; and becoming involved in the activity of community or political institutions). Despite the relative simplicity of this classification, it brings to light several significant differences between the lifestyles of various income groups. While both simple and traditional leisure is typical of the overwhelming majority of all income groups, when it comes to active leisure, significant differences begin to surface: in low-income groups at least one of these activities is practiced only by one in every five people, whereas in the lower mid-income group the figure reaches one third and in the upper mid-income group it is already one half. This largely impacts the specific features of these groups' lifestyle (in high-income groups, the figures are just barely higher, reaching 55%).

Among various types of active leisure, mid-income respondents are mostly going to concerts, theaters, and movies (this practice is common for 16% of the lower subgroup and 22% of the upper subgroup), cafes and restaurants (13% and 20%), and gyms and training sessions (8 and 16%), as well as clubbing and dancing (6 and 10%). All other types of active leisure are typical of <10% of respondents from

Table 8.10 Active leisure pursuit dynamics across mid-income groups, 2003–2014, in %

Types of leisure activities	Lower mid-income			Upper mid-income		
	2003	2010	2014	2003	2010	2014
Active pursuits, including:	*36*	*27*	*32*	*45*	*48*	*50*
Attending concerts, theaters, movie theaters	16	12	16	24	24	22
Going to cafes or restaurants	6	6	13	15	16	20
Attending gyms and training sessions	7	7	8	12	16	16
Clubbing or attending dance parties and other entertainment events	5	5	6	13	9	10
Visiting museums and going to exhibitions	9	4	6	9	8	9
Attending extra education courses	11	8	6	16	13	8
Contributing to community organizations	4	2	2	4	3	4
Contributing to political organizations	1	1	2	1	1	4
Going to hobby clubs	2	1	1	3	3	2

mid-income groups. *People with middle income tend to enjoy a greater variety of active leisure in their free time compared to people with low income, and the lack of time for relaxation and entertainment is partly compensated by the diverse range of opportunities that they have.*

If, however, we turn to the dynamics characterizing active leisure pursuits, we may observe some discrepancies between the two income subgroups: in the upper subgroup, the share of people engaged in active types of leisure had been growing steadily ever since 2003, while in the lower subgroup, the figures fluctuated during different periods (Table 8.10). Regarding certain specific types of active leisure, we may note that both subgroups of mid-income Russians are seeing a rise in the share of people who go to cafe and restaurants, while the upper subgroup has also experienced an increase in the number of people who attend gyms and train for sports. At the same time, the share of people who dedicate their free time to additional education and skill improvement has shrunk noticeably in both subgroups of the mid-income strata. This is consistent with the aforementioned data on the decrease of investments in the human capital among members of both subgroups.

When we turn to traditional leisure, we note a dramatic surge in the share of computer-related activities: from 9% in the lower mid-income subgroup and 17% in the upper mid-income subgroup in 2003 to 30% and 36% respectively in 2014.

Finally, let us consider the ways in which Russians with middle income tried to adapt their consumption patterns to the economic crisis of 2014–2016, which was characterized by the longest period of decrease in real incomes in Russia's modern history. Our data shows that saving on the consumption of various goods and services turned out to be the population's most widespread strategy of adapting to the new economic conditions. Quite symptomatically, all income groups were forced to resort to this strategy: the crisis prompted cuts in expenses among 78% of people from low-income groups, 74% of people from low mid-income groups, 71% of people from upper mid-income groups, and 66% of people from groups with relatively high income.

The extent to which people cut down on their spending differed depending on the income group: all types of economy strategies were more likely to occur among Russians from low-income groups and far less likely among those from high-income groups, while mid-income groups found themselves between the two extremes. On average, representatives of low-income groups used 3.2 out of the 9 possible strategies for cutting their expenses, while representatives of high-income groups used 2.2 strategies; for the two mid-income subgroups, the average figures reached 2.8 and 2.4 out of 9, respectively.

Russians from mid-income groups tended to save on buying clothes and footwear (54% of the lower mid-income group and 46% of the upper mid-income group), food (45 and 36%), and vacations (42 and 45%). A large share of the population also started cutting down on leisure activities (35 and 34%) and durable goods (32 and 27%).

Economy strategies that Russians used under those economic circumstances may be classified into several large groups. The first group may be described as *saving on routine consumption,* for instance on food and purchases of clothes, footwear or durable goods (even though the need for food and clothes is more basic than for buying costly durable goods, uniting these needs within one category is still justified, as saving on food or clothes may mean not only that the person can no longer meet their own basic needs, but also that they might be switching to cheaper counterparts, temporarily putting off planned purchases, etc., in other words, adapting by means of changing routine consumption patterns). The second group includes *saving on leisure,* i.e. on hobbies or vacations. The third group may be described as *saving on investments in human capital,* i.e. cutting expenses on healthcare and education services. A category somewhat apart from the rest of the classification is *saving on material help* to family and friends. As we review these large groups of economy strategies, it becomes quite clear that during the crisis, most Russians from mid-income groups cut their expenses in several areas at once (Fig. 8.3). Saving on routine consumption is the most widespread strategy for all income groups, followed by saving on leisure and vacations.

It is important to note that cutting down expenses has also impacted investments into human capital (such as education and healthcare), thus exacerbating the negative

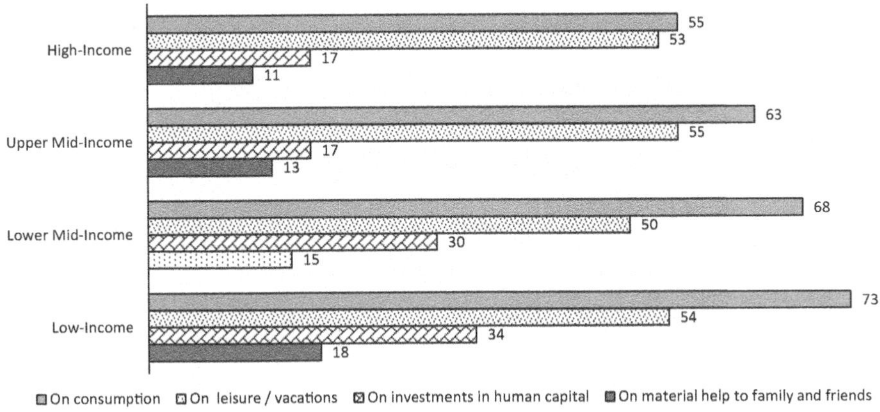

Fig. 8.3 Austerity strategies during the crisis across income groups, Fall of 2016, in %

trends that had already surfaced before the crisis. In terms of saving on human capital investments, members of the lower mid-income group differed substantially from members of the upper mid-income group: this strategy was far more typical of the former (impacting 30%) than of the latter (17%). In this respect, lower mid-income Russians were closer to low-income Russians, while upper mid-income Russians were closer to those with high income, once again reaffirming the heterogeneous nature of the mid-income strata.

Nevertheless, similar statements about what people save on may refer to qualitatively different processes with varying outcomes—and data confirms this. Even though respondents from the upper mid-income groups claim to have started saving on consumption en masse, it is worth recollecting that their evaluation of their situation with food, clothing, and housing was almost identical both in the spring of 2014 and the fall of 2016 (although the figures did experience a certain downward trend between the two surveys, in the year of 2015). At the same time, they responded quite painfully to the need to cut down on leisure and vacations, which was reflected in the downgrade of the corresponding assessments, since saving on these positions meant changes in their lifestyle.

As we conclude our discussion of consumption patterns typical to mid-income groups, we must point out that the social well-being of the population is impacted not only by the objective indicators of their standards and quality of living, but also by the comparison they draw between their own consumption standard and that of the people around them. Therefore, it is important to note that even during crisis, most members of both the upper and the lower subgroups of the mid-income strata believed that they were not living any worse than others or that the goal of living no worse than others lied well within their capabilities (Fig. 8.4).

Let us summarize. The mid-income population groups are heterogeneous both in terms of their consumption patterns and their relevant capabilities. In some aspects they are closer to one another than to low-income or high-income groups; in others,

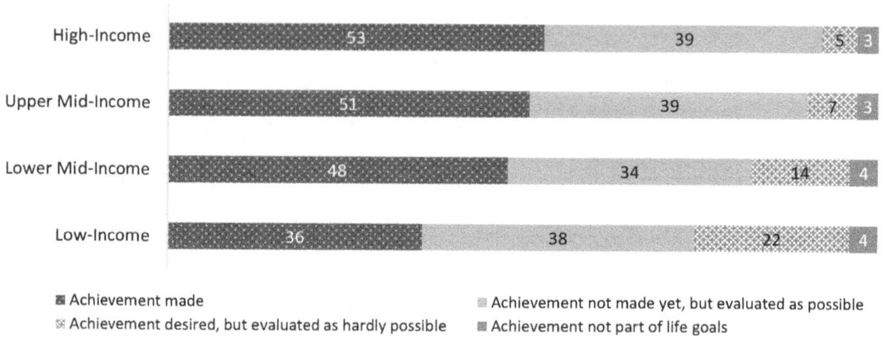

Fig. 8.4 Evaluation of own ability to live no worse than others across various income groups, Fall of 2015, %

by contrast, the lower mid-income group is more similar to the low-income level, while the upper group approaches the high-income level. The position of the lower mid-income group is characterized not only not only by a more modest consumption standard (although far from the standard of survival), but also by greater vulnerability which results in qualitative changes in their consumption habits when crises strike. The status of the upper mid-income group is more favorable (which is reflected, among other things, by the opportunity to enjoy stylized consumption) and characterized by greater stability. The crisis did influence this group's consumption capabilities, but it impacted only those lifestyle aspects that concern stylized consumption and the opportunities to achieve a desired lifestyle.

The mid-income groups' self-assessment of various life aspects linked to consumption has improved greatly over the past decade and a half, which reveals a significant positive trend in its consumption standards compared to the early 2000s. Furthermore, the dynamics of durable goods sets' ownership in households shows that this lifestyle aspect has also improved notably compared to 2003. However, the positive dynamics associated with mid-income groups' consumption patterns has mostly been limited to upgrading the sets of household goods and improving the quality of routine consumption (food, clothing, etc.). The level of more notable achievements in this area remained practically unchanged from 2003 to 2014, and even dropped due to the crisis of 2014–2016. Furthermore, people with middle income are decreasing their investments in human capital which negatively impact their prospects in the long run.

During the crisis, Russians with middle income, just like the rest of the population, actively used various economy strategies, which mostly involved saving on routine consumption, followed by saving on leisure and vacations. Cutting down expenses has also greatly impacted investments into human capital, such as education and healthcare (this type of economy was more typical of Russians from the lower mid-income group than from the upper mid-income group). Even though mid-income respondents use paid healthcare rather actively, the reason for that increasingly turns out to be the lack or inaccessibility of free counterparts far more often than the search for better-quality services, i.e. the respondents are, to an extent, forced to resort to using paid services.

On the other hand, even during an economic recession, mid-income groups keep exhibiting willingness to familiarize themselves with innovative goods, which will facilitate the gradual transfer of these products from the innovative category to the expanded set of basic durable goods for all population.

Svetlana V. Mareeva Head of Center for Stratification Studies at National Research University Higher School of Economics and Leading Researcher at the Federal Center of Theoretical and Applied Sociology of the Russian Academy of Sciences (former Institute of Sociology, Russian Academy of Sciences). Holds Ph.D. in Sociology (2009). Her main areas of interest include social structure, social stratification, middle class, socio-cultural modernization and social policy. Author of over 90 publications, incl. monograph "Middle Class: Theory and Reality" (2009, co-authored, in Russian); chapters in monographs on the results of international projects ("Health and Health Care in the New Russia" (2009), "Handbook on Social Stratification in the BRIC Countries. Change and Perspective" (2013), "People's Dreams in China and in Russia" (2015)); chapters in Russian monographs and articles in scientific journals. Participant of prominent research projects, incl. international, on the problems of the social structure of Russian society, social policy, cultural dynamics and modernization processes.

Chapter 9
Intergenerational Mobility of Middle Income Group in China: A Perspective from Household Registration and Education

Peng Lu and Xiaoguang Fan

9.1 Urban–Rural Segmentation and Reproduction of Education in the Perspective of Intergenerational Mobility

The anxiety of middle income group in China has never been such a hot spot spotlighted by the media like today. It was not only brought upon by the new Internet environment but also the intergenerational solidification of their social status people could feel by themselves. For many, their middle income identity is just achieved in their own generation. To maintain their quite fragile sense of security, the middle income group has over-drafted from expenditures for their middle income lifestyle to housing and children's education—housing in many metropolitans indicates both the holding of urban household registration (hereinafter "*hukou*") and the children's education that may ensure their offspring to urban middle. In short, the intergenerational mobility is a key to understand the middle class' anxiety.

There are basically two main angles or measurements shared by the sociology circle for the investigation of the intergenerational mobility. One is the economic aspect, mainly on the (household) intergenerational mobility of income (Chen and Yuan 2012; Liu and Hu 2014; Wang and Qian 2009; Wang and Li 2012; Wei 2009), with the wealth intergenerational mobility taken into consideration occasionally (Liu

P. Lu (✉)
Institute of Sociology at Chinese Academy of Social Sciences (CASS), Beijing, China

Shanghai Academy, Shanghai, China

X. Fan
Department of Sociology, School of Public Affairs, Zhejiang University, Hangzhou, China

Center for Local Governance Studies, Zhejiang University, Hangzhou, China

P. Li and M. K. Gorshkov (eds.), *The Middle Income Group in China and Russia*, Research Series on the Chinese Dream and China's Development Path,
https://doi.org/10.1007/978-981-16-1464-4_9

and Hu 2014). The other is the social aspect, mainly on the intergenerational mobility of occupations (Li and Zhu 2015; Qin 2011) and education (Li 2002, 2014a; Liu and Fan 2013; Wu 2016; Xin 2016).

No matter the judgment of the rate of intergenerational mobility in China is high or low, most researches have mentioned the key role of the hukou. For those scholars who see a low intergenerational mobility, the hukou is the systematic basis for the reproduction of the urban–rural dual structure, which constitutes the main systematic barrier for the mobility of population and therefore the social integration (Li and Ren 2011; Liu and Fan 2013). Two closed circle loops were formed by the registration system, which further enlarges the already existing urban–rural discrepancy (Yu 2005).

The hukou however sometimes can be changed by individual endeavors. For those scholars who believe the rising trend of the intergenerational mobility, it is an important institutional design so that the Chinese society can maintain its openness to the whole society (Zhang 2004). It has to be admitted that, for many people, especially "the first generation of urban middle class ", to change hukou from rural to urban marks a key step of realizing their intergenerational mobility. Some researchers think that high intergenerational mobility of current rural population and the openness of mobility in cities can be attributed that some well-educated people born with rural *hukou* can gain their city registration household (Wu 2007). Other researchers further point out that major rising paths for the new generation are education, getting a CPC membership and getting employed in a state organ (Yang and Lian 2015).

In most case, mobility brought by educational attainment serves the first checkpoint for hukou mobility. As education is found by many researches as the vital variable for realizing upward mobility of an individual, educational attainment is quite influenced by the family background (Zhang et al. 2016). Although some scholars think that more public spending on education enables better intergenerational flow (Li and Zhou 2015; Xu and Yi 2014), it cannot happen automatically by only enlarging higher-education enrollment (Yang 2016). Fair and equal reform in the education system is a key. This, in return, requires the breakthrough of hukou by the flow of education. But the tricky part is: many researchers think that the intergenerational mobility of education is going downward (Li 2014b; Liu 2005; Liu and Fan 2013; Tang 2015; Wu 2013, 2016). It is more and more difficult for those rural students to realize upward mobility by gaining higher education (Xin 2016). The above indicated that we have to include the interactive results of education and hukou on intergenerational mobility into the analysis.

In addition to urban–rural discrepancy on education opportunities, whether there is such gap in different sectors (those who work for the government or public sectors and those work in the private sectors) is a noteworthy issue. For instance, although a young person of rural hukou may gain higher social status through education and a middle-class occupation, whether he or she can get an urban hukou still mostly depends on whether he or she works for a state organ.

The paper analyzes relations between hukou and education mobility, between education and sector segmentation of education as well as the correlation of education and hukou. Contrary from many studies that view the hukou and education as either the hindrance or incentives of intergenerational mobility, we make separate analysis of hukou and educational attainment as the result of the mobility above mentioned. In the second and the third parts, we shall first talk about the middle income group's hukou flow, and then the education flow. For each part, we showcase the flow chart first, then make parallel analysis of education, hukou and the system together. And finally, the Goodness-of-Fit tests of hukou and the education for Log-Linear Models shall be provided. Conclusions and discussions shall be carried out in session 4.

This paper uses the data from China Social Survey 2015 (CSS 2015), which was carried out by the Institute of Sociology at Chinese Academy of Social Sciences (CASS). With the method of multi-stage random sampling, the subjects of this survey are the citizens above 18 years old in the urban and rural areas of 30 provincial regions in the China's mainland. The total number of samples is 10,243.

The income median value is used as reference to define different levels of class positions. People whose incomes is below 0.75 times of the median are defined as the low income group, while those whose income is between 0.75 times and 1.25 times (included) of the median is defined as the lower middle income group. Those whose income between 1.25 times and 2 times of the median is the upper middle income group and those whose values are above 2 times of the median is the high income group.

9.2 Intergenerational Mobility of Hukou

Hukou mobility is the generational discrepancy of hukou. According to the statistics, among those middle income group whose parental generation hold agricultural type of hukou, 85.52% still fall in the agricultural category, with only 15.48% of them acquire non-agricultural category; 89% of those whose parental generation hold a non-agricultural type remained the identity by their parental generation, with the rest of approximately 10% holding agricultural identity (refer to Fig. 9.1.) Those analysis indicates that the inflow and outflow are pretty low for either the non-agricultural and agricultural household types. The flow shows both evident intergenerational transmission or social reproduction.

Table 9.1 is about the hukou distribution of middle income group with different educational attainment. For those middle income residents who receive education of primary school or lower, 90.58% of their parental household hold the agricultural household type, which is 80% percent higher than those peers of the non-agricultural household type; more than 80% (82.82%) of the filial generation hold the agricultural household type, which is 60% higher than those of those peers of non-agricultural household type. For those middle income residents who receive junior high school education, 78.17% of their parental generation hold agricultural household type and 21.83% hold non-agricultural household type; correlated filial generation hold the above household types respectively 67.25% and 32.75%. For those who receive senior high school education, 55.74% of their parental generation hold the agricultural household type, which is approximately 10% more than the non-agricultural

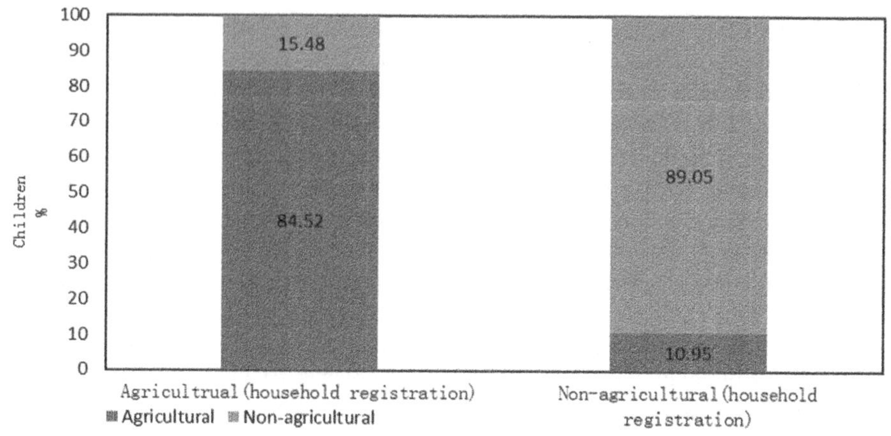

Fig. 9.1 Hukou flow of middle income group

household type; however, the percentage of agricultural household type is lower than those non-agricultural household type for the filial generation, which forms a strong contrast against those groups who receive junior high school education or even below. For those middle income group who attended junior colleges or higher schools, their parental generation who belong to agricultural household type is a little higher than those hold non-agricultural household types. The filial generation who hold non-agricultural household type is twice of those who hold agricultural household type.

As for the index of dissimilarity, only when more than 20% of middle income group (from all educational attainment) whose parental generation changed their hukou type, can the equal percentage of hukou be realized. Or, the equal distribution can be realized when almost 19% of middle income group (from all educational attainment) has filial generation to changed their hukou type.

To further analyze the flow discrepancy of hukou, we make the following definition: if the parental and the filial generations share the same hukou type, this can be treated as a stable or smooth flow; otherwise they shall be treated as an upward or downward flow. Given the cities in China have been long enjoying the biased resources allocation, in most cases, people value more their non-agricultural identification than the agricultural one. Therefore, the conversion of an agricultural to a non-agricultural identify shall be defined as an upward flow while the other conversion shall be defined as the downward flow.

Table 9.2 shows the study of household mobility and education segmentation. For those middle income group with stable agricultural hukou (the agricultural one for both filial and parental generations), 9.24% of the filial generation receive junior college education or higher, 75% of the filial generation receive junior high school education or below and 15.2% receive senior high school education; for those middle income group with stable non-agricultural hukou, more than 30% percent (31.82%) receive junior college education or higher, and only 32.15% receive junior high school or below.

Table 9.1 Marginal distribution of hukou distribution of residents with different educational attainment (in: %)

	Primary school and below		Junior high school		Senior high school		Junior college		Δ
	Agricultural	Non-agricultural	Agricultural	Non-agricultural	Agricultural	Non-agricultural	Agricultural	Non-agricultural	
Parental generation	90.58	9.42	78.17	21.83	55.74	44.26	52.67	47.33	20.56
Filial generation	82.82	17.18	67.25	32.75	41.77	58.23	30.91	69.09	18.72

Note Δ is the index of dissimilarity of hukou in terms of educational attainment

Table 9.2 Education division of Hukou flow of middle income group (in: %)

Filial generation (agricultural)					
Parental generation		Primary school	Junior high school	Senior high school	Junior college
	Agricultural	31.01	44.56	15.20	9.24
	Non-agricultural	17.33	56.00	16.00	10.67
	Filial (non-agricultural)				
		Primary school	Junior high school	Senior high school	Junior college
	Agricultural	9.70	28.36	27.61	34.33
	Non-agricultural	6.01	26.14	36.04	31.82

For those who move downward (filial generation are agricultural hukou and parental generation are non-agricultural), those who receive junior middle school education have the highest share, which is more than half. So, the total share of those who received primary school education and junior high school education is beyond 70%, while those who receive junior college education and above is merely 10% plus. For those who move upward (filial generation of non-agricultural hukou and parental generation of agricultural), those receive junior college education and above show the biggest share, with more than 1/3—the reason behind is probably the higher education the filial generation have gone through has altered their hukou type, from an agricultural one to a non-agricultural one.

Table 9.3 analyzes the sector segmentation of hukou flow. For those middle income group who has been through the horizontal "agricultural to agricultural" flow, 94.19% of them are working in the private sector, and only 5.81% work in the governmental or public; for those middle income group who has been through the horizontal "non-agricultural to non-agricultural" flow, more than 70% (71.84%) of them are working in the private sector, and more than a quarter (28.16%) work in the governmental or public sector. For those middle income group who has been through the upward "agricultural to non-agricultural" flow, 30.22% of them are working in the governmental or public sector; for those middle income group who has been through the downward "non-agricultural to agricultural" flow, 11.84% of them are working in the governmental or public sector; In all, those middle income group who has been through the upward hukou flow enjoy a higher employment rate in the governmental

Table 9.3 Sector segmentation of hukou mobility of middle income group (In: %)

		Filial generation			
		Agricultural		Non-agricultural	
		State owned	Private	State owned	Private
Parental generation	Agricultural	5.81	94.19	30.22	69.78
	Non-agricultural	11.84	88.16	28.16	71.84

or public sector; those who has been through the downward flow only show higher employment percentage the governmental or public sector than those who get their agricultural hukou from their parental generation.

The following is the research on the segmentation of hukou mobility of middle income group As in Table 9.4, we use the independent model (Model 1) as the starting point and adjust the other models one by one. An association item of parental hukou with educational attainment is added to Model 2; an association item of educational attainment and filial hukou is added to Model 3; an association item of parental-filial hukou is added to Model 4; association items of parental household with educational attainment and filial household with educational attainment are added to the Model 5; based on Model 5, the association item of parental-filial hukou is added to Model 6. G^2 of Model 1 is 1686.16, with 34.06% error recognition of the samples. BIC is 1608.25. Of Models 2–Model 4, Model 4 showcases the lowest unexplained variance and relatively small BIC. Model 1–Model 5 show significant difference from the original contingency table ($p < 0.000$). Only Model 6 shows no significant difference. With the goodness of fit comparison, there is no significant difference between Model 4 and Model 5, while the former is pretty simple. As there is significant difference between Model 6 and Model 4 at the same time, when combined with BIC value, Model 6 is the optimal model. Therefore, when the parental hukou is controlled, the filial educational attainment is associated with the hukou and does not change with the parental hukou; when the filial hukou is controlled, the parental hukou is associated with the filial hukou and does not change with filial educational attainment; when the filial hukou is controlled, the parental hukou is associated with the filial educational attainment and does not change with the filial hukou.

Table 9.4 The goodness-of-fit comparison of log-linear models of hukou mobility and educational attainment

Model	Parameter setting	G^2	df	p	Δ	BIC	Model comparison	rG	rdf	p
1	F, E, S	1686.16	10	0.000	34.06	1608.25	1 versus 2	264.11	3	0.000
2	F, E, S, FE	1422.05	7	0.000	30.80	1367.51	1 versus 3	195.65	3	0.000
3	F, E, S, ES	1226.4	7	0.000	30.05	1171.86	1 versus 4	769.17	3	0.000
4	F, E, S, FS	457.23	9	0.000	19.39	405.10	5 versus 4	505.06	5	> 0.050
5	F, E, S, FE, ES	962.29	4	0.000	24.08	931.12	4 versus 6	454.89	6	0.000
6	F, E, S, FE, ES, FS	2.34	3	> 0.05	0.82	−21.04	–	–	–	–

Note F stands for parental hukou, E stands for filial educational attainment and S stands for filial hukou

Table 9.5 Goodness-of-fit comparison of log-linear models of hukou mobility and employment sector

Model	Parameter setting	G^2	df	p	Δ	BIC	Model comparison	rG	rdf	p
1	F, R, S	1055.36	3	0.000	25.65	1031.98	1 versus 2	25.1	1	0.000
2	F, R, S, FR	1030.26	2	0.000	25.57	1014.67	1 versus 3	34.21	1	0.000
3	F, E, S, RS	1021.15	2	0.000	24.15	1005.56	1 versus 4	938.2	1	0.000
4	F, E, S, FS	117.16	2	0.000	4.68	101.57	1 versus 5	47.64	2	0.000
5	F, E, S, FR, RS	1007.72	1	0.000	23.81	999.92	4 versus 5	890.56	1	> 0.050

Note F stands for parental hukou, R stands for filial employment sector and S stands for filial hukou

Table 9.5 is the analysis of the goodness-of-fit of log-linear models of the hukou mobility and the employment sector. According to the statistics, there is 25.65% error recognition of the samples in Model 1, Model 2 and Model 3 have the similar index of dissimilarity, while Model 4 has only 4.68% error recognition with its degree of freedom standing at 2, which is much smaller than all other Model's goodness of fit; the comparison of BIC has no difference with the coefficient of variation. Cross-model comparison indicates that there is no significant difference between Model 4 and Model 5. But Model 4 is the optimal one when sticking to the principle of parsimony. Therefore, the employment sector is independent of the parental and filial hukou while the parental and filial hukou correlate with each other.

9.3 Intergenerational Mobility of Education

Similar to hukou mobility, education mobility refers to the intergenerational change of education attainment. For the filial generation whose parental receive primary school education or below, 30.59% receive primary school education, 42.23% junior high school education, 8.05% senior high school education, and a mere 9.13% receive college education or above. For the filial generation whose parental receive junior high school education, only 9.44% receive primary school education or below, while more than half receive senior high school education, college education or above. For filial generation whose parental generation receive junior high school, primary school education or below, those whose parental education is senior high school, junior college or above enjoy an evident advantage. For instance, nearly 70% of the offspring whose parental generation receive senior high school education have the educational attainment of senior high school or above, and as high as 79% of the offspring whose parental generation who receive junior college education or above have the educational attainment of junior college education or above. According to the statistics, the general mobility rate is 67.59%, the upward mobility rate is

60.40% and the downward mobility rate is 7.19%. This indicates that the dominant education flow of the middle income group is upward, which is a strong contract to the reproduction mode of hukou flow.

Table 9.6 shows the descriptive statistics of sector segmentation of educational attainment. Of those filial generation who work in the governmental or public sector, nearly 50% of their parental generation receive primary school education, 26.82% junior high school education, 21.28% senior high school and 5.25% junior college education or above; while of these working in such sector, as high as 45.64% of them receive junior college education or above, 28.64% and 19.69% of them separately hold senior and junior high school education. A minimum of 6.04% receive primary school education. Of those filial generation who work in the private sector, over 60% of their parental generation receive primary school education, 21.72% junior high school education, 10.78% senior high school and only 2.54% (which is below 5%) junior college education or above; while of these working in such sector, over 70% of them receive primary school or junior high school education. But most of the filial generation receive primary school education, rather than the primary school education that dominates their parental educational attainment.

Table 9.7 analyzes the sector segmentation of education flow. For those filial generation who work in the governmental or public sector, 41.51% of them receive junior college education or above as their parental generation receive primary school education. The percentage is lower than that of those whose parental generation receive other education. For those filial generation who work in the private sector, primary school (33.62%)/junior high school (40.28%) education dominate those whose parental education attainment shows the same distribution. Filial generation work in the private sector share the educational attainment distribution with their parental generation who receive senior high school education, junior college education or above. The comparison indicates that the education mobility for those who work in the governmental or public sector is mainly upward and the education mobility for those work in the private sector tend to share the education attainment with their parental generation.

Table 9.8 analyzes the hukou segmentation of education flow. For those who hold agricultural hukou, 29.10% of the offspring whose parental generation attend primary school still receive their primary school education, and the education percentages of the junior high school, senior high school, junior college and above are respectively 45.03%, 30.16% and 33.33%; these who hold agricultural hukou show low percentage of senior high school education and above when the parental generation attend primary or junior high school. For those who hold non-agricultural hukou, the "transmitted" educational attainment of primary, junior high school, senior high school and junior college are separately 10.85%, 18.46%, 32.70% and 61.11%; compared with those who hold agricultural hukou, the filial generation shows higher percentages of senior high school education and above when their parental generation received primary school and junior high school. The comparison indicates that the education flow for those agricultural hukou holders is mainly downward and those non-agricultural hukou holders, mainly upward.

Table 9.6 Marginal distribution of educational attainment of residents with different employment sectors (In: %)

State owned					Private				
	Primary school	Junior high school	Senior high school	Senior college or above	Primary school	Junior high school	Senior high school	Senior college or above	Δ
Parental generation	46.65	26.82	21.28	5.25	64.95	21.72	10.78	2.54	21.27
Filial generation	6.04	19.69	28.64	45.64	34.32	38.65	18.66	8.37	22.32

Note Δ is the index of dissimilarity of educational attainment in terms of hukou

Table 9.7 Sector division of education flow of middle income group (In: %)

Filial generation		State owned				Private			
		Primary school	Junior high school	Senior high school	Senior college or above	Primary school	Junior high school	Senior high school	Senior college or above
Parental generation	Primary school	6.29	24.53	27.67	41.51	33.62	44.44	16.85	5.09
	Junior high school	2.17	9.78	30.43	57.61	11.01	40.28	27.4	21.31
	Senior high school	-	9.59	30.14	60.27	7.55	30.19	32.08	30.19
	Senior college or above	-	11.11	11.11	77.78	4.08	20.41	28.57	46.94

Table 9.8 Hukou segmentation of education flow of middle income group (in: %)

Filial generation		Agricultural				Non-agricultural			
		Primary school	Junior high school	Senior high school	Senior college or above	Primary school	Junior high school	Senior high school	Senior college or above
Parental generation	Primary school	39.10	44.90	11.30	4.70	10.85	36.03	33.72	19.40
	Junior high school	11.49	45.03	22.98	20.50	5.64	18.46	36.41	39.49
	Senior high school	10.32	39.68	30.16	19.84	1.89	13.21	32.70	52.20
	Senior college or above	16.67	33.33	16.67	33.33	-	14.81	24.07	61.11

Table 9.9 Goodness-of-fit comparison of log-linear models of education mobility and hukou

Model	Parameter setting	G^2	df	p	Δ	BIC	Model comparison	rG	rdf	p
1	F, H, S	880.46	24	0.000	24.23	694.68	1 vs 2	126.27	3	0.000
2	F, H, S, FH	754.19	21	0.000	22.30	591.63	1 vs 3	301.34	3	0.000
3	F, H, S, HS	452.85	21	0.000	16.61	290.29	4 vs 3	29.20	6	0.000
4	F, H, S, FS	482.05	15	0.000	19.42	365.94	4 vs 5	155.47	3	> 0.050
5	F, H, S, FH, HS	326.58	18	0.000	13.49	187.24	4 vs 6	467.40	6	0.000
6	F, H, S, FH, HS, FS	14.65	9	0.101	1.79	-55.02	5 vs 6	311.93	9	0.000
7	unidiff	13.70	8	0.080	2.00	-48.3	5 vs 7	312.88	10	0.090

Note F stands for parental educational attainment, H stands for filial hukou and S stands for filial educational attainment

Now we begin the analysis of education flow segmentation of middle income group. As in Table 9.9, we still use the independent model (Model 1) as the starting point and adjust the other models one by one. An association item of parental education with hukou is added to Model 2; an association item of hukou and filial education is added to Model 3; an association item of parental-filial education is added to Model 4; association items of parental household with hukou and filial education with hukou are added to the Model 5; based on Model 5, the association item of parental-filial education is added to Model 6. Model 7 is a log multiplicative modeling. G^2 of Model 1 is 880.46, with 24.23% error recognition of the samples. BIC is 694.68. In Models 2–Model 4, Model 4 showcases the lowest variance and relatively small BIC. Model 1–Model 5 show significant difference from the original contingency table ($p < 0.000$). Only Model 6 and Model 7 show no significant difference. With the goodness of fit comparison, there is no significant difference between Model 4 and Model 5, while the former is even simpler and is therefore optimal. Model 6 showcase the smallest BIC, whose goodness of fit is optimal when compared to that of Model 4 and Model 7. Therefore, when the parental hukou is controlled, the filial educational attainment is associated with the hukou while does not change with the parental educational attainment; when the filial hukou is controlled, the parental educational attainment is associated with the filial educational attainment and does not change with filial hukou; when the filial educational attainment is controlled, the parental educational attainment is associated with the filial hukou and does not change with the filial educational attainment.

Table 9.10 Goodness-of-fit comparison of log-linear models of education mobility and employment sector

Model	Parameter setting	G^2	df	p	Δ	BIC	Model comparison	rG	rdf	p
1	F, R, S	748.19	24	0.000	21.27	562.35	1 vs 2	49.39	3	0.000
2	F, R, S, FR	698.80	21	0.000	20.91	536.19	1 vs 3	287.02	3	0.000
3	F, R, S, RS	411.78	21	0.000	16.42	249.18	3 vs 4	62.13	6	0.000
4	F, R, S, FS	349.65	15	0.000	11.77	233.50	5 vs 4	12.75	3	0.005
5	F, E, S, FR, RS	362.40	18	0.000	14.32	223.02	5 vs 6	351.42	9	0.000
6	F, E, S, FR, RS, FS	10.98	9	0.277	1.76	-58.71	5 vs 7	4.28	10	0.570
7	unidiff	6.70	8	0.680	1.00	-55.30				

Note F stands for parental educational attainment, R stands for filial employment sector and S stands for filial educational attainment

Table 9.10 is the analysis of the goodness-of-fit of log-linear models of the education flow and the employment sector. According to the statistics, there is 21.27% error recognition of the samples in Model 1, Model 2 and Model 3 have the similar index of dissimilarity, while Model 4 has only 11.77% error recognition with degree of freedom standing at 15, which is much smaller than all other Models' goodness of fit. Cross-model comparison indicates that there is no significant difference between Model 5 and Model 7. And Model 6 shows no significant difference from the original contingency table ($p > 0.1$), which is optimal when compared with Model 5. So, Model 6 is the optimal model. Therefore, there is association between employment sector and both the parental and filial educational attainment while the parental and filial educational attainment correlate with each other.

9.4 Conclusions and Discussions

This paper employ data from China Social Survey 2015 (CSS 2015) to carry out exploratory investigation on hukou and education in intergenerational mobility. In terms of hukou, social reproduction is dominant regardless types of the hukou. But it is noteworthy that in terms of education, most middle income group people have an upward mobility, which casts a strong contrast against reproduction of hukou mobility.

We do not want to deny the existence and enhancement of education reproduction. But interestingly enough, at least for some middle income group member, the hukou is still a strong barrier, while education mobility is relatively a feasible solution. Evidently, education serves an important mechanism for the younger generation to improve their social status.

The tricky part is, the future vision can be reversed for the next generation: with the ever-stronger barrier of education reproduction, the barrier of hukou is getting eased in recent years. This is both manifested by years of faster income growth of the rural residents than that of the urban residents (Li and Zhu 2015), and the receded or even abolished urban–rural hukou by some local governments, which is attracting more migrant population into these cities. For the intergenerational mobility in the future, just like the expanded enrollment of higher education that would not have necessarily brought upon intergenerational mobility, the active improvement of public goods supplies as well as the promotion of international mobility stay the key to the issue.

Education can serve as the lubricant of intergenerational mobility due to the payoff of human capital on the labor market. The paper finds that the younger generation whose parental generation has little education capital tend to go to the state sector when they achieve upward education flow; and the middle income group who has been through the upward hukou mobility show even higher employment percentage in the governmental and public sector. The employment percentage in the state sector of the downward mobility generation is only higher than those younger generation who share the agricultural hukou with their parental generation. This may as well explain the importance of fair talent systems, especially that of the civil servant system. Simultaneously, when the hukou is getting loose, the key to promote the intergenerational mobility lies in the labor market.

Currently, the GDP per capita in China is estimated to be over USD 8500, and is heading toward the very threshold of USD 10,000. In this process, whether China can overcome the middle income trap has become a hot spot for top government leaders, the academic circles and the media. The consensus is to keep the momentum of national income increase and an open society under fair systems; in such as society, ascribed barrier (such as the hukou) should be naturalized and the acquired achievements (such as the individual educational attainment and skills) should be boosted. More importantly, the correlation between the two factors (such as household and education) shall be lowered to break the intergenerational transmission barrier in both the urban–rural discrepancy of education and the sector segmentation of hukou.

References

Chen L, Yuan Z (2012) To teach one how to fish rather than just offering one a fish?—Wealth capital, social capital, human capital and intergenerational mobility in China. Fudan J (Social Sciences Edition) 4

Li L (2002) Institutional transformation and changes in stratification structure—continued reproduction of the pattern of relative relations among social strata. Social Sciences in China 6

Li L (2012) Institutional transformation and changes in stratification structure—continued reproduction of the pattern of relative relations among social strata. Social Sciences in China 6

Li C (2014a) The trending of education inequality 1930–2010—re-investigation on urban-rural inequality of education opportunities. Sociological Studies 2

Li C (2014b) Education experience and inequality of opportunity for Post-80s in China—also comment on quiet revolution (Wusheng De Geming, Liang Chen et al.). Social Sciences in China 4
Li L, Zhou G (2015) Household loan restrictions, public education expenditures and social mobility. China Econ Q 14(1)
Li T, Ren Y (2011) Reform of urban hukou and social integration of floating population. South China Popul 26(3)
Li P, Zhu D (2015) Endeavor to form an olive-shaped distribution pattern—Based on the statistics from Chinese General Social Survey 2006–2016. Social Sciences in China 1
Liu J (2005) The state, social class and education. China Renmin University Press, Beijing
Liu Z, Fan Y (2013) Analysis of influencing factors on educational generational mobility. J Edu Sci 1
Liu J, Hu Y (2014) Study of intergenerational transmission of residents' income based on household wealth capital. Zhejiang Finance 9
Qin G (2011) Intergenerational mobility and discrimination against out-group: an empirical study based on statistics from Chinese General Social Survey 2005. Chin J Sociol 4
Tang J (2015) Underprivileged starting line of life—re-discussion of educational inequality in Chinese society. Sociol Studies 3
Wang Y, Qian Z (2009) Literature review of measurement bias of income intergenerational flow. Product Res 21
We Y (2009) Study of intergenerational income flow and income inequality. China Financial and Economic Publishing House, Beijing
Wu X (2007) Hukou and intergenerational occupation flow. Sociol Studies 6
Wu Y (2013) Education streaming system and education stratification in China. Sociol Studies 4
Wu X (2016) Current higher education in China, the formation of elite and the social stratification—primary finds of Beijing College Students Panel Survey (BCSPS). Chin J Sociol 3
Xin K (2016) Urban-rural discrepancy of intergenerational flow of education in China. J Southwestern Univ Finance Econ
Xu J, Yi X (2014) Will the increase of public education expenditures mitigate influence from the "second generation" issue?—an analysis of intergenerational income mobility based on the China Health and Nutrition Survey, CHNS. J Finance Econ 11
Yang Z (2016) Is the intergenerational mobility improved by expanded enrollment of higher education? Chin J Sociol 6
Yang Y, Lian Y (2015) A dynamic analysis of social intergenerational mobility in China—empirical evidence from pooled cross-section data of CGSS (Chinese General Social Survey) and CLDS (China Labor-force Dynamics Survey). Manage World 4
Yu X (2005) Reproduction of urban-rural dual structure—an analysis of the education policy between 1978 to the end of 1990s. Res Educ Dev 4
Zhang Y (2004) The attainment of chinese social status: class succession and intra-generational mobility. Sociol Studies 4
Zhang G, Zhang D, Zhou W (2016) Effects of multi-generational mobility: an evidence from China. Chin J Sociol 3

Peng Lu is now an associate professor at Institute of Sociology, Chinese Academy of Social Sciences. He earned his Ph.D. degree in sociology at Tsinghua University in 2010, plus a visiting student experience at Yale University from 2007–2008. He worked at New York University Abu Dhabi (NYUAD) as a postdoctoral research fellow from 2011 to 2012. He works in the fields of social stratification and class analysis, business-government relationship, Chinese entrepreneurship, and comparative studies in post-communist and new emerging economies.

Xiaoguang Fan associate professor of the Department of Sociology in Zhejiang University, Ph.D. He was the winner of Sixth ISA Worldwide Competition for Junior Sociologists. His primary research interests are social stratification and mobility and political sociology. Major publication includes Permeability of Boundaries and Inequality, Discordance between Subjective and Objective Social Class in Contemporary China.

Chapter 10
Intergenerational Mobility of Middle Income Groups and the Role of Family in This Process

Y. P. Lezhnina

A significant part of the social structure analysis is the study of social mobility nature. The beginning of the transformational period which Russia entered more than a quarter of a century ago was associated with the emergence of new instruments and channels of social mobility. Under these circumstances the intergenerational dynamics of social status was conditioned by the situation of Russian citizens' parents to a lesser extent. Strengthening the meritocratic principles of social and economic life organization in the society and gradual normalization of the institutional environment by the mid-2000s led to the fact that in the context of generations upward social mobility exceeded the downward one, although the preservation of the parents' social status remained the dominating trend of social dynamics. Thus, in 2006, when referring to their own situation, just under half of Russians (42%) noted that their status corresponded to the parents' one, while one third (35%) evaluated it as a higher one compared to their parents' situation in the same age, and only 23% evaluated it as a lower one.[1]

However, the population of the country has faced several economic crises over the past 10 years (in 2008–2009 and 2014–2016). Economic restructuring had generally come to an end before the crisis of 2008–2009, which led to the disappearance of many means of social mobility. As a consequence, Russians' evaluation of their own status compared to the situation of the family they grew up in was generally lower: in

[1] Hereinafter, the data for 2006 is given according to the study "Social Inequality and Public Policy", carried out by the Institute of Sociology of the Russian Academy of Sciences in April–May 2006. The selection included 1750 respondents, who represented the Russian population by gender, age, settlement type and region. For more information, please refer to: https://www.isras.ru/analytical_report_Social_inequality_0.html.

Y. P. Lezhnina (✉)
HSE University, Institute of Sociology of FCTAS RAS, Moscow, Russia

P. Li and M. K. Gorshkov (eds.), *The Middle Income Group in China and Russia*, Research Series on the Chinese Dream and China's Development Path,
https://doi.org/10.1007/978-981-16-1464-4_10

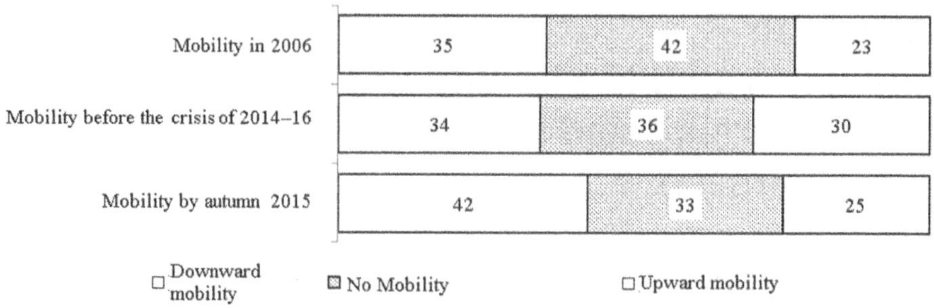

Fig. 10.1 The nature of Russians' intergenerational mobility and the impact of 2014–2016 crisis on it, IS RAS, 2006, 2015, %

autumn 2015[2] 42% of Russians referred to their downward intergenerational mobility and only a quarter referred to the upward one, while one third (33%) noted the lack of the relevant dynamics.[3] Even if we consider the situation before the crisis of 2014–2016, with its greater overall favorableness than at the time of crisis, the share of those who faced downward intergenerational mobility was higher at that period than the share of those who had a higher social status compared to their parents (34% and 30% respectively according to the Russians' self-assessment in 2014), with a very slight prevalence of those who did not show any intergenerational dynamics of social status (36%) (Fig. 10.1). *Thus, the social and economic transformations during the last decade led to the reduced opportunities of the population in terms of upward intergenerational mobility.*

It is worth mentioning that compared to upward mobility the downward one has a wider scope not only in terms of the covered population of Russia, but also in the distance of this mobility. The main distance within which upward intergenerational mobility is realized almost entirely lies in the range of adjacent social groups: 96% of Russians who evaluated their current situation on a 10-point scale as a higher one compared to their parents' status set this difference within 3 points, while the most of them (60%) set it within only one point. The correlation between Russians with a long-distance (difference is more than 3 points) and a short-distance (1–3 points) downward mobility did not seem so dramatic and was fivefold (7% and 35% respectively).

All of the above means that, on the one hand, the Russian population has currently limited opportunities of upward social mobility, and on the other hand, the deterrents of downward dynamics in social status and moving down the social scale do not work

---

[2] Hereinafter, unless stated otherwise, the data of the third wave of IS RAS Monitoring, carried out in autumn 2015, is provided. The selection included 4000 respondents, who represented the adult population of Russia by gender, age, settlement type and region.

[3] The nature of social mobility is defined by means of comparing the social status of Russians according to their self-assessment and the situation of the family they grew up in on a 10-point scale.

well. Such situation mainly developed before the social and economic crisis of 2014–2016. The crisis in its turn had a negative impact both on the nature of social mobility and its distance, having somewhat exacerbated the status of almost all Russians.

Social reproduction of parents' status in only a third of cases indicates that the Russian society has a relatively open character and the boundaries between social groups within this society are relatively transparent. However, the dominance of downward social dynamics in the society makes us talk about "hatches" of social mobility that mainly lead downwards, rather than "social lifts" with equal opportunities to move in both directions.

In general, the intergenerational status dynamics of Russians over the age of 55 years is the most unfavorable: only 18–21% of them referred to a higher social status compared to their parents and about a half of them (47–54%) referred to a lower one. It is largely due to the fact that these people are generally retired, and in modern Russia retirees have already become a traditionally vulnerable group as opposed to the USSR.

The population of middle working age (26–55 years) feels their advantage over the parents slightly more often than the older generation, although their evaluation of intergenerational mobility as the downward one prevails over the positive evaluation as well (39–43% and 27–30% respectively). Young people under 26 years, who are not yet largely separated from their parents' households, refer to intergenerational reproduction of social status more frequently than others (43–45%). *Thus, intergenerational social mobility of the Russian population is largely determined not only by the efforts of the population itself (children and their parents), but also by the fact that the succession of generations took place against transformation of the economic life in the country and the system of functioning means of social mobility, as well as fundamental change of the social structure.*

Nevertheless, it is expectable that Russians are to some extent hostages of their parents' status: the higher it was the lower their chances of upward social mobility and the higher the risks of the downward one are. Thus, the majority (58%) of those who evaluated their parents' status with 1–3 points out of 10 showed upward social mobility, while only 31% of those who evaluated it with 4–5 points showed the same result. Russians whose parents have a relatively high status (6–7 and 8–10 points) showed a significant prevalence of downward social mobility (56% and 65% respectively).

Under these circumstances in nearly half of the cases the status of low-income population groups is the result of downward mobility, which is also true for the representatives of lower middle income groups. The social status of more economically advantaged groups is almost equally the result of both upward and downward social mobility, as well as the lack of it (Table 10.1).

The situation of the most well-off income groups is mostly the result of a higher status compared to their parents one (32 and 38% for upper middle income and high-income groups). Those who evaluate their status as lower than the parents' one (49 and 45% for low-income and lower middle income groups) prevail within less privileged income groups. The shares of those who had preserved the same social status as their parents made up about a third in all groups.

Table 10.1 The nature of intergenerational mobility in different income groups of Russians, IS RAS, 2015, %

Intergenerational mobility type	Low-income	Lower middle income	Upper middle income	High-income
Long-distance downward mobility (4 and more points)	10	6	5	3
Short-distance downward mobility (1–3 points)	**39**	**39**	28	28
No mobility	30	32	**35**	31
Short-distance upward mobility (1–3 points)	20	22	31	**33**
Long-distance upward mobility (4 and more points)	1	1	1	5

The representatives of low-income and lower middle income groups generally evaluated the status of their parents in the same way: the average point for their social status was 5.59 and 5.57 respectively (median results—5 points). The share of those who evaluated the parents' status with 6–10 points out of 10 made up less than a half (48–49%) in both groups. At the same time the representatives of these income groups differentiated their own status quite clearly: the average points were 4.73 and 5.64 respectively. *Thus, low-income and lower middle income groups consist of people from a similar social and economic environment, who have currently reached a certain status in adjacent social groups, while some of theme were slightly more successful than others.*

In upper middle income and high-income groups the evaluation of parents' status was slightly different from the corresponding evaluation in less well-off groups, reaching 5.82 and 6.13 respectively (median was 6 points). The share of those who attributed their parents to the 6th–10th levels of the social scale made up 52% and 59% respectively. These groups representatives' evaluation of their own status differed much more noticeably amounted to and 5.03 and 6.22 points respectively. This means that the environment the representatives of upper middle income and high-income groups came from was generally the same as well, and some of these people were more successful than others.

The average distance of intergenerational dynamics was positive only for high-income groups amounting to 0.11 (on a 10-point scale); in other groups it varied from −0.18 for upper middle income to −0.86 for low-income groups. At the same time, during the crisis period, the differentiation between these groups in terms of intergenerational mobility characteristics only increased—the declining income of Russians directly affected their ability to maintain their social and economic status. Thus, from the beginning of 2014 to the autumn of 2015 the Russians' evaluation of

Table 10.2 Russians' income status depending on education level of their parents, IS RAS, 2015, %

Income group	Not higher than general secondary education	Secondary professional or incomplete higher education	Higher education
Low-income	43	35	19
Lower middle income	37	34	32
Upper middle income	15	23	31
High-income	5	8	18

their own place in the society varied from −0.43 for low-income to −0.13 for high-income groups (−0.36 and −0.28 for less and more well-off categories of middle income groups). In addition, the share of those who faced a decline in their social and economic status during the crisis according to their self-assessment on a 10-point scale exceeded one third in low-income and lower middle income groups (33–37% with 24–31% in other groups).

It is worth mentioning that the differentiation between the current status of various groups representatives with a similar integral social status of the parents was influenced by the education level of their parents' families. Thus, if in low-income groups the parents' education level in most cases[4] did not exceed general secondary education (45%), the shares of parents among lower middle income who had general secondary (or lower) and secondary professional (or incomplete higher) education both amounted to 38%. 15% and 24% of representatives' parents in these income groups respectively received higher education. As for other income groups, the dominating type of parents' education in upper middle income groups was secondary professional, which was comparable to a higher one in prevalence (39% and 37% respectively); the Russians' parents in high-income groups had higher education in almost half of the cases (48%). *Thus, the parents' education level has an impact on the Russians' income status* (Table 10.2). However, regardless of the parents' education level, a third of Russians reproduced their social and economic status, a quarter showed upward mobility, and the rest (40–44%) were characterized by downward mobility, which once again confirms the openness of the Russian society, but more in the terms of downward subjective social dynamics.

Naturally, the higher the status of parents in the society, the more difficult it is to surpass them. Therefore, in middle income groups a "fine" for the parents' higher education is reduced chances of upward intergenerational mobility—22% with 27–31% of Russians whose parents had a lower education level. At the same time this "fine" also exists in upper and lower middle income groups—27% and 17% of them respectively had a higher status compared to their parents with 32–41% and 23–27% of those whose parents received education of other levels. However, as we can see, the value of this "fine", which is inevitable, should not be underestimated.

[4] This refers to the highest education level among parents.

Table 10.3 Russians' mobility vector depending on correlation between their own and parents' education levels, IS RAS, 2015, %

Intergenerational mobility vector	Lower education level than that of parents	The same education level as that of parents	Higher education level than that of parents
Long-distance downward mobility	4	7	7
Short-distance downward mobility	35	**36**	**34**
No mobility	**37**	34	31
Short-distance upward mobility	23	22	26
Long-distance upward mobility	1	1	2

Perhaps, the most interesting result of our analysis is the conclusion that getting education has not only ceased to play a role of a "social lift" for intergenerational mobility for Russians, but it also does not deter downward social dynamics. Those Russians whose education level is not lower than that of their parents have higher chances of downward social mobility compared to chances of improving or preserving the social status of the parents' family (Table 10.3). Getting education of a lower level allows to preserve the parents' status as well as increasing of education status does. Moreover, the education level which is not lower than that of the parents does not guarantee similar working positions under the conditions of economic life change and ongoing transformation of working relations system over the past 25 years. *Thus, in the context of the massive spread of higher education in Post-Soviet Russia and the consequent devaluation of its values, the "rent" on cultural capital in the interpretation of P. Bourdieu*[5]*(parents' education) appears to be higher for modern Russians than the "rent" on their human capital (their own education). And this means the processes of social reproduction become more active and the social structure of the Russian society will become less open in the long term.*

Thus, the resources of the families modern Russians grew up in set certain limits for their future opportunities, although they are still transparent enough. In addition, a relatively high parents' social status does not "launch" upward mobility of their children, and also becomes a kind of "high basis", which is rarely incremented by Russians. At the same time a "low basis" is an incentive and a factor of upward intergenerational mobility. In middle income population groups, where the parents' situation in terms of social and economic status and education level has an intermediate character compared to the polar income groups, this "basis" has a middle level and thus barely affects intergenerational dynamics opportunities.

It is worth mentioning that the characteristics of the Russians' own families rather than the parents' ones play a significant role in social status dynamics as well. They can act both as deterrents and catalysts of their social status dynamics. Family is a

[5] Bourdieu (2001).

traditionally terminal value for the representatives of all groups within the Russian society,[6] and consequently it is an integral attribute of everyday life. Moreover, according to the 2016 data of IS RAS, starting a family and childbearing[7] determine the success in Russians' life (56%) and goes ahead of such factors as financial well-being (54%), job and business (50%), and self-realization (45%). In middle income population groups the corresponding situation is fundamentally the same, and family is also the main key element of the success in its representatives' life (56% for upper and 58% for lower middle income groups).

If we talk about the family situation of middle income population groups, it is worth noting that in 2016 the major part of them were married (55–56%) and had relevant obligations of providing economic support to their family. This share was higher than in high-income groups, but lower than in low-income ones (49% and 63% respectively). At the same time the representatives of middle income groups were more likely to include widowed persons and less likely single persons (15% and 15% respectively) than the representatives of the upper category of the same group (5% and 22% respectively), which is connected to the difference between the age of the group representatives'.

On the one hand, the number of relatives living together in the same household in middle income groups (on average 2.65 and 2.62) in 2016 was bigger than in high-income groups (2.21), but on the other hand, it was considerably smaller than within the disadvantaged population (3.18). The number of households, which is smaller than the average one in the country (2.8), indicates that the representatives of these groups have opportunities to separate from the parents' families.

Only the representatives of high-income groups evaluated the relations in their own families in 2016 considerably better than on average: 73% of them referred to them as good ones. In middle income families this indicator amounted to 61–65% (with 57% in low-income groups). 3% of the representatives in middle income groups and 5% in low-income groups referred to them as bad ones.

Regardless of family relations transformation and family ties weakening, which are characteristic of modern societies, family in the broad sense remains the main source of support for Russians in difficult life situations. Thus, according to the 2016 data of IS RAS, in case of serious difficulties, Russians will firstly seek help from their relatives (64%) and only then from their friends or colleagues (46%). At the same time in middle income groups these indicators were at the level of the all-Russian ones: 63–64% and 44–49% respectively. Bad family relations reduce Russians' inclination to seek help from relatives. Thus, in case of good family relations, relatives were seen as a source of help in difficult situation by 67–68% of the

[6] Varlamova (2006); Rossiyskaya povsednevnost v usloviyakh krizisa [Russian everyday life during a crisis]/edited by Gorshkov M. K., Krumm R., Tikhonova N. E.—Moscow: Alpha-M. 2009; Gotovo li rossiyskoye obschestvo k modernizatsii? [Is Russian society ready for modernization?]/edited by Gorshkov M. K., Krumm R., Tikhonova N. E.—Moscow: Ves Mir. 2010, Gurko (2011), Kartseva (2003), Lezhnina (2016), Mitrikas (2004).

[7] Hereinafter, the 2016 data is provided according to the forth wave of IS RAS Monitoring, carried out in spring 2016. The selection included 4000 respondents, who represented the adult population of Russia by gender, age, settlement type and region.

representatives of middle income groups (69% in low-income groups), and in case of bad relations—by 33 and 48% in the upper and lower categories of this group (45%). This means that, *regardless of the declarative family value, family help in middle income groups depends on the situational atmosphere in it*. Such correlation between the availability of help from an extended family and the relations character was not observed among high-income groups, where the deterioration of family relations from good to bad increased the possibility of seeking help from relatives in case of serious life difficulties from 56 to 67%.

In 2016 seeking help from family and friends (18%) was the third most common strategy to overcome prolonged deterioration in the financial situation during the crisis[8] following thrift (54%) and searching for additional earnings (45%) in lower middle income groups (as well as in low-income ones—24%). In case of bad family relations this indicator dropped to 9%. In upper middle income groups the strategy of seeking help from family and friends did not enter the top three strategies[9] (thrift—52%, additional earnings—50%) and was displaced by the job change strategy (22%), although it had a quite similar spread (19%). This represents *the limited availability of instruments for solving financial problems outside the circle of family and friends in lower middle income groups, which brings them closer to low-income ones.*

The downside of the fact that Russians can seek help from relatives is the obligation to support family members if necessary. At the same time they are as strict as possible when it comes to the own household members. As the number of dependents directly affects the per capita income of the family, it is not surprising that in middle income groups dependency ratio had intermediate indicators compared to that of low- and high-income groups. Thus, in 2016 the average share of working persons in the families of upper and lower middle income groups amounted to 0.68 and 0.76 respectively, while in more and less well-off groups it was 0.53 and 0.87 respectively. At the same time, almost a third (29%) in upper and 42% in lower middle income groups had a high[10] or rather high dependency ratio in their families. *A high dependency ratio affects not only the Russians' status, but also the risk of downward social mobility.* Thus, in 2015, for the Russians in whose households the share of not employed family members exceeded three quarters this risk amounted to 54%, while for others it was 38–42%.

With the increase of income, the dependency load reduced both in quantity and diversity. Thus, the average number of dependency types out of 6 considered (the unemployed, disabled persons of groups I and II, chronically ill persons without

---

[8] The study examined such strategies of improving one's financial situation during the crisis as change of job, change of profession, professional skill improvement, renting of dwellings or other property, thrift, additional earnings, belongings sale, moving within Russia, moving abroad, growing food, dishoarding, credit, help from family and friends, as well as from state social welfare bodies, charitable and religious organizations.

[9] Nevertheless, the representatives of high-income groups also regarded help from family and friends as a source of solving financial problems in 14% of cases.

[10] Dependency ratio was calculated as the ratio of working household members to the total number of household members. High dependency ratio includes a range from 0 to 0.33, rather high—from 0.34 to 0.5, rather low—from 0.5 to 0.75, low—from 0.76 to 1.

Table 10.4 Different dependency load types in the households of Russians from various income groups, IS RAS, 2016, %

Nature of dependency load	Low-income	Lower middle income	Upper middle income	High-income
The unemployed	19	6	5	3
Disabled persons of groups I and II	7	5	2	3
Chronically Ill persons without disability	1	1	1	0
Not employed retirees	42	39	21	12
Not employed students	14	13	18	9
Minor children	50	30	21	13
For reference: there are no such dependents	*8*	*23*	*43*	*65*

disability, unemployed retirees, unemployed students, and minor children) amounted to 1.3 in low-income groups, 0.94 and 0.68 in lower and upper middle income groups respectively, and 0.4 in high-income groups. At the same time 24% in low-income groups, 15% and 8% in lower and upper middle income groups respectively, and 4% of high-income groups had more than one dependency type. In general, the diversity of dependency load distinguished low-income groups from those who had it: 7% of its representatives had at least three and 30%—at least 2 dependency types (1–3% and 11–18% in other income groups respectively). However, the dependency load character was more noticeably differentiated in various income groups and had its own peculiarities in middle income groups.

In 2016 only 8% of low-income group representatives did not have dependents of the types mentioned above among their family members. In middle income groups this indicator amounted to 23% and 43% for the lower and upper categories respectively (65% in high-income groups) (Table 10.4).

The dependency load with the unemployed, disabled and chronically ill persons without dependency is present in less than 10% of Russian households, and this indicator is even lower in middle income groups amounting to 6%. At the same time these dependency types are usually accompanied by other family members who do not participate in the economy (they were the only household dependency form in not more than a third of cases).

Minor children are the dependency type that does not concentrate in certain income groups (as well as unemployed students though). At the same time, according to the 2016 data, with the increase of income, the share of households with minor children reduces (Table 10.4). In general, at that time the dependency load included minor children in 37–54% of the Russians' households, burdened by its certain type, regardless of income. This dependency type is the most common in all groups, except the households of lower middle income groups where the share of families

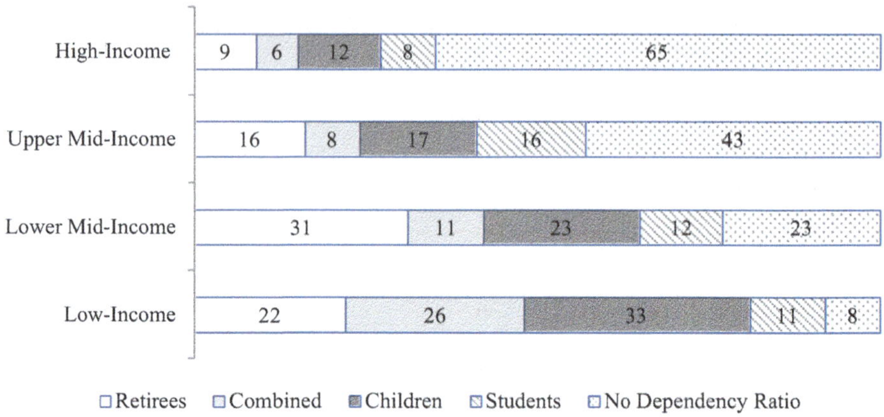

Fig. 10.2 Structure of dependency types in the households of Russians from various income groups, IS RAS, 2016, %

with retirees prevailed (50% among the families having dependency ratio). The share of households with three and more children on the whole amounted to 3% in low-income groups; in other groups this share was much smaller. The share of families with two minor children amounted to 20% in low-income groups (less than 10% in other groups).

18% of Russians living with minor children had not employed retirees in their families. The dependency load with not employed retirees was the most common in low-income and lower middle income groups. At the same time the share of households with 2 and more retirees without work amounted to 15% in low-income groups, 13% and 5% in lower and upper middle income groups respectively, as well as 3% in high-income groups.

Generally, we can distinguish 5 types of households depending on the character of dependency load in them[11]: (1) with no dependency load, with dependency load (2) with only not employed retirees, (3) with mainly children, (4) with mainly students, (5) with a combined dependency ratio (Fig. 10.2). In addition, 16% of households with children dependency load also had not employed retirees among their family members; 18% of households with student dependency load had retirees and 29% had minor children; 67% of households with a combined dependency load had the unemployed, 31% had disabled persons of groups I and II, 7% had chronically ill persons without disability, 31% had unemployed retirees, 11% had students, and 40% had minor children.

A combined dependency load is not only diverse in its structure, but is also associated with large quantities: it was high for 44% of Russians with this type of dependency ratio in their households and rather high for 36% of the representatives. For other dependency types these indicators jointly amounted to 53–65%. A combined

[11] The typology is developed using two-step cluster analysis, a silhouette measure of cohesion and separation is 0.7.

dependency load was the most common in low-income groups (26%). The particularity of lower middle income population groups is the prevalence of retiree dependency load, which has financing in the form of pensions, and upper middle income groups in their turn are characterized by the lack of its clear profile: in this population group dependency load with retirees, students, and minor children was distributed quite equally.

At the same time, the existence of dependency load plays a decisive role for income status: two thirds (65%) of high-income Russians do not have it, and as we move to the groups with lower income the share of unburdened Russians significantly decreases—up to 8% in low-income groups. Nevertheless, children dependency load is also a weighty factor of the economic status lowering, however, the share of this dependency type among the most and the least financially well-off groups differ only 3 times (Fig. 10.2).

Thus, the quantitative dependency load parameters generally affect the Russians' belonging to a certain income group, but at the same time in both categories of middle income groups there is dependency load in the majority of households. As for the nature of dependency load, the situation in lower middle income groups is relatively more balanced, because the dependency load of not employed retirees, i. e. the group supported by state social transfers, roughly corresponds to the total dependency load of students and minor children, which is nominally or by no means supported by the state social instruments. In upper middle income groups the overbalance towards the latter is almost entirely compensated by household resources.

According to the 2015 data, the most critical limiter of social mobility vector is the dependency load by not employed retirees and the unemployed (Table 10.5). More than a half of Russians with this dependents reported their lower social status compered to the parents' one. It is not surprising, because *it is these dependency types that characterize the condition of "family labor resources" and, consequently, the potential of its members to achieve privileged positions in the social structure in terms of both individual and intergenerational mobility.*

Thus, the particularities of the Russians' own family, fist and foremost the characteristics of dependency load when it characterizes the household "labor potential" as a whole or has a very high level, are an important factor of their social mobility.

Other factors of social mobility, especially the upward one, include moving to the locations that are more promising in terms of labor markets. Regardless of the characteristics of the original and host cities, the migrants' situation is quite vulnerable during the period of resettlement at a new location. Thus, in 2015, among those who moved to the current place of residence[12] more than 5 years ago, but not as children with their parents, the share of people showing upward social mobility exceeded the all-Russian one (29–36% depending on the time of moving and 25% respectively). In addition, in middle income groups as a whole "a bonus for moving" 5–10 years ago was maximal—according to their self-assessment, 36% of the representatives were characterized by upward social mobility compared to their parents. However, this "bonus" was one of the lowest for those who moved less than 5 years ago, and

[12] Regardless of the types of the original and host settlement.

Table 10.5 Nature of social mobility depending on dependency load type, IS RAS, 2015, %

Groups with different dependency types	The unemployed	Disabled persons of groups I and II	Chronically Ill persons without disability	Unemployed retirees	Unemployed students	Minor children	For reference: overall pop*ulation*
Long-distance downward mobility	**9**	9	7	**9**	6	6	*7*
Short-distance downward mobility	**41**	38	35	**42**	28	33	*35*
No mobility	31	**37**	33	28	**36**	32	*33*
Short-distance upward mobility	17	16	24	20	**29**	**28**	*24*
Long-distance upward mobility	2	0	1	1	1	1	*1*

upward social mobility in this group was 1.7 times less frequent than the downward one (23% and 42% respectively). *Thus, a 5-year term is a kind of "adaptation period" of Russians at a new location.*

The representatives of different income groups showed equal territorial mobility: 64–71% of them did not change the residence for more or less large settlement, 19–27% moved to larger territorial units, and 7–13%—to smaller ones. On the whole, the change of settlement for a relatively larger one occurred 2–3 times more often than the change for a smaller one in all income groups.

Nevertheless, the importance of territorial mobility for social dynamics, including the intergenerational context, should not be exaggerated. Among the Russians who did not move within the country, as well as those who moved to more or less large settlements, the share of people who showed upward social mobility varied in the range of 25–28%, and 40–45% for the downward one. Moreover, it was among those who moved to a certain settlement during the last 10 years that the share of low-income and lower middle income groups was less than two thirds (60–62% with 66–73% in other groups), and the share of high-income groups exceeded 15%. Only some points gave noticeable differences in social status dynamics depending on moving to a settlement of a fundamentally different type. Thus, for example, the change of residence from the regional center to a smaller settlement reduced the chances of upward intergenerational mobility, which was largely due to the limited working positions in small settlements. Megalopolises, on the contrary, opened to the newcomers relatively large prospects, even compared to their native residents: the possibility of upward social mobility for them amounted to 30% and 20% respectively. First of all, this is due to the fact that newcomers to megalopolises are the most active and promising representatives of the work force from other original settlements.

10 years ago, the nature of social mobility after the migration was also considerably influenced by the conditions of Russians' socialization, including the type of settlement, where they went to school.[13] Thus, the socialization in rural environment limited the mobility prospects outside of it, and the socialization in large settlements served as a supporting factor of upward social dynamics. Currently the territorial particularities of mobility, as well as the family education status, are an indicator of a person's "starting point", in regard to which it is either easier or more difficult to show upward mobility, rather than a factor of social dynamics. Thus, for example, in middle income population groups the socialization in a megalopolis means lower chances of upward mobility: in upper and lower middle income groups the representatives from Moscow and St. Petersburg showed upward social mobility in 13 and 18% of cases respectively, while the socialization in smaller settlements increased these shares up to 22–25% and 32–38% for these categories respectively. *Thus, currently the change of residence is no longer a means of social mobility, including the intergenerational context. Over the past decade, the economic system of the country has developed*

[13] For more information, please refer to: Lezhnina (2008).

in such a way that the territorial imbalances of available jobs and remuneration of labor are smoothed over by the difference in moving costs, cost of living and consumption standards in different settlements.

Let us summarize

From the mid-2000, Russians' perception of their own status dynamics in the intergenerational context has changed fundamentally. If 10 years ago they were more optimistic in their assessments, today the general turbulence in the country's social and economic environment together with the disappearance of "social lifts" has led to their negative perception of this dynamics. At the same time, the system of mechanisms that deter deep status "gaps" of the population, as well as a set of the instruments that support upward social mobility of Russians do not work well. And although the nature of the parents' social status reproduction indicates still existing general openness of the Russian social structure, the dominance of downward social dynamics over the upward one makes us talk not so much about "social lifts" with equal opportunities to move upwards and downwards, but about the widespread distribution of social mobility "hatches" that mainly lead downwards and increasingly dominate over the upward "lifts."

The crisis of 2014–16 revealed the worsened state of "social lifts" even clearly, although this worsening had happened before it began. Nowadays only a half of the population can talk about the correspondence of their and the parents' statuses or about its successful surplus. However, an important factor of negative social status dynamics in the intergenerational context is the fact that the parents of the majority of respondents achieved their status in a different social and economic context. Thus, for example, modern retirees are practically a priori among vulnerable social groups in contrast to the Soviet period.

Middle income groups break up into two categories due to the nature of social mobility, as well as other characteristics of social situation. Lower middle income groups are close to the low-income ones in terms of their mobility vector: their representatives' status is largely the result of downward mobility from similar social and economic "starting points" with the differentiation of the final results of this dynamic. The same is true for upper middle income groups, though their origin is close to high-income groups.

At the same time Russians are a kind of "hostages" of their parents' status in intergeneration mobility: the higher the status of the previous generation is, the more difficult it is to improve it in following generations. Although the parents' education level has a positive impact on achieving privileged positions in the system of income stratification, it can play a role of "high basis" which complicates the chances of upward mobility for the next generations. In addition, the intergenerational education trajectory, including higher education level compared to the parents' one, does not have a definite impact on social mobility, as the meaning of a certain education level and its value for achieving relevant positions in the system of relations of production were different in various historical periods in the life of our country.

Generally, in the context of social dynamics the "rent" on the parents' education is now higher than the "rent" on one's own education, i. e. the role of cultural capital is relatively higher than that of the human one in modern Russia. This can reduce the openness of the Russian social structure in the long term. At the same time parents' family sets certain range for the next generation opportunities, but it does not guarantee relevant positions. All this suggests that, although the Russian social structure can still be classified as an open one, the process of social reproduction in some population groups is on the rise in our country.

Russians' status and their social mobility are influenced both by the parents' and their own family situation. Family serves both as a source of support, and as a system of additional obligations of a person in relation to family members, especially living with him or her. Family ties are generally a reliable source of insurance against social and economic risks for Russians, but in lower middle income groups its use is limited both by the low resources of their families and its dependence on the character of family relations. However, their situation is partially saved by the fact that the households belonging to these groups have a relatively balanced structure of dependency load, although it is rather increased—children and students dependency load, generally unsupported by noticeable social transfers, is balanced with the dependency load of retirees receiving pensions that are to a certain degree comparable to the income of working population. At the same time the scale of dependency load and its nature bring lower middle income groups closer to low-income Russians, rather than to upper middle income groups. In the context of intergenerational social mobility the most critical dependency type is the load which is related to the inclusion of household members in real employment, rather than to their working capacity—not employed retirees and the unemployed are most likely to reduce the chances of positive intergenerational dynamics.

References

Bourdieu P (2001) Forms of capital. In: Granovetter M, Swedberg R (eds) The sociology of economic life, 2nd ed. Westview Press, Boulder

Gurko TA (2011) Institut semyi v postindustrialnykh obshchestvakh [Institute of family in post-industrial societies]. Tsennosti i smysly [Values and Meanings] 4(13):26–44

Kartseva LV (2003) Model semyi v usloviyakh tranformatsii rossiyskogo obschestva [Family model during the transformation of Russian society]. Sotsiologicheskie issledovaniia [Sociol Studies] (7):92–100

Lezhnina YP (2008) Sotsialnye neravenstva i sotsialnaya mobilnost [Social inequality and social mobility]. Sotsialnye neravenstva i sotsialnaya politika v sovremennoy Rossii [Social inequality and social policy in modern Russia]. Nauka, Moscow

Lezhnina YP (2016) Institut semyi v Rossii: na puti transformatsii [Family institution in Russia: on the path of transformation]. Sotsiologicheskaya Nauka i Sotsialnaya Praktika [Sociol Sci Social Practice] (2):70–90

Mitrikas AA (2004) Semya kak tsennost: sostoyaniye i perspektivy tsennostnogo vybora v stranakh Evropy [Family as a value: current status and future possibility of value choice in European countries]. Sotsiologicheskie issledovaniia [Sociol Studies] (5):65–72

Varlamova SN, Noskova AV, Sedova NN (2006) Semya i deti v zhiznennykh ustanovkakh rossiyan [The place of family and children among Russians' life goals]. Sotsiologicheskie issledovaniia [Sociol Studies] (11):61–73

Yulia P. Lezhnina Assistant Professor at the National Research University Higher School of Economics and Senior Researcher at the Federal Center of Theoretical and Applied Sociology of the Russian Academy of Sciences (former Institute of Sociology, Russian Academy of Sciences). Holds Ph.D. in Sociology from the Higher School of Economics (2010). Her main areas of interest include social policy, ageing, socio-demographic modernization, socio-cultural dynamics. Author of over 50 articles and chapters in scientific monographs. Her publications in English include articles "The Family in Value Orientations" in Russian Education and Society (2011), "Sociodemographic Factors Determining the Risk of Poverty and Low-Income Poverty" in Sociological Research (2011), "Socio-demographic characteristics of Poverty" in Sociological Studies (2014). Her recent publications in monographs in Russian are Impact of the Crisis on the position of Social and Demographic Groups of the Population/Russian Society and Challenges of the Time. Book Five. Ed. by Gorshkov M.K. 2017; Main Problems of Everyday Life in Crisis/Russian Society and Challenges of the Time. Book Three. Ed. by Gorshkov M.K. 2016; Family, Love, and Children in Russian People's Dreams and Their Everyday/Lives Dreaming an Ideal Society in Russia and China" Ed. by Gorshkov M.K., Li Peilin. 2016.

Chapter 11
Social Insurance of the Middle Income Group in China

Yi Zhang

As an emerging group, the middle income group was born in the wider context of fully advancing of the reform and opening-up. It is still fragile and weak to a certain extent. In order to ensure each social member of the middle income group to stay in the middle as enduring and stable as they can, it is essential to design a series of social protection networks to prevent them from falling into low-income group. Among social protection network, social insurance should be the most effective net.[1]

As a matter of fact, social insurance is playing an increasingly powerful role in underpinning everyday life of social members. Whether it is retirees or employees with a job, without social insurance, there will be no important backbone to resist and prevent social risks. As a result, the evaluation of insurance coverage for various income groups has both remarkable theoretical significance and practical meaning in measuring social support and safeguarding peaceful development. In the process of stabilizing and expanding middle income group, the supporting role of social insurance can never be underestimated.

11.1 Regional Overall Planning of Social Insurance

Before the reform and opening-up of China, social insurance was provided mainly by public institutions or state-owned enterprises. Civil servants and employees of urban enterprises enjoy a certain amount of pension given out by their employers when they reach the mandatory age for retirement. However, this was changed to pension insurance system and social insurance system after the reform and opening.

[1] See Li and Zhang (2014).

Y. Zhang (✉)
Beijing Association of Sociology, Beijing, China

P. Li and M. K. Gorshkov (eds.), *The Middle Income Group in China and Russia*,
Research Series on the Chinese Dream and China's Development Path,
https://doi.org/10.1007/978-981-16-1464-4_11

The purpose was to eliminate the pension pressure brought by the rapidly rising ratio between retirees and in-service personnel. Pension insurance system separates the receiving of insurance fund from its granting. The employers pay insurance on behalf of their employees while the pension will be handed out by social security department. In this way, regardless of the profit made by public institutions or companies, as long as the social insurance fee is paid on schedule for employees at work, insurance protection can be guaranteed. However, there are big differences in regard to payment status among the five types of insurance, namely endowment insurance, medical insurance, employment injury insurance, unemployment insurance and maternity insurance because insurance payment is still a selective option rather than a mandatory one.

Since the end of 2014, social insurance for staff of public institutions and employees of urban companies has been merged into one, but the capital pools are still differentiated. For social members, payment channels are designed for each and every one when it comes to social insurance. Institutionally speaking, insurance coverage is nationwide. However, social insurance for civil servants is directly transferred and paid by public institutions or government departments through accountants without the need of asking for their consent. It is mandatory to some extent. But the payment of insurance for company employees is sometimes interrupted or declined. In addition, for other rural or urban residents who are working neither in public institutions nor companies, there is resident insurance system that combines government financial inducting with personal choices to attract residents to get themselves enrolled in social security program.

Furthermore, there is proportional differentiation between individual account and social pooling account due to the nature of the social security system. In principle, the central government requires that companies pay 20% of social average wage of the previous year for pension insurance while individuals pay 8%. However, this is not the case in reality as each region has certain administrative power to decide on different plans. From Table 11.1, we can see that companies or public sectors pay 19%, 20% and 14% respectively in Beijing, Shanghai and Guangzhou. Individuals of all three cities contribute 8% for pension insurance. This kind of regional differences and ratio discrepancy also happen in medical insurance, unemployment insurance, work-related injury insurance and maternity insurance.[2]

Regional differences of social insurance also make it difficult for employees to move from one province to another and from one region to another. From the perspective of institution, it is a growing trend to have potable and transferable insurance. It is also an institutional norm that can be implemented now. However, the practical operation can be more complex, making it barely possible to carry and transfer social insurance. For instance, a migrant worker who obtains employment in Guangzhou receives 14% of his pension insurance from the company. If he were to move to Shanghai, the proportion contributed by the company should be 20% and thus the discrepancy is 6%. It is therefore difficult to integrate the workforce between Guangzhou and Shanghai. What's more, the minimum wage of payment

[2] The data is set out based on the author's investigation and survey.

Table 11.1 The payment proportion of social insurance for urban workers (%)

	Beijing		Shanghai		Guangzhou	
Insurance item	Company contribution	Individual contribution	Company contribution	Individual contribution	Company contribution	Individual contribution
Endowment insurance	19	8.00	20.00	8.00	14.00	8.00
Medical insurance	10	2.00	9.50	2.00	7.00	2.00
Unemployment insurance	0.80	0.20	0.50	0.50	0.64	0.20
Employment injury insurance	0.40	0.00	0.20	0.00	0.20	0.00
Maternity insurance	0.80	0.00	1.00	0.00	0.85	0.00

Note Due to weak overall planning, the proportion of payment varies from region to region. What should be noted here is that flexible employees (unemployed, self-employed and part-time workers with no fixed company or institution to pay for their insurance) need to contribute 20% of their pension insurance and maximum wage of payment determined by last year's average social wage also varies from region to region. As a result, the amount of social insurance acquired by employees also varies from region to region. Even in one region, the minimum and maximum wage of payment also differ from one type of insurance to another.

The fragmentation of social insurance makes it difficult for the academic field to calculate the differences of social insurance amount among various income groups on a nationwide scale. However, if we change to a different research perspective, we can discuss the differences between the middle income group and other income groups in terms of their participation in various types of social insurance.

In the following research, CSS data of 2015 is mainly used to classify wage-earners into different income groups. People whose income is lower than 75% of the income median are defined as low-income group. Those with income between 75 and 125% of the median fall into medium–low income group. Income that is between 125 and 200% of the median is medium–high income. Those whose earnings are higher than 200% of the median belong to high-income group. There are sometimes huge income differences between members of the middle income group. It is therefore necessary to further classify respondents into middle-low income group and middle-high income group.

11.2 The Middle Income Group and Labor Contract Signing Rate

According to the labor contract law, employers must sign labor contracts with their employees. Some companies adopt collective negotiation system and sign collective labor contract while other companies sign labor contracts with each individual. Companies that have signed labor contracts must pay social insurance fee for their employees in accordance with the law.[3] As a result, different types of labor contracts mean different social insurance access. Labor contracts play an important role in safeguarding the employees' rights to social security.

Table 11.2 shows that the variable of income group imposes remarkable influence on whether the contracts signed are of a fixed term or not. The higher the income is, the bigger chance of signing a labor contract will be. For people who have signed labor contracts of fixed term, 20.28% are low- income group, 25.68% are medium–low income group, 28.44% are medium–high income group and 37.72% are high-income group. For those who have signed contracts of non-fixed term, 6.76% are low- income group, 7.43% are medium–low income group, 6.48% are medium–high income group and 11.61% are high-income group. It is obvious that the possibility of high-income group to sign labor contracts is the highest.

---

[3] Based on the 17th clause of "Labor Contract Law", there are 9 items under "the following should be included in a labor contract"and the 7th is social insurance.

Table 11.2 Income level and different status of signing labor contracts (%)

	The status of signing a formal labor contract with your employers						Total
	Fixed term	No fixed term	Probation period	No contract signed	No need to sign	Not sure	
Low-income group (Income lower than 75% of the income median)	20.28	6.76	1.69	67.04	3.66	0.56	100.00
Medium–low income group (75%–125%)	25.68	7.43	1.01	57.09	8.11	0.68	100.00
Medium–high income group (125%–200%)	28.44	6.48	0.95	51.50	11.85	0.79	100.00
High-income group (income higher than 200% of the median)	37.72	11.61	0.19	30.06	19.75	0.67	100.00
Total	33.07	9.76	0.57	40.39	15.54	0.68	100.00

Note In regard to employees with agricultural residence registration, migrant workers who are employed in non-agricultural sectors are included in the statistics while those working in agriculture are not taken into account

It can also be seen from Table 11.2 that workers who haven't signed labor contracts still account for a large proportion, 67.04% of low-income group, 57.09% of medium–low income group, 51.5% of medium–high income group and 30.06% of high-income group.

As a result, in order to expand and stabilize the middle income group to build our society into a moderately prosperous one, we must ensure that people of medium–low income and medium–high income have stable jobs gained by signing labor contracts. People without labor contracts tend to change their jobs more frequently. This is not good for them to accumulate work experience, nor for the continuity of social insurance. If work-related dispute happens, it is also difficult to ensure their interests if they do not have labor contracts. Therefore, to expand middle income group, it is essential to enable workers to have stable jobs. If middle income people do not have stable jobs, it is likely for them to fall into low-income group due to lack of earnings either because they are out of work or they attempt to change their job. It is also impossible for middle income group to maintain a certain living standard without stable jobs. Their spending power might be jeopardized, so is the expansion of domestic demand.

11.3 Social Insurance Participation Rate of Middle Income Group

The expansion of the middle income group is highly relevant to the construction of a moderately prosperous society. Participation rate and the coverage scale of social insurance plays an important role in facilitating the enlargement of the middle class. It is easier for a person entitled to the rights of social insurance to withstand social risks and maintain his or her social status. On the contrary, a person that lacks social insurance tends to descend into a lower social class with inferior living quality. As a result, the status of having social insurance or not is a significant index in evaluating how developed a modern society is.

Table 11.3 shows that 46.65% of the low-income group, 59.43% of the medium–low income group and 63.33% of the medium–high income group and 68.36% of the high-income group have been registered for pension insurance. Comparatively speaking, medical insurance can ensure a better chance to resist current social risks, which explains high participation rate of nearly 90% for all income groups.

However, group discrepancies between unemployment insurance, work injury insurance and maternity insurance is huge. For instance, the participation rate of unemployment insurance for low-income group is merely 1.89% while the figures for medium–low income group, medium–high income group and high-income group are 6.75%, 12.42% and 30.05% respectively. In regard to work injury insurance,

Table 11.3 Social insurance participation rate of various income groups (%)

	Pension insurance	Medical insurance	Unemployment insurance	Work injury insurance	Maternity insurance
Low-income group (Income lower than 75% of the median)	46.65	87.36	1.89	1.87	1.57
Medium–low income group (Between 75 and 125% of the median)	59.43	89.77	6.75	7.89	4.91
Medium–high income group (Between 125 and 200% of the median)	63.33	88.60	12.42	14.01	10.24
High-income group (Above 200% of the median)	68.36	90.29	30.05	33.00	24.45

participation rates for the low-income group, medium–low income group, medium–high income group and high-income group are respectively 1.87%, 7.89%, 14.01% and 33%. In terms of maternity insurance, those rates are 1.57%, 4.91%, 10.24% and 24.45% respectively.

Though participate rates of unemployment insurance, work injury insurance and maternity insurance are low for most income groups, high-income group still outnumber others. It is quite strange that the participation rates of those three types of insurance for middle income group are quite limited. What need to be explained is that during the process of social changes, workers may need to consider more about wage earnings in cash for the time being rather than insurance for the future. In the circumstance of relatively stable employment, having unemployment insurance or not does not matter so much for their current living. Job security at many departments is also guaranteed and thus it makes sense why the participation rate of work injury insurance is low. However, once there is big fluctuation with economy and unemployment raises, unemployment insurance will play its role of security and maintain social stability. People who have completed the task of reproduction tend to leave out the option of maternity insurance and hence the low participation rate.

Needless to say, there is also a circumstance where respondents are not aware of whether they have unemployment insurance, work injury insurance and maternity insurance. From Table 11.1, we learn that the insurance institution reform makes it possible for companies or employers to pay work injury insurance and maternity insurance for their employees instead of the former circumstance of deducting directly from their wages. Unemployment insurance is an exception.

Even so, the stability and enlargement of middle income group should be our concern.

Firstly, if the objective is to expand the middle income group, the income level of the low-income group must be improved continuously under the condition of controlled prices. In addition, their pension insurance participation rate must also be elevated. There is certain contraction on the level of social individuals. If people participate in pension insurance, their cash earnings might become less. But if they do not, then their future life cannot be safeguarded. Many peasant workers travel to the city to work after they've participated in pension insurance for rural residents. Some of them or the great majority of them choose pension insurance for rural residents over pension insurance for employees of urban enterprises. Pension insurance for rural residents is comparatively low and can hardly support a senior to live in urban cities if they retire in cities. But if they choose pension insurance for employees of urban enterprises, a high insurance fee must be paid and their cash earnings will be decreased for certain.

Secondly, many problems related to companies and employers must be resolved to expand middle income group. As we all know enterprises and employers contribute a bigger part than individuals to social insurance. It is also up to employers rather than employees to decide whether to increase salaries or wages. However, with limited improvement of labor productivity and rising labor cost, companies' profitability and competitiveness in the market may be weakened. The improvement of social dynamics of the middle income group relies not only on the enlargement of the share taken up by workers in the distribution process, but also on the increase of labor productivity and technological progress. Measures taken at present to reduce the premium rate only take effect to some extent.[4]

11.4 Middle Income Group's Satisfaction with Social Insurance

At different stages of development, the need of various income groups for social insurance and other social policies varies from each other. At a certain phase of development, different income groups may have different choice preferences regarding social insurance and other social policies. Generally speaking, the lower the income, the more concerned they are about current cash earnings and job stability. Stable employment means relatively stable earnings for low-income group. However, for people with higher income, whether it is income from properties or income from wages or salaries paid in work, so long as they have stable income that can help them resist general social risks, they tend to focus on other aspects such as providing for old age and medical care (Table 11.4).

From Model 1—the endowment insurance model of the Table above, we can see that neither medium–low income group nor medium–high income have high significance while high-income group shows high significance with negative value indicating that they are extremely unsatisfied with current situation of pension insurance. Correspondingly, in regard to education level, when we take "junior high school and below" as control group, both "high school and technical secondary school" and "junior college" show statistical significance with negative value which shows that both groups with higher education level are not quite pleased with their current pension insurance.

In Model 2—the medical insurance model, "medium–low income group" and "medium–high income group" show low significance while "high-income group" shows higher significance with negative value. In terms of the variable of "education level", when we regard "junior high school and below" as control group, both "high school and technical secondary school" and "junior college" show great significance.

If we take a look at the employment supportive policy, i.e. Model 3, the picture is quite the opposite. Compared to "low-income group", "high-income group" has statistical significance with positive value, indicating that they are extremely satisfied

[4] When the profitability of companies is low, the government will reduce the premium rate of social insurance. The premium rate of pension insurance paid by enterprises will drop from 20 to 19%, the rate of work injury insurance drop from 2 to 0.4% or below and the premium rate of unemployment insurance will be reduced to 0.5% or below. Maternity insurance will be merged into medical insurance. However, the most complicated of all is work injury insurance which varies from industry to industry. There are eight different industries classified in many regions. Standard rates after adjustment for industry 1–8 are 0.8%, 1.0%, 1.3%, 1.5%, 1.8%, 2.0%, 2.8%, 5.6% respectively of the total wage of staff and workers of that industry (5.6% for coal mining industry). The standard rate of employment injury insurance for construction industry by project is 1.8%.

Table 11.4 How satisfied different income groups are with social insurance and employment promotion policy

	Pension insurance (Model 2)		Medical insurance (Model 2)		Employment promotion policy (Model 3)	
	Non-standardized coefficient	Significance	Non-standardized coefficient	Significance	Non-standardized coefficient	Significance
Constant	6.077	0.000	6.212	0.000	4.761	0.000
Education (Control group: junior high school and below)						
High school and technical secondary school	−0.213	0.001	−0.176	0.006	0.146	0.026
Junior college	−0.201	0.021	−0.213	0.011	0.420	0.000
Undergraduate	−0.060	0.497	−0.021	0.805	0.581	0.000
Income group (Control group: low-income group)						
Medium–low income group	0.013	0.889	−0.011	0.903	−0.003	0.972
Medium–high income group	−0.090	0.233	−0.125	0.088	0.049	0.525
High-income group	−0.160	0.008	−0.174	0.003	0.293	0.000
Gender (Male = 1)	0.103	0.041	0.024	0.628	−0.064	0.207
Registered permanent residence (Non-agricultural = 1)	−0.135	0.025	−0.236	0.000	0.010	0.864
Confirmed coefficient after adjustment	0.004		0.005		0.014	

with employment policies. In regard to education, when compared with "junior high school and below", "high school and technical secondary school", "junior college" and "undergraduate" all have great significance with positive value which shows that those people are more content with employment promotion policies.

An interesting phenomenon then occurs. Though low-income group, medium–low income group and medium–high income group all have low participation rates regarding pension insurance and medical insurance, they are moderately satisfied or at least they have not expressed any dissatisfaction while high-income group are not pleased with current situation of pension insurance and medical insurance despite high participation rates. It is also quite fascinating to see that when it comes to the assessment of employment promotion policies, high-income group are more satisfied than low-income group.

One possible explanation is that job stability and quality not only determines whether the income is stable, but also decides to a large extent excess to various social insurance. In current labor market, though private sectors may pay a higher salary, they often avoid the payment of social insurance fee deliberately or unintentionally while public sectors provide stable social insurance despite limited salary income. In addition, employees of state-owned enterprises and public institutions also have access to steady occupational annuity. In companies of urban cities, only a few top managers and capitalists are entitled to enterprise annuity. This explains the prioritization of college graduates in choosing jobs. The first choice is to work as a civil servant or in public institutions, the second choice is state-owned enterprises and the last resort is other private sectors.

The government has achieved continuous growth of pension insurance in 12 years in a row through hard work. However, institutional bonus generated by enhanced insurance resilience is decreasing gradually. If the growth rate of national economy is difficult to maintain the anticipation of continuous growth of social insurance, there will be more discontent and dissatisfaction. Under this circumstance, it is necessary for us to reflect on the growth mechanism of pension insurance and build on principles of equity and justice between generations to work out adjusting policies where pension insurance is in line with the increase of commodity prices and national economy.

11.5 Discussion and Policy Suggestions

The original intention to set up social insurance system is to resolve and prevent possible risks to guarantee stable income and living of social members. The concept is originated from the West and connotes the meaning of social security in and of itself. In order to expand the middle income group, our policies should not only focus on those who have already been defined as the "middle income group", but also be interpreted broadly as "to increase the earnings of the low-income group, enlarge the proportion of the middle income group and ensure stable income of the high-income group". To succeed in this, it is essential to put both social insurance and stable employment in equally important positions. Thus policy suggestions proposed in the paper are as the following.

First, we must strengthen social insurance for college graduates and peasant workers. We must bear in mind that as long as there are competition in job market, there will be risks of unemployment. Social insurance is an institutional assurance that reduces or mitigates risks of unemployment and occupational change. It now seems that social insurance has had nation-wide coverage institutionally, but more effort should be made to expand to a larger group and sound measures should be taken to tackle insurance interruption. Even for people who have already made it to the middle class, unemployment and insurance interruption occur from time to time as a result of economic fluctuation. The expansion of pension insurance coverage cannot be successful without strong and powerful institutional support. The key work from now on should be social insurance for fresh graduates and peasant workers. There are only 75.1 million peasant workers with work injury insurance so far.[5] If we aim to lift those high-tech people among peasant workers, we must ensure more peasant workers participate in social insurance of urban company employees. Furthermore, the turnover rate of college graduates is very high,[6] which in reverse has impact on rates of signing employment contracts of fixed-term and non-fixed term. CSS survey shows that the middle income group has a very low rate of signing employment contracts of non-fixed term, which is a social policy issue that urgently requires to be attended to.

Second, it is important to handle well the relationship between the expansion of coverage and the premium. There is no doubt that at present China is going through rapid population aging. In order to respond to it in the correct way, it is necessary to build a sustainable social insurance system as quickly as possible. However, fragmentation of the current pension insurance system and the levying body has strongly impacted the sustainability of social insurance system. Measured based on the current population structure, China's workforce still takes up nearly 70% of the entire population. Population of employment also accounts for a high proportion of the workforce. If every person in the labor force has social insurance, we can easily deal with the current problems even if the prestation system of "pay-as-you-go" is implemented. The reality is that the pension insurance participation rate is still low for urban workers and there exists serious regional inequality. Pension supply is abundant in regions with more influx of labor force whereas regions with more outflow of migrant population find it very difficult to make ends meet in regard to pension. If the rate is reduced, the operating cost of companies might be alleviated which is good for the expansion of coverage.[7] However, certain areas may find it hard to sustain current premium if the rate is reduced. It is essential to upgrade the overall planning

[5] By the end of 2015, the population with employment injury insurance had increased to 218.87 million, up by 4.55 million. The number of peasant workers is 75.1 million, up by 210,000. https://www.stats.gov.cn/tjsj/zxfb/201702/t20170228_1467424.html.

[6] Li (2013).

[7] Feng (2013).

and form basic pension system planned at the national level. Otherwise, more labor force will flow into developed regions such as Guangdong province. There will be abundant supply of insurance fund and the rate will be decreased, which in return can reduce the burden on enterprises to a great degree and enhance their market competitiveness. Inland areas have to maintain a higher rate due to outflow of labor force. As a result, labor cost might rise institutionally and market competitiveness of companies will be weakened. The Matthew Effect of the development process thus appears where early players join the game without any burdens while late comers find themselves caught in an awkward and difficult position. Those early-developing areas have more middle income people while those who joined later have more the low-income or medium–low income population.

In addition, certain support must be provided to middle income group which is still a fragile group. On the one hand, economic fluctuation might drive a part of the group to fall into the low-income group. On the other hand, a large number of the middle income group is not fully covered with social insurance. Participation rate of the medical insurance is high while the participation rate of pension insurance is quite low, making it difficult for them to resist possible risks at the social and individual levels, such as disease-caused impoverishment and old age poverty.

Fourth, in the process of industrial transformation and consumption upgrade, the needs of income groups vary from one another. The high-income group hopes for improved pension insurance and medical insurance while the low-income group prefers to keep stable employment and income. The high-income group is active in participating in various social insurance, and yet they are least satisfied. The low-income group is not pleased with employment supportive policies, but they do not care about the configuration of social insurance. This is the inevitable result of the modernization of China. Social development and income disparity will definitely cause differentiated expectation of social policies, adding more national governance system and modernization of the governance capability. If we fail to tackle policy anticipation of different income groups, there will be a social gap that is difficult to be eliminated.

Last but not the least, two problematic thoughts must be prevented to improve social security system and enlarge the middle income group. One is the idea of "robbing the rich to feed the poor" which will not only harm the interest of high-income group but also affect the enthusiasm of the middle income group to strive for affluence. The more obvious the income gap is, the easier for populism that stresses the thought of "robbing the rich to feed the poor" to take root and flourish. The other idea is to curtail excessive welfare that is prone to weaken the drives of the low-income group and add burden to development. The government should focus on providing the basic public service. The low-income group should take advantage of social policies to get a fair share of the fruits of economic development of the modern society. They should also explore new ways to improve their income and carry out the ideology of employment being the foundation of people's livelihood so that the middle income group can be enlarged step by step and the middle income trap can be overcome.

References

Feng J (2013) Participation incentives of social insurance system for urban employees in China. Econ Studies (7)

Li Y (2013) Empirical research of job-hopping of college graduates and reasons behind. Employment of Chinese Undergraduates (7)

Li P, Zhang Y (2014) The study of building an olive-shaped distribution pattern. Jiangsu Social Sci (5)

Yi Zhang is a research fellow on Institute of Social Development of Chinese Academy of Social Sciences (CASS), and director of Institute of Social Development. He is the chief-editor of JOURNAL OF SOCIAL DEVELOPMENT, and the Executive Chief Editor of the Journal of Chinese Sociology. He is also the Vise-President of Chinese Social Psychology Society, and Vice Secretary-General of Chinese Association of Sociology, Vise-President of Beijing Association of Sociology. Recent years he focuses his research in the fields of class structure, population sociology, family sociology and so or. He published his works as below: Clanized state-Owned Enterprises, Political attitude of Middle Class in Present China, The Research of Class Conflict Consciousness in Chinese Cities, The attainment of Chinese Social Status: Class Inheritance and Intergenerational Mobility, The attainment of Social Class Status and Education Was Affected by Family Background, and Population Floating and Family Risks of Migrant Workers.

Chapter 12
Social Security and the Risk Resistance Capacity of Middle Income Groups in Russia

P. M. Kozyreva and A. I. Smirnov

As society undergoes dynamic and controversial development, accompanied by the surge in the variety and scope of threats and dangers, principal focus is given to higher awareness of social security issues, which reach a critical point during the most acute shocks. This is exactly the type of situation Russia has been going through over the past decade. The influence of current events on the social sphere has exacerbated many of the previous dangers and threats, while also causing new ones, which has destabilized all areas of life. Such threats include, first and foremost, the steady rise of poverty, higher unemployment risks, a deepening of social polarization, worsening working conditions along with more cases of labor rights violations, and a plummet in the efficiency of most social security and support institutions. Far fewer families and individuals currently have access to social benefits and count on social support.

The social aspect of security may be understood both in the broad and narrow sense. In the broad sense, social security is often equaled to national security. In this case, it is interpreted as the fundamental unifying category of human existence,[1] which, in one way or another, includes all the other types of security,[2] as well as the way in which the social system functions and the way of ensuring its resilience and sustainability as its structural elements interact among themselves and with external factors throughout society, development, etc.[3] By contrast, when social security is reviewed in the narrow sense, special attention is given to safeguarding the interests

[1] Zinchenko (2007).

[2] Social Security in Russia in an Information Reality: A Monograph] / S. I. Samygin, A. V. Vereshchagina, I. V. Pechkurov. Moscow. RU-SCIENCE, 2016.

[3] Kuznetsov (2008).

P. M. Kozyreva (✉)
HSE University, Institute of Sociology of FCTAS RAS, Moscow, Russia

A. I. Smirnov
Institute of Sociology of FCTAS RAS, Moscow, Russia

P. Li and M. K. Gorshkov (eds.), *The Middle Income Group in China and Russia*, Research Series on the Chinese Dream and China's Development Path,
https://doi.org/10.1007/978-981-16-1464-4_12

of individuals, families, communities, and other actors in the social sphere, as well as to developing the social structure, social interactions, and the means of supporting the human sustenance system, socialization, and lifestyle. Social security is interpreted as "the state of society that provides the maximal level of social benefits and conditions, determines the overall quality of life, and undertakes to minimize the threats to people's life and wellbeing".[4] Social security covers a diverse range of social life aspects that not only reflect a broad spectrum of social issues but also, first and foremost, determine an individual's social position.

The narrow interpretation of social security presupposes the protection of an individual's and society's interests from the unacceptable or unwarrantable risks, challenges, dangers, or threats; the opportunity to exercise essential rights in the social sphere (such as the rights to life, paid labor, free healthcare and education, accessible vacations, guaranteed social support, etc.); and effort to maintain the optimal or at the very least agreeable and satisfactory living and working conditions. One of the key concepts in this respect is "acceptable risk", which, if we follow the methodology of social risk studies, may be defined as "the indicator of individuals and entities' certain level of protection against harmful influences from various sources".[5]

In the past few years, with the economic crisis having gotten especially prolonged and adverse, the level of individuals', families', and communities' protection against the rising dangers and threats, along with their ability to withstand the greater challenges and risks, is largely defined both by the critical state of Russia's social sphere and by the people's access to certain resources and assets that could allow them to weather the harsh environment. The crisis reality and the qualitative changes in the system and in the scope of threats and dangers lead to adjustments in the social security priorities and to a demand for new approaches to providing the said security.

In many ways, the resolution of social security issues depends on the efficiency of the state's social protection system; i.e., on the way the state implements programs aimed at helping people in dire circumstances; on whether or not all people have guaranteed access to certain types of social services and the minimal amount of social benefits, regardless of how well they contribute to the production process; and on whether or not all people are provided with the services that meet their social needs (education, healthcare, social services, etc.). A robust and efficient social security system that properly protects the people may prove quite useful for addressing a number of social issues, boosting social cohesion, and prompting sustainable economic growth.

In a stable society, social support moves towards acquiring the traits of social development that is aimed not only at supporting the most vulnerable members of the community and dealing with the traditional tasks of providing social benefits for the poor, but also at achieving the highest results in each individual's development. The unquestionable priorities of such support come to include personal growth, social freedoms, gender equality, employment support and fair wages, equal access

[4] Chernikova et al. (2015).

[5] Mozgovaya and Shlykova (2016).

to education and jobs, healthcare, etc.[6] Social services undergo modernization, and social policy benefits from innovative approaches aimed at introducing new means, strategies, and technologies that may satisfy the population's current needs. On the other hand, an economic crisis, especially a prolonged one, shifts the focus in an opposite direction. The importance of traditional social support issues increases, along with the number of people in need, as the lasting crisis turbulence zone sucks in not only the poor but also some of the wealthier groups that no longer feel socially and economically secure.

In the current challenging circumstances, special research and practical emphasis is given to the social security issues of the mid-income groups, which cannot be classified as either the rich or the poor but, "due to their internal diversity, cannot be viewed as a single social entity".[7] Even though the mid-income population groups are highly heterogeneous and their members have different worldviews, mindsets, life goals, consumption styles, adaptive strategies, etc., all of them are brought together by the fact that they are more or less successful. Success is mostly evidenced by people's ability to provide for themselves materially and financially. Another factor in favor of this conclusion is the research that shows that the high level of social differentiation in today's Russia is influenced the most by the high level of material inequality.[8]

The research of relevant issues concerning the social security of mid-income groups allows, on the one hand, to determine the degree to which the vital needs and interests of the largest population strata are met, to reveal and analyze the key processes taking place within the social and structural interactions of the Russian society, and to trace these processes' link to the changes in the country's economic status. On the other hand, this research also provides an opportunity to evaluate the efficiency of the current social policy, as well as to clarify and shift the course of improving the system that provides social protection to individuals and families that have either slipped below the poverty threshold or are balancing on the edge, and to people that are facing unemployment, worsening labor conditions, and lower accessibility of healthcare and education services.

In this chapter, we have attempted to focus on the range of issues specified above, basing our study on the data provided by the RLMS-HSE monitoring of the Russian population's economic status and health.[9] The analysis of this data has allowed to single out four groups of respondents, defined by different income levels: low-income groups (0.75 income median or lower); lower mid-income groups (from over

---

[6] The Modernization of Russia: Social and Humanitarian Changes/ed. by N. Ia. Petrakov/Russian Foundation for the Humanities; Russian Academy of Sciences. Moscow, St. Petersburg: Nestor-Istoriia, 2011, pp. 196–201.

[7] Middle Class in Modern Russia. The Summary of Many Years' Worth of Research / ed. by M.K. Gorshkov and N.E. Tikhonova. Moscow. Ves Mir, 2016, p. 9.

[8] Rimskii (2013).

[9] Russia Longitudinal Monitoring survey, RLMS-HSE», conducted by National Research University "Higher School of Economics" and OOO "Demoscope" together with Carolina Population Center, University of North Carolina at Chapel Hill and the Institute of Sociology RAS. (RLMS-HSE websites: https://www.hse.ru/rlms, https://www.cpc.unc.edu/projects/rlms).

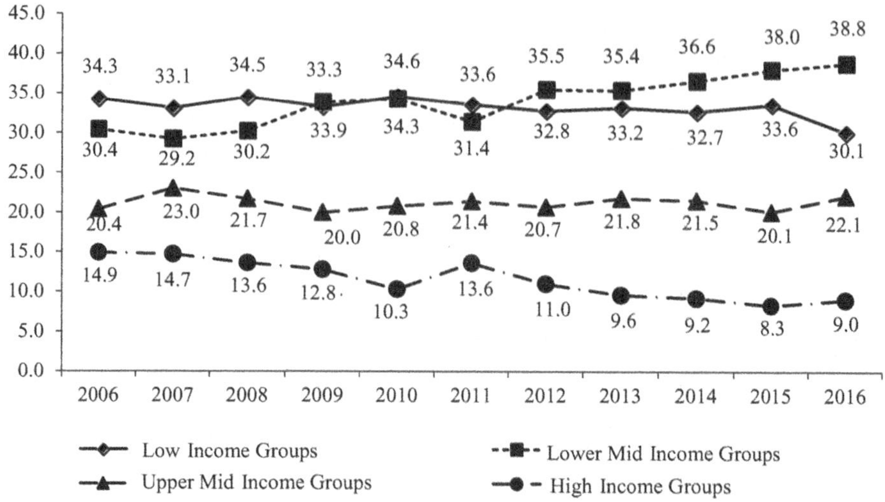

Fig. 12.1 The dynamics of income group ratio, 2006–2016, % (Similar trends are also evident in other bodies of data. See e.g.: the data provided in Chap. 1 hereof.)

0.75 to 1.25 median); upper mid-income groups (from over 1.25 to 2 medians); and high-income groups (over 2 medians).

The analysis of the respondents' group distribution dynamics (see Fig. 12.1) shows that the degradation of most Russians' economic status, which occurred after the country entered a stretch of economic instability in 2008, lead to the noticeable shrinkage of high-income population groups (from 14.7% in the pre-crisis year 2007 to 9% in 2016) and the expansion of the lower mid-income groups (from 29.2% to 38.8%, respectively). *Over the course of these shifts, which transpired against the background of slower income growth, followed by income decrease (thus signaling a rise in the number of Russians with limited or depleted resources that are often insufficient for successfully withstanding the dangers and threats that come with a crisis), the lower mid-income groups turned into the most numerous category of respondents. Together with the respondents from the groups with the lowest income, these groups now amount to almost three quarters of all respondents.*

The danger of low-income groups' expansion rises at an especially dramatic speed as the population's income shrinks during the most adverse periods of economic crises. Even the relatively well-off families cannot escape the economic challenges in the country. For instance, the income crisis and the subsequent inevitable drop in purchasing demand, which fully manifested itself in the particularly challenging years of 2014 and 2015, gave rise to a whole range of negative effects, linked to the steep rise in the population's material disparity, the polarization of the labor market, and the far higher proportion of those unable to obtain even the basic social benefits for themselves and their families.

Following the drop in their actual income, many people from the lower mid-income groups started experiencing significant material challenges or even balancing precariously on the edge of poverty, which noticeably exacerbated the issue of unequal access to education, healthcare, and other surfaces, especially in the context of efforts[10] to make the social sector less state-dependent and more commercialized. As before, the list of the most urgent issues that caused special concern for underprivileged Russian was headed by rising prices, poverty, and the risk of unemployment. Healthcare became one of the most pressing matters for people over the retirement age, who complained about costly medication and the absence of free medical products in hospitals. For some of those people, lower income meant not only the shortage of the necessary material goods but also the loss of the habitual lifestyle and the opportunity to properly exercise certain basic rights. These processes were directly reflected through the emergence of social pessimism as a mass trend in the Russian mindset.

According to RLMS-HSE, from December of 2013 to December of 2015, the average actual income of Russian households[11] dropped by 6.5%, and then rose by more than 11% in December of 2016. This was due to the significant decrease in the size of low-income groups (from 33.6% in 2015 to 30.1% in 2016) and the expansion of upper mid-income groups (from 20.1% to 22.1%, respectively), which, however, did not make Russians' perception of their social well-being more optimistic. *Throughout the entire year 2016, the population's attitude was mostly governed by the current stagnant state of the economy, while the economic crisis still continued to determine Russians' attitudes as an absolutely dominant factor. The unstable and controversial economic situation affected almost all of the Russian population.* While the economy continued to go through a crisis, the families' resources kept draining faster and faster. The vast majority of Russians viewed economic issues as the main domestic threat and felt insecure about their families' ability to make it through economic incidents. Many people grew notably more pessimistic both about the country's economic state and their own resent and future. And this pessimism is not something that surfaced only recently. A significant share of Russians had been going through prolonged stress for many years before.

The changes described above were most dynamic in largest cities—the capitals of Republics, Krais and Oblasts, where over the course of 2007–2015, the population groups with the highest income shrank twofold, from 22.7 to 11.6%, while the size of upper mid-income groups decreased almost by one third, from 33.4 to 27.6%. At the same time, the lower mid-income groups grew bigger by around a half, from 28 to 40.3%, and the low-income groups grew from 15.9 to 20.6%. Nevertheless, in late 2016, when the income of Russian families rose, the low-income groups shrank to 16.9%. In other cities and towns, the only more or less notable changes were exhibited by low-income groups (which in size from 34.3% in 2006 to 41.2% in 2016) and topmost high-income groups (which shrank by a third, from 13.9 to 8.9%). It is also worth noting that the lowest income level was a constant trend in

[10] Aleshina (2013).

[11] We have based our calculations of the income levels on the Index of Consumer Prices for Goods and Services, available on the official website of the State Statistics Service. URL: https://www.gks.ru/free_doc/new_site/prices/potr/tab-potr1.htm (accessed on 03/31/2017).

rural areas, where over half of the population got sorted into lowest-income groups year after year. There is another interesting and more positive fact: namely, that the share of these respondents shrank from 56.3% in 2007 to 50.1% in 2016, while the number of rural community members from the lower mid-income groups increased by one third, from 25.9 to 34.1%, during the same period.

The distribution of respondents across income-driven groups has allowed us to analyze the consistency of their objective and subjective material status. The self-evaluation scale of material well-being, which includes 9 brackets (the lowest being "destitute" and the highest being "rich"), is based on how respondents view their current financial status. Our study is split into three hierarchic levels, the lower, the middle, and the upper, with 3 brackets in each. We define status consistency as a significant or substantial overlap between the subjective status perception (scale level) and the actual income group.

The analysis of RLMS-HSE data shows that the most consistent self-evaluation is typical of respondents from mid-income groups, while the least consistent self-evaluation is typical of respondents from high-income groups (Table 12.1). Overall, the general picture of status consistency barely changed from 2006 to 2015 and experienced significant shifts in 2016. The most notable shift is that respondents from all income groups except those with the highest income started describing themselves as underprivileged far more often.

The large size of respondent groups with unrealistically low or high estimates of their own social and economic status may serve as evidence of both notable shifts in the material well-being of the majority of Russians, and of the profound inconsistencies rooted in the mass mindset, which is typical of an unstable society. In late 2016, approximately one in every four respondents from high-income groups, one in every three respondents from upper mid-income groups, and one in every two respondents from lower mid-income groups experienced feelings of belonging to the lowest social strata, which, more often than not, lead to depressing notions of predetermined and inescapable fate, of becoming a social outcast or being discriminated against. These notions stemmed from the respondents' lack of satisfaction with their own material status and quality of life. At the same time, far fewer respondents from the lower and middle income cohorts described themselves as well-off and confident about braving the past social barriers and expanding their social horizons.

Overall,[12] *the overwhelming dominance of the negative status consistency over the positive proved that, throughout the past decade, the income of a significant number of Russians, including those from groups with high income and the most material resources at their disposal, remained low or at the very least quite limited, preventing Russians from meeting their needs and acting on their interests, which were, for the most part, quite modest.*

At the same time, if we look at the monitoring data reflecting a number of long-term trends, we may conclude that the general status of Russians' social security has

---

[12] We do not take into account the topmost 2–3%, which are not featured in the population samples for mass surveys.

Table 12.1 The consistency of objective and subjective material status, 2006–2016, %

Income groups	Scale levels and brackets								
	Lower level			Middle level			Upper level		
	Bottom bracket	2nd bracket	3rd bracket	4th bracket	5th bracket	6th bracket	7th bracket	8th bracket	Top bracket
2006									
High-income groups	2.2	6.2	18.0	22.0	33.5	11.1	4.9	0.8	1.3
Upper mid-income groups	3.8	7.7	20.0	27.5	27.0	8.9	4.4	0.6	0.1
Lower mid-income groups	5.6	11.2	24.8	25.8	23.6	6.6	2.0	0.2	0.2
Low-income groups	8.8	16.3	24.8	24.2	19.1	4.3	2.1	0.3	0.1
2015									
High-income groups	2.5	5.8	16.5	25.2	31.8	12.8	4.9	0.4	0.1
Upper mid-income groups	2.8	7.3	20.1	28.1	26.5	10.2	4.5	0.5	0.0
Lower mid-income groups	3.5	10.0	25.2	25.3	22.1	9.7	3.9	0.3	0.0
Low-income groups	7.6	16.0	23.5	19.0	19.6	11.0	3.1	0.2	0.0
2016									
High-income groups	2.1	4.5	18.5	28.2	30.1	11.6	4.6	0.3	0.1

(continued)

Table 12.1 (continued)

Income groups	Scale levels and brackets								
	Lower level			Middle level			Upper level		
	Bottom bracket	2nd bracket	3rd bracket	4th bracket	5th bracket	6th bracket	7th bracket	8th bracket	Top bracket
Upper mid-income groups	2.3	8.1	25.7	27.2	25.5	8.3	2.4	0.5	0.0
Lower mid-income groups	5.2	15.0	29.3	24.8	18.2	5.7	1.7	0.1	0.0
Low-income groups	10.2	20.5	26.6	18.1	16.9	6.6	0.8	0.3	0.0

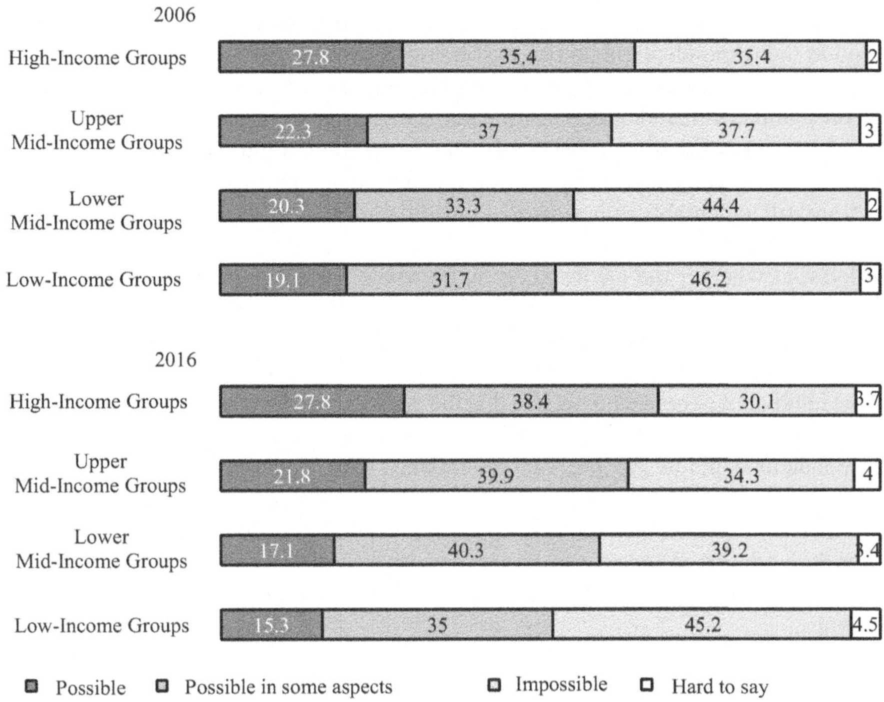

Fig. 12.2 The dynamics of evaluating the likelihood of mutual understanding between the rich and the poor across various income groups, 2006–2016, %

still improved for the better in the past ten years, even despite the major negative developments noted during the latest economic crisis.

The gradual shifts of large population groups from high-income to mid-income groups, together with the considerable expansion of lower mid-income groups thanks to the influx of those relatively well-off, has not lead to the critical exacerbation of the social inequality issue. On the contrary, we have revealed yet another case of income gap reduction among Russian household. While from 2006 to 2008, the income difference between the upper and lower quintiles rose from 6 to 6.7 times, and then slowly dropped to 2.7 times by late 2016. Such a downward trend, against the background of a drop in actual household income, may serve as evidence that the income of most of the population is leveling off, but at an insignificant rate.

The changes we have noted helped improve relations between people belonging to groups with different income levels and, consequently, contributed to social capital growth and better social cohesion, which is evidenced by the positive dynamics of mutual understanding and cooperation estimates regarding the relations between the rich and the poor (Fig. 12.2). Even though the coordination of differing (and sometimes polar opposite) interests was viewed as a complicated and even painful issue on every level of the social hierarchy, we managed to witness a clear positive trend as the respondents' material well-being improved.

In addition, the analysis of monitoring data convincingly shows that Russians have not only gained a clearer understanding that social cohesion is necessary, but have also learned to commiserate with each other better and find common ground faster. And even though these shifts are not too significant, and sometimes even unnoticeable, they are still undeniably important for consolidating society during times of hardship. There is a universal variable that helps reveal the level of trust in society overall and understand whether the environment is favorable for harmonizing the interactions between various social entity—namely, generalized trust, which reflects how much people trust strangers, i.e. people they do not know.

According to RLMS-HSE, all the cohorts being analyzed are experiencing a rise in the number of people who believe that the decision to trust or mistrust those around them should be influenced by what kind of person one is dealing with (Table 12.2). Respondents with low income are more inclined to be welcoming towards strangers, while those with high income are the most wary. As for respondents from the middle tier, they tend to trust the people around them without any additional conditions far rarer than other respondent categories, and lean slightly more towards a weighed, cautious approach, believing that trust or lack thereof has to depend on personal qualities.

Our research across all of the income groups shows a notable improvement of such social well-being factors as satisfaction with both life overall and the different aspects of life; that said, the relevant figures have started dropping after the beginning of the current economic crisis (Fig. 12.3). The most painful response to the negative changes in life came from the low-income respondents. From 2013 to 2016, the share of those more or less satisfied with their life overall dropped from 50 to 45.9% in the lower mid-income cohort of respondents, and from 44.7 to 37.1% in the low-income cohort. This drop was far more dramatic than during the previous economic crisis of 2008 and 2009, but the annual slump rates remained relatively the same. At the same time, the mounting feelings of anxiety and pessimism among the mid-income groups were most often intermingled with the willingness to steadfastly weather through all hardships.

Today, the economic and social issues that concern Russians the most include low income and meager retirement payments, rising prices, the threat of unemployment, and the lacking quality and accessibility of healthcare and education services. Research carried out by the RAS Institute of Sociology shows that the personal issues that worry Russians may be grouped into three most common categories: financial problems, factors that contribute to social and economic vulnerability, and health problems.[13] As the economic crisis aggravated these issues, this impacted the standards and quality of life of most Russians, including those from the mid-income population groups. Many of them were forced to limit most of their needs and give

[13] Russian Society and the Challenges of the Time. Book Three / M.K. Gorshkov [et al.]; edited by Gorshkov, M. K.; Tikhonova, N. E. – M.: Ves Mir, 2016. p. 62, 9–72.

Table 12.2 The dynamics of trusting other people, 2006–2016, %

Alternative statements	High-income groups			Upper mid-income groups			Lower mid-income groups			Low-income groups		
	2006	2009	2016	2006	2009	2016	2006	2009	2016	2006	2009	2016
Most people can be trusted	13.0	18.0	15.6	15.9	17.0	13.8	15.9	18.0	14.4	16.0	24.0	21.7
Caution is always necessary when dealing with other people	59.4	44.6	44.1	57.2	45.4	44.7	55.0	44.6	44.5	55.1	39.3	39.3
Both are applicable depending on the person and circumstances	26.7	36.2	39.9	26.0	36.0	40.6	27.6	36.2	39.9	25.5	33.9	37.4
Hard to say	0.9	1.2	0.4	0.9	1.6	0.9	1.5	1.2	1.2	3.4	2.8	1.6

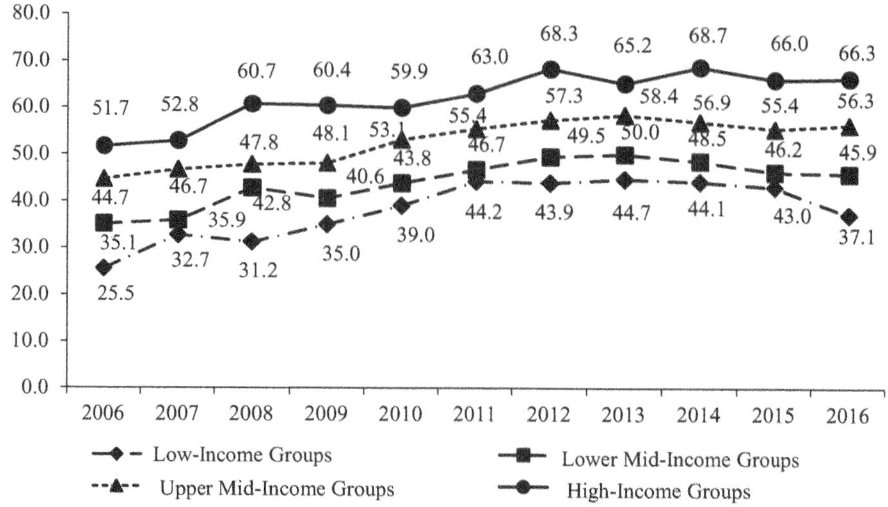

Fig. 12.3 The share of respondents fully and mostly satisfied with their overall life among different income groups, 2006–2016, % (A similar trend may also be deduced from other large bodies of sociological data that have been analyzed with the use of slightly different methodologies. For instance, the conclusion that the level of satisfaction with life among mid-income population groups may be derived from the dynamic analysis of the gap between good and poor attitudes to life that we gave in Chap. 1.)

up their routine spending habits, while the topmost strata of the population, regardless of hardships and losses, for the most part retained their secure status.

Table 12.3 shows that in the category comprised out of lower mid-income groups, the share of respondents that noticed an at least marginal improvement of their families' material well-being in the past 12 months decreased more than by one third, from 20.4% in 2013 to 12% in 2016, while the share of those who remarked on things getting worse grew more than twofold, from 15.6 to 32.8%. The shifts in the opinions of upper mid-income groups were even more significant. In this category, the share of respondents that remarked on the improvement of their families' material status dropped by over a third during the same period, from 28.2 to 17.5%, while the share of respondents who sensed a degradation of their families' well-being grew by almost three and a half times, from 11.4 to 37%. Such a substantial negative trend, which impacted almost all population groups, first surfaced in 2006. An improvement in the evaluation of changes in the families' material status is notable only among respondents from high-income groups.

At the same time, the level of mid-income respondents' dissatisfaction with their material well-being has also grown. This is clearly illustrated by the data in Table 12.4. Another interesting trend is that, despite the lasting economic crisis, the level of these respondents' satisfaction with their material well-being has still remained higher than in 2009.

Table 12.3 The dynamics of evaluating the changes in the material well-being of the respondent's family over the last 12 months, 2006–2016, %

Income groups	2006		2009		2013		2015		2016	
	Got better	Got worse	Got better	Got worse	Got better	Got worse	Got better	Got worse	Got better	Got worse
High-income groups	43.7	8.7	36.2	11.3	34.3	10.6	18.1	31.7	21.6	25.8
Upper mid-income groups	35.0	11.4	32.5	13.6	28.2	11.4	16.4	27.6	17.5	27.0
Lower mid-income groups	26.0	14.1	28.1	15.0	20.4	15.6	14.2	32.0	12.0	32.8
Low-income groups	17.4	25.5	18.2	21.9	19.1	21.5	14.0	34.2	10.4	34.5

Table 12.4 The dynamics of satisfaction with the respondent's material well-being, 2006–2016, %

Income groups	2006		2009		2013		2015		2016	
	Satisfied	Not satisfied	Satisfied	Not satisfied	Satisfied	Not satisfied	Satisfied	Not satisfied	Satisfied	Not satisfied
High-income groups	29.7	48.5	37.3	43.6	39.1	38.6	34.1	46.8	34.4	41.4
Upper mid-income groups	24.7	56.1	26.2	51.9	29.7	46.2	28.3	49.1	25.8	52.6
Lower mid-income groups	17.9	62.3	18.2	61.0	22.9	56.5	20.5	59.7	16.6	63.6
Low-income groups	10.2	75.2	15.6	70.1	16.2	67.7	17.9	66.9	12.5	71.5

It is quite obvious that the higher the people's income, the more they are inclined to spend. In this case, the crucially important factor is the gap between the opportunities provided to groups with different income levels. When the gap is too big, this shrinks the foundation for improving social cohesion and prompts greater social exclusion. The sheer size of this gap in today's Russia is revealed by the Monitoring data that concerns the dynamic of various income groups' evaluation of their ability to buy costly goods and services.

Table 12.5 shows that, each time we move to the next income level, the share of respondents that can afford saving up for major purchases, like a car or a country cottage, grows twofold. That said, the relative share of people with such purchasing ability is no higher than 42.9% even among the respondents with the highest income; while among those with the lowest income, this figure reaches a mere 6.1%. An even more striking discrepancy is revealed between the figures that describe various income groups' ability to afford a family holiday abroad. In the context of our analysis, it is especially interesting to note that there is an almost threefold difference between the lowest and highest income groups (6.4% and 22.2%, respectively).

When it comes to willingness to pay for the more crucial or less costly items and services, however, the figures are much higher across all income groups and the shifts from group to group are significantly smoother than in the previous cases. For instance, paying their child's college fees is something that can be afforded only by around one quarter of respondents from low-income groups, slightly less than a third of respondents from lower mid-income groups, around 44% of respondents from upper mid-income groups, and almost 60% of the wealthiest respondents. Paying for their children's extracurricular classes, such as music lessons, foreign language courses, sports clubs, etc., is affordable for 47.7% of respondents from the lowest income category up to 75.8% of respondents from the topmost cohort.

When reviewing the above data, it is important to bear in mind that, first and foremost, the concepts of a good apartment, house, or car, of a prestigious college or vacation abroad, differs vastly from one income group to another. That is, while the ultimate dream of the poor or financially disadvantaged respondents is to send their child to study at any higher education institution at all, wealthier respondents aim for the most prestigious colleges and universities. And saving up for a Russian-made second-hand car is not the same thing as buying a brand new luxurious vehicle from a foreign manufacturer. In addition, as the adverse economic crisis resulted in a steep drop in the population's actual income and an explosion of prices, many Russians found themselves forced to economize and to change their consumption patterns and other habits. Most families started saving on clothing and footwear, on eating out, servicing their cars, etc.; chose a more cautious approach to picking out and buying food; deprived themselves of expensive items and goods; and began to switch from vacations abroad to cheaper counterparts. All the money they thus saved went to keeping up their consumption on the level they were used to.

As the crisis phenomena grew more adverse, against the background of increasingly poorer conditions for meeting vital needs and interests, more Russians turned into economic pessimists. The negative processes in the social and economic sphere

Table 12.5 The dynamics of evaluating the ability to buy costly goods and services, 2006–2016, % (out of cases where this is applicable)

Able to	High-income groups				Upper mid-income groups				Lower mid-income groups				Low-income groups			
	2006	2009	2013	2016	2006	2009	2013	2016	2006	2009	2013	2016	2006	2009	2013	2016
Improve their living conditions	15.1	11.6	13.3	17.6	7.2	8.4	7.1	10.1	5.4	3.4	5.0	4.2	3.7	5.2	3.4	3.8
Pay for their children's extracurricular classes	73.0	74.2	78.9	75.8	63.6	68.1	71.6	70.3	52.5	56.5	62.5	59.9	35.7	48.3	44.6	47.7
Save up for large purchases	34.0	35.5	38.9	42.9	19.3	24.5	23.3	26.6	10.4	11.8	12.8	11.2	5.8	9.1	6.4	6.1
Take the whole family on vacation abroad	24.6	32.9	45.2	46.2	7.1	14.6	22.0	22.2	2.9	4.8	7.8	6.4	1.0	1.6	2.6	2.6
Take the whole family on vacation to a Russian resort	–	–	–	57.3	–	–	–	38.9	–	–	–	20.6	–	–	–	8.1
Pay for their child's college tuition	57.7	62.7	56.5	59.9	43.1	49.7	46.5	43.9	32.4	33.9	34.3	29.5	18.1	30.5	20.4	18.7

prompted a change in the outlook across a broad range of social groups, causing the people to feel more insecure about their future.

In 2016, most Russians did not expect their status to improve quickly and prepared for the worst: a new rise in prices and unemployment level, a new drop in income, etc. The proliferation of pessimistic notions is further confirmed by the answers that respondents gave when asked, "Do you think you and your family will live better or worse than now in 12 months' time?" (see Table 12.6). When analyzing this data, we must note that every year, approximately one in every five respondents in every group being researched found it hard to give a definite answer, while other respondents (around 40%) predicted hat nothing would change in their lives. In addition, in 2016, the estimates of personal and family prospects shared by respondents from low-income and lower mid-income groups reflected a negative trend, while the upper mid-income and high-income groups started exhibiting a more positive look on their prospects more often. The dominance of negative expectations is also reaffirmed by the rise in the number of respondents who are, at least to some extent, anxious about failing to obtain the bare necessities during the next 12 months. For instance, from 2013 to 2016, the share of such respondents increased from 64.7 to 69.5% in the lower mid-income groups and from 56.3 to 62.2% in the upper mid-income groups.

It goes without saying that the processes we have revealed, along with any others, are far from reflecting the mindset of all population groups equally. Even during the more or less stable years of the so-called recovery growth, there were still some rather sizable population segments that were barely affected by the improvement in the quality of life and still remained deeply troubled by the sensation of their own financial insecurity. Throughout this period, the changes in the standards of living were accompanied by social and psychological tension; thus, people had to constantly over-exert themselves to meet their needs and interests. Nevertheless, the notable decrease of actual income and degradation of living conditions after a new curve of the crisis, even despite their relativity and incomparable scope, often prompted people, including those with low social status, to feel a certain set of premonitions regarding negative trends not only in the economic but also in the social aspect of their lifestyle. The increase in the number of people suffering from dire destitution gradually began to have a negative impact on the social and psychological attitudes of the wealthier population groups.

An important feature of the mindset of large population groups during the crisis years have been the rising concerns over employment issues and heightened fear of unemployment, which is among the most crucial issues that trouble Russians on a permanent basis. Many sociologists believe that the reason for such intense anxiety over the unemployment threat is primarily the "high level of uncertainty over the future economic situation and employment prospects, given that most people's level of income and savings is not enough to make up a safety cushion in case they lose their job".[14] But we can agree with this conclusion only in part. The monitoring results show another, no less important reason: the lack of well-paid jobs that would

---

[14] Ibragimova D. Kh., Akindinova N. V., Aukutsionek S. P., Bataeva A. E. The Formation of Unemployment Expectations and Their Influence on the Economic Behavior of the Population

Table 12.6 The dynamics of evaluating personal and family prospects in life, 2006–2016, %

Income groups	2006		2009		2013		2015		2016	
	Will live better	Will live worse	Will live better	Will live worse	Will live better	Will live worse	Will live better	Will live worse	Will live better	Will live worse
High-income groups	38.9	5.5	31.1	9.8	30.9	8.5	21.1	18.8	25.1	15.2
Upper mid-income groups	29.5	6.3	29.5	9.2	25.2	10.8	19.5	17.9	21.5	14.0
Lower mid-income groups	23.4	8.4	25.4	9.9	21.6	10.2	19.3	19.4	17.4	16.8
Low-income groups	19.1	11.0	26.7	10.7	24.1	10.8	20.4	17.8	16.3	16.4

Table 12.7 The dynamics of concern over possible job loss, 2006–2016, %

Income groups	2006		2013		2016	
	Concerned	Not concerned	Concerned	Not concerned	Concerned	Not concerned
High-income groups	49.6	38.0	47.7	38.9	60.7	27.3
Upper mid-income groups	48.3	36.4	52.6	34.3	60.8	25.1
Lower mid-income groups	51.5	32.0	57.8	28.5	65.7	20.7
Low-income groups	58.8	27.0	64.8	21.7	71.4	16.6

allow the employee to fulfill their potential, which leads to significant hurdles during job hunting, even for highly qualified professionals. And all of this at a time when the labor force deficiency in the country reaches 16% and keeps surpassing the deficiency of production assets.[15] Consequently, the creative potential of the mid-income population tier is often neglected or used inefficiently.

The unemployment threat causes more concern for employees with low wages, but the number of wealthier people who are worried about this issue is also quite high (Table 12.7). Furthermore, after the start of the crisis, negative outlooks became far more widespread among the population masses with the highest income. From 2013 to 2016, the share of respondents that were very concerned or slightly concerned about the prospect of losing their jobs increased by a mere 6.6 percentage points in the poorest population groups, by 7.9 and 8.2 percentage points in the lower and upper mid-income groups respectively, and by 13 percentage points in the highest income groups. But even counting these changes, the elements of anxiety and fear over the rising unemployment risks still occupied the minds of the poorest respondents far more than those of the wealthiest respondents.

The mounting economic challenges tends to draw the employers' attention to "unorthodox" forms of behavior in the labor market, which cull the rise of unemployment. These were especially widespread in Russia during the 1990s. The distinguished Russian economist R. I. Kapeliushnikov describes these behavior forms as various adaptive mechanisms that have asserted themselves in the Russian labor market and "either do not occur in other economies (in both transitioning and developed nations) or are quite limited elsewhere".[16] Specifically, this concerns such spontaneous adaptive strategies as administrative leaves, limited hours, side jobs, systemic wage delays, "covert" payments, etc. The use of such mechanisms allows employers

// Social Policy: the Realities of the 21st Century]. Collection of works by winners of the Fourth Grant Competition. Moscow: Independent Institute for Social Policy, 2004. p. 134–135.

[15] Enterprises Satisfied with Capacities and Sales // Expert. 2016. Issue 42. p. 72.

[16] Kapeliushnikov (2001).

to emerge from a crisis with minimal losses, but at the same time jeopardizes social security, as it leads to labor rights violations. And the lower the respondents' place on the wealth scale, the more often their rights get violated.

The analysis of RLMS-HSE data shows that among those employed and receiving average income, the share of respondents whose wages or working hours had been cut against their will over the 12 months preceding the survey, along with the share of those that were sent on forced unpaid leave, grew twofold over the 2013–2015 period, but then decreased by approximately one third in 2016. By contrast, the rise in the number of such employees during the previous economic crisis of 2008–2009 was even more significant (Table 12.8). Research also highlights a surge in the number of people from low-income and lower mid-income groups that work without registering their status officially. But a great many respondents from this category were also found among the wealthier Russians, many being young people that agree to work long and hard without an official labor contract, provided they are paid well.

Such employees are, in essence, deprived of their rights in the relationship with their employers: they have no employment guarantees, not healthcare and retirement coverage, and they cannot count on any social benefits. And even though many of them belong to relatively high-income groups and do not experience a lot of financial difficulties, they all may still be deemed vulnerable in terms of labor rights protection. As demonstrated by some research, even though poverty and rights violations overlap, the state of being disenfranchised, which implies "limited access to vital resources that are available to most of the population",[17] occurs far more often than poverty.

The latest positive trends include the significant decrease in the urgency of wage delays as an issue. From 2006 to 2016, the share of upper and lower mid-income employees whose wages got delayed shrunk from 5.3% to 2.8% and from 7.8% to 2.8%, respectively. The wage delays occurring in 2014–2016 only marginally exceeded the pre-crisis level and did not turn into a pandemic, as it had occurred during the previous crises. On a nationwide scale, the amount defaulted wages was relatively small. It equaled around 1% of the monthly labor compensation pool for various economic activity types. In a way, the drop in employees' actual earnings, caused by the surge of inflation, served as a protective shield, preventing employers from resorting to mass lay-offs and a wider spread of the wage delay practice.

Previous analysis shows that by the early 2010s, the vast majority of employed respondents, regardless of income status, had all been working for companies and organizations that provided their employees with guarantees and benefits under the applicable law: paid annual leaves, paid sick leaves, paid maternity leaves (for pregnancy, childbirth, and caring for a child under 3), etc.[18] (Table 12.9). At the same time, only one in every five employees had an opportunity to enjoy the guarantees

[17] Income and Social Services: Inequality, Vulnerability, Poverty / G. E. Besstremiannaia, A. Ia. Burdiak, A. S. Zaborovskaia [et. al.]; author team led by. T. N. Ovcharova; Independent Institute for Social Policy. M.: Higher School of Economics National Research University Publishing House, 2005, p. 253.

[18] That said, during the past years, the provision of such benefits has been experiencing a slightly negative trend (Tikhonova 2015), and those who did retain such benefits do not always enjoy them in full.

Table 12.8 The scale of labor rights violations, 2006–2016, %

	High-income groups			Upper mid-income groups			Lower mid-income groups			Low-income groups		
	2006	2009	2016	2006	2009	2016	2006	2009	2016	2006	2009	2016
The percentage of respondents who did not receive wages in full	5.5	5.4	3.0	5.3	6.3	2.8	7.8	6.1	2.8	15.9	11.8	3.9
Distribution of worker groups based on wage delay terms												
1 month or less	65.2	46.2	60.0	67.9	51.7	65.6	70.2	53.4	73.2	56.3	47.6	68.3
From 1 to 2 months	26.1	22.7	13.3	15.1	20.0	9.4	20.2	17.8	14.6	24.2	21.4	17.1
From 2 to 3 months	4.3	8.6	2.1	9.4	6.7	3.1	3.6	13.7	7.3	6.7	11.7	9.8
3 months or more	4.4	22.5	24.6	7.6	21.6	21.9	6.0	15.1	4.9	12.8	19.3	4.8
Experienced wage or working hours cuts over the past 12 months	4.8	11.2	6.2	5.1	12.0	8.5	5.9	12.3	7.6	7.4	13.7	8.8
Sent by the management on unpaid leave over the past 12 months	2.3	3.1	1.3	1.6	3.2	2.6	2.3	5.7	2.7	3.4	5.8	3.6
Working without getting officially registered	6.9	7.2	6.0	7.5	6.9	5.7	6.8	5.6	8.8	8.2	8.6	9.7

Table 12.9 Benefits for employees of industrial enterprises and other organizations, 2010, %

Guarantees and benefits	Income groups			
	High-income	Upper mid-income	Lower mid-income	Low-income
Paid routine leaves	88.7	90.5	90.3	87.6
Paid sick leaves	86.3	88.7	87.7	86.0
Paid maternity leaves (for pregnancy, childbirth, and caring for a child under 3)	71.4	74.1	73.3	72.2
Free treatment at government-owned medical facilities, full or partial coverage of treatment at other medical facilities	21.9	20.7	20.3	16.4
Full or partial coverage of visits to health resorts, retreats, tourist camps, and children's camps	20.0	22.0	22.1	19.1
Free children's education at government-owned preschool facilities, full or partial coverage of education at other preschool facilities	3.9	3.7	4.2	3.1
Free or discounted meals, meal coverage	12.9	10.8	9.6	7.8
Travel allowance, travel expenses coverage	13.3	11.5	8.7	5.6
Training at the organization's expense	23.4	22.8	20.2	17.1
Advance payments and loans for home construction or repair work, discounts for construction materials	6.2	4.2	3.7	2.7
Compensation for renting premises	2.2	1.6	2.0	1.6

and benefits that are not required by law but have traditionally been widespread across Russian companies and organizations, such as free treatments at state-owned medical facilities and full or partial coverage of treatment at other types of facilities, or full or partial coverage of vacations at health resorts, retreats, tourist camps, and children's camps. In turn, all other benefits, which are provided by employers on a voluntary basis, are mostly typical of successful companies, and are enjoyed by the more valuable and promising employees.

Faced with a dire economic crisis, employers have started optimizing their production and cutting losses, which has resulted in fewer expenses on personnel, including expenses on the "non-obligatory" benefits. At the same time, employers have started increasing the workload, assigning more duties without a wage increase and imposing more stringent control over their employees. The desire to increase efficiency and workload without raising wages and incurring other personnel expenses has been damaging to work conditions, resulting in a rise in labor rights violations. Among the most affected, are those employees that are not considered valuable assets and are the least protected, i.e. those engaged in unskilled or low-skilled labor and receiving low wages.

People's attitudes today are being impacted negatively by the dissatisfaction by a whole range of the government's social policy aspects and the impression that the measures taken by the state in the sphere of healthcare and education are not effective. Furthermore, the exacerbation of the budget crisis, which is pushing government officials to make unpopular decisions, such as limiting a number of social initiatives, causes growing concerns over whether or not these and other programs will remain in place in the future. There is a certain growing sense of social insecurity, linked to the development of the social security system.

The results of the monitoring of the population's attitude to optional insurance are especially indicative in this respect, as they reveal a certain wariness. Russians from the mid-income tier, just as most others, are largely distrustful towards insurance companies, which stunts the development of the entire Russian insurance system, which is supposed not only to bolster the people's social security and guarantee proper coverage in case they lose their ability to work or their income, but also to meet the various population categories' demands for insurance services as fully as possible.

In 2016, only 17.4% of respondents from lower mid-income groups and 15.6% of respondents from upper mid-income groups exhibited a certain level of trust towards insurance companies. In other words, approximately just as many as in the wealthiest cohort and slightly fewer than in the poorest cohort (16.1% and 22.3% respectively). What is more, the situation has remained almost unchanged throughout the past decade. The only notable trends are a barely significant growth of trust towards insurance companies among the poorest and underprivileged groups and a just as small decrease of trust among respondents with the highest income.

The number of people that use various types of optional insurance services still remains relatively low. Still, their general share increases along with their income. For example, in 2016 the share of respondents that signed an additional private medical insurance policy with an insurance company or healthcare facility amounted to a mere 2.8% (from 0.9% of the lowest income group up to 10.6% in the highest income group). In the vast majority of cases, the policy was covered by the companies or organizations that the respondents were working for.

Only 4.2% of those responding to the survey took out life insurance for accidents (from 2 to 9%, respectively). 5.4% of the relevant group of respondents insured their apartments or houses (from 3.1 to 11.3%). 3.8% of those respondents that owned property in the countryside insured their summer cottages (from 0.7 to 8.2%); while 4.8% of car owners took out extra insurance in addition to the Compulsory Automobile Liability Insurance (from 2.6 to 8.8%). A scant few respondents residing in rural areas insured their farm equipment, cattle, or other livestock.

Let us summarize

A drop in the quality of life and degrading living conditions, correlating to the exacerbating economic crisis, has diminished the protection of Russians' vital rights and interests, regardless of material well-being. Though, of course, the population groups with the lowest income have found themselves in especially dire straits. As for mid-income groups, while the upper mid-income tier has remained relatively stable, the lower mid-income tier has grown rapidly (by over one third) after the country entered the zone of economic turbulence. Though from a closer angle, it is evident that the make-up of upper mid-income groups has changed substantially, as their ranks have been bolstered by a number of people previously belonging to the high-income groups; while those who used to belong to the upper mid-income groups have slipped down into the lower mid-income groups. All of this points at the social and economic degradation of a large share of the mid-income tier, which only recently was considered relatively privileged compared to most other Russians. Over the past years, the mid-income groups have been losing their economic foothold and resilience against the threats and dangers of a society that is battling through a crisis. The process has been especially intensive in large cities.

A drop in actual income, the rising threat of unemployment and an uncertain future all exacerbate the dissatisfaction among people belonging to vastly different levels of the social ladder. This dissatisfaction concerns both life overall and the various aspects thereof. The most painful response to the negative changes in life comes from the mid-income respondents, who put special emphasis on their personal security and the security of their families. The lasting economic crisis has greatly undermined their social optimism and shaken their positive certainly in their social position. There has been a drop in the number of mid-income citizens that hope for economic improvement and a better quality of life for their families in the nearest future. Many have been forced to abandon the lifestyle they have been accustomed to, and to resort to austerity measures. The number of people from mid-income groups that are facing basic labor rights violations has increased twofold.

But even despite the emergence of a number of negative trends, the mid-income groups' social security situation does not appear to be critical. Many figures characterizing the protection of vital rights and interests of Russians from mid-income groups during the 2014–2016 economic crisis remained higher than during the 2008–2009 economic crisis.

References

Aleshina MV (2013) Social cohesion: the conceptualization of the notion and the social and cultural realia. A monograph. Variant OJSC Publishers, Moscow, p 109

Chernikova SA, Cherdantsev VP, Vshivkova GA (2015) Contemporary issues of social security. Fundamental Studies 11(part 4):836

Kapeliushnikov RI (2001) Russian labor market: adaptation without restructuring—M. Higher School of Economics National Research University, pp 7–8

Kuznetsov VN (2008) Social security, sociological dictionary. In: Osipov GV, Moskvichev LN (eds). Norma, Moscow, p 48

Mozgovaya AV, Shlykova EV (2016) Regional security as the target of sociological monitoring. Bulletin of Russian Peoples' Friendship University. The Sociology Series 16(4):834

Rimskii VL (2013) The market rationality and social arrangement. In: Patrushev SV (ed) The civic and the political in Russian social practices. Russian Political Encyclopedia (ROSSPEN), Moscow, p 85

Tikhonova NE (2015) Overt and covert consequences of economic crises for Russians. Sociol Res (12):16–27

Zinchenko NI (2007) The social dimension of security in Russia. Sociol Studies (2):137–140

Polina M. Kozyreva Doctor of Sociology, is First Deputy Director of the Federal Center of Theoretical and Applied Sociology of the Russian Academy of Sciences (former Institute of Sociology, Russian Academy of Sciences). She also serves as Director of the Center for Longitudinal Studies at the Institute of Social Policy of the National Research University Higher School of Economics. She is the Editor-in-Chief of the journal "Sotsiologicheskiy Zhurnal". P. Kozyreva directs one of the largest longitudinal surveys in Russia—"The Russia Longitudinal Monitoring Survey of HSE" (RLMS-HSE), which has been conducted since 1994. Selected publications in English: Ethnicity and Trust: Evidence from Russia // American Political Science Review, 2005 (in co-authorship with D. Bahry, M. Kosolapov and R. Wilson); "Consumption and Lifestyle in Russia" in Handbook on Social Stratification in the BRIC Countries. Change and Perspective/Editors: Peilin Li (Chinese Academy of Social Sciences, China), M.K. Gorshkov (Russian Academy of Sciences, Russia), Celi Scalon (Brazilian Sociological Society, Brazil), K.L. Sharma (Jaipur National University, India) // World Scientific Publishing Co. Pte. Ltd. 2013 (in co-authorship with A. Smirnov and A. Nizamova); Economic Change in Russia: Twenty Years of the Russian Longitudinal Monitoring Survey // Economics of Transition. 2015. Vol. 23. No. 2. (in co-authorship with Klara Sabirianova Peter); Data Resource Profile: The Russia Longitudinal Monitoring Survey—Higher School of Economics (RLMS-HSE) Phase II: Monitoring the Economic and Health Situation in Russia, 1994–2013 // International Journal of Epidemiology. 2016. Vol. 45(2) (in co-authorship with Kosolapov M., Popkin B.).

Alexander I. Smirnov Doctor of Sociology, Senior Researcher at the Federal Center of Theoretical and Applied Sociology of the Russian Academy of Sciences (former Institute of Sociology, Russian Academy of Sciences). His major interests include political sociology, social factors of Russian society consolidation (including institutional changes in army, family, etc.), dynamics of socio-economic conditions of Russian population. His publications are wide range, for example, "Factors forming Trust in Russian Army" // Sociological Studies. 2009, Issue 2, "Labyrinths of Development of Democracy in Russia", 2007 (in co-authorship with Kozyreva P.), "Consumption and Lifestyle in Russia" in Handbook on Social Stratification in the BRIC Countries. Change and Perspective / Editors: Peilin Li (Chinese Academy of Social Sciences, China), M.K. Gorshkov (Russian Academy of Sciences, Russia), Celi Scalon (Brazilian Sociological Society, Brazil), K.L. Sharma (Jaipur National University, India) // World Scientific Publishing Co. Pte. Ltd. 2013 (in co-authorship with P. Kozyreva and A. Nizamova).

Chapter 13
The Analyses of Objective Social Status and Subjective Identification of Middle Income Group in China—Also on the Construction of the Subjective Identified Olive-Shaped Society

Yan Cui and Yongliang Huang

13.1 Theoretical and Practical Meanings of the Research on Identification of Middle Income Group

The research on identification of middle income group has significant meaning on the social stability and sustained economic growth. In recent years, the expansion of the middle income group in the population has become a national strategy and the construction of the olive-shaped society has already gained recognition from both the academic circle and the mass people. Li Peilin thinks that the key to form an olive-shaped distribution pattern is to expand the share of the middle income group along with other measurements, such as state governance, comprehensive market control, re-distribution by the government and reinforcement of intra-household distribution (Li 2015; Li and Zhang 2014). But it is worth noting that to form the olive-shaped distribution pattern, we shall not only achieve higher share of the middle income group in the income structure but also the consistency of their subjective identification with their income. In other words, the objective formation of the olive-shaped distribution pattern does not equal to the identification of social position and social identity of the middle class by middle income group. And neither could the olive-shaped society brought by economic and income groups be automatically understood as the formation of a stable social structure. Examples of western countries indicates that the middle class can serve as a stabilizer of social development as the group has stable social values and mature social recognition. But it is a stabilizer only when

Y. Cui (✉)
Institute of Sociology in CASS, No.5 Jian Guo Men Nei Street, Beijing, China

Y. Huang
Graduate School of Chinese Academy of Social Sciences, No. 11 Changyu street, Beijing 102488, Fangshan District, China

P. Li and M. K. Gorshkov (eds.), *The Middle Income Group in China and Russia*, Research Series on the Chinese Dream and China's Development Path,
https://doi.org/10.1007/978-981-16-1464-4_13

the middle income group identifies themselves with the middle-class identity. As for our national reality, the downward identification of social status by the group tends to happen. That is, even with middle or higher income, people simply put themselves in the lower middle class or the underclass as their identification. This is also true for their tendency of social recognition. So, to an achieve a stable social structure, the identification of middle class by the middle income group, more than the objective construction of the olive-shaped society, shall be properly addressed. The consistency of the subjective identification and the objective income index shall help eliminate the mismatch of subjective and objective social stratum recognition, thus realizing a truly stable social structure.

13.2 Literature Review of the Downward Moving of Identification of Current Middle Income Group

With the re-structure of our social stratification and the reform of our economic system, we achieve fast industrialization. The emergence and development of the middle class come along with the fast process. As the number of people grows within the group, the strata consciousness begins to take form. Most domestic researches on the domestic middle class highlight the classification standard, scale, characteristics and components of them. For instance, some scholars believe that the aspects such as occupation, income, consumption, lifestyle and subjective identification are the determinant of whether an individual belongs to the middle class (Li 2003). There are other scholars who believe the middle class is the product of modern society, that stays just between the basic social classes (Liu 2007). Still, there are other scholars who use three indexes, i.e., income level, category type of employment and the education capital to divide the middle class into three kinds: the core middle class, the semi-core middle class and the marginal middle class (Li and Zhang 2008). It can be see that the research on the class consciousness, especially on the identification of middle class is relatively little. The so-called identification of class, is the recognition and feel of the members in the class for their status in the social strata. Despite the growing share of the middle class in the social strata, the identification of middle class is lagging behind. That is, the social roles, status, participation and functions of the middle class have not been fully recognized amongst people.

As for current downward moving of identification of the middle class, scholars contribute their separate analysis and discussion from varied perspectives. Gao Yong believes that the "change of the reference group" is the main reason of the downward identification of class (Gao 2013). Liu Xin uses "relative sense of deprivation" to provide explanation for the subjective recognition of the class (Liu 2002). Li Chunling takes that the influence of the collective anxiety alienates many middle-class people from their middle-class identity (Li 2016). From the "fragmented identification" aspect, Li Peilin points out the certain correlation between the objective stratification index and the subjective strata identification. But the correlation is weak, and the rupture of the social identification among strata could happen. Besides, there will be the complication of the solidification of Chinese social strata and the fragmentation of the strata consciousness (Li 2005).

As the population of 1980s and 1990s generations are joining the labor market, rapid changes are taking place in the structure of the middle income group. There are certain researches that would treat those people above as an entity when carrying out analysis of the middle income group. But the perspective of either the "relative deprivation" or the "collective anxiety" has provided future analysis on the internal discrepancy of different groups. We believe that different generations of population feature varied growth background and life experience. Those who were born in 1940s, 50s and 60s, and experienced the complete central planned economic era, have a special understanding and memory of the "class". Their life journey has certain influence on their identification of their social stratum. While for those 1970s, 80s and 90s generations, their life is mostly about the comprehensive reform and opening up. Almost zero "Communist Memory", which was shared by previous generation do they have. They identify themselves more with the western ideology and values. In the market economy wave, the concepts of "class" and "strata" are more about economic than political implications for people. These kind of life does exert certain influence on their middle-class identification. So, when carrying out the general analysis of the middle income group in this paper, deepened discussion on various intergenerational groups are carried out. This shall help locate the intergenerational differences and similarities.

13.3 Discussion on Influencing Factors of Middle Income Group Identification—Hypothesis, Data and Models

1. Identification of middle class strata of the middle income group and the influence factors on such identification

The analyses of this paper are entirely based on the data from China Social Survey (CSS 2015) by Chinese Academy of Social Sciences. The PPS (Probability Proportionate to Size Sampling) combined with indoor questionnaire methods were used with more than 10,000 urban and rural residents as samples. In the questionnaires of CSS, measurements such as the middle income group's identification, relative sense of deprivation and life burden were carried out. As for the definition of the middle income group, we made division among the interviewed households. Based on the objective index and the median of the income distribution as the standard, the total samples were then divided into the lower class, lower middle class, higher middle class and upper class. Of which, the lower middle and the higher middle income classes were defined as the middle income group. We then made comprehensive analysis and discussion on the identification and social recognition of the middle income group.

We analyzed first on whether the middle income group identify themselves as middle class. The statistics showed that 38.0% of the interviewees believed that they were the middle class, 33.5% believed that they were lower-middle class and 24.6% believed that they were the lower class of the society. When asked about whether they believed that their household belonged to the middle class, only 28.1% thought so while 71.9% denied it. The downward moving of their middle-class identification in most of the middle income group in China could therefore be seen. The downward-moving of identification of the middle income group was analyzed by three issues: "sense of relative deprivation", "collective anxiety" and social discrimination and institutional barriers.

As from the measurement of the sense of relative deprivation, one of the indexes is the sense of fairness on both wealth and income distribution. According to the statistics, the middle income group basically believed that the current social reality was relatively fair. For instance, 83.4% of the middle income group think the higher education entrance exam in China (Gaokao) was relatively or very fair, and only 16.6% of the people thought the opposite. But when questioned about wealth and income distribution, 57.1% of the people, more than half of the group thought that it was relatively or very unfair. Of which, 12.5% of the middle income group thought that the wealth and income distribution was very unfair; the statistics also showed that, 54.1% of the people, also more than half of the group thought that it was relatively or very unfair in terms of the urban–rural rights and entitlement. Of which, 10.5% of the middle income group thought that the urban–rural rights and entitlement was very unfair (Table 13.1).

Secondly, as for the collective anxiety of the middle income group, the statistics showed that quite a group of people felt the anxiety to a certain extent. Specifically, as for the social security, 18.5% of the group agreed very much that "the low level of current social security does not actually work" and 46.7% of the group relatively agreed so. Apart from the anxiety of the basic social security, quite a group of people

Table 13.1 The cognition of social equity and sense of relative deprivation of the middle income group (in: %)

	Very unfair	Not fair	Relatively fair	Very fair
Higher education entrance examination system	3.6	13.0	64.2	19.2
Real political rights citizens are entitled	5.7	27.7	58.6	8.0
Jurisdiction and law enforcement	4.9	28.6	58.8	7.7
Public medicare	4.3	23.4	64.4	7.9
Employment and job opportunities	6.6	40.3	49.3	3.8
Wealth and income distribution	12.5	44.6	39.4	3.5
Social security such as old-age security	6.8	30.5	55.4	7.3
Rights and entitlement between the urban and rural areas	10.5	43.6	42.6	3.3
General social equity	2.8	25.8	68.5	2.9

with middle income bore stressful economic and living burden. For instance, among the middle income group, 20.1% confessed that their children education spending was too high to be accepted; 30.4% stated that their family members were suffering from unemployment or unstable jobs; 33.6% expressed that their medicare expenditure was too high to be paid; 34.4% thought that their living condition poor and their ability to improve is less; 38.5% said that their routine life was difficult to be sustained due to their low income; there were 54.4% people complained about fast growing good prices that had already affected their living standards. In summary, nearly 1/3 of the middle income group encountered huge economic pressure, especially in the basic livelihood areas, such as employment, medicare, housing and price of commodities.

And as for the social discrimination and institutional barriers, the statistics showed that the two factors had affected the identification of the middle income group on their middle class very much. For the social discriminations, 11.3% of the middle income group stated that they were discriminated against their ages; 13.9% expressed that they were discriminated against their education level; 5.7% said that they were discriminated against their household registration (hereinafter "*hukou*") types; 13.9% thought that they were discriminated against their family backgrounds and social relationship. Meanwhile, 20.5% of the middle income group said that they were discriminated against their ages very much or pretty much; 16.2% expressed that they were discriminated against their gender very much or pretty much; 34.3% said that they were discriminated against their educational attainment very much or pretty much; 14.5% expressed that they were discriminated against their hukou types very much or pretty much, and 33.8% thought that they were discriminated against their family backgrounds and social relationship very much or pretty much.

It is worth noting that of all the current middle income group, 8.8% of them were migrant residents holding non-local hukou, and 6.7% were urban workers holding agricultural hukou. Meanwhile, 19.5% of the middle income group holding agricultural hukou and non-local hukou holder expressed that they were discriminated against their hukou very much or pretty much, and 28.1% expressed that they were discriminated against of such very much or pretty much. The two percentages were both much higher than that of the general middle income group. The hukou system was supposed to be the statistic tool of social management, whereas the social welfare and citizen rights are deeply confined by such currently. So, even some middle income group, although economically ranked in the middle class, did not enjoy equal rights only because of their rural or non-local hukou type. This definitely affected their middle income identification of their class.

2. Further discussion of identification of middle income group through models

(1) Hypothesis

With previous literature, we have set up a Logistic Regression Model to help analyze the influence of variables on the middle income group's identification. In the model, the dependent variable is a dichotomous variable of the identification of the middle income group (1, identification of the middle class; 0, no identification of the middle class) and the independent variables, mainly include the age group, urban–rural, education level, social cognition, etc. With which, we make the core study hypothesis:

Hypothesis 1: more sense of relative deprivation of the interviewee tends to lead to higher possibility of denial of their middle-class identity;

Hypothesis 2: more sense of institutional discrimination of the interviewee tends to lead to higher possibility of denial of their middle-class identity;

Hypothesis 3: more sense of anxiety and living pressure of the interviewee tends to lead to higher possibility of denial of their middle-class identity;

(2) Logistic Measurement Model of current middle income group identification in China

The paper has examined all the hypotheses using models. For details, please refer to Table 13.2. From the model, in terms of the control variable, the educational attainment has certain influence on the middle income class identification, as higher education background tends to bring about middle-class identification. Specifically speaking, when other variables are controlled, with each one year added to the educational attainment, the sample odds of the individuals that identify themselves with the middle class shall grow 1.031 times of those who identify themselves as middle class with less education ($\exp\beta = 1.031, \rho < 0.05$). Meanwhile, great discrepancy of such middle-class identification can be found within different age groups. Typically, with those 1970s generation as the control group, those 1940s and 1950s generation tend to identify themselves with middle class ($\exp\beta = 1.768$, $\rho < 0.01$; $\exp\beta = 1.567$, $\rho < 0.001$), while those 1980s and 1990s generation tend to deny the identification of middle class ($\exp\beta = 0.777$, $\rho < 0.100$; $\exp\beta = 0.564$, $\rho < 0.05$).

The model testifies the hypothesis, "more sense of anxiety and living pressure of the interviewee tends to lead to higher possibility of denial of their middle class identity". To be more specific, those who tended to believe that the low level of current social security did not actually work tended to show higher possibility of denial of their middle-class identity. ($\exp\beta = 0.872$, $\rho < 0.050$). Meanwhile, those who showed higher satisfaction over the old-age pensions and medicare tended to identify themselves with middle class ($\exp\beta = 1.070$, $\rho < 0.050$; $\exp\beta = 1.060$, $\rho < 0.100$).

The model testifies the hypothesis, "more sense of relative deprivation tends to lead to higher possibility of denial of their middle-class identity". Specifically, those who tended to believe the inequality of the current social wealth and income had higher possibility to deny their middle-class identity ($\exp\beta = 1.403$, $\rho < 0.000$). Meanwhile, urban residents tended to show lower identification rate than those rural residents ($\exp\beta = 0.716$, $\rho < 0.01$).

The hukou had its significant role in the institutional discrimination. Specifically, the migrant workers, the rural hukou holders working in the urban area tend to deny their middle-class identification ($\exp\beta = 0.620$, $\rho < 0.001$); Previous hypothesis above mentioned is supported herein.

As for the occupational identity, those who work for the "in-system" government departments tended to identify themselves with the middle class ($\exp\beta = 1.371$, $\rho < 0.100$). And it is worth noting that the self-hired businessman also tended to identify themselves as the middle class ($\exp\beta = 1.389$, $\rho < 0.050$).

Table 13.2 Logistic measurement model of current middle income group identification in China

	B	Standard error	Wald value	Significance	Exp (B)
Gender (Male: 1)	−0.312	0.100	9.675	0.002	0.732
Age group[a]					
Born in 1940s	0.570	0.182	9.788	0.002	1.768
Born in 1950s	0.449	0.141	10.116	0.001	1.567
Born in 1960s	0.076	0.136	0.315	0.575	1.079
Born in 1980s	−0.252	0.167	2.275	0.100	0.777
Born in 1990s	−0.572	0.247	5.349	0.021	0.564
Political identity[b]					
Member of Communist Youth League	−0.043	0.312	0.019	0.891	0.958
General public	−0.251	0.166	2.291	0.130	0.778
Yeas of education	0.031	0.015	4.030	0.045	1.031
Migrant workers	−0.478	0.127	14.210	0.000	0.620
Employment sector[c]					
Government department	0.316	0.300	1.110	0.092	1.371
State/Collective owned enterprise units and institutions	−0.166	0.212	0.616	0.433	0.847
Private enterprise	−0.194	0.151	1.639	0.200	0.824
Individual business	0.329	0.149	4.888	0.027	1.389
Inequality of wealth and income	0.339	0.066	26.223	0.000	1.403
Anxiety over social security	−0.137	0.064	4.528	0.033	0.872
Satisfaction of old-age security	0.067	0.034	3.892	0.049	1.070
Satisfaction of medicare	0.059	0.034	2.978	0.084	1.060
Urban residents (rural residents: 0)	−0.334	0.108	9.464	0.002	0.716
Constant	−1.038	0.356	8.499	0.004	0.354

Note [a] The control group is the group that were born in 1970s
[b] The control group is the China Communist Party members
[c] The control group is the unemployed ones

(3) Logistic Measurement Model of current middle income group identification among different age groups in China

We have also analyzed the middle income group identification among different age groups in China. We first made comparison of identification between 1940s, 1950s and 1960s generations with 1970s, 1980s and 1990s generations. See Table 13.3 for details.

As for the occupation sector, those who work for the "in-system" government departments tended to identify themselves with the middle class (exp$\beta = 2.52$, $\rho < 0.100$). And it is worth noting that the self-hired businessman tended to identify themselves with the middle class (exp$\beta = 2.35$, $\rho < 0.000$). This to some extent has

Table 13.3 Logistic measurement model of current middle income group identification among age groups in China

	Aged group				Young group			
	β	Standard error	Significance	Exp(β)	β	Standard error	Significance	Exp(β)
Gender (Male: 1)	−0.30	0.21	0.15	0.74	−0.74	0.24	0.00	0.48
Political identity[a]								
Member of Communist Youth League	2.29	1.39	0.10	9.84	0.64	1.17	0.59	1.89
General public	0.47	0.39	0.24	1.59	−0.47	0.41	0.26	0.63
Yeas of education	0.01	0.03	0.03	1.01	−0.01	0.04	0.08	0.99
Migrant workers	−0.54	0.28	0.05	0.58	−0.18	0.30	0.55	0.84
Employment sector[b]								
Government department	0.92	0.53	0.08	2.52	−0.08	0.74	0.91	0.92
State/Collective owned enterprise units and institutions	−0.49	0.43	0.26	0.61	0.32	0.42	0.45	1.37
Private enterprise	0.06	0.30	0.85	1.06	0.31	0.32	0.34	1.36
Individual business	0.33	0.24	0.17	1.38	0.85	0.28	0.00	2.35
Inequality of wealth and income	0.34	0.14	0.01	1.40	0.20	0.15	0.20	1.22
Anxiety over social security	−0.01	0.14	0.05	0.99	−0.16	0.15	0.31	0.86
Urban residents (rural residents: 0)	−0.49	0.22	0.02	0.61	−0.96	0.25	0.00	0.38
Constant	−2.68	0.86	0.00	0.07	−0.67	0.91	0.46	0.51

Note [a] The control group is the China Communist Party members
[b] The control group is the unemployed ones

verified the "change of the reference" raised by a scholar previously. Meanwhile, the sense of relative deprivation has less influence on the middle-class identification for the young generation (expβ = 1.22, ρ = 0.200) than the aged generation (expβ = 1.40, ρ = 0.010). From the anxiety hypothesis, the aged generation tended to show denial of their middle-class identification with stronger anxiety and higher life pressure (expβ = 0.99, ρ = 0.050); the young generation demonstrate less influence of their middle-class identification from their anxiety (expβ = 0.86, ρ = 0.310).

13.4 The Analyses of Mismatched Subjective Identification of the Middle Income Group in China

In all, the downward-moving of the subjective social status of the middle income group is testified in this paper. Many negatives can be brought upon the social stability and sustained development. If the middle income group does not identify themselves as the middle class in terms of their subjective cognition and tends to identify themselves with the lower middle class or the lower class, the dissatisfaction of such income group may find it properly expressed.

As for a stable social form, the middle class should be the major part. Generally speaking, the middle class tend to have high cognition of the social values. They are politically conservative and have high tolerance over the social reform. And in the middle class dominated society, the social ideology can be well maintained. They contribute constructive, instead of destructive or subversive feedback to the government. In addition, the middle class tend to participate in the country and social activities. They make their political appeals in an "in-system" channel.

It is found that there exists a mismatch between the subjective identification of social position and objective income. The downward-moving of status identification of the middle income group has already become a common phenomenon in our society. The objective formation of the olive-shaped society does not necessarily equal to the subjective cognition of the olive-shaped society.

On one hand, the mismatch of the subjective cognition and objective income reflect the sense of relative deprivation shared by the current middle income group. As the income has been raised for each member of the society along with the reform and opening up and the economic development in the country, the gap between the rich and the poor, the expanded discrepancy between the upper class and all the other strata have impaired the social identification of the middle class. Some scholar points out that the olive-shaped society is a relatively stable one (Li and Zhang 2014) (P7-16). In other words, a sustained social development can only be achieved when the middle class dominate the society and enjoy most of the social resources and wealth. But even the middle income group has benefited from the reform and opening up, our national reality is that the certain unfairness and partiality in the current social system has brought about the evident sense of relative deprivation by the social unfairness. The sense has aggravated the identification with the lower middle class subjectively by the middle class. This identification has made their social identification similar with the underprivileged group in terms of ideology, social values and political participation.

As we are maintaining high-speed economic development, the discordance of the social and economic development has torn apart the social security of many livelihood areas from the economic pace, leaving the middle class under huge pressures such as housing, medicare, old-age caring, employment, etc. Mounted life burden leaves the middle income group with incomplete identification of the middle class. This reflects the absence of the policy security in the livelihood sector, for which the middle-class lack sense of security. It can be observed from the data that the incomplete welfare and security system in the livelihood, part of the middle income group show huge anxiety in terms of the expectation of future and life burden.

And the institutional barrier and social discrimination have engraved the situation that some of middle income group does not completely accept their middle-class identity. From the statistics, the current hukou arrangement leads to evident identification difference as for different hukou type holders. Specifically, the current region division of the hukou casts a huge wall between the local and non-local hukou type holders. The non-local ones are bearing the significant difference in terms of employment, medicare, school attendance, etc. The differentiated institutional arrangement leads to the fact that those economically middle income group do not accept their middle-class tag when it is about the social identity mostly represented by the hukou types. In other words, the middle-class tag is also about the equal civil rights, complete citizenship, stable social mentality, positive comment on the government, relatively satisfactory life, etc. As for the non-local ones who are rated as the "Second Class Citizen" because of the hukou reason, they cannot identify themselves with the middle class when they does not enjoy equal civil rights. For the non-locals who live in the first-tire cities, such as Beijing, Shanghai, Guangzhou, etc., even when they have higher educational attainment and techniques and skills, have positions in the high-tech enterprises and earned a lot, they are just drifting there mentally. This is not the satisfactory lifestyle what middle class deserves and the active and health social mentality that naturally represented by middle class is on the non-locals' mind.

In all, the downward-moving of the identification by the middle income group reflects both the sense of relative deprivation and social inequality felt by the middle income group, and the inner anxiety for the missing social security during the reform and opening up process. Meanwhile, the alienation of the hukou has undermined the basis of identification of middle class for some of the middle income group.

13.5 Policy Suggestions on Improving the Identification of Middle Class by the Middle Income Group

It is found that the downward-moving of social position identification of the middle income group still exists in our society. Quite many people who economically belong to middle income group think themselves more as a lower class. They do not identify themselves as the middle class. As for the policy suggestion, this paper believes that, to improve the identification of the middle class, the following aspects should be attended to by the government.

First, the income distribution structure shall be further implemented, and the systems such as the state fiscal and taxation system should have more favor for the middle income group and the underprivileged group. The elimination of unequal benefit transfer and the reduction and the removal of the privileged class shall help realize the equalization of economic, civil, political and legal rights for the whole strata. If the privileged class exists, favored social and economic resources distribution favor the privileged class, the unbalanced social mentality and sense of relative deprivation of the public shall only be engraved. To re-adjust the unreasonable social structure, the equal distribution among all social groups should be addressed, which requests both the use of market measures to distribute the social wealth and the improvement of legal system, elimination of gray income channel and proper adjustment of wealth re-distribution. Those can promote the equity and justice of the income distribution.

And the social welfare arrangement for the people's livelihood should be enhanced to really improve the social security level and raise the public's sense of security. The raise of the welfare and security in the social security polity and the elimination of the age-caring and medicare issues can help improve identification of the middle income group. From the statistics, the main part of the middle income group are the people who are working in the government, technicians, small and medium enterprises, some individual businessman, middle or highly skilled workers, land contract rural household operators or professional farmers on plantation or breeding, and some of them do not enjoy the exclusive "in-system" social welfare and security. For the middle income group, they do not enjoy the complete social security as those hired "in-system". Critical incidents in their life may even destroy their life quality and reduce them into low income group or the group of poverty. Therefore, to promote the identification of the middle income group, the social security system should be further improved. A well-constructed social security system shall free the middle income group from their great worries as mentioned above in the paper.

Meanwhile, social policies that cast institutional discrimination should be abolished gradually. The equal rights of the citizens should be safeguarded. The bias of social identification of the public due to the discrepancy brought by the hukou system should be called off too. The disconnection of the link between the hukou system and social welfare, the elimination of identity definition and negative division on civil right of the hukou, and the restoration of its social management function of the system are all required by the realization of social fairness and justice, the harmony and stability of the society and the cohesion of the society.

To sum up, only when the policy reform and system innovation in those above areas are implemented, could the current negative social mentality be effectively reversed. The wealth and income distribution can be kept up in pace with the construction of the olive-shaped society in China following that. Thus, the harmony and stability shall be maintained and the development shall be sustained.

References

Gao Y (2013) Why the downward moving of social status and strata—also on the transformation of the social status and strata identification basis. Society 4

Li C (2003) The construction and percentage of current middle class in China. Chin J Pop Sci 6

Li P (2005) Social conflict and class consciousness: a study of current social contradictions in China. Society 1
Li P (2015) The expansion of middle class and an olive-shaped society. Int Econ Rev 1
Li C (2016) The sense of insecurity and anxieties. Beijing Cult Rev 4
Li P, Zhang Y (2008) The scale, identification and social attitude of the middle class in China. Society 2
Li P, Zhang Y (2014) A study of issues concerning the construction of an olive-shaped distribution pattern. Jiangsu Social Sci 5
Liu X (2002) The relative sense of deprivation and the recognition of the strata. Sociol Study 1
Liu X (2007) The urban strata and the positioning of middle class in China. Sociol Study 6

Yan Cui assistant professor of the Institute of Sociology in CASS, Ph.D, specialized in social development research and social research method. Major publication includes Research on the Motivation of Citizens' Environmental Organization Participation, The General Public's Urban Attributes During the Process of Urbanization.

Yongliang Huang student of the Graduate School of Chinese Academy of Social Sciences, Ph.D, specialized in social development research and sociology of consumption.

Chapter 14
The Identities of the Middle Class

N. V. Latova

When studying society and its members, researchers are bound to face the problem of classifying individuals into social groups, sooner or later. And while the matter of formal group classification is always more or less clear, what is far less evident is the way people identify themselves in relation to various social groups (i.e. which groups they see themselves belonging to), along with the way they perceive the groups ("us" or "them") and the role the groups play in people's lives (whether they bring them together or draw them apart). All of these questions may be answered by means of analyzing social identity.

A person's social identity[1] means that a person identifies himself with a specific community (a professional, gender, status, or any other group). On the one hand, it is the result of a person's self-perception and outlook on social reality; and on the other hand, it is the force the cements this perception and outlook, turning it into a foundation of life's activity. A person's actual behavior depends on who they think they are and which community they identify with the most, as well as on the number and nature of groups that they believe they belong to.

There is a broad range of methods that can be used to study identity. One of them is placing the individual into a predetermined framework, i.e. singling out a certain group before hand and offering the respondent to describe their position therein. This way of studying social identity is the best option for defining vertical social structures. For instance, it is used for studying respondents' status anchoring in a vertical social hierarchy. The assumption here is that people who evaluate their social standing in

[1] Back in 1972, Henri Tajfel, founder of the social identity theory, described the category of social identity as individual knowledge that one belongs to a specific social group, as well as the emotional and axiological value of belonging to this group (Turner 1982). Later on, the followers of the British scholar expanded and further enhanced this theory.

N. V. Latova (✉)
Institute of Sociology of FCTAS RAS, Moscow, Russia

P. Li and M. K. Gorshkov (eds.), *The Middle Income Group in China and Russia*, Research Series on the Chinese Dream and China's Development Path,
https://doi.org/10.1007/978-981-16-1464-4_14

a certain way also tend to follow the precise behavior patterns that are customary among groups with the social status that they believe to be similar to theirs.

However, this type of self-identification informs us only about the respondents' most generalized notions of their place in the society they live in. When offering respondents to identify themselves according to this method, it is necessary to bear in mind that the resulting data will reflect the individual's general level of satisfaction with their place in society, rather than the conscious and rational choice of position in the social structure and the application of "us" and "them" terms to specific social subgroups. In order to gain an understanding of individuals' specific identities and of their actual self-identification, it is not enough to determine how they view their social status. What is needed is a ranking system of groups that the individual feels close to. This method reveals the horizontal social structure. When applied to income groups, the first approach shows us the characteristic features of various income groups' self-anchoring on a vertical scale, while the second approach allows us to single out the roles that people attribute to themselves and are ready to act upon on a horizontal scale.

Let us apply both methods to the Russian middle class, which we have defined in an economic sense.

To help respondents identify their position in society, we used a vertical ten-point social status scale (the "ten-step social ladder") that respondents needed to position themselves on. This method is quite widespread in international practice and has long been in use in a range of different versions.[2] Based on the data derived, we have built social structure models for different income groups in Russia (Fig. 14.1), where the 1st level stands for the lowest position in the vertical social hierarchy, while the 10th stands for the highest.

[2] The original source of this method is the so-called "Cantril's Ladder" (Kilpatrick and Cantril 1960), which is used for evaluating the level of a person's satisfaction with their life. The method has a number of varieties, including the MacArthur Scale of Subjective Social Status (Adler and Stewart (2007), which is the methodology we used as a base for our research. In the classical methodology, the questions contain hints on what the respondent should associate the scale's topmost level with: a lot of money, the best education, and a prestigious job. In our case, we merely used the terms "the top of society" and "the bottom of society", without any correlation to specific social and economic parameters.

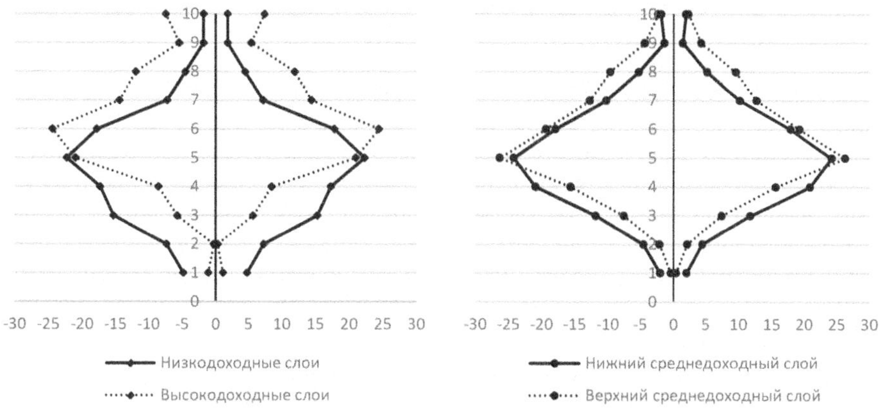

Fig. 14.1 The models of social structure of income groups in Russia, based on self-evaluation of people's social status, 2015, %[3]

Table 14.1 Figures describing the self-evaluation of social status in different income groups of Russians, 2015

Groups	Average social status score	Median social status score	The share of people on the lower 5 levels of the social scale, %
High-income groups	6.2	6	37
Upper mid-income group	5.6	5	52
Lower mid-income group	5	5	63
Low-income groups	4.7	5	67

Overall, as seen in Fig. 14.1, *most Russians from all social positions describe themselves as belonging to the middle groups.* Nevertheless, the higher the income rank of a respondent group, the more its subjective social structure model moves up the scale.[4] That said, the model only transitions into a new quality (as the median social status evaluation equals 6 and the share of Russians on the bottom 5 levels of the social scale amounts to a mere 37%) among high-income groups (Table 14.1). As for the two subgroups of the mid-income groups, their notion of their social status is, in a way, somewhere in between before the notions of Russians with low and high income (Fig. 14.1 and Table 14.1).

[3] The model was built as follows: as the status scale is vertical, we used the datum axis for ranging the percentage of people who chose the relevant score; and then, to make the figure symmetrical, we flipped it into the negative value plane.

[4] There is a number of preceding papers on this peculiarity of respondents' personal social status evaluation, including: Lindemann (2007). To learn more about the way this pattern exhibited itself in Russia during different periods, see: Tikhonova (2014).

At first glance, the difference between the models of subjective social structure, as perceived by the upper and lower mid-income groups (Fig. 14.1), is minimal. However, a closer inspection reveals certain specific features. The lower segment of the lower mid-income model (4th level) has a tendency to "sag down", which vaguely resembles similar trend in the low-income model. The upper mid-income model, on the other hand, shoots up around the 8th level, which, albeit less pronounced, is still reminiscent of the upward curve on the 8th level of the high-income group model.

Consequently, *despite being quite close, both subgroups of the mid-income group are not completely similar in terms of their members' status identity.* Russians from the lower mid-income group are somewhat closer to those from the low-income group, while members of the upper mid-income group are more inclined towards presenting themselves as people with high status, which is more typical of Russians from the high-income group. In general, however, *members of both subgroups of the mid-income group evaluate their social status in a way that is closer to low-income than high-income groups.* Even in the case of the upper mid-income group, there still are some differences, both qualitative and quantitative, in terms of the average social status score, the median social status score, and number of people on the lower 5 levels of the social scale, as compared to similar figures in the high-income group (Table 14.1).

We have already remarked upon the close link between income level and Russians' self-identification of their status. The importance of this factor is reaffirmed by the degree to which Russians from different income groups are satisfied with their social status (Fig. 14.2). The patterns that we noted before, while reviewing the models of subjective social structure in different income groups, get fully reproduced when we look at the level of people's satisfaction with their status in their respective groups. First of all, the patterns are reflected in the striking discrepancies between low-income and high-income groups (they differ twofold in terms of perceiving their status in society as good and eightfold in terms of perceiving their status as "bad"). Furthermore, the lower mid-income groups is relatively close to the low-income group (the number of "good" responses differs by 5 percentage points, and the number of "bad" responses differs by 7 percentage points). And finally, we can note that the upper mid-income group combines traits that are typical of both high-income groups (one third of the respondents has described their status as "good") and of lower mid-income groups, with a slight dominance of similarity to the latter (in terms of "bad" responses).

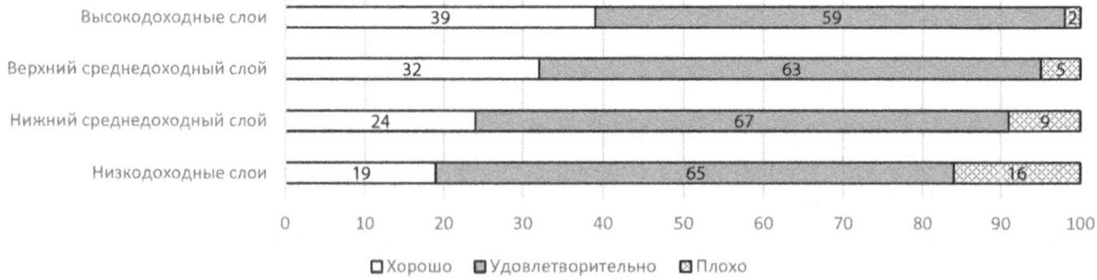

Fig. 14.2 Level of Russians' satisfaction with their social status across income groups, 2015, %

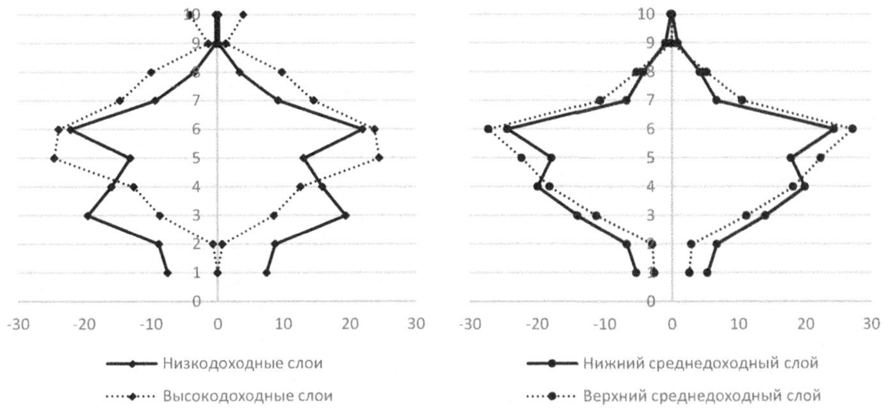

Fig. 14.3 Models of social structure of income groups in Russia, based on self-evaluation of people's social status, 2011, %

Table 14.2 Figures describing the self-evaluation of social status in different income groups of Russians, 2011

Groups	Average social status score	Median social status score	Share of people on the lower 5 levels of the social scale, %
High-income groups	5.8	6	46
Upper mid-income group	5	5	57
Lower mid-income group	4.7	5	64
Low-income groups	4.4	4	65

But how stable are the patterns we have discovered in modern Russia, and can they change with time? We shall attempt to answer this question by using 2011 data.[5] Let us now build several models of income groups' social structure for the Russia of then (Fig. 14.3), similar to the ones we based on the 2015 data.

We can see that, even though all models of social structure have undergone certain changes over the past 3 years, in general, *they have still retained all their characteristic features. This reflects the stability of both the subjective structure of Russian society as a whole, and the identities of mid-income groups.*

As evidenced by Table 14.2, the low-income group has been the only one to experience significant changes in status identification over the past 4 years. Even

[5] It must be noted that our choice of the April data for 2011 is grounded, in part, in the peculiarities of our tool set (our survey includes questions on status self-anchoring and a number of different role identities), as well as in the stability and optimism that were the general mood that year (see: Latova (2016). During this period, on the one hand, the 2008 crisis had already given way to economic growth, and on the other hand, the political protests of late 2011 were yet to come. Consequently, we must conclude that in Russians' cultural mindset in the April of 2011 way not fogged over by any political or economic cataclysms.

though the average social status score increased across all income groups, the median social status score increased only in the low-income group (from 4 points in 2011 to 5 points in 2015), which brought this group somewhat closer to the lower mid-income group.

To summarize: the way Russians from different income groups identify themselves based on their social status is greatly impacted by their income level: the higher the income group's ranking, the higher the place respondents choose for themselves on the social scale. In this respect, both mid-income subgroups are very close to one another and stand apart from all other income groups. Even despite the fact that *the lower mid-income group tends to gravitate towards Russians from the low-income group, and the upper mid-income group exhibits certain traits typical of the high-income group.* These patterns remained stable from 2011 to 2015.

To gain a better understanding of the identities of Russians from the "economic" middle class, however, we must define not only their status anchoring but also their role-based identities. We can derive these figures by asking respondents to say which groups of people they can describe as "us", i.e. as people that they easily find common ground with, communities that are close to them and inspire a sense of belonging.

The 2015 survey provided a list of 11 groups that respondents were asked to define as "us" or "them". They had to make their pick out of 3 answers: if the respondent believed that the group fit into the "us" category, they had to choose "significantly close"; if they did not feel too close to the group but at the same time would not have identified the group as "them", they had to choose "somewhat"; and if the respondent did not feel like they belonged in the group at all, they had to choose "do not feel close". The respondents' choices can be termed as follows: "significantly" as sustainable positive identification; "somewhat" as unsustainable positive identification; and "do not feel close" as negative identification. The two extremes, the sustainable positive identification and the negative identification, are of the most interest when analyzing self-identification of different income groups.

We shall now contrast mid-income groups against the other income groups through the prism of their sustainable positive identities (Table 14.3).

Overall, we have not discovered major difference between income groups' identity structures, which means that *differences in income do not have a notable impact on the nature of communities that Russians prefer to interact with.* And this is hardly surprising, taking into account the relatively recent shared Soviet past, when everyone was oriented on the same worldview standards and priorities. Moreover, we must acknowledge that, when it comes to education level and professional position, income groups are very heterogeneous in nature, which also impacts their worldviews, either binging them close or drawing them apart.

The most popular group identities among Russians with middle income include: "people with the same life stance", "people with the same hobbies and passions", and "people with the same job". No less than 50% of each group's members prefer to identify with one of these groups. One third of the respondents both in the lower and in the upper mid-income group also feel close to "people in the same financial circumstances", "Russian citizens", and "people of the same ethnicity". By contrast,

Table 14.3 Ranking structure of sustainable positive self-identification in different income groups of Russians, 2015, %

Identities	Lower Mid-income group	Upper Mid-income group	Mid-income groups overall	For reference	
				Low-Income groups	High-Income groups
People with the same life stance	62	59	**60**	55	57
People with the same hobbies and passions	54	57	**55**	50	54
People with the same job[a]	46	54	**49**	39	53
People in the same financial circumstances	36	35	**36**	34	34
Russian citizens	32	35	**33**	29	33
People of the same ethnicity	29	28	**29**	28	27
Members of the working class	23	18	**21**	25	17
Members of the middle class	19	20	**19**	20	17

[a]It bears noting that we have re-calculated the data in this category for employed respondents only. This has lead to a slight increase of the figures in the table, but has not impacted the ranking structure of sustainable positive identification. As most unemployed Russians are retirees, this prompts a conclusion that, as a person retires, their job-based identification ceases to be as strong, but does not diminish enough to influence the overall pattern. Moreover, in the upper mid-income group, job-based identification among retirees barely diminishes at all. All the above considered, the data in Table 14.3 is given as percentage of all respondents.

the least popular identities are based on social class: "members of the working class" and "members of the middle class".

Even though income groups are generally close to one another in terms of how strongly they express their different identities, these identities are somewhat more prominent on the mid-income level. This mostly concerns such identities as "people with the same life stance", "people with the same hobbies and passions", "people in the same financial circumstances", and "people of the same ethnicity". As for identities like "people with the same job" and "Russian citizens", they are, in general, expressed by mid-income groups no stronger than by other income groups. Nevertheless, if we look at the level-based structure, we will see that on the upper mid-income level these identities are also more salient than in other groups.

There is only one identity that entails notable changes across income groups: "people with the same job". This means that job-based identity can be viewed as a certain marker for differentiating income groups. Overall, this identity is expressed the least in low-income groups (39%) and the most in the upper mid-income and high-income groups (54% and 53%, respectively). The same identity also differentiates

Table 14.4 Ranking structure of negative self-identification in different income groups of Russians, 2015, %

Identities	Lower mid-income group	Upper mid-income group	Mid-income groups overall	For reference	
				Low-income groups	High-income groups
Europeans	56	46	**52**	64	46
Members of the lowest class	51	54	**52**	49	57
The poor	48	54	**50**	48	59

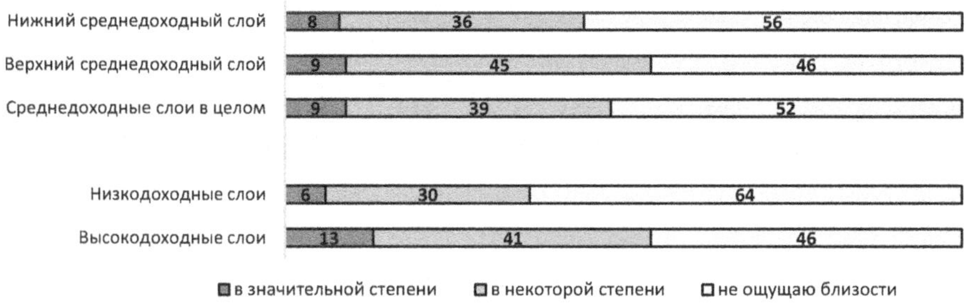

Fig. 14.4 Self-identification as Europeans across income groups, 2015, %

the two subgroups of the mid-income group (by 8 percentage points), although in terms of expressing other identities, they are more similar than not.

Now we shall dwell on the differences within mid-income groups from the point of view of negative self-identification (Table 14.4). What we see here are groups that Russians reject, perceiving them as "them" rather than "us". There are three such identities: "Europeans", "the poor", and "members of the lowest class".

As it happens with sustainable positive identification, the ranking structure of negative self-identification is generally similar across all income groups. Mid-income groups, as Russians overall, tend to perceive Europeans as "them" the most. Other groups that get rejected include "members of the lowest class", with "the poor" rounding up the list. However, we can note that all negative identities depend on income group ranking. The lower the income group rank, the less inclined its members are to deny feeling close to "the lowest class" and "the poor".

European identity is a separate matter entirely. Overall, this issue has always been traditionally controversial for Russia. Going back to disputes between the "slavophiles" and the "westernizers", it currently takes the form of trying to rationalize Russia's place in the West vs East civilization paradigm. Let us take a closers look at mid-income groups' self-identification in this respect (Fig. 14.4). Feeling close to Europeans (sustainable positive identification) is typical only of a very small share of Russians, although these figures increase together with income. Furthermore, despite this identity being quite rare among all groups of Russians, it is still expressed by members of high-income groups far more often than by members of low-income groups. Mid-income groups are in the middle in this respect. Moreover, as we see in Fig. 14.4, *negative responses regarding European identity may be treated as a differentiating marker for income groups* (the gap between the number of "do not feel close" responses given by low-income and high-income groups reaches 18%). Even in mid-income groups, where the identity expression of the lower and upper subgroups tends to differ very little, the matter of identifying as Europeans has started exhibiting a certain discrepancy. For instance, 56% of respondents from the lower mid-income group do not feel close to Europeans at all, whereas in the upper mid-income group, the figures reach a mere 46%. To summarize, *the split in society's views on European identity runs through the mid-income groups.*

We have noted before the class-based identification is not too popular in Russian society. Nevertheless, one fifth of the population seems certain in its belief that they feel close to groups of people joined within the same class. The traditional social class theory stipulates that different classes have different worldviews. As a result, when expressing sustainable positive identification with a certain social class, a person must feel close to this particular class and reject all others. Otherwise, we will have to conclude that even those respondents who claim to have class-based identity do not, in fact, have any class-based mentality. To best determine whether this is the case in modern Russia, we have decided to bring together all three class-based identities and to consider the way Russians view them as a whole (Table 14.5).

We should note that around 20% of respondents from each income group, when claiming to have a sustainable class-based identity, actually have a combined identity, feeling like they belong to all three classes at once. Dual identity is an even more common occurrence. At the same time, cases when a respondent might identify both as a person from the lowest class and a person from the middle class (i.e.

Table 14.5 Self-anchoring in different social classes across income groups, 2015, %

Groups	Consistent identification as			Combined identification as			
	Lowest class	Working class	Middle class	Lowest/working/middle class	Lowest/working class	Working/middle class	Lowest/middle class
High-income groups	4	30	30	19	1	16	0
Upper mid-income group	2	18	27	22	6	25	0
Lower mid-income group	2	26	20	18	9	24	1
Low-income groups	6	18	13	20	9	33	1

as having two opposite, mutually exclusive identities) are extremely rare. Furthermore, as respondents' income increases, we can note a drop in the share of those who feel that they have such types of dual identity "lowest class/working class" and "working class/middle class". In general, dual class-based identity is typical of 43% of respondents from low-income groups, 34% of respondents from the lower subgroup of mid-income groups, 31% of respondents from the upper mid-income group, and 17% of the high-income group. In other words, the higher the income, the smaller the share of people with "dual" class-based identity. In this respect, *Russians from mid-income groups are similar to one another while differing from the low-income group; nevertheless, they are, in general, much closer to the latter than to the high-income group.*

We must highlight that respondents' professional status plays a crucial role in their combined class-based identification. People with less prestigious jobs tend to form a so-called "spoiled identity".[6] For instance, 27% of people who sustainably identify with all three classes come from rural areas, while 21% are blue-collar workers without a higher education. Another 19% are retirees from urban areas, whose current identities overlap with their former ones. In turn, among people whose responses indicate a dual "working class/middle class" identity, 28% are blue-collar workers without a higher education, 27% are people from rural areas, and 16% are urban retirees.

As for consistent identification with a single social class, the patterns here are much clearer: *as their income increases, Russians become more aware of their class-based identity.* For example, significant correlation between income and identity is quite evident among respondents who consistently identify themselves only as the middle class: the higher their income, the more often they describe people from the middle class as "us". Incidentally, regarding this matter, the upper mid-income group is definitely closer to the high-income group, whereas the lower mid-income group, while not quite reaching the high-income group yet, is already a long way apart from the low-income groups. To conclude, if we review respondents' conscious *identification as different social classes, we shall discover that identification as the middle class depends on income level the most.* And it is quite certain that *mid-income groups' class mentality brings together the lower and upper mid-income groups,* placing them between the low-income and high-income levels.

If we analyze the class-based identification of the "multi-criteria" middle class[7] (Table 14.6), the situation will become even more clear and transparent. When interpreted according to this approach, this group exhibits the most obvious identity as a clearly articulated middle class (37%). In addition, 23% of respondents from the middle class present themselves as both the middle and working class. Class-based identification of the rest of the population is not as clear and is characterized by the overwhelming dominance of the "working class" identity: 28% respondents from the remaining population groups identify themselves as only the working class, and 29% more have dual identity, as the working class and the middle class.

---

[6] Goffman (2017).

[7] See Chap. 1 of this book.

Table 14.6 Self-anchoring in different social classes among members of the multi-criteria middle class and other Russians, 2015, %

Social groups	Consistent identification			Combined identification			
	Lowest class	Working class	Middle class	Lowest/working/middle class	Lowest/working class	Working/middle class	Lowest/middle class
Middle class	2	12	37	21	4	23	1
Remaining population	4	28	8	20	10	29	1

Thus, the analysis of the middle class's positive and negative identities has revealed the following patterns:

1. Mid-income population groups, just like all other income groups, share a unified structure of group identities, i.e. the ranking of groups that they are most inclined to refer to as "us" or "them", which points to a high homogeneity of both the mid-income groups and the nation as a whole.
2. The most striking differences between income groups, and between the subgroups of the mid-income group in particular, become apparent when we look at sustainable positive and negative European identities. These identities serve as markers of income stratification, though one should not exaggerate their role in this respect.
3. The "economic" middle class, which we have singled out during this study, has a rather moderately expressed class identity, with income stratification driving the frequent identification with the middle class and middle class alone. This "blurred" class-based self-identification picture is largely the result of the middle class encompassing blue-collar workers without higher education but with high income, who have a dual class identity. A much more clearly defined class-based mindset is typical of the middle class that falls under the multi-criteria approach.

But how stable are the above features of income groups in general and mid-income groups in particular? When comparing Russians' group-based self-identification in 2015 to similar data for 2011,[8] we can notice that the situation has changed significantly (Table 14.7), even though these changes follow a single direction in all income groups.

First of all, in 2011, civic identity was prevalent in all income groups, whereas in 2015, the "life stance" identity took the lead. Secondly, in 2011, civic identity also served as a marker for income stratification; in 2015, its place was taken by job-based identity (in 2011, it also exhibited some income-driven patterns, but they were less obvious). Thirdly, even though European identity was an income marker both in 2011 and in 2015, by 2015, its significance in this role increased greatly.

[8] In 2011, the set of identities offered to Russian respondents was slightly different, but it did include all the basic key parameters that are needed for comparative analysis.

Table 14.7 Structure of sustainable positive identities and negative identities in different income groups of Russians, 2011, %

Identities	Lower mid-income group	Upper mid-income group	Mid-income groups overall	For reference	
				Low-income groups	High-income groups
Sustainable positive					
Russian citizens	72	68	**70**	76	64
People with the same life stance	55	53	**54**	49	56
People of the same ethnicity	51	48	**50**	50	54
People in the same financial circumstances	43	43	**43**	40	47
People with the same job[a]	41	40	**40**	35	44
Negative					
Europeans	55	57	**55**	54	38

[a]The data is given as percentage of all respondents.

As a final note, we must also focus on another important characteristic feature of different income groups' identities. When analyzing sustainable identities in 2015, we already noted that, more often than not, mid-income groups express these identities stronger than other groups of Russians. In order to have a clearer understanding of which income group has a more wide-spread sustainable identification as different communities (i.e., is more included into the social sphere), we must calculate the integrated average degree of social identity expression (SIE) for each income group both in 2015 and in 2011 (Table 14.8). For our analysis, we have singled out only those identities that are popular among no less than a quarter of all Russians, which means that the classification does not include such barely expressed identities as "the poor", "the lowest class", "Europeans", "working class", and "middle class".

As seen in Table 14.8, in 2015, sustainable identification was less prominent than in 2011. Furthermore, *while in 2011 the integral degree of social identity expression was roughly the same in all income groups (around 50%), by 2015, low-income groups stood out in stark contrast with the rest of the population, which suffered from a dramatic drop in their sense of social integration, expressed by a dramatic drop in the share of their identities as members of basic social groups.*

We believe that these changes may be explained both by the events that occurred in Russia from 2011 to 2015 and by the dramatic changes in foreign policy, including the economic crisis that started in 2014. There was a sheer drop in civic identification (especially in the low-income group) and national identification (especially in the high-income group). Another typical trend was the slight decline of European identity, which shrank by 9% in the low-income group, 6% in the lower mid-income group, and 4% in the upper mid-income group, while not experiencing any changes whatsoever in the high-income group.

Table 14.8 Degree of sustainable social identity expression in different income groups of Russians, 2011 and 2015, %[9]

Identities	Low-income groups	Lower mid-income group	Upper mid-income group	High-income groups
People with the same hobbies and passions	– /50	– /54	– /57	– /54
People with the same life stance	49/55	55/61	53/59	56/57
People with the same job	35/39	41/46	40/54	44/53
People in the same financial circumstances	40/34	43/36	43/35	47/34
Russian citizens	76/29	71/32	68/35	64/33
People of the same ethnicity	50/28	51/29	48/28	54/27
Integral SIE value	50/39	52/43	50/45	53/43

Let us now summarize our study of status- and group-based self-identification of mid-income groups.

When defining their place in the structure of Russian society, Russians are strongly driven by what income group they belong to. Members of mid-income groups, as a rule, give a fairly rational evaluation of their social status, placing themselves between low-income and high-income groups. Furthermore, the two mid-income groups are, in general, closer to one another than to low- or high-income groups, despite sharing some common traits with the former or the latter.

In terms of mid-income groups' group identity, we can see a clear division into "us" and "them" among the communities they were offered to associate themselves with. "Us", the familiar and understandable communities, included 8 groups, "people with the same life stance" and "people with the same hobbies and passions", first and foremost. Based on the degree of identity expression as of 2015, these were followed by "people with the same job", "people in the same financial circumstances", "Russian citizens", "people of the same ethnicity", "members of the working class", and "members of the middle class". The "them" category included three groups that mid-income respondents perceived as alien to them. These groups were "the poor", "members of the lowest class", and "Europeans". Overall, all income groups share similar opinions when it comes to accepting or rejecting various communities. This results from a shared historic past and speaks of a high degree of homogeneity in the public mindset. Those differences in Russians' self-identification that we did manage

[9] To make the juxtaposition of sustainable social identity expression clearer, we shall list the data as fractions, where the numerator shows the figures for 2011 and the denominator shows the figures for 2015. For example, in the low-income group, the feeling of being close to "people with the same life stance" was expressed by 49% of respondents in 2011 and as many as 55% in 2015. We do not have the data on identifying with "people with the same hobbies and passions" for 2011, as this identity was not listed as one of the options in the 2011 survey. The integral SIE value was calculated as a simple average of the set of identities corresponding to the respective year.

to discover concern the degree of expressing social identity rather than its ranking structure.

On the whole, the differences between income groups become most apparent when we look at the sustainable job-based identity and negative European identity. The same parameters also reveal differences between the lower and upper mid-income groups, which tend to be more similar with respect to other identities.

Mid-income groups' class-based identities are barely notable, compared to all other positive identities. Those respondents from mid-income groups who claim to feel very close to various social classes are often characterized by "blurred" class-based identity, as they identify as members of both the working and middle class to an equal degree. Turning to clear, consistent class-based identification, we see that, as we move from the lower mid-income group to the upper mid-income group, the share of people identifying with the working class drops and the share of those identifying with the middle class rises. At the same time, we should note that singling out the "economic" middle class is not the optimal solution for defining class-based identities. To gain a better understanding of the latter, a far better strategy is the "multi-criteria" approach, which makes the correlation between society's class structure and the respondents' class-based self-identification much clearer.

If we juxtapose the data derived from status identification analysis (a more formal approach) and the results of group identity studies (an approach that accounts for respondents' conscious self-examination), we shall arrive at a conclusion that the lower mid-income groups are close to the upper, although not in every respect: in some matters, the lower mid-income group gravitates to Russians from low-income groups, while the upper mid-income group comes closer to the high-income groups.

References

Adler N, Stewart J (2007) The MacArthur scale of subjective social status. Web resource, The MacArthur research network on socioeconomic status and health. https://www.macses.ucsf.edu/research/psychosocial/subjective.php. Accessed 22 Apr 2017

Goffman E (2017) Stigma: notes on the management of spoiled identity. Part 1. Stigma and social identity. Web resource, Federal Education Portal. Economics. Sociology. Management. https://ecsocman.hse.ru/text/17687311/ Accessed 22 Apr 2017

Kilpatrick F, Cantril H (1960) Self-anchoring scaling: a measure of individuals' unique reality worlds. J Indiv Psychol 16(2):158–173

Latova NV (2016) Russians' satisfaction with their life during a crisis: 2015 as the year of bifurcation. In: Public opinion monitoring: economic and social changes (3):25

Lindemann K (2007) The impact of objective characteristics on subjective social position. Trames 11:54–68. https://www.kirj.ee/public/trames/trames-2007-1-4.pdf. Accessed 22 Apr 2017

Tikhonova NE (2014) Sotsialnaya struktura Rossii: teorii i realnost. Russia's Social Structure: Theories and Reality]. Novy Khronograf, Moscow, pp 63–64

Turner J (1982) Towards a cognitive redefinition of the social group. Social identity and intergroup relations. Cambridge University Press, p 18

N. V. Latova Senior Researcher at the Federal Center of Theoretical and Applied Sociology of the Russian Academy of Sciences (former Institute of Sociology, Russian Academy of Sciences). Holds Ph.D. in Sociology from Institute of Sociology (2011). The author of more than 80 articles and chapters in scientific monographs, she also annually participates in scientific grants. Her professional interests are: comparative studies, sociology of education, economic sociology and migration problems such as "brain drain". Co-author of the monograph "Continuing Education as a Stimulus for Human Development and a Factor of Socio-Economic Inequalities" (2014). Her resent publications include chapters in scientific monographs Satisfaction with Life: Dynamics and Factors / Russian Society and Challenges of the Time. Book Five. Ed. by Gorshkov M.K. 2017; General Mood in the Country and Russians' Social Attitudes/Russian Society and Challenges of the Time. Book Four. Ed. by Gorshkov M.K. 2016; Middle Class Migration Behavior / Middle Class in Modern Russia. Ed. By Gorshkov M.K., Tikhonova N.E. 2016.

Chapter 15
Values and Social and Political Attitudes of the Middle Income Group

Wei Li

To include most of the population into the middle income group is both the key remark of a healthy modern society and the requirement of a society of justice, equity and harmony. Examples from home and abroad indicate that except those overall poor or affluent countries, the gap between the rich and the poor is a long last phenomenon. Whereas the olive-shape social pattern with minimized affluent and poor people and the maximized middle income group shall be the proper configuration of a rational and peaceful society.

Although concept of the middle income group is different from that of the "middle class", which is defined by the occupations, the group and the class do share a large portion of overlapping population. The reason, according to researchers is that personal income correlates closely to the occupation and educational attainment and the group who enjoys intermediate income generally has the medium occupation status and educational attainment (Li and Xu 2017).[1] Therefore, to study the characteristics of the middle income group, the social function beyond the economic aspect shall be involved.

In the classic studies of the middle class, it is generally believed that the middle income group has influenced the politics and democracy and that it is the major strength in democratization and driving social reform. Lipset believes that the social affluence is highly related with the economic level and the political democracy of a country. The emerging of the middle class from the affluent society shall certainly come along with political democracy (Lipset 1959).[2] When Samuel Huntington was investigating the modernization procedure of developing countries, he found that the urban middle class was the most proactive supporters of the said democratization

[1] Refer to Li and Xu (2017). How to Define the Middle Income Group. Social Sciences of Beijing, vol. 7.

[2] Lipset (1959).

W. Li (✉)
Institute of Sociology, Chinese Academy of Social Sciences, Chaoyang District, Beijing, China

P. Li and M. K. Gorshkov (eds.), *The Middle Income Group in China and Russia*, Research Series on the Chinese Dream and China's Development Path,
https://doi.org/10.1007/978-981-16-1464-4_15

procedure almost in every country. A society with high political participation level of the middle class in the social transformation tends to endure fluctuation (Huntington and Nelson 1989).[3] Similarly, some domestic scholars also believe that the middle class in China has even stronger critical consciousness as it harbors doubts of the government and social institution. So, using the expansion of the middle class as s social stabilizer is not practical (Zhang 2008).[4] On the other hand, some other scholars in China think that the middle class is equipped with rational, warm and conservative ideology, and therefore they are the buffer and stabilizer between the upper and lower classes, which decreases the possibility of social conflicts (Li 2001).[5] They are considered the "defenders in the politics pitch"[6]. Li Chunling's research indicates that sub-groups of the middle class in China with different attitudes play different social functions. There are multiple values inside the middle class, where the conservatism and the liberalism co-exist. As an entity, they are satisfied with current situation and are supportive for the government. Meanwhile, a part of the group expects more political democracy and social justice. The complex and contradictory social attitudes forecast a third path for the middle class to take—a progressive and stable social and political transformation (Li 2011).[7]

There has been rich and diversified research on the social functions of the current middle class/middle income group in China. However, as previous research mainly focused on its political function, that is, the radical or conservative aspect of the community and critics or support for the current institution, there has been little observation of the group's social values except the determination of its political inclination. So, the paper makes the analyses of the middle income group in China in terms of its basic characteristics, social origination, social and political attitudes, etc.

15.1 Values Orientation of the Middle Income Group

This paper uses the statistics from Chinese Society Survey 2015 (CSS 2015), which was carried out by the Institute of Sociology, Chinese Academy of Social Sciences (CASS) and divides the samples into 4 groups with person income. Those whose income equals to or below 0.75 times of the median are defined as the low income group; those with income between 0.75 times and 1.25 times (included) of the median are defined as the lower middle income group; those earn between 1.25 times and 2 times (included) of the median are defined as the upper middle income group, and

[3] Huntington, Samuel. Political Order in Changing Societies. Huaxia Publishing House, 1989.

[4] Zhang (2008). Current Political Attitudes of the Middle Clas in China. Social Sciences in China, vol. 2.

[5] Li (2001).

[6] Zhou Xiaohong. Survey of the Chinese Middle Classes, Social Sciences Academic Press (CHINA), 2005.

[7] Li (2011).

those who earn above 2 times of the median are the high income group. The lower and upper middle income groups are both "the middle income group".

The constitution of the middle income group is closely related to the non-agricultural transformation of the rural residents over the last 4 decades in China. The population carrying out non-agricultural work with agricultural hukou (household registration type in China), i.e., the migrant workers in a broad sense have the highest possibility of entering the middle income group. From Fig. 15.1, it can be seen that of the current employed population, 49.7% of the migrant workers were the middle income group and 34.4% were the high income group; for the population participated in the non-agricultural work with non-agricultural hukou showed even higher percentage as in the high income group, which was 44.2%. But correspondingly, their percentage in the middle income group was 46%, lower than that of the migrant workers; for the non-agricultural hukou holders who had the agricultural work, the percentage that became the middle income group fell to 39.6% and most of them (49.9%) were the low income group; whereas for the agricultural hukou holders who had the agricultural work, the percentage that became the middle income group was even lower, which stood at 20.1%.

In general, the main body of the middle income group were those young adults who lived in the urban area, received middle school or higher education and worked in the non-agriculture sector. 50% of them were transformed from those with the traditional agricultural hukou and they were the group of new citizens.

In 1970s, American scholar Alex Inkeles, through his intercultural comparison research of multiple countries, concluded that the modern industrial and commercial society had not only changed the traditional social structure but also shaped the social members with the modern personality. In his opinion, the factory experience, mass

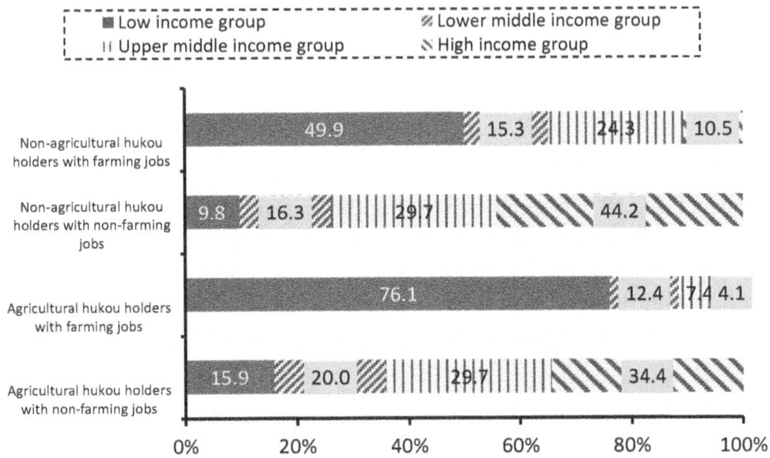

Fig. 15.1 The income group distribution of population with different hukou types and occupation types

Table 15.1 Rights consciousness for various income groups (%)

	One should reason when the rights are undermined	One should remain silent when the rights are undermined	Total	Sample size
Low income group	59.3	40.7	100.0	3,012
Lower middle income group	68.2	31.8	100.0	651
Upper middle income group	72.1	27.9	100.0	1,001
High income group	77.1	22.9	100.0	2,499
Total	67.3	32.7	100.0	7,163

media communication, urban life and education in schools enabled the modern characteristics to the people and they went modern (Inkeles 1992).[8] The demographic characteristics of the middle income group reflected that they were the new citizens of young adults that had experienced the urbanization and industrialization. So, whether their social values reflected cultural and psychological characteristics of the modern personality shall be discussed below. Alex Inkeles generalized 12 characteristics of the modern personality.[9] In the research, as inspired by the measurement of the individual modern personality, we check the tradition-modern value orientation the middle income group with the following: rights consciousness, competence and equity awareness, planning consciousness, innovation consciousness and social transformation consciousness.

(1) Rights consciousness

According to Table 15.1, the middle income group generally had higher rights consciousness, as 68.2–72.1% of them approved that "one should reason for the rights if they are undermined", which was far above the approval rate of 59.3% by the low income group.

(2) Competence and equity awareness

According to Table 15.2, over 60% of the middle income group believed that "only the individual competence and efforts shall lead to success in China", showing that they attached importance to the "achieved factors" such as individual efforts. Whereas 60% of the group believe that money, power, social network and other resources were great support in achieving social status. It is noteworthy that the middle and

[8] Inkeles (1992).

[9] Among the traits, they are: openness to new experience; prepared for social reform and transformation; open minded and respective to different ideas; focus on present and future, punctuated and valuing time; strong sense of personal efficacy; being positive towards people and society; planning ahead; valuing education and technical competence; believing in reasoning and society running under reason; high degree of autonomy in dealing with the family, clan, and religious authority; mutual understanding, respect and self-respect; understanding production and is procedure.

Table 15.2 Competence consciousness of various income groups (%)

	Only the individual competence and efforts shall lead to success in China	Only those people with power and wealth shall lead a good life in China	Total	Sample size
Low income group	64.6	35.4	100.0	2,994
Lower middle income group	60.5	39.5	100.0	647
Upper middle income group	60.9	39.1	100.0	996
High income group	60.2	39.8	100.0	2,485
Total	62.1	37.9	100.0	7,121

high income groups showed 4 points percentage higher than that of the low income group in the above viewpoint. This, to a certain extent, reflected their perception of the scarcity of social resources that brought about the current inequity of social status for different groups in China.

As the group believed in individual competence and the unequal resource distribution in the current society, half of them argued that "the income and social status should be determined by individual competence" and they did not ask for an average society each was entitled to equal income and social status. The belief that the social status should be determined by individual competence was even stronger among the upper middle income group, as 58.4% of the group approve the point. That was evidently higher than the approval rate of 50.1% as shared by the low income group (see Table 15.3). From the point above, the middle income group showed certain marketism orientation.

Table 15.3 Equality consciousness of various income groups (%)

	The income and social status gaps only be limited as the equal the better	The income and social status should be determined by individual competence	Total	Sample size
Low income group	49.9	50.1	100.0	2,995
Lower middle income group	48.0	52.0	100.0	647
Upper middle income group	41.6	58.4	100.0	992
High income group	36.0	64.0	100.0	2,489
Total	44.9	55.1	100.0	7,123

Table 15.4 Time planning consciousness of various income groups (%)

	I don't plan my life because it is hard to plan ahead	I have the plan for 1–2 years of my life	I have the plan for 3–5 years of my life	I have the plan for 5–10 years of my life	Total	Sample size
Low income group	58.8	21.3	14.3	5.6	100.0	2,995
Lower middle income group	53.3	22.8	18.4	5.5	100.0	647
Upper middle income group	42.1	25.5	27.6	4.7	100.0	992
High income group	30.2	27.0	33.8	8.9	100.0	2,489
Total	48.3	23.7	21.9	6.1	100.0	7,123

(3) Planning consciousness

As what was remarked by Fromm, the concept of time was one of the main features of the social characters in modern industrial society (Fromm 2007),[10] and the associated use is the planning of a life. Time planning indicates the confirmation of life and work targets and behavior of rational management. In the survey of the time planning consciousness of each income group, it was found that the middle income group, when compared to the low income group, had an explicit sense of time planning. 46.7% of the lower middle income people had a long-term planning of life ranging from the short-term 1–2 years to 5–10 years. And the planning of the upper middle income group was even better at planning: the short-term to long-term life planners accounted for 57.9% of them. Only 41.2% of the low income group had the time planning awareness (Table 15.4).

(4) Innovation consciousness

According to Table 15.5, the middle income group generally showed higher enterprise consciousness, as 65.4–71.31% of them agree "one should be progressive and make breakthrough in work and life and being innovative is a critical character". They did not let the traditional custom dominate them. The values for the above attitudes is evidently higher than that of the low income group (58.4%).

[10] Fromm (2007).

Table 15.5 Innovation consciousness of various income groups (%)

	One should be progressive and make breakthrough in work and life and being innovative is a critical character. They do not let the traditional custom dominate them	Respecting the traditional custom is the most important	Total	Sample size
Low income group	58.4	41.6	100.0	2999
Lower middle income group	65.4	34.6	100.0	651
Upper middle income group	71.3	28.7	100.0	999
High income group	78.5	21.5	100.0	2499
Total	66.6	33.4	100.0	7147

(5) Social transformation consciousness

According to Table 15.6, the middle income group expected the stability of the country and the society, as 65% of the group believed that "stability is most critical to China" and only around 33–35% of the people were in favor of "despite of all kinds of risks, a social transformation is needed in China". The group pursued innovation in their individual life and work while expected stability of the country and the society, which was the proof to some extend of its identity as the "defender in the politics pitch" as labelled by some domestic scholars.

From the above data analysis, we can see that the people of contemporary Chinese middle income group had a strong sense of individual rights, focused on competence orientation, emphasized time planning and were willing to make progress and innovation, for which they showed obvious modern personality. They expected state and social stability and were prudent towards social transformation.

Table 15.6 Social transformation consciousness of various income groups (%)

	Stability is most critical to China	Despite of all kinds of risks, a social transformation is needed in China	Total	Sample size
Low income group	66.3	33.7	100.0	3,002
Lower middle income group	66.6	33.4	100.0	648
Upper middle income group	64.6	35.4	100.0	994
High income group	59.2	40.8	100.0	2,492
Total	64.5	35.5	100.0	7136

15.2 Social Attitudes of the Middle Income Group

What kind of society does the middle income group expect as they are living in the modern industrial and commercial civilization and urbanization? How is their social participation? What about their evaluation of the real world? The following is the survey contents of their social attitudes. Social attitudes refer to people's perception, emotion and behaviors towards social matters, which reflect the perception and opinion of social members in their social context in a more specific level. From the psychological—behavioral perspective, the view of society indicates their position and action tendencies. In the survey, we examine the social attitudes of middle income group from five aspects: social trust, social inclusion, social equity, social participation and social appraisal.

(1) Social trust

The level of public trust is an important indicator of the steady development of social economy, the prevention of social risks and the resolution of potential crises. In the theory of social trust, trust is divided into interpersonal trust between acquaintances, and the institutional trust between the objects and the institution or the representatives of the institution (such as doctors, judges, police, etc.). As for the stranger society created by marketization, the establishment of institutional trust is the more basic content of social integration.

In the survey, we measured the degree of trust in 11 categories of social roles. From Table 15.7, it can be seen that (1) as other groups, there existed the "Pattern of Different Sequence" of interpersonal trust among the middle income group, that is, the trust on their relatives was almost 100%. Following that were the trust on friends,

Table 15.7 Social trust of various income groups (%)

	Low income group	Lower middle income group	Upper middle income group	High income group
Relatives	97.2	97.8	98.4	98.6
Friends	84.0	83.6	88.4	90.4
Teachers	88.6	83.4	84.5	85.3
Neighbors	84.0	79.5	79.2	77.9
Doctors	82.4	76.4	76.0	73.6
Colleagues	64.3	74.4	77.0	79.9
Police	72.4	65.8	64.4	64.9
Judges	65.2	59.7	56.5	58.6
Personnel in charge of public departments	59.7	50.7	51.0	50.4
Merchants	31.4	29.8	28.1	30.2
Strangers	5.9	4.4	4.8	7.5

neighbors, colleagues, which reflected the cultivation of trust in the kinship, friendship, neighborhood and career; (2) as for the institutional trust, teachers and doctors generally enjoyed the highest trust, and the percentage of the figure stood between 75 and 85%; the police, the judges, the personnel in charge of public departments roughly enjoyed the trust rate between 60 and 70%; the trust percentage of merchants was low, which was only 30%; the lowest trust percentage went to strangers, which was below 10%; (3) The institutional trust from the middle income group was generally lower than that of the low income group, among which the trust level of the police and the judges was 5–8 percentage points lower than that of the low income group, and the trust of the personnel in charge of public department was nearly 10 percentage point lower than that of the low income group. The lack of trust of the public power and its representatives of roles such as the police, judges and the personnel in charge of public departments reflected their caution and fear of the government.

(2) Social inclusion

Social inclusion refers to the tolerance of social members with different social characteristics and their manifestations of social behavior, equal participation and support for the weak, the elimination of discrimination and equal opportunities for development. This is the required citizen's spirit to ensure social harmony and to achieve social justice must have the spirit of citizenship. In the survey, we inquired whether the respondents had experienced social discrimination due to factors such as hukou, age, gender and educational level, and the degree of acceptance of some special social groups. The current social discrimination and social inclusion situation were both examined.

Survey data showed that the middle income group actually encountered rare social discrimination, as the highest rate was still below 20%, which was much lower than the discrimination towards the low income group. As indicated in Table 15.8: (1) the overall assessment of each income group on the current social discrimination severity was consistent, as they all thought that the degree of social discrimination was not very high, the highest percentage staying below 40%. (2) It was general believed that the most frequent social discrimination was due to educational attainment and family background and social relations, with a proportion of about 35–36%; the second social discrimination is due to age, gender and hukou, which is around 16–20%; the social discrimination due to race or nations was the least with a proportion of about 7%. (3) Survey data showed that as the middle income group actually encountered less social discrimination, they rated the prevalent of the discrimination in the society higher than that from the low income group. The assessment of the severity of social discrimination resulting from family background and social relations was rated 3–4 percentage points higher by the middle income group than that of the low income group.

The data in Table 15.9 show that the degree of acceptance (separately fully acceptable and comparatively acceptable) of all the special social groups that are easily perceived as "heresy" positively correlates to the income level. The social acceptance from the middle income groups was significantly higher than that of the low

Table 15.8 Rate of social discrimination by various income groups (%)

	Age	Gender	Educational attainment	Race and nations	Hukou type	Family background and social relationship	Sample size
Low income group	19.8	16.1	34.5	7.0	16.0	31.8	3,385
Lower middle income group	19.2	15.5	35.7	8.7	15.1	36.7	1,446
Upper middle income group	20.3	17.4	37.3	6.0	15.2	34.8	1,674
High income group	20.7	17.5	37.9	8.3	19.0	39.5	1,844
Total	20.0	16.5	36.0	7.4	16.3	34.9	8,349

Table 15.9 Acceptance of special social groups by various income groups (%)

	Premarital cohabitation	Homosexuality	Beggars	Emancipist	People with different religious beliefs	AIDS carriers	Sample size
Low income group	39.9	11.4	61.7	57.9	64.3	25.9	3,440
Lower middle income group	49.9	10.1	58.8	62.6	71.2	27.9	1,465
Upper middle income group	57.6	11.4	54.3	63.9	75.9	29.1	1,699
High income group	66.6	18.2	57.4	67.7	82.8	34.4	1,866
Total	51.1	12.7	58.8	62.1	71.9	28.8	8,470

income group. For example, the acceptance rate of pre-marital cohabitation from the low income group was below 40%. Whereas that from the income of middle-income groups was about 49.9–57.6%; as the degree of acceptance of the emancipists, the rate from the middle-income group was 5–6 percentage points higher than that from the low income group; the acceptance of people with different religious beliefs was also 7–12 percentage points higher than. The only exception was that the acceptance rate from the middle class was lower than that of the low income group. The data above showed that the middle income group had a higher social inclusion spirit, which as a positive drive for the development goals of the "inclusive growth".

(3) Social equity

The following question was included in the survey: "How you think of the social equality in the following categories", and 8 detailed aspects such as gaokao (higher education entrance exam in China) and public medical service were included. Answers include "very fair, fair, unfair and very unfair". From Table 15.10, it can be seen that (1) over 65% of all income groups had positive evaluation on the social fair situation, as the percentages of all categories were more than 65%. The fairness

Table 15.10 Sense of social equity trust of various income groups (%)

	Low income group	Lower middle income group	Upper middle income group	High income group
Gaokao (higher education entrance examination system)	85.0	83.8	80.5	77.3
Public medicare	73.8	69.6	70.1	66.8
Jurisdiction and law enforcement	70.3	65.9	61.1	59.3
Real political rights citizens are entitled	67.2	63.9	61.7	57.9
Social security such as pension	66.3	60.8	61.7	60.5
Work and job opportunities	53.8	50.7	52.5	55.8
Rights and entitlement between the urban and rural areas	42.9	42.3	45.7	45.7
Wealth and income distribution	43.2	42.2	41.4	44.6
General social equity	70.5	68.9	68.2	65.6
Sample size	3,000	1,327	1,556	1,763

assessment of education ("very fair" + "fair" percentage) was relatively high, while that of people's livelihood and social security, politics and public power was the second highest. The fairness assessment of urban and rural gaps and rich and poor gaps stayed the lowest, which were below 50%. (2) With the increase of income level, the evaluation of social fairness showed a downward trend. Actually, the middle income group provided lower evaluation in almost all the items. This is evident in the Jurisdiction and law enforcement area, for which the middle income group had a fair assessment of 5–9 percentage points lower than that of the low income group; in the practical political rights as enjoyed by the citizens, the fairness assessment from the middle income group was 4–6 points lower than that from the low middle income group; the fairness assessment of the social security and welfare from the middle income group was 5–6 percentage points lower than that from the low income group.

The above data reveals that the social group with lower social and economic status had a higher sense of social fairness, and the group enjoyed higher socio-economic advantage provided lower rate. This indicates that the "sense of unfair society led by the unequal status" shall no more apply to the difference between groups for the social inequality in China.

(4) Social participation

In the survey, we listed 9 types of social participation and asked respondents whether they had a corresponding involvement in the past two years. From Table 15.11, we can see the characteristics of the social participation by the middle income group: (1) The discussion of political topics was much higher than that of the low income group. There were 37.2 and 45.2% of the lower middle and higher middle income groups who discussed political issues with others, while the percentage for the low income group was only 27.9%, which was 10–18 percentage points lower. The social participation of volunteer activities and social activities for public good was significantly higher than that of the low income group. There were 17 and 23.5% separately of the lower middle and higher middle income groups participated in the volunteer activities and social activities for public good as organized by the government or institutions, which was 2–8 percentage points higher than that of the low income group. while the percentage for self-organized activities for public good by the middle income group was also 1–4 percentage points higher than that of the low income group. (3) Although the middle income group showed the highest participation rate in the election of village committees, the percentage was significantly lower than that of the low income group. There were 68.1% and 55.8% separately of the lower middle and higher middle income groups participated in the election of village committees in the past two years, which was 6–17 percentage points lower than that of the low income group.

Table 15.11 Social participation of various income groups (%)

	Low income group	Lower middle income group	Upper middle income group	High income group
Discuss political issues with others	27.9	37.2	45.2	53.7
Call the newspaper or radio station to reflect social issues	3.5	3.8	5.9	6.2
Make petitions to government departments on social issues	11.9	12.5	13.3	13.2
Participate in the volunteer activities as organized by government, schools or other institutions	14.9	17.0	23.5	28.3
Participate in the election of village committees	73.2	68.1	55.8	48.3
Participate in religious activities	12.7	10.3	10.9	11.4
Participate in self-organized social activities for public good	23.0	24.8	27.3	34.1
Make petitions to government departments on social issues	5.2	5.3	5.6	4.7
Participate in protest demonstrations or on strikes	1.0	1.9	1.2	2.2
Total	100.0	100.0	100.0	100.0
Sample size	3,000	1,327	1,556	1,763

People's intention of social participation was also surveyed herein. From Table 15.12, it can be seen that the participation intention of self-organized and formal institutions organized activities for the public good was the highest, which respectively surpassed 60% and 50%. There were as high as 67.2 and 70.2% separately of the lower middle and upper middle income groups showing the participation intention, which was 7–10 percentage points higher than that of the low income group. And the percentage formal institutions organized activities for the public good by the lower and upper middle income group were also 8–10 percentage points higher

Table 15.12 Social participation intention of various income groups (%)

	Low income group	Lower middle income group	Upper middle income group	High income group
Discuss political issues with others	25.4	26.9	26.4	26.0
Make phone calls to newspaper or radio station to reflect social issues	32.5	36.4	37.3	38.6
Make petitions to government departments on social issues	36.9	37.5	40.9	39.9
Participate in the volunteer activities as organized by government, schools or other institutions	51.4	58.4	60.5	60.8
Participate in the election of village committees	49.0	48.5	52.8	46.5
Participate in religious activities	8.0	8.3	8.8	11.1
Participate in self-organized social activities for public good	60.5	67.2	70.2	70.8
Make petitions to government departments on social issues	17.2	18.5	16.2	15.9
Participate in protest demonstrations or on strikes	5.0	4.4	8.0	7.4
Total	100.0	100.0	100.0	100.0
Sample size	3,000	1,327	1,556	1,763

than that of the low income group, staying separately 58.4 and 60.5%. In addition, their tendency of informing the social issues to the mass media was respectively 36.4 and 37.3%, 4–5 percentage points higher than the low income group. It can be seen from the above data that the social participation behavior and intention of the middle income groups mainly fell in the activities for public goods and they had a preference for self-organized activities. That indicated that they had a higher intention for expressing opinions and social participation and they were capable of acting. They were the backbone of social participation.

(5) Social appraisal

In the survey, we learned about the respondents' appraisal on the current social situation. Use 1–10 as the scale of appraisal, 1 point for the worst and 10 points for the best. The data showed that: (1) People's appraisal of the current social situation was not very high, ranging between from 5–7 points. On the whole, the highest rate went to the overall social situation, with the average being 6.37 points. Following that were the social compliance level (6.17 points) and social tolerance (6.11 points). The lower score went to the moral level of society (5.84), the lowest was social trust (5.49). (2) People from higher income groups generally had lower appraisal of social conditions. Actually, the middle income group provided lower appraisal in almost all the items of social situation. Such as, the appraisal of social trust from the low income group scored 5.62, while that from the lower and upper middle income groups were respectively 5.40 and 5.43; the appraisal degree of social morality by the low income group scored 6.01, and that by the lower and upper middle income groups were 5.77 and 5.71 (see Table 15.13).

From the above aspects of social attitudes, the middle income group showed strong social inclusion spirit, high intention of opinion expression and social participation. They preferred the self-organized activity for the public good. The appraisal of the real society was unsatisfactory, as they showed evidently lower the social trust rate (especially the trust of the institution of the public power), the sense of social fairness and the appraisal of the overall situation of today's society than those of the low income group.

Table 15.13 Appraisals of social situation by various income groups (%)

	Degree of trust	Degree of tolerance	Level of social morality	Compliance of laws and regulations	Overall social condition	Sample size
Low income group	5.62	6.14	6.01	6.30	6.44	3,433
Lower middle income group	5.40	6.12	5.77	6.16	6.25	1,468
Upper middle income group	5.43	6.12	5.71	6.06	6.39	1,699
High income group	5.36	6.04	5.67	6.03	6.33	1,866
Total	5.49	6.11	5.84	6.17	6.37	8,466

15.3 Political Attitudes of the Middle Income Group

We examined the middle income group's political attitudes in terms of political attitudes and democracy awareness, political path of the state, political efficacy and appraisals of government work.

(1) Consciousness of political liberty and democracy

We designed a pair of contrasting statement in the survey to understand people's inclination on political liberty and government power. From Table 15.14, it can be seen that the middle, low and high income shared the same idea that they attach more importance to a mighty government that maintained the social order rather than the appealing for political liberty and democracy. Over half of the middle income group believed that "A mighty Chinese government is required to maintain the public order". However, even the appeal for political liberty and democracy was weaker than the reliance on the state power. The middle income did show an evidently higher percentage of such appeal. There were 43.4 and 47.7% separately of the lower middle and higher middle income groups who believed that "the political liberty and democracy shall never be undermined in any case", which was 1–5 percentage points higher than that of the low income group as 42.2%.

(2) Choice of the political path of the state

From Table 15.15, it can be seen that, nearly 90% of the respondents believed that "China should take their own path as it has its own particularity" and only 10% chose "China shall follow the development path as that of the West in the future". The middle income group showed similar choice to other groups'. This indicated the high acceptance of the current political institution and path in China by the middle income group.

Table 15.14 Consciousness of political liberty and democracy of various income groups (%)

	The political liberty and democracy shall never be undermined in any case	A mighty Chinese government is required to maintain the public order	Total	Sample size
Low income group	42.2	57.8	100.0	2,961
Lower middle income group	43.4	56.6	100.0	644
Upper middle income group	47.7	52.3	100.0	987
High income group	48.9	51.1	100.0	2,481
Total	45.0	55.0	100.0	7,072

Table 15.15 Recognition of political paths by various income groups (%)

	China shall follow the development path as the that of West in the future	China should take their own path as it has its own particularity	Total	Sample size
Low income group	9.8	90.2	100.0	2,979
Lower middle income group	8.4	91.6	100.0	645
Upper middle income group	11.0	89.0	100.0	992
High income group	13.9	86.1	100.0	2,482
Total	10.7	89.3	100.0	7,099

(3) Political efficacy

Political efficacy is the citizens' faith and trust in government and their belief that they can understand and influence political affairs. It is worthy of the individual's ability to practice his civic responsibility (Campbell et al. 1954).[11] For individuals, political efficacy is the most important factor affecting their political participation. In general, people with high political efficacy are more likely to be involved in politics than those with low political efficacy. Political efficacy is then divided into two parts: internal political efficacy and external political efficacy. The former refers to individuals who believe that they have the ability to influence political decision-making. The latter refers to the individuals' belief that the government's response to public participation and attention (Li 2010).[12]

In the survey, 4 questions were used to measure the political efficacy of the respondents and Table 15.16 provides their approval percentage ("very approval + approval"). The public showed low political efficacy. Except the high income group, less than 50% of the other stated that "they have the ability and knowledge to comment and participate in political activities; the internal efficacy of the middle income group was 4–5 percentage points higher than that of the low income group. Whereas over 50% of the people stated that they were not interested in politics and would not spend time and energy on it, which reflected the public's indifference and alienation towards politics.

As for the external efficacy, the middle income group showed little difference than other groups, with more than 50% of people thought that participation in political activities was useless and little influence would be generated on the government. This showed that they felt the lack of appropriate political participation channels and opportunities. It is noteworthy that more than 40% of the middle income group believed that the liberty to participate in political activities would be subject to

[11] Campbell et al. (1954).

[12] Li (2010).

Table 15.16 Political efficacy of various income groups (%)

	Low income group	Lower middle income group	Upper middle income group	High income group
I have the ability and knowledge to comment and participate in political activities	41.3	45.9	46.7	50.1
I'm not interested in politics and I wouldn't spend time and energy on it	55.4	54.1	52.9	52.4
Participation in political activities is useless and it has little influence on the government	54.3	53.5	54.7	54.2
The liberty to participate in political activities would be subject to restrictions from government departments	44.2	43.2	48.9	47.7
Sample size	3,376	1,447	1,667	1,830

restrictions from government departments, of which the high income group felt the most, 48.9%, 4 percentage points higher than that of the low income group.

(4) Appraisals of government work

The public's appraisal on government work could be interpreted as the practical indicator of people's political attitudes. In our survey, we inquired of the public's appraisal on local governments' (which refer to county-level governments in the survey, including county, Banner, county-level cities and urban districts) 11 categories of basic functions and their overall performance Table 15.17 shows the percentage of people who held positive appraisal (very good + good) of the local governments' work. From the table, we can see that (1) Lower income groups provided higher appraisals with the middle income group providing intermediate appraisal; (2) The overall appraisal for the local governments by the middle income group stayed around 63%. In which, "combat criminals and maintain social order", "provide medicare service", "provide social security", and "safeguard citizens' political rights" received high appraisals, with an approval percentage between 63 and 75%; the lowest appraisal was "response to the public's appealing with service awareness", which stayed below 50%. And the other 6 categories such as "lawfully administrate business and carry out law enforcement" and "protect environment and treat pollution" were rated as intermediate approval, with the percentage between 50 and 60%.

Table 15.17 Political efficacy of various income groups (%)

	Low income group	Lower middle income group	Upper middle income group	High income group
Combat criminals and maintain social order	78.4	74.8	74.3	75.3
Provide medicare service	72.7	69.9	71.7	70.7
Provide social security	69.1	66.9	65.1	65.3
Safeguard citizens' political rights	67.7	66.7	63.6	63.5
Lawfully administrate business and carry out law enforcement	63.8	58.9	56.7	58.6
Protect environment and treat pollution	60.1	55.4	54.2	51.2
Grow economy and people's income	54.6	55.0	56.5	59.0
Serve the public's interests and combat corruption	59.0	55.3	53.9	53.0
Create new jobs	49.5	51.0	55.6	58.2
Keep the public informed of government affairs	54.1	54.3	53.0	48.8
Response to the public's appealing with service awareness	52.2	49.0	49.8	49.6
Overall appraisal on government work	64.5	63.1	63.7	60.5
Sample size	3,000	1,327	1,556	1,763

(3) Compared to the low income group, the upper middle income group showed lower appraisal of the government work. Its appraisal of "maintain social order", "provide social security" and "safeguard citizens' political rights" were 3 percentage points lower than that of the low income group; and the gap was 3 percentage points when it comes to "lawfully administrate business and carry out law enforcement", "protect environment and treat pollution" and "Serve the public's interests and combat corruption", the appraisal was 6 percentage points lower.

To sum up, the middle income group highly stressed that China's political development should take a different path than that of the West. Despite their urge for democratic liberty than that of the low income group, they expected a stable state and social order by a mighty government; they had the ability to state their interests and political participation, but they showed a considerable degree of alienation towards politics because of their limit influence on real politics; their appraisals for the local governments were basically positive, but all below those of the low income group.

15.4 Conclusion

At present, China's middle income group is mainly composed of non-farm workers living in urban areas, and its main social origination is the original agricultural population. About 45% of them are under the age of 40, roughly the generation born after the reform and opening up (1978) and they bear the marks of times such as high-speed industrialization, marketization and urbanization. Because the majority of the low income group live in rural areas, the nationwide "middle income group" are actually those urban "low income" and "lower middle income" groups. Studying China's "middle-income groups" therefore requires a deep understanding of the characteristics of the "new citizens".

Most of them received a high school or above level of education as required by urban employment on human capital. Modern education, work in the industrial and commercial organizations and urban lifestyle have shaped their "modern personality". They have a clear sense of individual rights, focus on ability, make plans for themselves, accept innovation and are willing to forge ahead. This has brought increasing difference between them and the rural low income group with main livelihood of the farming.

The new citizens bear the mark of urban–rural social identity: Although about 80% of the middle income groups are engaged in non-farm labor, more than 60% of them hold the agricultural household registration. The diversification of urban life has made them highly inclusive and they are against discrimination of all kinds of members of society. Urbanization had transformed the traditional acquaintance society into stranger society, which has affected their social trust. Especially for the personnel in charge of the public departments, they had insufficient trust. They think that China is a generally fair society and they are sensitive to all kinds of social issues. As they have strong appealing for equity, they didn't rate the current social equity situation high. In areas such as especially in jurisdiction and law enforcement and citizens' political rights, social security, they hold that the equity level is far below expectation. Similarly, they are dissatisfied with the whole society's trust, tolerance, morality, and compliance of laws and regulations.

In the process of urbanization, the new citizens' living space has also been reconstructed. Urban community living environment has provided them with different urban social identity and social participation than before. In recent years, the activities for public welfare has been quickly gaining support in all areas and social organizations, volunteer service organizations, etc., are growing quickly. Those above provide the middle income groups better social participation environment at a lower cost, which enables part of the middle income people who are keen on public affairs to participate in non-political social activities. Through all kinds of activities, the "new citizens" roles are enhanced. In terms of social participation, they discuss actively of political and social issues, have a sense of volunteer service, and are willing to participate in various activities for the public good. The middle income group has shown potential for becoming undertakers and practitioners of new citizen values.

In terms of political attitudes, the middle income group show a certain degree of mixed and contradictory mentality. To sum up, the middle income group highly stresses that China's political development should take a different path than that of the West despite of their urge for democratic liberty. That indicates its more reliance on the current political and economic structure as a shareholder; they have the ability to state their interests and political participation, but they show a considerable degree of alienation towards politics because of their limit influence on real politics; their appraisals for the local governments are basically positive, but they rate lower the aspects such as public order, social security, environment protection and pollution treatment, citizens' political rights, jurisdiction and law enforcement, serving the public's interests and combat of the low income group than the low income group does.

In all, the middle income group in China currently basically belong to the "new citizens" community and this community is experiencing growth and the deepened urbanization process. During the urbanization, the group of people have gone through the stage of non-agriculturalization of jobs. Now they are gradually entitled to homogeneous urban public services, accessing to complete civil rights and achieving the psychological and cultural integration into the urban civilization.

References

Campbell A, Gurin G, Miller WE (1954) The voter decides. Row Peterson and Company, p 187

Fromm E (2007) The sane society. Shanghai Translation Publishing House

Huntington SP, Nelson JM (1989) No easy choice: political participation in developing countries. Huaxia Publishing House

Inkeles A (1992) Becoming modern: individual change in six developing countries. China Renmin University Press

Li Q (2001) On the middle class and middle intermediate stratum. J Renmin Univ China 2.

Li R (2010) Review of oversea studies of political efficacy. Foreign Theor Trends 9
Li C (2011) To seek reform of stay content with things as they are-measure of social and political attitudes of the middle class. Chin J Soc 2.
Lipset SM (1959) Some social requisites of democracy: economic development and political legitimacy. Am Polit Sci Rev 53:69–105
Li Q, Xu L (2017) On defining the middle income group. Social Science of Beijing, No 7
Zhang Y (2008) Political attitudes of current middle class in China. Social Sciences in China, No 2.

Wei Li is a Research Fellow of Institute of Sociology of Chinese Academy of Social Sciences (CASS), and director of the Department of Social Development in the Institute. His main research field is sociology of development, social research methods and social survey. He is also executive director of the China Social Survey.

Chapter 16
Social Values of Middle Income Group

N. N. Sedova

The middle class in present-day Russian society is not only an economic driving force that ensures social and political stability but also concentrates the most important functions connected with transformations in the field of social values. Setting the standards of the way of life and activity that others, first of all, less successful strata, may look at, the mid-class Russians thus take the role of a leader in formation, mastering and translation of relevant social ideals and goals, ideas of the world and the person's role in it.

The Russian middle class is very young in historical terms and dynamically developing social subject, heterogeneous in its origin. It is developed against a background of total changes in all spheres of the society with regard to which it is both an object and a subject, that is, it simultaneously forms new realia and is the first to adapt to them. Thus, the middle class is a group with a potentially high level of value transformation dynamics.

Of course, social values and standards in the society and its separate groups are quite conservative and change with noticeable delay, giving all new things an opportunity to be proven by time. However, values undergo transformations, even if they do so slowly, and their changes are of deep nature and they bring serious, fundamental shifts to the development of the society, reflecting change of generations, social-and-economic and social-and-political transformations, changes in the social structure of the society. The situation is aggravated by financial and economic crises and instability of external political situation in recent years.

Let us take the basic sociocultural trends which describe the current drift of the systems of norms and values, singled out by N. Tikhonova, as the initial point of analysis that generally characterizes the main tendencies of value transformations

N. N. Sedova (✉)
Institute of Sociology of FCTAS RAS, Moscow, Russia

P. Li and M. K. Gorshkov (eds.), *The Middle Income Group in China and Russia*,
Research Series on the Chinese Dream and China's Development Path,
https://doi.org/10.1007/978-981-16-1464-4_16

of present-day society.[1] These trends are revealed in the growing importance of practical, pragmatic motives in the evolution of value systems[2]; propagation of self-assertion values (personal success, high social status, domination, etc.) and decreased popularity of values that express the interests of the group[3]; in high importance of safety and wealth in Russia as compared to other countries and low importance of "going beyond personal ego" (tolerance, well-being of other people, etc.)[4]; in movement of Russia towards the type of cultures focused on result achievement at any price[5]; in gradual increase in the number of "Modern Men" in our country (analog of the western movement) which now make up a little less than a quarter of the population.[6] On the whole, the results of studies record growing values of achievement (as self-assertion, not self-realization) and individualism in Russia to the detriment of focus on group interests and cooperation, drift of regulation and value systems from the cultures of collective type to individual-based cultures.[7]

The sociocultural drift above may be placed in the value continuum between the two poles which may be conditionally determined as traditional and modernist ones. The pole of traditional values includes the maxims characteristic of deep-rooted system of norms in a traditional society based on customs and ideas of "due", "self-evident", on generally accepted life goals and strategies of their achievement

[1] Tikhonova, N.E. Peculiarities of Russian Modern Men and Prospects of Russian Cultural Dynamics. Article 1 // Social Sciences and Modernity. 2012. No. 2. pp. 38–52.

[2] See more about this and other conclusions of the group of N. Lapin and L. Belyaeva: Dynamics of Values of the Population in Reformed Russia. Moscow, 1996; Lapin, N.I. Russian Ways: Sociocultural Transformations. Moscow, 2000.; Lapin, N.I. Functional-Orienting Clusters of Basic Values of Population in Russia and Russian Regions // Sociological Studies. 2010. No. 1.; Regions in Russia: Sociocultural Portraits in General Russian Context. Moscow, 2009 et al.

[3] See more about this and other conclusions of the group of N. Lebedeva and A. Tatarko: Lebedeva, N.M., Kozlova, M.A., Tatarko, A.N. Psychological Research of Sociocultural Modernization. Moscow, 2007; Lebedeva, N.M., Tatarko, A.N. Culture as the Factor of Social Progress. Moscow, 2009; Lebedeva, N.M., Tatarko, A.N. Values of Culture and Society Development. Moscow, 2007 et al.

[4] See more about this and other conclusions of the group of V. Magun and M. Rudnev: Magun, V., Rudnev, M. Basic Values of Russians in the European Context // Social Sciences and Modernity. 2010a. No. 3.; Magun, V., Rudnev, M. Basic Values-2008: Similarities and Differences between the Russians and other Europeans // WP6. Higher School of Economics, 2010. No. WP6/2010/03 et al.

[5] See more about this and other conclusions of the group of N. and Yu. Latov: Latova, N.V., Latov, Yu.V. Peculiarities of Russian Economic Mentality // Economic Subjects of Post-Soviet Russia (institutional analysis). Part 1. Moscow, 2003.; Latova, N.V., Latov, Rossiyskaya, Yu.V. Russian Economic Mentality on the World Background // Social Sciences and Modernity. 2001. No. 4; Latova, N.V., Tikhonova, N.E. Modernization and Characteristics of the Russian National Mentality // Is the Russian Society Ready for Modernization? Moscow, 2010 et al.

[6] See more about this and other conclusions of the group of M. Gorshkov and N. Tikhonova: Changing Russia in the Mirror of Sociology / Edited by Gorshkov, M., Tikhonova, N. Moscow, 2004.; Russian Identity in Sociological Terms / Edited by Gorshkov, M., Tikhonova, N. Moscow, 2008.; Russian Identity under Transformation Conditions. Experience of Sociological Analysis / Edited by Gorshkov, M., Tikhonova, N. Moscow, 2005.; Is the Russian Society Ready for Modernization? / Edited by Gorshkov, M., Tikhonova, N. Moscow, 2010 et al.

[7] Tikhonova, N.E. Peculiarities of Russian Modern Men and Prospects of Russian Cultural Dynamics. Article 1 // Social Sciences and Modernity. 2012. No. 2. pp. 38–52.

Table 16.1 Worldview attitudes of middle class representatives, 2016, %. (*choice in the pairs of alternative statements*)

First statements in pairs (modernism)	Degree of consent with the first or second statement				Second statements in pairs (traditionalism)
	Definitely with the first	More with the first	More with the second	Definitely with the second	
I can sustain myself and my family and I don't need any state support	17	31	31	21	My family and I cannot survive without state support
You have to fight actively for your interests and rights	25	32	30	13	You have to be able to adapt to reality rather than spend efforts on fighting it
The main thing is initiative, enterprise, search for the new	21	38	27	14	The main thing is to respect the existing customs and traditions
Personal interests is the main thing for any person	23	37	32	7	Personal interests should be restricted in the interests of the country and the society

(for example, in the interpretation of I. Kuznetsov[8]), often resonating with "survival values" (according to R. Inglehart[9]) and predetermining the position of a "philistine".[10] The other pole is characterized by values of a modernist type characteristic of the modern society resulting not only from economic, cultural and political but also from social and sociocultural modernization (as determined by N. Tikhonova and S. Mareeva[11]); reliant on the rational type of thinking (values of the secular rational type or self-realization values according to R. Inglehart) that form an active position in life, "passionate" model in the extreme (according to N. Sedova).

Let us consider the peculiarities of social values of Russian middle class representatives in the continuum from traditionalist to modernist world concepts, emphasizing the parameters which characterize self-sufficiency or dependence on the state, degree of (non-)conformism, focus on protection of personal interests or adaptation to reality, personal or social interests (Table 16.1). Each studied parameter was measured by choosing one of a pair of statements by respondents which represented a rigid alternative; you could express a different degree of consent with the selected statement (full or partial).

The analysis of obtained data shows that representatives of the Russian middle strata are divided in their preferences. A relative majority (57–60%) supports modernist attitudes, and thinks that personal interests are the main thing in life;

[8] Kuznetsov (2016).

[9] Inglehart and Welzel (2011).

[10] Sedova (2016).

[11] Tikhonova and Mareeva (2009).

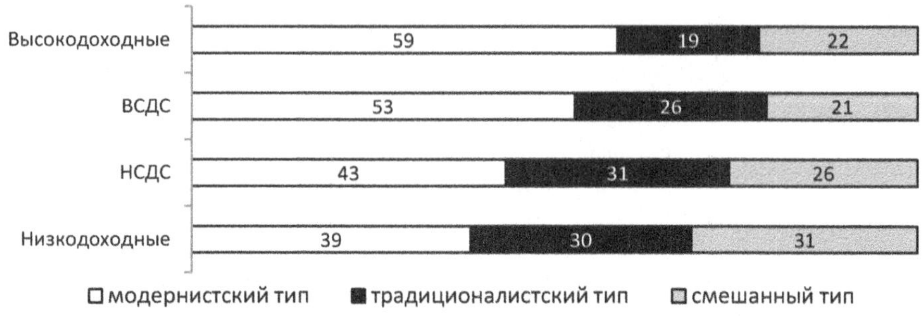

Fig. 16.1 Distribution of modernist and traditionalist types of world view among representatives of mid-income, low and high-income strata of the population, 2016, %

initiative, enterprise, search for the new; readiness to fight for your interests and rights. However, there are quite considerable (40–43%) shares of those who choose the statements that reflect a traditionalist position, considering it correct to adapt to the reality rather than fight it; respect the existing customs and traditions. As regards the statements which characterize self-sufficiency or dependence of a person on the state, the present-day middle class is divided practically into halves: a little less than a half (48%) declare their ability to sustain themselves and their families, independence from state support in this issue, and a little more than a half (52%) declare, on the contrary, that they and their families cannot survive without state support (Table 16.1).

Research of IS RAS shows that some strengthening of activist positions in most parameters has been in trend among the Russians in the development of worldview attitudes over the past 15 years.[12] As regards the possibility to be self-sufficient, independent of state support, a real revolution has taken place during this time: in 2005, the group of "self-sufficient Russians" was practically twice smaller than the group of Russians that felt dependent on the state support (34 against 66%), but today these groups are almost the same (48 and 52%). The "self-sufficient" Russians from the evident minority have turned into a group whose place under the sun has become comparable with the place of the "dependent" group that dominated earlier.

How general is this tendency? This question is to some extent clarified by comparison of value attitudes of middle class representatives with those of low-income and high-income groups, and also with lower and upper mid-income strata. To make such a comparison, groups of respondents have been singled out prone to modernist/activist and traditional/passivist values, as well as groups of mixed orientation.[13] As we may see in Fig. 16.1, not a single population stratum classified by income may be called homogeneous today in terms of distribution of modernist or

[12] Sedova (2016).

[13] The respondents that selected the relevant statements more than in 3 of 4 pairs were also classified as the supporters of modernist/activist traditionalist/passivist types of world view. The others were classified in the group of mixed attitudes.

traditional values; at the background of relative predomination of modernist attitudes (39–59%), there is a considerable share of those who share traditional values (19–31%). At the same time, 21–31% of different income groups representatives are prone to mixing traditionalist and modernist values in their ideas of life. Nevertheless, *there is an evident connection between the level of citizens' income and their system of values—the share of "modern men" increases by one time and a half (from 39 to 59%) and the share of "traditionalists" falls (from 30 to 19%) from low-income to high-income groups. This tendency also finds its reflection within the middle class—its lower strata are more "traditional", while the upper ones are more prone to modernist/activist attitudes.*

Thus, from the viewpoint of instrumental system of values[14]*in the modernism-traditionalism continuum, mid-income strata are characterized in Russia by combination of different types of value systems with predominant modernist attitudes. AT the same time, they occupy a mid position among low- and high-income population strata on the "value drift" ladder.*

The key factor of values formation is the age: its influence dominates in all income groups singled out for analysis, including middle-class ones. The maximum distribution of modernist values is typical of youth that starts life with focus on self-sufficiency and independence, active fight for personal interests and their priority over social interests, with striving for everything new. The modernism of the youth is expressed the most brightly among representatives of mid- and high-income groups (67–69%), but even in low-income strata, modern men dominate among the youth aged 18–30 (59%). With age, people are becoming more prone to traditional values – respect for customs and traditions, desire to adapt to the surrounding environment, readiness to limit personal interests for the sake of social ones and focus on the state support. The share of "traditionalists" reaches 53–55% among the respondents of older age across different income groups (Table 16.2).

Now let us look at the data on the social values of mid-income strata expressed in their attitude to other people. What human characteristics do they value, what do they lack in actions, communication and attitude to themselves on the part of the others? According to surveys (Table 16.3), today's middle class representatives value most of all honesty (74%), industry (62%), responsibility for yourself and your closest people and justice (52% each) in people. That is, today they are mostly after the characteristics of the people that show, first of all, in private life, in the sphere of direct interpersonal relations. The other characteristics are far behind the top group. For example, there is much less demand for the characteristics connected with business activity of people (enterprise and ability to achieve success was noted by 28% of those polled, initiative and activity–22%). The middle class representatives are considerably inferior to high-income group representatives in evaluating relevance, initiative and activity. Increased interest of high-income respondents in the values of initiative and activity (as well as rationality and pragmatism) seems to be connected

---

[14] Instrumental values (using the term of M. Rokeach) define the principles of everyday behavior, implying existence of the higher-level values – imperatives of abstract ideological nature or terminal values. Ref.: Rokeach, M. The Nature of Human Values. N.Y., 1973.

Table 16.2 Distribution of modernist and traditionalist types of world view among representatives of different age groups in different strata of the population, 2016, %[15]

Types of world view	18–30 years old	31–40	41–50	51–60	Over 60 years old
Low-Income Groups					
Modernist type	**59**	41	42	22	20
Traditionalist type	18	21	23	40	53
Mixed type	23	38	36	38	27
Mid-Income Groups					
Modernist type	**67**	**53**	**52**	38	20
Traditionalist type	14	24	23	32	55
Mixed type	19	24	24	30	25
High-Income Groups					
Modernist type	**69**	**71**	**64**	34	20
Traditionalist type	10	16	17	27	55
Mixed type	21	13	19	39	25

with a considerable share of people among them that occupy managerial positions and thus translate the demands to their subordinates. Written and non-written norms of interaction between people are also in the low-relevance zone: orderliness, reliable principles and ideals are important for only 18% of mid-income strata representatives, following traditional moral norms–for 15%. Even fewer votes were given to the characteristics that imply a possibility of collective civil activities (solidarity, readiness to help people–16%, personal involvement in the problems of your city–13%, collectivism, readiness to participate in resolution of general problems–5%).

Let us dwell on the general situation for different groups of Russians that looks contradictory at first sight. On the one hand, the leading positions in the list of the most demanded characteristics are occupied by those related to moral categories: honesty, industry, justice. On the other hand, general principles of conduct and actions that imply reliance on moral and legal norms are not very relevant. It seems that the demand for system compliance with the rules of the game would be more logical than support of separate positive characteristics pulled out from the general context of morals or state law. This contradiction seems to reflect the realities of present-day life where it is often impossible to achieve success without violation of these or those accepted norms. It is the representatives of mid-income groups, especially its upper subgroup, who become the main hostages to this dilemma: the majority of them (59% among the lower and 61% among the upper subgroups of mid-income groups) recognize the relevance of moral norms, agree with the necessity of state participation in supporting favorable moral climate in the society (72% among the lower and 61% among the upper subgroups of the mid-income group), and practically the same

[15] The bold indicators exceeding 50% are highlighted.

Table 16.3 Human characteristics valued most in people by representatives of different strata of population, 2016, % (*up to 5 answers were possible; regularized by importance for Mid-Income Group on the whole*)

Characteristics	Low-income	Lower mid-income group	Upper mid-income group	*Mid-Income Group as a whole*	High-income
Honesty	77	76	73	*74*	72
Industry	63	63	59	*62*	61
Responsibility for yourself and your closest people	52	52	52	*52*	50
Justice	57	51	54	*52*	55
Enterprise, ability to achieve success	26	26	30	*28*	29
Initiative, activity	19	22	21	*22*	30
Patriotism	17	18	20	*19*	21
Orderliness	17	19	18	*18*	13
Existence of clear principles and ideals	17	18	18	*18*	22
Solidarity, readiness to help people	18	16	16	*16*	13
Love of freedom, self-esteem	14	15	17	*16*	22
Following traditional moral norms	13	13	17	*15*	11
Personal involvement in the problems of your city, settlement	16	15	10	*13*	9
Tolerance to people of another nationality	9	10	9	*10*	7
Rationality, pragmatism	7	9	8	*9*	16
Religious commitment, belief in God	7	6	5	*6*	6
Collectivism, readiness to participate in resolution of general problems	7	5	5	*5*	5
Obedience, humility	4	4	4	*4*	7

number of people (57% and 60% respectively) have to agree that achievement of success sometimes requires stepping outside of these norms (Table 16.4).

Summarizing the analysis of the request that middle class representatives set to the people around them, let's pay attention to the manifestation of self-oriented model of the world view when the person's private life comes to the foreground, and something that is oriented outside and regulates the person's interaction with the outer world is at the periphery of interests. This correlates with the trends mentioned earlier for values drift towards individually-oriented sociocultural environment. Distribution of request for human characteristics of the surrounding people among the representatives of different age groups of the middle class also correlates here: young people aged 18–30 demand such qualities as enterprise and ability to achieve success more often than older people (18% more often than in the group of 60-year-olds and older), initiative and activity (by 15%), love for freedom and self-esteem, rationality and pragmatism (by 9–11%).

One more aspect of the social values system of the Russian middle class is seen in understanding of success in life by its representatives. *The three whales on which the view of normative model of success in life by the majority of low-income group representatives rests is family and children (57% gave 5 points on a five-point scale—"very important"), financial well-being (55%), work, business (50%, Fig. 16.2). This model of success is supplemented with such criteria as self-realization and a possibility to show yourself (45%), education (43%), health, beauty, sports (33%). Thus, the top list of life success indicators is focused on the person's individual goals in life.* The only relatively popular marker of success, connected with what is happening in the "outer world" rather than with the personal life circumstances of the person is "life in the society arranged in a more just and reasonable way" (23%). The criteria that presuppose the person's active social position determine success in life much less frequently.

The Russian middle class is quite homogeneous in evaluating the criteria of life success, and there are no considerable deviations in the answers of representatives of upper and lower mid-income group. However, they still have some peculiarities. Thus, representatives of the upper subgroup of the mid-income group attach a higher importance to such a criterion of success in life as self-realization, showing yourself (51% and 42%, respectively) more frequently as compared to the representatives of the lower subgroup. In its turn, the answers of lower subgroup representatives of the mid-income group contain more frequent high evaluations of such a life criterion as life in a more just and reasonably arranged society (26% with 19% in the upper subgroup). These two vectors lie within the trends mentioned earlier for movement of high-income strata towards modernist values and individual-based cultures, and also to wider distribution of traditionalist values in low-income strata of the society.

Table 16.4 Moral values of representatives of different population strata, 2015, % (*choice in the pairs of alternative statements*)

Pairs of alternative statements	Low-income	Lower mid-income group	UPPER mid-income group	*Mid-income group as a whole*	High-income
We live in a different world today and many moral norms are obsolete	41	41	39	*40*	36
The main moral norms are not influenced by time, they are always relevant and up-to-date	59	59	61	*60*	64
The present-day world is cruel, and achieving success in life sometimes requires stepping outside of moral norms and principles	46	43	40	*42*	45
I'd better not achieve success in life than act beyond moral norms and principles	54	57	60	*58*	55
Morals and ethics is the sphere of the person's private life, and the state should not interfere with it	33	28	31	*29*	30
Keeping up the favorable moral climate in the society is impossible without state participation	67	72	69	*71*	70

Mid-income groups are quite close to low-income Russians in their evaluation of success in life, while comparison with high-income groups shows certain differences in ideas of what may be considered success. First of all, the model of life success in high-income groups looks somewhat more intense due to a whole range of criteria included in them more often: career, self-realization, friendship and communication, music and culture, love and sex, access to information. The frequency of mentioning them as life success criteria in the group of high-income Russians is higher by 5–9% as compared to mid-income groups. As a result, the model that serves as a basis for

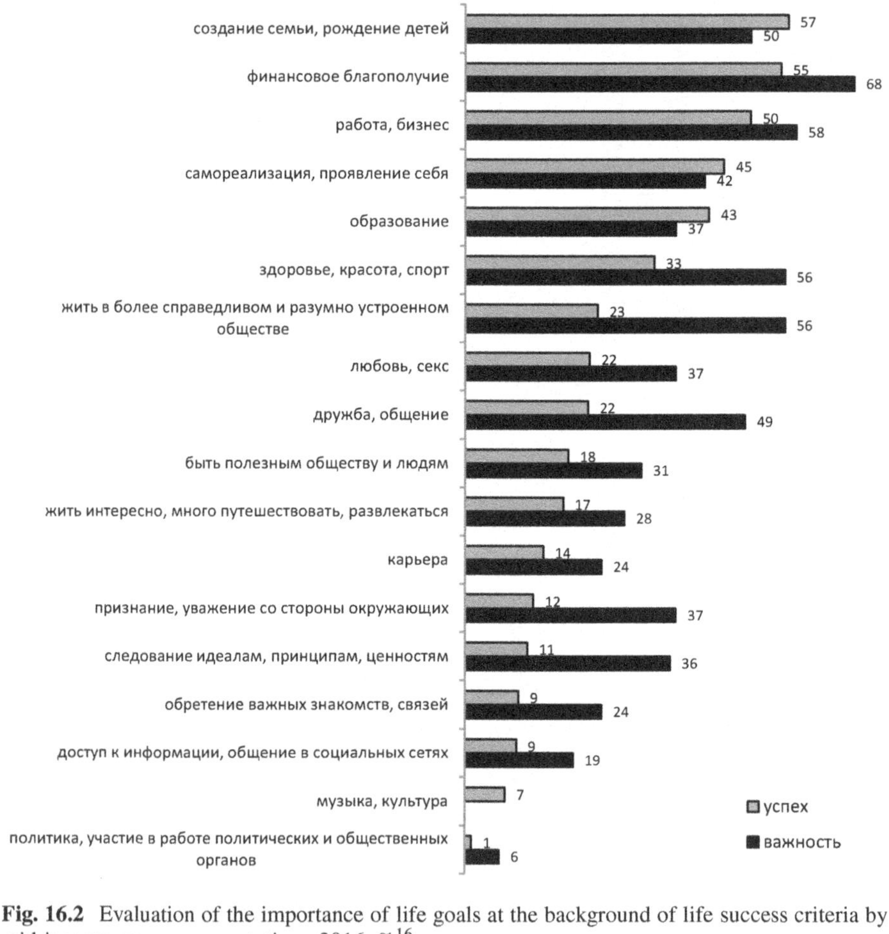

Fig. 16.2 Evaluation of the importance of life goals at the background of life success criteria by mid-income group representatives, 2016, %[16]

[16] Answers to the questions: "How important is … at present for you personally?" (there is a choice of importance (5 points on a 5-point scale) and "In your opinion, what determines the person's success in life in the first instance?" (up to 5 variants of answers were admitted).

high-income Russians seems more diverse and harmonious. Moreover, an important role in the normative model of life success in the mid-income group is played by two criteria from the top list: first of all, creation of a family and giving birth to children, and secondly, financial well-being (distribution higher by 7 and 11% than in the high-income group). *These differences may be interpreted as the evidence of the fact that mid-income group of the Russian population finds itself today within a strictly focused model of life success, concentration of efforts in clearly defined directions. Meanwhile, high-income groups are drifting towards a more diverse and harmonious model of success based on the achieved level of material and social well-being.*

Representatives of different age groups of the mid-income group have their peculiarities in the ideas of life success. As compared to the older groups, the youth includes love and sex (27% more often than those polled aged 60 and older), self-realization (17% more), interesting life with travels and entertainment, career (12–13% more) in the success criteria on a more frequent basis. For older age groups, health, life in a more just society (20–23% more), financial well-being, a possibility to be useful to the society and people, respect of the surrounding people, following the ideals, principles and values (8–12% more) are much more relevant than for the youth.

The normative model of success is a kind of a guideline that sets the main vector of life strategies for several group members. However, particular conditions and life circumstances of people, group and country on the whole adjust these strategies, specifying the profile of life focus of the mid-income group. This is clearly seen if we compare the normative model of success considered above and particular life goals set by their representatives (Fig. 16.2).

The first thing that draws our attention if we compare the data given in Fig. 16.2 is the growing relevance of the majority of parameters when people shift from considering them as abstract criteria of success in life to inclusion of particular goals in the list that are important personally. The general tendency is ruined by only three parameters that display some reduction of relevance: creation of a family and giving birth to children, self-realization and self-actualization, education. The particular personally important life goals of the mid-income group representatives include most often financial well-being (68%), work and business (58%), health (56%), life in a more just and rational society (56%), creation of a family and having children (50%), friendship and communication (49%). *Thus, as compared to the normative model of life success, the list of highly important personal ambitions shows more variety in middle class representatives as it contains such items as health, friendship and communication, social justice.*

Besides the items that are highly relevant for half and more middle class representatives, the set of relatively widespread life goals also includes self-realization (42%), education, love and sex, recognition and respect of the surrounding people, following the ideals, principles and values (36–37% each). Another third of polled group representatives included contribution to the society and people (31%) into the list.

At the general background, the most important life goals noticeably more rarely include an interesting life with travels and entertainments (28%), career, getting important acquaintances and connections (24% each), access to information, communication in social networks (19%). As regards politics and contributing to the activity of social and political organizations, they are included in the relevant life goals by only 6% of the middle class representatives.

Now let us look at the differences in particular ambitions of the middle class as compared to the low- and high-income groups (Table 16.5). When mid-income group representatives transit from general understanding of success in life to personal life goals, they display a higher degree of actualization of such parameters as life in a more just society, friendship and communication, contributing to the society and people, recognition and respect of the surrounding people, following the ideals, principles and values. As regards low-income strata, they are characterized by the highest possible actualization of the issue of financial well-being at the background of middle- and high-income groups.

The hierarchy of life values in the mid-income strata has its peculiarities for "Modern Men" and "traditionalists". Thus, abstract understanding of success in life by "Modern Men" is more often connected with personal and professional development (love and sex, work and business, self-realization, interesting life with travels and entertainments, career) than is the case with "traditionalists". As regards personal life goals, the "Modern Men" are in the lead as compared to the "traditionalists" by the absolute majority of items, including them in the number of those very important personally. There are also several priorities in the group of "traditionalists" that they include in the understanding of life success more often than the "Modern Men": health by 15%, contributing to society and people by 9%, creating a family and having children by 6%. On the level of personal life plans, the relevance of all goals among the "traditionalists" is lower than in "Modern Men".

At the same time, the analysis of hierarchic peculiarities of life values formed in mid-income "Modern Men" and "traditionalists" testifies to the fact that these two groups have no considerable differences in this issue. In both groups, the leading priorities in life include work and business, creation of a family and having children, financial well-being. The second tier of priorities also coincides in both groups, including self-realization, education and health. However, peculiarities of the groups are seen in the evaluation of importance of life priorities in the third tier (which occupy 7th and lower places in the ratings of life success criteria importance). For instance, the items connected with personal interests, such as love and sex, interesting life, career (the places in the rating are higher by 3–4 positions than in "traditionalists") are found higher in the rating of life success criteria as provided by "Modern Men". The rating of "traditionalists" is characterized by higher ranking of such items as living in a just society, making a contribution to the society and people, recognition and respect of surrounding people, following ideals, principles, values.

Table 16.5 Changes related to transit from normative evaluation of life success criteria to the choice of important personal life goals among representatives of different income groups, 2016, % (*arranged by the goals of mid-income group*)

Criteria of success in life/life goals	Low-Income			Mid-income group			High-Income		
	Success[a]	Goa[b]	Difference[c]	Success	Goal	Difference	Success	Goal	Difference
Financial well-being	53	**71**	*18*	55	**68**	*13*	44	**59**	*14*
Work, business	49	**55**	*6*	50	**58**	*8*	47	**59**	*12*
Living in a more just society	28	**63**	*35*	23	**56**	*33*	22	47	*25*
Health, beauty, sport	35	**54**	*19*	33	**56**	*23*	31	**51**	*19*
Creation of a family, having children	58	**49**	*−9*	57	**50**	*−7*	49	46	*−3*
Friendship, communication	23	**50**	*27*	22	**49**	*27*	29	**50**	*22*
Self-realization, self-actualization	41	41	*−1*	45	42	*−3*	52	41	*−11*
Recognition, respect of the people around	13	45	*32*	12	37	*25*	11	24	*12*
Education	40	33	*−6*	43	37	*−6*	40	40	*0*
Love, sex	20	36	*16*	22	37	*15*	27	38	*11*
Following the ideals, principles, values	11	41	*30*	11	36	*25*	9	27	*18*
Making a contribution to society and people	21	33	*12*	18	31	*13*	17	24	***6***
Live an interesting life, travel a lot, have a good time	19	26	*7*	17	28	*11*	21	32	*11*
Career	16	27	*11*	14	24	*10*	21	29	*7*

(continued)

Table 16.5 (continued)

Criteria of success in life/life goals	Low-Income			Mid-income group			High-Income		
	Success[a]	Goa[b]	Difference[c]	Success	Goal	Difference	Success	Goal	Difference
Getting important acquaintances, connections	9	28	*19*	9	24	*15*	6	20	*13*
Access to information, communication in social networks	9	21	*12*	9	19	*10*	14	20	*5*
Politics, contributing to political and social organizations	1	7	*5*	1	6	*5*	1	3	*2*

[a]Success—the share of respondents that include this parameter in the criteria of life success
[b]Goal—the share of respondents that gave 5 points to this parameter on a 5-grade scale (as a highly important one) as a life goal that is personally important
[c]The difference between the share of respondents that specified this parameter as a personally important goal and the share of those who mentioned it as an abstract criterion of success in life. A positive value means that this parameter is more relevant as a particular life goal than a criterion of success. A negative value means that this parameter is more important as a criterion of success in life, not as a personal life goal
The values of life goals that are highly relevant for half (49–50%) and more representatives of the group, are shown in bold

To develop analysis of the social value systems of middle class representatives, let us turn to evaluation of the basic notions which describe in their perception the past, thc present, and idea of the future of the Russian society. Among 34 notions proposed for evaluation, positive feelings of mid-income group representatives are raised in most cases by justice, Motherland, freedom, Russians, patriotism, compassion, human rights, morals, faith, progress, tradition, equality, property, solidarity (positive reaction in 62–88% of cases). The negative reaction follows more often if we mention "revolution" (negative feelings in 48% of those polled), West, capitalism (34–35%), power (30%), conservatism, reforms (18–19%). As we see, *the set of notions that raise the highest positive response shows the pronounced patriotic and moral dominant ideas of values in the mid-income strata*, while *politically and ideologically loaded notions are rejected, no matter whether they are connected with the previous, Soviet stage of the country's life, or with the present day*. At the same time, the notion of Democracy is in the zone of "emotional mastering": 41% take it as positive, and 49% as neutral, showing the possibility of a positive or a negative scenario. It is also interesting to note that there are more of those among mid-income strata representatives who experience positive emotions if we mention such notions as Socialism, USSR (more positive answers by 12–13 points), past, solidarity (by 8–9 points), church, progress (by 6 points).

On the whole, mid-income strata are quite close in their evaluations to low-income strata (differences within 5–6 points). At the same time, the mid-income group representatives express a positive attitude to the notions of progress, USSR, Socialism, collectivism (by 9–10 points), human rights, equality, state (by 7 points), patriotism (by 6 points) than the high-income Russians. In their turn, the representatives of the high-income strata positively perceive the notions of individualism (by 12 points), West (by 10 points), self-government (by 7 points), nation (by 6 points) more often.

The attitude to the proposed list of notions among the "Modern Men" and "traditionalists" presents two different world views. The specifics of positive description of the world by the "Modern Men" is determined by such notions as business, individualism, competition, self-government, reform, democracy, West, market. At the same time, they show on the whole a positive attitude to the progress, property and human rights. Attention is drawn by the fact that the set of notions which are positively perceived by the "Modern Men" has, first of all, two backbone accents: economy and democracy; secondly, it relates to the active part of life, describes the conditions and rules of this activity. As regards the "traditionalists", the set of notions they take positively is different: USSR, church, tradition, state, faith, compassion, patriotism, nation, Russians, morals, Socialism, past, collectivism. Here we see the values turned to the past of the country, with the vision connected with the concepts of statehood and unity (Table 16.6).

Evaluations of separate statements about it by the mid-income group representatives (Table 16.7) allow to present the images of the desired future for Russia more fully. On the whole, they show a moderately conservative approach, standing for preservation of stability and gradual reforms (71%), for revival of Russian national traditions, moral and religious values (67%), for Russia to be the state that unites different peoples; for development of a democratic state in Russia which provides human rights and freedom of expression (63% each). Today, radical changes attract only 28% of the middle class representatives, and those who reject the possibility of democratic development of Russia and stands for solid individual rule, creation of the Russian national state (36–37% each) or for the European way of development

Table 16.6 Top groups of notions that raise positive feelings in the mid-income group on the whole and its different subgroups, 2016, %[17] *(arranged by the share of those who showed a positive reaction)*

"Modern Men"	Mid-income groups overall(top group of notions by the share of those who noted them as raising positive feelings)	"Traditionalists"
Business	Justice	*USSR*
Individualism	Motherland	*Church*
Competition	Freedom	Socialism
Progress	*Russians*	Past
Property	*Patriotism*	*Tradition*
Self-government	*Compassion*	*State*
Reform	*Morals*	*Faith*
Human rights	**Human rights**	*Compassion*
Democracy	*Faith*	*Patriotism*
West	**Progress**	Collectivism
Market	*Tradition*	*Nation*
	Equality	*Russians*
	Property	*Morals*
	Solidarity	
	State	
	USSR	
	Nation	
	Church	

[17] The emphasis zones show intersection of the positions relevant for the whole middle class, with "Modern Men" and "traditionalists". The Table shows only the notions that accounted for the difference in the positive reactions between the "Modern Men" and "traditionalists" by more than 5 points.

in the economy and way of life (32%) also form a minority. The only thing that splits the positions of mid-income group representatives by almost a half is the question of what is the first priority for Russia now – restoration of the state power with relevant armed forces and a possibility to influence the political processes in the world (55%) or care about the well-being of citizens (45%).

Table 16.7 World views of the representatives of different subgroup representatives in the mid-income strata, as well as low- and high-income groups, 2016, %[18] (*choice in the pairs of alternative statements*)

Pairs of alternative statements	Low-income	Mid-income groups					High-income
		Lower mid-income group	Upper mid-income group	"Modern Men"	"Traditionalists"	*Mid-income groups overall*	
The country needs changes, radical economic and political reforms	29	30	25	37	16	**28**	29
The country needs stability, gradual reforms	69	70	74	63	84	**71**	71
Russia should become a democratic state which provides human rights and freedom of expression	62	61	65	71	50	**63**	72
Democracy does not come to stay in Russia. The country needs solid individual rule that ensures order, unity and sovereignty of the country	37	39	34	29	50	**37**	28

(continued)

[18] The values are the sums of answers "strongly agree" and "rather agree" with regard to each statement.

Table 16.7 (continued)

Pairs of alternative statements	Low-income	Mid-income groups					High-income
		Lower mid-income group	Upper mid-income group	"Modern Men"	"Traditionalists"	*Mid-income groups overall*	
Russia needs revival of Russian national traditions, moral and religious values	66	68	67	61	75	**67**	59
Russia should move forward, to the modern economy and way of life, like in Europe	33	32	33	39	25	**32**	40
Russia has to be a great power with strong armed forces and influence all the political processes in the world	50	53	58	56	55	**55**	63
Russia should take care of the well-being of its citizens rather than strive for consolidation of the state power	49	47	42	44	45	**45**	37
Russia should first of all strive to create the Russian national state	37	37	35	41	33	**36**	37
Russia should be the power that unites different nations	62	63	64	59	67	**63**	63

The groups of the mid-income strata representatives that adhere to modernist or traditionalist values share this view on the whole, but add their accents. Traditionalists are more conservative in their social and political ideas: 84% of them stand for stability, 75% – for reliance on traditions, morals and religion. Moreover, every other of them denies Russia the possibility to establish a democratic state and stands for solid individual rule (50%). Despite the dominating values of stability and traditions, there is a considerable share of "Modern Men" who are ready for substantial changes in the course of the country's development (radical economic and political reforms are supported by 37%, European line – 39%). On the whole, the positions of "Modern Men" and "Traditionalists" are characterized by a high degree of conformity with regard to the moderate conservative vector and the "Russian way" of the country's development.

Summarizing the analysis of different aspects that characterize the system of social values in the mid-income strata of the Russian society in the space between traditionalist and modernist poles, we should note some discrepancies existing in it. Thus, the principles of everyday activity in the social and economic sphere, selected by their representatives, imply co-existence of different types of value systems in their environment with predomination of modernist attitudes (non-conformism, readiness to fight for personal interests, focus on the initiative, enterprise, search for something new; personal interests).

The section of values, received by analyzing the human characteristics that enjoy the highest demand by representatives of the mid-income group, showed that such characteristics as honesty, industry and justice are demanded most of all. The characteristics that presuppose reliance on the moral and legal norms are noticeably less relevant. This discrepancy is also seen in the dilemma "success in life vs morals" faced by middle class representatives: recognizing the relevance of moral norms, they have to step over them to achieve success. As a result, their environment forms a request for active state participation in supporting the favorable moral climate in the society which may be interpreted as the request for compliance with the existing "rules of the game" first of all, including on the part of the state. On the whole, the request of the mid-income strata for certain human characteristics testifies to their development of a self-oriented world view model with dominating personal interests.

Understanding of success in life, which shows one more side of the social value system in the mid-income strata, is also focused today on person's individual life goals (family and children, financial well-being, work/business, self-realization, education, health) and emphasizes low relevance of the success criteria connected with the surrounding world (political and social participation, acquaintances and connections, access to information, respect by the surrounding people).

Within the system of personal life goals, the middle class representatives show a considerably higher and systemic proneness to traditional values as compared to high-income strata; among the key vectors of life efforts, the values of survival, safety, building your own "castle" (financial well-being, work and business, health, living in a just society, family and children, friendship and communication) come to the foreground.

The set of values that describe the past, present and the ideas of the Russia's future, shows a pronounced tendency of mid-income group for the traditionalist type of perception, patriotic and moral dominant ideas in their minds. However, mid-income strata are not homogeneous in this respect. The specifics of the world description by the "Modern Men" from their number is determined by the system-forming accents on the economy and democracy. The vision of "traditionalists" is more focused on the past of the country and connected with the concepts of statehood and unity.

On the whole, the middle class realizes the moderately conservative approach, standing for stability, return to the national, moral and religious traditions, for the great power statehood and the "Russian" way, connecting it all with the possibilities of democratic development and economic prosperity of the country.

References

Inglehart R, Welzel C (2011) Modernization, cultural change and democracy: the human development sequence. Novoye Izdatelstvo, Moscow

Kuznetsov IM (2016) Evolution of value orientations in the tradition-modernity continuum. In: Gorshkov MK, Petukhov VV (eds) Russian society and challenges of the time. Ves Mir., Moscow, pp 86–104. (Book Four / Gorshkov, M.K. [et al.]).

Sedova NN (2016) Life priorities: from needs and interests to taking action. In: Gorshkov MK, Petukhov VV (eds) Russian society and the challenges of time. Ves Mir., Moscow, pp 105–130. (Book Four / Gorshkov, M.K. [et al.]).

Tikhonova NE, Mareeva SV (2009) The middle class: theories and reality. Ves Mir., Moscow

Natalia N. Sedova Senior Researcher at the Federal Center of Theoretical and Applied Sociology of the Russian Academy of Sciences (former Institute of Sociology, Russian Academy of Sciences), and Scientific Assistant to VCIOM General Director (Russian Public Opinion Research Center), and Deputy Editor-in-Chief of the journal The Monitoring of Public Opinion: Economic and Social Changes. Her main areas of interest include economic sociology, dynamics of moral attitudes, leisure sociology, the role of mega-events on territories' social development, public participation and Spontaneous order. N. Sedova the author of more than 50 scientific papers published either in Russia or abroad, including chapters in scientific monographs "Russian Everyday Life During a Crisis" (2009), "Is Russian society ready for modernization?" (2010),

"Rich and Poor in Contemporary Russia" (2014), "Russian Society and Challenges of the Time" (Books 3–5, 2016–2017). She takes part of several research projects devoted to a wide range of issues: public participation and issues of political activity, social structure, modernization processes.

Chapter 17
Social and Political Participation of Middle Income Group in China

Yan Cui

As China goes through profound reform and rapid social-economic transformation, its structure of interests starts to show a diversified characteristic. Various social problems begin to reveal themselves gradually while some conflicts become intensified. Meanwhile, confrontational social political activities happen from time to time. Examples are petition, protest, workers' strikes and shopkeepers' strikes. They have posed negative influence on social harmony, stability and sustainable development. Middle income group is essential to social stability as they are the stabilizer of our political and social life.

On the one hand, middle income group are well-educated and well-off in economic terms. They have access to more information and social-economical resources with higher social cognitive competence and social mobilization ability. On the other hand, they usually have stable social connections, making it more likely for them to achieve individual appeal through constructive and non-confrontational means. To the contrary, low income group tend to adopt radical and confrontational act to push the government when their individual interests are violated because of lack of relevant channels and information. Consequently, it is highly on the agenda of our political development and social construction to strengthen social and political participation by removing information asymmetry and to give play to institutional participation of civil groups by building various mechanism and platforms to coordinate interests.

In the past decades, China's social governance is mainly government-oriented and lacking institutional channels and opportunities for active public participation. Meanwhile, weak social empowerment makes it difficult for the public to actively engage in social and political life. In other words, the current social structure fails to provide abundant resources and channels for social and political participation for social members. Individuals are not motivated to actively engage in social and political affairs and their sense of effectiveness is quite low. In the following part, this

Y. Cui (✉)
Institute of Sociology in CASS, Beijing, China

P. Li and M. K. Gorshkov (eds.), *The Middle Income Group in China and Russia*, Research Series on the Chinese Dream and China's Development Path,
https://doi.org/10.1007/978-981-16-1464-4_17

paper will mainly focus on three aspects: social participation, political participation and sense of effectiveness.

17.1 Social Participation of Middle Income Group in China

17.1.1 The Significance of Social Participation

As the society develops rapidly, it is essential to build a sound self-management mechanism to enable a good match between social governance ability and social-economic development to ensure optimal allocation of social resources. It is inevitable for us to expand social participation to better react to increasingly complex social needs. Only through proper guidance by government departments can we equip social members and organizations with better self-management skills in dealing with affairs in various social and public domains as well as public welfare courses to respond to social changes during the process of social development and transformation. In the meantime, we must transform from a single subject of social governance to multiple ones. Only by doing this can we fully implement the goals of social governance under new circumstances and further enrich means of social governance. Middle income group play a very crucial role in this process as they are equipped with high social cognitive competence and organizational capability. If middle income group are fully motivated to participate in social affairs, it can help to remit the scarcity of public management resources to effectively offset the vacuum zone of social management under traditional social system.

In political participation, interactions between the public, the state and government are emphasized from time to time while social participation mainly focuses on interactions between various social communities. Social participation cannot only meet diversified needs of the public, especially day-to-day individual needs, but can also satisfy their demand of social interactions. Therefore, the essence of social participation is self-management and self-service in social lives. It is a combination of social participation and social service of individuals. In a sense, the nature of social participation is social service which includes both service for oneself and others.

In addition, the process of social participation embodies self-actualization of one's social meaning and the fulfillment of social value through social interactions. By engaging in social affairs, individuals can build good interactive relations with other social members and expand his or her social circle. Individuals can also be involved in the management of public affairs through proper platforms and approaches to achieve unification between personal values and social values. As a result, social participation is essential to the reinforcement of social cohesion, facilitation of social consensus and promotion of social identity.

17.1.2 Social Participation Level and Types

At present, there are two types of social participation, organizational and mobilized participation and public spontaneous participation. Organizational and mobilized participation is mostly initiated by government sectors, schools and grassroots autonomous groups. One representative is village or neighborhood committee. Under traditional social management model with lots of public institutions, the public are objects of management. They mainly participate in social affairs through top-down governance model initiated by the state or government. This kind of model can pose great influence on participation mechanism, motivation, scope, effect and the form of participation as mobilizers as authority are dominant in all aspects of participation. As scholars once said, "in activities mobilized by the community, participants have specific personal interests or expectations. They usually rely on the community or neighborhood committee for some benefit or expect to gain certain identification or reward by participating in those activities. Those who are not looking for material or psychological reward tend to be passive and don't expect much from the participation." (Xiang and Wang 2012).[1]

Spontaneous public participation is mainly self-organized driven by individual and social needs. It embodies an effective combination of individual interests and social interests. It is a bottom-up social governance and participation model formed by voluntary groups. Organizations formed through spontaneous participation serve as a bridge between the state and society or between government and citizens with good interactive mechanism. On the one hand, joint management of public affairs can be better achieved through consultative cooperation. On the other hand, public spontaneous organizations can maximize public interest and optimize resources allocation to avoid mismatch of social resources and government failure that happened frequently under traditional social system. They also prevent waste of public resources caused by mistakes in allocation to effectively implement social participation mechanism with shared benefits and risks. Social participation built on voluntary willingness can enable participants to identify with the significance and value of social activities to the greatest extent and thus form their social identity more effectively to fully realize social cohesion through individual interaction.

When we look at the overall picture of social participation in China, data shows that only 10.7% of people have taken part in voluntary activities organized by the government, companies or schools. 15.8% have joined self-organized social activities of public welfare such as voluntary environment cleaning, helping out the senior, the disabled and the sick, etc. In regard to participation willingness, quite a number of people are willing to be involved in social activities of public welfare. For instance, about 58% people say they want to attend voluntary activities organized by the government, companies or schools and 65% are willing to participate in self-organized activities of public welfare.

[1] Xiang and Wang (2012) (Vol 199 in all), P 43-45.

Table 17.1 Social participation and willingness of different income groups

	Reveal certain social issues to media	Participate in voluntary activities	Participate in religious activities	Participate in self-organized public welfare activities
Percentage of participation in various social activities				
Low-income group	1.85	7.37	9.32	14.22
Medium–low income group	2.6	9.58	6.76	14.47
Medium–high income group	2.91	12.33	5.44	16.64
High-income group	4.17	18.77	8.32	21.09
Willing to participate				
Low-income group	31.5	51.01	7.25	59.55
Medium–low income group	35.13	55.6	8.23	65.95
Medium–high income group	32.98	58.6	8.62	65.56
High-income group	36.03	58.66	9.78	69.29

Unit Percentage

The data also shows differences of social participation and willingness among various income groups (see Tables 17.1 and 17.2). Medium–high income group are more active in social participation than low income group. 18.77% of high income group and 12.33% of medium–high income group have taken part in voluntary activities while 9.58% of middle-low income people and 7.37% of low income group have done the same. In terms of the participation in self-organized social welfare activities, the picture is quite similar. 21.09% of high income group have attended self-organized social activities while only 14.22% of its low-income counterparts have done the same.

Regarding participation willingness, medium–high income group are more willing to participate in social activities than low income group. For example, 58.66% of high income people say they are willing to take part in voluntary activities while the figure for low-income group is 51.01. 69.29% of high-income people expressed willingness to attend self-organized public welfare activities while only 59.55% of low income people did the same.

Table 17.2 Political participation and willingness of different income groups

	Discuss political issues with others	Offer suggestions to government divisions	Attend village or neighborhood committee election	Petition at government departments	Attend march
Percentage of participation					
Low-income group	17.13	8.38	53.17	3.77	0.64
Medium–low income group	21.05	8.13	45.67	3.51	0.63
Medium–high income group	24.25	6.99	37.03	3.61	0.75
High-income group	31.96	8.25	32.44	2.62	0.91
Willingness of participation					
Low-income group	25.11	34.73	48.25	17.33	4.75
Medium–low income group	26.83	39.22	51.07	18.11	5.67
Medium–high income group	24.3	35.35	48.24	13.47	4.97
High-income group	25.63	38.54	47.79	15.69	6.76

Unit Percentage

17.2 Political Participation of Middle Income Group

17.2.1 Political Participation Reflects Individual Initiative

As one of the major manifestation of individual initiative, political participation refers to a situation when citizens rely on certain means to pose influence on government, political power system, public society and political life. Put in another way, it means citizens attempt to get involved in social and political life and decision-making process to convey individual or collective wishes in order to affect rule-making, decision-making and performance evaluation of a country's political system and social management through a certain organizational form and procedure (Sun and Liao 2010).[2] Huntington pointed out that political participation includes all the acts civilians use to pose influence on the government and it does not matter whether

[2] Sun Huan, Liao Xiaoming, "Political Participation Subject:from ethic perspective, including environmental ethics", Social Sciences Edition of Beijing Normal University Journal, vol. 6 in (2010) (vol. 222 in all), pp. 82–90.

those acts are legal, violent and voluntary or not. Huntington not only differentiated two important categories of voluntary participation and mobilized participation, but also distinguished concepts between legal participation and illegal participation, between conventional political participation represented by poll and unconventional ones, such as boycott and public demonstration.[3] Unlike Huntington, Noman H. Nie and Sidney Verba et al. hold narrower opinions. They believe political participation is an legitimate act taken by civilians to influence government personnel. Under this definition, political participation is a legal act that includes only voluntary participation.[4]

The author believes that the study of political participation should pay equal attention to both legal and conventional act as well as illegal and unconventional act. First of all, the legality of the act itself depends on specific social political structure. Illegal act in one society may be legal in another. The concept of political participation should have a wide coverage and not be limited by political system, legal regime and ideological form. Meanwhile, the act of political participation, some "illegal act" in particular, is direct feedback of individuals on social structure. It reflects the initiative of individuals and structural problems in social governance. Only by fully examining the rationality of "illegal act" can we conduct comprehensive research on the mechanism of action of social participation.[5]

If we take a glimpse of the reality of China, the public become increasingly more proactive in political activities, especially those middle income people with higher economic level and social status. On the one hand, their interests demonstrate a multilevel and multidimensional characteristic. On the other hand, middle income group are equipped with certain social resources and mobilization capability that enable them to negotiate with the state and government to seek a balance point and the greatest common divisor among interests of all parties. They use all types of information channels to build effective interaction with the government through collective act in real and virtual public sphere within the scope of the system. As a scholar once put forward, groups of higher social status tend to be active in political participation as they possess abundant social resources and are more demanding when it comes to whether the authority responds to their appeal or needs promptly. They also have stronger capability to act and are usually called active participators in political participation[5]. However, in regard to the acts of political participation of middle income group, most of them are about maintaining legal rights. There are few conventional and institutional political acts. This phenomenon has been brought

---

[3] Samuel. P. Huntington, Jorge I. Dominguez, "Political Development", in handbook of Political Science, ed. Fred I. Greenstein and Nelson W. Polsby, translated by Chu Fuyun, Commercial Press, 1996 edition, pp. 188–189.

[4] Sydney Verba, "Political Participation", in in handbook of Political Science, ed. Fred I. Greenstein and Nelson W. Polsby, translated by Chu Fuyun, Commercial Press, 1996 edition, p. 290.

[5] Kajima Kaoruo, "Political Participation", translated by Xie Lili, Economic Daily Press, 1989 edition, p. 108.

to the forefront in the academic world (Zheng and Wu[6] 2005; You[7] 2008; Huang[8] 2010).

17.2.2 Level and Form of Political Participation

In terms of the overall level of political participation, the public mainly get involved in political affairs through institutional elections. For instance, around 43.3% of respondents said they have attended village or neighborhood committee elections. Other forms of activities of political participation are less common. Only 8.1% have offered suggestions to governments divisions.

If we analyze in details, we can see that middle and high income groups are not actively involved in grassroots elections. Only 32.44% of high income group and 37.03% of medium–high income group participated in grassroots elections while the figure for low income group is 53.17%. However, when it comes to general political discussions, middle and high income groups are more enthusiastic than low income group. 31.96% of high income group and 24.25% of medium–high income group discusses political issues with others while 21.05% of mid-low and 17.13% of low income group do that (see Table 17.2).

In regard to willingness of political participation, the differences between various income groups in all kinds of political activities are not very evident. For instance, among groups that haven't participated in grassroots elections, irregardless of income level, there are merely 50% of people say they are willing to take part in grassroots elections (see Table 17.3).

In conclusion, political participation in China is still not mature with weak willingness. Middle income group who are supposed to be active in social-political life actually are less involved in grassroots elections in comparison to lower income group. No matter which form of political participation, the willingness of middle income group is not remarkably different from that of other groups. In order to further study middle income group in terms of low participation level and lack of willingness, we conducted deep analysis of their sense of political effectiveness.

---

[6] Zheng and Wu (2005).

[7] You Chuanyao, "Internet: an Essential Way of Political Participation", Development Research, vol. 9, 2008, pp. 96–98.

[8] Huang Ronggui, "Internet and Resistance: Theoretical Model, Chinese Experience and Research Progress", Society, 2010, vol. 30(2), pp. 178–197.

Table 17.3 Political participation willingness of different income groups

Willing to participate	Low income group	Mid-low income group	Medium–high income group	High income group
Discuss political issues with others	25.11	26.83	24.3	25.63
Provide suggestions to government sectors	34.73	39.22	35.35	38.54
Attend village or neighborhood committee election	48.25	51.07	48.24	47.79
Petition at government departments	17.33	18.11	13.47	15.69
Attend march	4.75	5.67	4.97	6.76

Unit Percentage

17.3 Analyzing the Sense of Political Effectiveness of Chinese Middle Income Group

17.3.1 Definition of Sense of Political Effectiveness

The premise of political participation is the high sense of effectiveness which as an internal motive largely decides how active the political life of a society can be. So the public's sense of political effectiveness will be further discussed here. We believe the measurement of sense of political effectiveness includes the following:

Sense of effectiveness of grassroots organizations: it mainly reflects how respondents think of the sense of effectiveness of elections and autonomous activities held by grassroots organizations. The public mainly participate in political activities through grassroots organizations. Here we mainly refer to the village or neighborhood committee which serves as a bridge between the public and government for communication and information exchange. The main political activities inside the institution are democratic elections of grassroots. The village or neighborhood committee is the organizer and host of those elections. Only when the public have a higher sense of effectiveness can they get involved in those elections more proactively.

(i) Sense of effectiveness of individuals is also called internal sense of effectiveness. It mainly reflects how respondents assess themselves in terms of their knowledge in political field, cognition of political rules and ability in attending political activities. If the public feel they don't know much or have weaker ability, they are less willing to participate in political activities and vice versa.

(ii) The level of political indifference is mostly about how passionate and active those respondents are about political activities. In current literature, scholars studied on the phenomenon of political indifference. Yang Guangbin pointed out the reasons for political indifference are psychological, cultural and political and they can be summarized into four specific factors, namely, how the political subject evaluates the reward, how they decide on choices and what is the sense of effectiveness and whether they are happy about the result (Yang 1995[9]). American Scholar Huntington said: "For most of the people, political participation is only a means to achieve other goals. If a person can achieve those goals through means like migrating to cities, climbing to a higher position in the company or obtaining a better economic welfare, those will become the substitution of political participation to some extent." (Huntington and Nelson 1989, p. 56[10]). Therefore, some scholars believe the public are indifferent to politics mainly because individuals are more focused on economic benefit and interests. "the society is not quite affluent and people tend to pay more attention to economic and material gains. They do not have much time, ability or interest to learn about decision-making procedure, to analyze the effect of decision-making and obtain decision-making information", "It is easier for people to meet their personal interests in economic field than in political life. That's why they choose to quite participating in political activities" (Liu 2002a[11]). From the perspective of citizen group theory, some scholars believe that civil groups and social organizations not developed in modern China. In regard to social governance model and the main body of social management, the government is controlling every aspects of our economic and social life. Government-oriented model makes it difficult for voluntary interest groups to flourish. The level of social self-governance and civic voluntary organization is comparatively low. Huang (2014[12]) As Huntington said: "If someone join a certain organization and participate actively, then he or she has a bigger chance to be involved in politics." (Huntington and Nelson 1989, p. 91[13])

(iii) Sense of effectiveness of the government is mainly a reflection of respondents' evaluation of government departments in terms of their ability to react to individuals' political appeal. On the one hand, it can reflect the anticipated evaluation of whether individual's political activities will influence the government and on the other hand, it can also show whether individuals believe their political actions might be restrained under current political system.

[9] Yang (1995).

[10] Huntington and Nelson (1989) edition, p. 56.

[11] Liu (2002b).

[12] Huang Jian, "The Study of Chinese NGOs under the Perspective of Democratic Politics". Doctoral thesis in Party School of the CPC Central Committee, 2014.

[13] Huntington and Nelson, "No Easy Choice: Political Participation in Developing Countries", Ningxia Publishing House, 1989 edition, p. 91.

17.3.2 Analysis of Sense of POLITICAL effectiveness of Chinese People

When we take a look at the overall picture of the sense of political effectiveness of Chinese people, we can see from the data the sense of participation effectiveness is quite low. For example, 49.9% respondents say in village or neighborhood committee elections, the votes of voters have no effect on the final result. 48.7% people think it is of no use to participate in political activities as they have no substantial influence on government departments. For quite a big part of the public, political apathy still exists to a certain extent. 53.2% of interviewees show no interest in politics and they are not willing to spend time and energy on it (see Table 17.4).

With detailed analysis of various income groups, it is not difficult to see there are no significant differences between those groups regarding the sense of political effectiveness. First of all, medium–high income group are less interested in grassroots elections. They are less likely to acknowledge the role of voting. 52.37% of high income group and 55.08% of medium -high income group focus on grassroots elections. This number for low income group is 65.15%. When we ask about whether the votes make a difference, no matter it is high income group or low income group, nearly half of each group believe the voters' votes have no effect on the final result.

In terms of political indifference, 51.62% of high-income group show no interest in politics and are not willing to spend time and energy on it while 53.67% of medium–high income group are indifferent to politics in a certain degree. The number for middle-low income group and low income group is 51.74% and 53.83% respectively.

The public's low sense of effectiveness of the government is one reason for political indifference. In this regard, no matter high income group or low income group, 50% of people say it is no use to participate in political activities as they pose no fundamental influence on government department. Meanwhile, among high income group, 39.88% say their freedom to participate in political activities might be restrained by government departments. This number for middle income group is 37.5% (see Table 17.5).

Extensive social and political participation of middle income group is the foundation of a nation's democratization and legalization. It is also the premise of innovation of social governance model. Only when middle income group as the most dynamic group have higher passion and motivation to participate in social political life can our society become more vigorous as a whole. However, in terms of the reality of China, the level of participation of middle income group is quite low in general. Data shows there are two main reasons. First of all, the public have a lower sense of effectiveness and a big part of the people believe there is no use to participate in political activities as they have no effect on government departments. Secondly, there are not enough channels of participation. In particular, there are not enough space for routine participation inside the institution. One third of middle income group even say their freedom to participate in political activities might be confined by government departments.

Table 17.4 Sense of political effectiveness of the public in China

		Very much willing to	Willing to	Not willing to	Strongly against it	Not sure
Sense of effectiveness of grassroots organization	I pay attentions to village or neighborhood committee elections	17.8	41.6	29.8	8.7	2.1
	In those elections, voters' votes does not affect the final result	12.0	37.9	34.4	7.8	8.0
Individuals' sense of effectiveness	I have the capability and knowledge to comment on and participate in political activities	6.6	33.7	41.5	12.3	5.8
Political indifference	I am not interested in politics and i don't want to spend my time and energy on it	13.0	40.2	35.6	6.8	4.4
Sense of effectiveness of the government	There is no use to participate in political activities as they have no fundamental influence on government departments	10.5	38.2	35.5	6.0	9.8
	My freedom to participate in political activities will be restrained by government departments	6.4	30.9	39.3	7.5	15.9

Unit Percentage

Table 17.5 Analysis of sense of political effectiveness of different income groups

Agree with what is being said here	Low income group	Middle-low income group	Medium–high income group	High-income group
I focus on elections of village (neighborhood) committee	65.15	60.32	55.08	52.37
In those elections, voters' votes have no effect on the final result	52.11	50.51	48.16	47.6
I have the capability and knowledge to comment on and participate in political activities	37.67	41.26	39.68	45.96
I have no interest in politics and i don't want to spend time and energy on it	53.83	51.74	53.67	51.62
There is no use to participate in political activities as they have no fundamental influence on government departments	49.14	49.57	49.07	50.26
My freedom to participate in political activities might be restrained by government departments	36.49	38.28	37.07	39.88

Unit Percentage

To sum up, middle income group in China have a low level of political participation. Political indifference is prevailing among the public including but not limited to the middle income group. In order to improve our social governance level and modernize our governance capability, we must further improve the rate of political participation of the public, especially of middle income group. Individuals should be encouraged to participate in political activities with institutional assurance. A benign coordination mechanism of interests can be formed to enable the success of constructive individual-society relations through multiple channels and organizations. In this way, individuals better interact with the nation, government and other social members in an organized and orderly manner. Meanwhile, from the perspective of national policy-making, only when the society encourages more political participation can the public be really involved in the process of political decision-making, gain information and resources more effectively and fully take part in the construction and transformation of the society.

17.4 Analyzing Political and Social Cognition of Chinese Middle-Income Group

Political and social participation of the middle-income group as well as their sense of political effectiveness are influenced by various factors. This paper will mainly focus on three aspects: sense of social justice, evaluation of governmental work and political orientation.

17.4.1 Analyzing of Sense of Social Justice

Overall speaking, the middle-income group possesses high awareness of social justice. To be specific, 2.78% of middle-income people believe that our society is quite fair and equitable and 68.52% think that current society is relatively fair and equitable. However, it is noticeable that the middle-income group also believes social justice is weak in certain areas. For instance, 57.14% think there is inequity and unfairness in the distribution of wealth and income, whereas 54.13% believe injustice exists in legal rights and privilege between rural and urban areas and 46.91% consider the area of employment and work is full of cases of unfairness(see Table 17.6). To sum up, the sense of unfairness in those three areas above approximates or

Table 17.6 Analyzing sense of social justice of middle-income group

	Not fair at all	Relatively not fair	Relatively fair	Fairy
College entrance examination system	3.62	13.01	64.22	19.15
Actual political rights of citizens	5.71	27.77	58.69	7.83
Judiciary and law enforcement	4.9	28.61	58.89	7.6
Public medical care	4.31	23.49	64.43	7.77
Work and employment opportunity	6.6	40.31	49.32	3.77
Wealth and income distribution	12.53	44.61	39.14	3.72
Pension and other social insurance	6.83	30.57	55.42	7.18
Legal rights and privilege between rural and urban areas	10.51	43.62	42.69	3.18
Overall social justice	2.89	25.81	68.52	2.78

Unit Percentage

surpasses 50%, indicating that a fairer and more equitable social-economic system must be constructed in fundamental domains of people's livelihood to further enhance public's sense of fairness.

The sense of social justice of the middle-income group is significant to social stability and sustainable development. Sense of fairness of social members is direct manifestation of social cognition and identification. If it is relatively low, it means there is serious socioeconomic inequality in our society. Social cohesion and social identification will be weakened as a consequence. Conflicts between various social groups will arise. In other words, sense of unfairness comes from differences in rights and opportunities perceived by social groups. By comparing with other social groups, people in certain group may realize that they are disadvantaged in aspects such as social status and social privilege. Sense of relative deprivation may occur, which may affect their perception of and action to social issues. In regard to social and political participation, sense of social injustice may result in social marginalization which may result in less involvement in socio-political life. Institutional injustice that exists for a long time may be the reason why partial social group find themselves caught in economic poverty, political powerlessness and resources scarcity leading to the decline of middle-income group through consolidation of existing social structure and reinforcement of polarization.

17.4.2 Analyzing How Middle-Income Group Evaluate Governmental Work

In general, the middle-income group gives positive evaluation to governmental work. 65.77% think the government has done an excellent or relatively good work. More specifically, middle-income group give high job rating in maintaining public security, providing medical care, providing social security and safeguarding people's political rights with 77.81%, 73.15%, 68.62%, 67.96% of respondents made positive evaluation on government's work on those four areas respectively.

However, some areas of governmental administration received low ratings. For instance, 46.91% of the middle-income group thinks the government needs to make more efforts to increase service awareness and respond to public demands more promptly. 46.40% believe there is still a long way to go in terms of creating more job opportunities while 44.73% believe the government has done poorly in making government affairs open and transparent. 42.87% of middle-income group think the government must make improvement in governing pollution to protect the environment (see Table 17.7). As middle-income group are improving economically and materially, their demand of government sectors also change from providing basic support to enhanced service and upgraded social governance capability.

The evaluation of middle-income group on government work is the perception of social reality and will also impose various kinds of impact on the socio-political life. On the one hand, if government departments cannot improve their work and respond

Table 17.7 How middle-income group are satisfied with the government

	Excellent	Good	Bad	Very bad
Provide medical care	8.63	64.52	23.37	3.48
Provide social security	6.68	61.94	27.79	3.59
Pollution treatment and environmental protection	9.12	48.01	32.58	10.29
Safeguard people's political rights	7.14	60.81	27.32	4.72
Fight crime and safeguard public security	13.23	64.58	18.00	4.19
Clean and honest governance that combats corruption	9.93	48.31	32.72	9.04
Act by law and fair law enforcement	8.65	53.78	31.92	5.65
Develop economy to increase people's income	7.74	50.31	35.73	6.22
Expand employment to create more jobs	6.86	46.74	39.66	6.74
Disclose government information to be more transparent	7.60	47.67	35.54	9.19
High sense of service and respond to public needs promptly	6.66	46.43	36.44	10.47
Overall evaluation of government work	5.73	60.05	29.92	4.31

Unit Percentage

to public demands more promptly, the public's evaluation of the government tends to be solidified. Part of the disadvantaged group will express negative opinions on the work of government sectors in social, economic and political areas, thus causing lower satisfaction rate. On the other hand, negative evaluation of governmental work may dampen people's enthusiasm in socio-political participation and weaken their sense of political effectiveness, which will affect the vitality and dynamics of social and political life.

17.4.3 Analyzing Social and Political Orientation of Middle-Income Group

This paper also measures the social and political orientation of the middle-income group from the following dimensions: national order versus liberal democracy, fighting for political rights versus compromise, maintaining national stability versus supporting social reform, Western road versus Chinese path. Two contradictory statements about each dimension are provided in the questionnaire and respondents are asked to choose which statement they agree more. For instance, the two statements about "maintaining national stability versus supporting social reform" are "stability is significant to China" and "China needs social reform despite various risks". Respondents are asked to choose which statement they identify with more and their political orientation is judged accordingly. By comparing middle-income group with other groups, we can see from statistics that the political orientation of middle-income group takes on the feature of respecting individual rights and political conservation. 65% of middle-income people said people should fight for it when their individual rights are impaired while nearly a third of them would rather accept the reality and compromise and this figure is 41.78% among low-income group. Middle-income group is also apt to order and stability in political attitude. For example, almost 60% of them believe a strong and powerful government is needed to maintain national order, 70% think stability is the most important to China while 90% of them believe that China should develop a path of its own with Chinese characteristics instead of imitating western countries in terms of their experience and patterns (see Table 17.8).

The table above shows the duality of political orientation of the middle-income group. On the one hand, middle-income group attach great importance to the maintenance of individual rights. They will take active actions to fulfill or maintain their own rights in the face of social injustice, institutional discrimination and unequal rights. On the other hand, they highly identify with the current state system and institution and are prone to conservative attitude. As a result, they prefer gradual change and improvement rather than social transformation. In conclusion, middle-income group plays a highly essential role in maintaining social and political stability as their political orientation contributes to social solidarity and national stability as well as sustainable development.

17.5 Suggestions Based on the Political Participation of Chinese Middle Income Group

In order to improve social governance and achieve social harmony and stability, we must further enhance the level of social and political participation of middle income group. Only when middle income group become the pivot of our social political life can we realize maximization in social dynamic and participant initiative and provide fundamental conditions for improving self-organizing ability of the society. However, data show that self-organizing and self-management ability of our society in current China is quite low. One of the manifestations is that the political and social participation of middle-income group is quite low, especially spontaneous participation. The sense of political effectiveness is also weak and a big part of middle income group believe social and political participation of individuals makes no difference as it has no effect on government decision-making. Nearly half people possess strong political indifference and show no interest in politics. All of these indicate that our social self-organizing level is low. On the one hand, middle income group has doubt about the meaning of social and political participation due to low sense of political effectiveness and lack of participation channels. On the other hand, political restructuring reform falls behind social economic development. In addition, government departments are not responding to public appeal promptly. As a result, a large quantity of middle income people is losing enthusiasm about political activities.

Table 17.8 Analyzing socio-political orientation of middle-income group

Political orientation	Agree with the statement or not	Low-income group	Medium–low income group	Medium–high income group	High-income group
National order versus Liberal democracy	China needs a powerful and strong government to maintain stability	58.09	61.28	58.21	53.82
	Political liberty and democracy must not be impaired in any circumstances	41.91	38.72	41.79	46.18
Fighting for rights versus compromise	One should fight for his or her rights if they are impaired	58.22	63.00	66.83	73.24
	One might as well accept the reality and compromise when rights are impaired	41.78	37.00	33.17	26.76
Maintain stability versus support reform	Stability is the most important for China	67.31	65.79	68.91	64.13
	China needs social reform despite all kinds of risks	32.69	34.21	31.09	35.87
Western road versus Chinese path	China will also take a development path which is similar to that of its western counterparts	8.11	10.56	6.73	11.14
	China should develop its own socialist path with Chinese characteristics	91.89	89.44	93.27	88.86

Unit Percentage

Political indifference becomes a common social mentality. Those factors have largely influenced the construction of political democratization in China, and hindered the building of a new social governance model and restrained the development of our society as a whole. Therefore, the author proposed the following suggestions:

First, we should expand channels of social and political participation and build multi-layered participation mechanism. At present, government sectors, enterprises and public institutions usually initiate social and political activities for the public to participate. There is little spontaneous participation. Furthermore, channels for political participation are quite limited and they are mainly elections and hearings, etc. In order to innovate social governance model, we must make sure the public has a bigger say in the process of decision-making. We must also enhance their right of supervision in execution. It is also necessary to make rules, regulations and organizations forms to guarantee public participation from aspects such as the right to know, to right to participate, the right to supervise and the right to inquiry.

Second, we should improve and safeguard social order and sustainability to transfer from mobilized and civil organizations to institutional and organized participation. Constituting a big part of the society, middle income group are usually more affluent with more social resources. They also are essential to social stability as they tend to resort to benign and progressive interaction model in social and political actions. In social and political life, provided with platform and space, they can play an important role in social governance and unleash huge potential in shelf-management of our society. Only when the middle income group is fully mobilized can we achieve a society of high political and social participation and improve the effectiveness and efficiency to eventually realize effective interaction between government and the public. On the other hand, organized participation can increase the sense of belonging of middle income group. Routinization of participation can help to enhance their subjective social awareness and social identity and thus facilitate active and constructive innovation of social governance.

Last but not least, we should make sure government departments respond to public appeal more promptly. Some government departments are sluggish in reacting to reasonable appeals from the public, which affects how people evaluate the government's work to a large extent and weakens their confidence in the government. In order to improve political and social participation, the primary task is to rebuild government authority and prestige by responding to public appeal faster and more promptly. Only in this way can the public become less indifferent about politics and start to get involved in the innovation of social governance as masters of the nation.

References

Huang R (2010) Internet and protests: theoretical model, China's experience and research progress. Chin J Soc 30(2)

Huang J (2014). Research of NGOs development in the democratic politics Horizont in China. Doctoral Dissertation. Party School of the Central Committee of CPC

Huntington SP, Nelson JM (1989) No easy choice: political participation in developing countries. Huaxia Publishing House.
Liu D (2002a) Analysis of reasons of indifference attitudes towards current Chinese politics. Shandong Soc Sci 1
Liu D (2002b) Analysis of reasons for political indifference in modern China, Shangdong Soc Sci 1:141–143
Sun H. Liao X (2010) Ethical dimension of the subjects of political participation–also on the perspective of environmental ethics. J Beijing Normal Univ (Soc Sci), 6
Xiang D, Wang Z (2012) Public participation of urban community management. Study Explor 2
Yang G (1995) On political apathy. J Renmin Univ China 3
Yang G (1995) The theory of political indifference. Collage J Renmin Univ China 3: 99–104
You C (2008) Internet as a critical for political participation of citizens. Dev Res 9
Zheng Y, Wu G (2005) Information technology, public space, and collective action in China. Comp Polit Stud 38(5):507–536

Yan Cui assistant professor of the Institute of Sociology in CASS, Ph.D, specialized in social development research and social research method. Major publication includes Research on the Motivation of Citizens' Environmental Organization Participation, The General Public's Urban Attributes During the Process of Urbanization.

Chapter 18
The Level of Social and Political Activities Among Middle Income Groups in Russia

Yu. V. Latov and V. V. Petukhov

In contemporary history, social and political science experts have viewed middle income groups as the steady core that ensures the social and political stability of Western societies. The very concept of the middle class emerged during a discussion on countering political radicalism. It is generally assumed that unlike the rich, people with mid-level income, are interested in change that would even out their chances at success in life, but unlike the poor, are not inclined to be radical.

A century ago, when middle income groups were rather small in size, radical revolutionaries subjected them to aggressive criticism for their "petty bourgeois" disinterest in politics. With time, however, it became apparent that a highly developed middle class can become a formidable social and political force, capable of self-organization and persistent activism on any level, from municipal to nationwide. The stronger the society's middle class, the more the path of gradual reforms dominates both over stagnation tendencies and a turn towards radicalism. It is the absolute prevalence of middle income groups in society that explains the combination of political stability and social and economic dynamics in developed nations. In a similar fashion, the serious issues faced by non-European civilizations are attributed to the weakness of middle income groups. Social and political activism of the emerging middle income groups is perceived as the safety anchor that will allow these civilizations to achieve social, political, social, and economic stability.

The above approach to reviewing the role of the middle class's social and political activism in the modern world is a general sketch, with many exceptions lying beneath the surface. For instance, the history of early twentieth century Russia demonstrates that the most radical revolution was, in fact, spearheaded by people from middle income groups (the "intelligentsia of the revolution", including Vladimir Ilyich Ulyanov-Lenin himself), while the stabilizing role of the Russian middle class was far less prominent. The paradoxical tendency of the middle class to initially cause

Yu. V. Latov (✉) · V. V. Petukhov
Institute of Sociology of FCTAS RAS, Moscow, Russia

P. Li and M. K. Gorshkov (eds.), *The Middle Income Group in China and Russia*, Research Series on the Chinese Dream and China's Development Path,
https://doi.org/10.1007/978-981-16-1464-4_18

an upheaval rather than stabilization in the social and political life is reaffirmed by examples from the history of other nations, even those more developed than Russia (like Germany in the 1930s).

To explain this discrepancy, it is worth remembering the Olson-Huntington Hypothesis (introduced back in the 1960s) on the "bell-shaped" relationship between the level of economic development and the social and political destabilization: as the so-called "catch-up growth" nations undergo modernization, the threat of political cataclysm only starts to decrease after rising first.[1] When applied to the social and political role of middle income groups, this hypothesis may be interpreted as follows: in the catch-up growth nations, the rise of middle income groups first turns into an additional stimulating factor that drives radical social protests, and subsequently helps stabilize the political life. This dual role of middle income groups stems from the fact that, initially, when they are small in size, members of these groups tend to identify more with low-income groups, where they have emerged from, and undertake it upon themselves to represent these groups' interests. It is not until later, when middle income groups expand and develop a sense of identity, that they begin to distance themselves both from the rich and the poor, protecting their own interests first and foremost. Consequently, it is very important for developing nations to survive this initial period, which poses the greatest danger as middle income groups generate more radicalism than stability.

In this chapter, we will used the empiric and sociological data collected in Russia as one of the major developing nations (alongside China, India, and Brazil) to determine how large-scaled and constructive the local social and political activity of middle income groups actually is. Our chapter will touch not as much upon political activity per se (such as party membership, participation in demonstrations, or voting) as upon civic activism in the broad sense. The case studies of developed nations show that this occurs because society becomes more stable when people with mid-level income stop delegating the resolution of all their issues to the government and not only start criticizing the failings of state authorities but also become personally involved in removing the obstacles that prevent them from living and working without incident. In other words, what we shall be dealing with here is the development (largely due to the activism of middle income groups) of a civil society that acts as a partner rather than an opponent of the democratic state. It is also important to bear in mind that, as aptly noted by O.N. Yanitsky, a formal categorization of collective actions is hardly a productive pursuit in our diverse and dynamic age. In today's world, there are almost no social movements that could be placed into a single strictly defined category. Even the so-called one-demand movements, which are geared towards meeting a single goal in a given sphere, time, and place, almost inevitably get transformed into something completely different, more lasting and large-scale.[2]

We shall look at the activism of middle income groups in Russia in the light of two aspects, first analyzing survey data on the actual involvement of these groups'

---

[1] See e.g.: Korotaev et al. (2017).

[2] Yanitsky (2013).

members in various types of social and political activity, and then reviewing their opinions on their possible future forms of such involvement.

The main development issue of post-Soviet Russia is that society felt tricked as far back as in the 1990's: the radical liberal reforms had a dramatic negative impact on most of the population's the material well-being, and new democratic institutions failed to bring the people any closer to those in power; on the contrary, they drew them even further apart. As a result, after a surge of political activism at the turn of the 1980s and 1990s, Russians quickly lost faith in their ability to influence what was going on in the country. This tendency, typical of most Russians, to alienate themselves from the state and to predominantly identify as "objects" rather than independent entities of policy-making, is yet to be fully conquered.

When asked during the survey in the spring of 2016 whether they were able to influence nationwide, regional, or at least municipal policy-makers, very few Russians selected the "Definitely yes" response: the higher share of people who responded this way, 5%, was among members of high-income groups in terms of influencing municipal policy; all other groups (including middle income groups) picked this option only in 2–3% of all cases. By contrast, the "Definitely no" response was selected by approximately one third of all Russians, mostly members of the lower subgroup of the middle income group. For instance, 40% of respondents from this group completely denied being able to influence nationwide policy, while in the upper subgroup of the middle income group, this opinion was shared by 34% of respondents; in the low-income group, by 36% of respondents; and in the high-income group, by 29% of respondents. A similar pattern characterized responses regarding the ability to influence municipal authorities: categorical denial of this ability was typical of 33% of respondents from the lower subgroup of the middle income group, 29% of respondents from the upper subgroup of the same group, 31% of respondents with low income, and 24% of respondents with high income.

If we look at the response array from a larger scale (Table 18.1), we will clearly note the specific features of high-income groups, which feel significantly less alienated from the government than all other Russians, albeit only on the regional and municipal level (and even here, as many as 60–70% of people with high income do not consider themselves involved in politics). *Respondents with mid-level income, in turn, feel almost as alienated from the state authorities as those with low income.* It is worth noting that the upper subgroup of middle income groups is slightly closer to high-income groups, while the lower subgroup is characterized by critical-level figures (the lowest degree of involvement and the highest degree of alienation).

Despite from the significant alienation from the state, social activism in modern Russia remains stable, if constrained. In the meanwhile, the line between political and non-political activism is becoming more and more vague, blurred, and arbitrary. Moreover, many forms of political activism grow increasingly closer to everyday forms of self-expression, which are, on the subjective level, not perceived as political; nor are they, in fact, wholly political (i.e. linked to a conscious desire to take part in a power struggle) by nature. What we mean here is contribution to the activities of various grassroots organizations and societies, usually for general cultural purposes. Even among people with low income level, who exhibit the highest degree

Table 18.1 Russians' opinions on their ability to influence political processes, spring of 2016, %

Set of questions for the respondents: do Russian citizens today have an opportunity to…	Share of "Definitely yes" and "Rather yes than no" responses				
	Lower middle income group	Upper middle income group	Middle income groups overall	Low-income groups	High-income groups
Influence the national policy overall	14	16	***15***	17	15
Influence the regional policy-makers	17	21	***19***	19	30
Influence the municipal policy-makers	21	28	***24***	24	39

of absenteeism, one in every five respondents claimed to be involved in the activities of a given organization or society, as compared to one in every four respondents among people with mid-level income and one in every three among people with high income (Table 18.2).

The grassroots organizations, unions, and communities that see widespread involvement among modern Russians can be divided into two relatively clearly defined groups. On the one hand, there is a small set (merely 5 types) of organizations that roughly 4–8% of Russians are involved in; and on the other hand, there is a far longer list of other entities, with the involvement not exceeding 1–2% of Russians in each case.

8% of respondents from middle income groups contribute to homeowners' associations, 7% are trade union members, and 5% are active charity workers; and these figures, without a doubt, merit our closest attention. It is important to emphasize that the involved respondent shares are even higher in large cities and among the youth.

In addition, Table 18.2 also reveals the following trend: *the higher the material well-being of a social group/subgroup, the more often its members contribute to grassroots organizations/unions/communities.* This steady growth of community involvement together with income level is especially evident if we, for instance, look at the data pertaining to youth/student groups: in low-income groups, the level of involvement is 3%, in the lower middle income subgroup it is 4%, in the upper middle income subgroup it is 5%, and in high-income groups, it is as high as 8%. That said, there are some exceptions, but they mostly concern organizations with rare involvement (volunteer movements, associations of veterans, etc.), which people from middle income groups contribute to slightly more often than those from high-income groups.

Table 18.2 Involvement of various Russian population groups and Strata in the activity of grassroots organizations, unions, and communities, 2016, %

Types of grassroots organizations, unions, and communities	Share of respondents, %				
	Lower middle income group	Upper middle income group	Middle income groups overall	Low-income groups	High-income groups
Relatively frequent involvement					
Neighborhood improvement groups and homeowners' associations	8	9	*8*	4	11
Trade unions	6	8	*7*	6	10
Internet communities (LiveJournal and Facebook groups)	4	8	*6*	4	12
Charity organizations (helping the disabled or children with special needs)	4	7	*5*	5	7
Youth and student communities	4	5	*4*	3	8
Rare involvement					
Professional interest clubs (for doctors, scientists, teachers, etc.)	1	2	*2*	2	2
Environmental protection groups	2	3	*2*	1	5
Social volunteer movements (helping fire, flood, etc. victims)	1	3	*2*	1	1
Consumer rights protection societies	1	2	*2*	1	2
Associations of seniors and/or veterans	2	2	*2*	1	0
Groups advocating for the protection and restoration of historical, cultural, architectural, etc. heritage sites	1	1	*1*	1	2

(continued)

Table 18.2 (continued)

Types of grassroots organizations, unions, and communities	Share of respondents, %				
	Lower middle income group	Upper middle income group	Middle income groups overall	Low-income groups	High-income groups
Religious (faith-based) communities	1	1	*1*	1	0
Groups advocating for the protection of community property (fighting against unauthorized/infill construction or the construction of highways and malls)	1	1	*1*	1	0
"One demand" movements (groups of defrauded shareholders, investors, or lenders; the Blue Bucket Society against the misuse of emergency lights, etc.)	0	1	*0*	0	2
National and cultural ethnic communities (diasporas)	0	1	*0*	0	0
No involvement	77	71	***74***	80	64

One must bear in mind that today, Internet communities have an especially broad reach both in Russia in general and among people with mid-level income in particular: this type of involvement is typical of 6% of middle income respondents overall (and even as much as 8% in the upper subgroup) and 12% of high-income respondents. In most cases, this is just a form of communicating with people who share the same interests (such as love for various types of escapist gaming), far removed from public or political life. At the same time, the practical experience of the past few years goes to show that self-organization via various online platforms increasingly serves as a catalyst of many grassroots initiatives, from rallying people to combat fires and floods or help children with special needs, to taking a stand against corruption. These online communities often are better organized and more efficient than the relevant state authorities.

It is quite notable that most Russians, middle income groups included, express quite a low demand for religious communities as a form of grassroots activity, with no more than 1% of any given income group or subgroup being involved in such organization. These insignificant figures that the post-Soviet "restoration of the religious mindset" takes effect only (if at all) in purely personal environments of the people of faith, while not impacting the life of civic society, which still has not started viewing the church as a major platform for social and political activity.

Another important observation regarding contributions to various grassroots organizations/unions/communities is *the striking rarity of involvement that is openly politicized.* Even though trade union membership is relatively widespread, modern Russia's trade unions are more like enterprises' routine maintenance departments than political organizations that protect the workers' rights. In the 2000s, political scientists started remarking on the genesis of new political movements in Russia, more flexible and practice-oriented than traditional parties, but surveys show that people rarely join such movements. For instance, "one-demand movements" (groups of defrauded shareholders and investors or movements protesting against road hogs) draw the attention of as few as 1% of respondents, even in upper middle income groups. In high-income groups, the involvement rate barely reaches 2%, and in other groups and subgroups it is completely inexistent. In the case of somewhat similar movements that advocate for protecting community property (by opposing unauthorized or infill construction, etc.), the situation is slightly different: the involvement rate reaches 1% among middle income groups (the upper and lower subgroup alike), just as it does among low-income groups, whereas people with high income do not contribute to such movements at all.

Nevertheless, according to the latest research of civic self-organization practices in Moscow, in large cities (the capital first and foremost), where the share of people with mid-level income is especially high, local communities gradually build up experience of fighting for civil rights, and create networks of active citizens, various professional associations, and activist groups driven by shared interests. People living in the same apartment complex create groups in social networks, communities create data bases with emails and phone numbers of neighbors from the same block or fellow homeowners who will be happy to help, etc.[3] This trend has already had a practical application when the people of Moscow organized themselves in the spring and summer of 2017 and went out to protect their interests regarding the city council's so-called "renovation" plans in several districts (large-scale demolition of condemned buildings and the tenants' relocation to apartments of inferior quality). Apart from the capital, new forms and practices of civic activism are emerging and/or actively developing in other Russian regions as well.[4]

Having compared and contrasted the survey data for the past three years (Table 18.3), we can conclude that overall, *the aforementioned features of Russians' involvement in grassroots organizations/unions/communities remain stable.* The only trend

---

[3] Volkov and Kolesnikov (2016).

[4] For more information, please refer to: L. Nikovskaya, V. Yakimets. Shaping and Protecting Public Interests in Russia: from the "Administrative" Model to the Partnership Model // Political Studies. 2015. Issue 5. pp. 49–64; V. Petukhov, R. Petukhov. The Democracy of Participation: Institutional Crisis and New Prospects // Political Studies. 2015. Issue 5. pp.25–49; N. Sedova. Russians' Life Goals and Strategies in the Passion-Driven Context // Sociological Journal. 2016. Issue 2. pp. 73–91.

Table 18.3 Dynamics of Russian population Groups' and Strata's involvement in the activity of some grassroots organizations, unions, and communities, 2014/2015/2016, %

Types of grassroots organizations, unions, and communities	Share of respondents, %				
	Lower middle income group	Upper middle income group	Middle income groups overall	Low-income groups	High-income groups
Neighborhood improvement groups and homeowners' associations	5/6/8	5/7/9	***5/7/8***	4/5/4	2/8/11
Trade unions	8/4/6	8/6/8	***8/5/7***	6/5/6	8/5/10
Internet communities (LiveJournal and Facebook groups)	6/7/4	7/10/8	***7/8/6***	4/5/4	10/13/12
Charity organizations (helping the disabled or children with special needs)	2/3/4	4/3/7	***3/3/5***	2/3/5	4/6/7
No involvement	***78|79|77***	***76|75|71***	***78|78|74***	***82|81|80***	***71|65|64***

that is clearly dynamic is the *notable surge of involvement in homeowners' associations, mostly among middle income groups* (more than twofold) and especially among high-income groups (more than fivefold). This is caused by the broad reach of this type of community among buyers of newly built homes, who predominantly belong to high-income groups and never to low-income groups. The trend towards a decrease of absenteeism (i.e. the drop of in the number of Russians who do not contribute to any grassroots organizations at all) is far less evident: it is notable only in the upper subgroup of the middle income group (the figures having dropped from 76% in 2014 to 71% in 2016) and in high-income groups (from 71 to 64%, respectively), mostly due to the aforementioned rise in formal contributions to home-owners' associations. Even less clearly defined are such trends as the decrease of active contributions to trade unions and the increase of active contributions to charity organizations.

As expected, purely political involvement is relatively rare for modern Russia (Table 18.4). That said, formal political involvement does occur more often than the participation in grassroots organizations/unions/communities that we have described above: only around 50% of Russians have stated that they do not contribute to the country's political life at all (with members of middle income groups doing this slightly more rarely than respondents from low- and high-income groups). But it is important to emphasize that the most frequent forms of political involvement are

Table 18.4 Involvement in Political Life Among Various Social Groups and Strata in Russia, spring of 2016, %

Types of political involvement	Share of respondents, %				
	Lower Middle income Group	Upper Middle income Group	Middle income Groups Overall	Low-Income Groups	High-Income Groups
Frequent involvement					
Voting at elections	34	31	***33***	33	22
Discussing political events with friends, coworkers, or fellow students	28	27	***27***	24	28
Rare involvement					
Contributing to election campaigns as an observer, canvasser, vote collector, etc.	6	4	***5***	4	5
Taking part in public and political events (rallies, demonstrations, etc.)	2	4	***3***	1	6
Working for local elective bodies	2	3	***3***	3	3
Contributing to political parties	2	2	***2***	1	5
Taking part in plebiscites and public hearings, making appeals to the authorities, etc	2	3	***2***	2	2
Extremely rare involvement					
Contributing to human rights advocacy groups	1	1	***1***	1	1
Keeping in touch with people who share the same political views via social networks or online forums	1	1	***1***	1	3

(continued)

Table 18.4 (continued)

Types of political involvement	Share of respondents, %				
	Lower Middle income Group	Upper Middle income Group	Middle income Groups Overall	Low-Income Groups	High-Income Groups
No involvement in political life	49	51	***50***	53	55

also the most passive ones, not grounded in personal initiative. These include voting (33% of respondents from middle income groups) and discussion of political events at home (27%). Even though members of high-income groups usually exhibit the highest level of activism, when it comes to voting, they are outstripped by mid- and low-income groups (22% vs. 33%). By contrast, in terms of household discussions of political matters, middle income groups (27%) barely differ from high-income groups (28%), while being somewhat ahead of the low-income group (24%).

When it comes to intensive activity that stems from personal initiative, the share of those involved usually does not exceed 5% of respondents from any social stratum or group. For instance, merely 2% of respondents from middle income groups were interested in working for political parties; while 3% were interested in contributing to public and political vents; and 5%, in helping run election campaigns as a volunteer (observer, canvasser, or vote collector). *There are very few differences in the political activism of the lower and upper middle income groups, but the middle income group overall is noticeably more active than the low-income group, and equally active or less active than the high-income group of Russians.*

It is crucially important to note that political activity in the Internet has turned out to be among the rarest types of activism: this means that the political segment of online communities is far smaller than it is often believed to be. While 6% of respondents from middle income groups and 12% of respondents from high-income groups describe themselves as members of online communities, only 1% and 3% of them respectively use these communities (social networks or forums) as a platform for conversations with like-minded individuals that share their political views.

An attempt to analyze the dynamics of political involvement by comparing the data for 2014 and 2016 (Table 18.5) reveals a real paradox. On the one hand, during these two years, the number of people who admitted to not being involved in political life shrank significantly (by almost one third, i.e. from 70 to 50%, in middle income groups, and even more so in low-income groups). On the other hand, if we look at the dynamics of certain specific types of political involvement, the growth was barely significant (discussions of political events, contributions to political parties), and in some cases, there was even a decrease (contributions to election campaigns).

The secret behind this paradox is that in 2016, the questionnaire was expanded via the addition of voting at elections as a type of political activity (which respondents had appeared not to perceive as proper political involvement before). As a result, respondents suddenly "realized" that they were contributing to politics far more

Table 18.5 Dynamics of involvement in political life among various social groups and Strata in Russia, 2014/2016, %

Types of political involvement	Share of respondents, %				
	Lower middle income group	Upper middle income group	Middle income groups overall	Low-income groups	High-income groups
Frequent involvement					
Discussing political events with friends, coworkers, or fellow students	22/28	26/27	***23/27***	14/24	32/28
Rare involvement					
Contributing to election campaigns as an observer, canvasser, vote collector, etc.	7/6	8/4	***7/5***	5/4	8/5
Taking part in public and political events (rallies, demonstrations, etc.)	2/2	2/4	***2/3***	2/1	2/6
Contributing to political parties	2/2	1/2	***2/2***	2/1	4/5
Extremely rare involvement					
Keeping in touch with people who share the same political views via social networks or online forums	3/1	3/1	***3/1***	1/1	2/3
No involvement in political life	***71/49***	***67/51***	***70/50***	***81/53***	***63/55***

actively. This statistical illusion aside, the only objective fact is that people with relatively modest income have started discussing political events far more often. The share of such people rose by a quarter in the lower subgroup of the middle income group (from 22 to 28%) and from 14 to 24% in the low-income group, whereas in the upper subgroup of the middle income group the figures remained almost completely unchanged, and in the high-income group, they even dropped. This is obviously a very passive form of political involvement, but the dynamics of the past few years do reveal a substantial increase of political inclusion among the least wealthy population groups (with the most wealthy groups experiencing an opposite downward trend).

Some researchers note that behind the low scale of political involvement, there is a hidden trend towards higher quality of said involvement. As demonstrated by the results of the 2014 nationwide of the RAS Institute of Sociology, titled "Civic Activism: the New Social Actors",[5] *this involvement is becoming more and more conscious, socially motivated, and (for most people) purely altruistic.* Indeed it is: in most cases, involvement in social and political activity (Table 18.6) is explained by truly "Promethean" motives, such as a desire to make the world better or to help people (approximately 10% across various groups and strata). A slightly smaller group includes motivations that are closer to healthy egoism: a desire to protect one's rights or to make one life experience more diverse by talking to like-minded people and trying to make new friends. Purely profit- and career-focused explanations are even rarer (1–3%), as is a desire to protest against the powers that be (3% in high-income groups, 2% in the upper subgroup of the middle income group, and 1% in the lower middle income subgroup and low-income groups).

It is essential to highlight the prevalence of altruistic motivations behind Russians' activism, since only recently, many people in the country, including the "progressive" minority of activists, used to view any political or social involvement that did not promise direct material or career benefits as a strictly fringe movement. The last few years have seen an opposite trend: an increasing interest towards various types of informal grassroots activity in and of itself, along with volunteering and contributing to "one demand" movements, most of which are based on gratuitous participation and altruistic principles. *The popularity of altruistically motivated forms of grassroots activism shows that Russia is gradually building up the potential for making its political life more democratic in the future.* Modern Russian grassroots activism is not yet paving the path to professional policy-making, but for the next generation of Russians, it may turn into one of the means of renewing the country's pool of politicians.

The relatively low figures pertaining to Russians' active and regular involvement in politics should not be interpreted as an indicator of their total depoliticization and of a long-term political status quo (with a potential threat of yet another stagnation period). What we are dealing with here is more akin to the transition of *significant amounts of social and political energy, which exists within large numbers of people, from kinetic to latent.* A reverse transformation is also possible; this is ensured by the inclusion of the majority of the population into politics, which allows to mobilize activists quickly when an urgent issue arises. After all, in modern information society, even the smallest groups of activists can utilize the latest means of communication in order to have a notable impact on the life of the nation, their home city or town, etc., thus detonating a political "explosion". But in order for these groups to inspire others to follow them, someone must keep listening to them and hearing what they have to

[5] Civic Activism: the New Social and Political Actors [Online resource] // Polit Analitika. Publication date – June 25, 2014. URL: https://www.politanalitika.ru/doklad/grazhdanskiy_aktivizm_novye_subekty_obshchestvenno_politicheskogo_deystviya/ (Accessed on: 04.05.2017).

Table 18.6 Motivations behind contributing to social and political life among various population groups and Strata in Russia, spring of 2016, %

Activism motivations	Share of respondents, %				
	Lower middle income group	Upper middle income group	Middle income groups overall	Low-income groups	High-income groups
Frequent motivations					
Sense of civic duty and a desire to make the world a better place	11	10	***11***	10	10
A desire to take specific action and get a chance to help people	8	12	***10***	8	9
Motivations occurring at an average rate					
A chance to protect my rights and the rights of my loved ones	6	9	***7***	5	10
A chance to make my life experience more interesting and diverse	7	7	***7***	5	7
A chance to meet people that share my values and opinions	6	8	***7***	7	7
A chance to make new friends	4	6	***5***	4	7
Personal growth and development, new experiences	4	5	***5***	5	10
Tagging along with my friends and relatives	5	4	***4***	2	5

(continued)

Table 18.6 (continued)

Activism motivations	Share of respondents, %				
	Lower middle income group	Upper middle income group	Middle income groups overall	Low-income groups	High-income groups
A chance to earn extra money	3	2	*3*	3	2
Rare motivations					
A desire to pursue a political or social career	0	1	*1*	0	1
A desire to protest against the government	1	2	*1*	1	3
Not interested in any political or social activity	73	68	*71*	75	62

say. Consequently, having even a basic interest in politics is a very important factor that reflects the potential of political involvement. For the longest periods of time, this interest may remain purely detached, but, given a high-profile enough headline-maker, impassive observers will "suddenly" transform into active participants of political processes.

Data derived from a nationwide survey in the spring of 2016 shows that, as we have already noted above, the circle of people who share a certain degree of interest in politics is far bigger than the circle of people who actually take part therein. Even though 71% of respondents from middle income groups do not find social and political activity to be particularly appealing, only 50% do not get involved in politics at all and only 33% are not interested in politics in the slightest (Table 18.7). *In terms of general interest in politics, middle income groups occupy their usual middle ground between the relative absenteeism of low-income groups* (where 38% of respondents are not interested in politics) *and the relative inclusion of high-income groups* (where only 30% are not interested in politics). At the same time, the largest share (22%) of middle income groups (including both the lower and upper subgroup) "closely follows" political updates. In this respect, middle income groups largely surpass both low-income (17%) and high-income (18%) groups.

That said, if we contrast data for different years, we see that interest in politics is experiencing a declining trend: for instance, in 2015–2016, middle income groups saw a significant increase of the share of people who are not interested in politics (from 27 to 33%), while the desire to follow political updates closely lessened almost by one third (although at the same time, there was a slight increase in the number of people who do not follow politics all the time but occasionally do discuss political

Table 18.7 Ways of expressing an interest in politics in various social groups and Strata in Russia, spring of 2015/spring of 2016, %

Attitudes to politics	Share of respondents, %				
	Lower middle income group	Upper middle income group	Middle income groups overall	Low-income groups	High-income groups
Closely follow the updates on the country's political life	28/22	33/22	***30/22***	25/17	33/18
Do not follow political events too closely, but occasionally discuss them with friends and loved ones	42/45	41/45	***42/45***	39/45	38/52
Not interested in politics	***29/33***	***25/33***	***27/33***	***35/38***	***26/30***

updates within their social circle). This decline, first and foremost, indicates a general relief of political tension and is likely to be a mere temporary fluctuation.

In order to better understand the development prospects of middle income groups' political activity, let us look at the structure of responses to questions regarding Russians' possible ways of retaliation against the hypothetical violation of their rights (Table 18.8).

Russians tend to plan their responses to possible violations within the law, which is very important. For instance, mid income groups' most frequent response to their rights being violated is eager readiness to appeal to the authorities with petitions (20%) or to contribute to local-federal elections by becoming involved in political parties' activities (13%). They are not nearly as ready to take part in peaceful protests such as strikes, rallies, or demonstrations of civil disobedience (a mere 10%). *Figures pertaining to potential readiness for political activism are relatively similar across all social groups and strata,* with discrepancies only amounting to 2–3% points (the figures are usually higher among high-income groups).

Another factor well worth noting is the very low percentage of ultra-radicals who are ready to stand up for their interests by taking up arms. In 2016, the share of such people in all social groups and strata fluctuated between 1 and 3%, with middle income groups barely differing from low- or high-income groups in terms of inclinations towards extreme radicalism. Evidently, the share of people prepared to take up arms reflects not as much the scale of political protest in modern Russia as the level of psychological tension, caused by factors that lie beyond this analysis.

Table 18.8 Political forms of readiness to respond to the violation of rights among various Strata and groups of Russians, spring 2016, %

Types of responses to possible violation of rights	Share of respondents, %				
	Lower middle income group	Upper middle income group	Middle income groups overall	Low-income groups	High-income groups
Frequently chosen types of possible political action					
Petitions and appeal to the authorities	19	21	***20***	18	19
Voting for local and federal officials, contributions to political parties	13	12	***13***	12	15
Rarely chosen types of possible political action					
Participation in strikes, rallies, demonstrations, and other social protest events	10	10	***10***	11	13
Peaceful civil disobedience (refusing to pay taxes, utility bills, etc.)	10	9	***10***	10	8
Participation in trade union rallies or in the activities of the work team councils	7	8	***8***	5	8
Contributions to non-political grassroots organizations (such as consumer rights protection societies)	6	6	***6***	6	7
Extremely rarely chosen types of possible political action					
Armed resistance	1	2	***2***	2	2
Political absenteeism					
No political action, because today, there are no efficient ways of influencing the government	30	23	***27***	28	19

(continued)

Table 18.8 (continued)

Types of responses to possible violation of rights	Share of respondents, %				
	Lower middle income group	Upper middle income group	Middle income groups overall	Low-income groups	High-income groups
No political action, because we are used to dealing with our problems on our own	25	26	***25***	25	34

Finally, we must draw attention to the views of some experts, who believe that Russians have already emerged from the[6] pit of disappointment in the Moscow demonstrations of 2011–2012, which means that we are in for a new wave of protests, especially since there already is a suitable headline-maker: the upcoming 2018 presidential elections open a new window of opportunity for criticizing the policies of the federal government. In this respect, it is essential to know under what circumstances and to what extent Russians might be ready to personally contribute to the mass protests that are likely to erupt in the nearest future.

A nationwide survey in the spring of 2016 showed that the most likely reason for such protests would be a desire to protect people's economic and social rights or oppose the authorities' abuse of power (Table 18.9). In case of the former, 30% of respondents from low- and middle income groups and 21% of respondents from high-income groups claim that they are ready, to a certain extent, to take part in rallies and demonstrations. In case of the latter, the overall share of potential protesters is slightly lower, but there is a greater number of more decisive people (those who are definitely ready to take part in protests): 10% of respondents from low-income groups, 7% of respondents from middle income groups, and 5% of respondents from high-income groups. But even under these circumstances, these respondents are greatly outnumbered by Russians who are definitely not ready to take part in rallies and demonstrations (approximately 40% across all income groups). The most politicized option, "Rallies and demonstrations in support of opposition parties and movements", has turned out to be the most unpopular, with readiness to go to such rallies and demonstrations being expressed only by 6% of respondents from low- and middle income groups (and definite readiness being expressed by as few as 1%) and 8% of respondents from high-income groups (3% if we look at definite readiness). By contrast, the share of people who are categorically against taking part in mass protests in favor of the opposition exceeds 50% in each income group. Supporting local and federal authorities is also one of the least popular prompts for taking part in mass demonstrations; but even so, the number of people who are ready to rally for this reason is bigger by half or even twofold than the number of opposition supporters.

[6] Middle Class in Modern Russia. Summary of Many Years' Worth of Research. Ed. Gorshkov, M.K. and Tikhonova, N.E. Moscow: Ves Mir, 2016. P. 307.

Table 18.9 Russians' opinions on the likelihood of their personal contribution to mass political events, spring of 2016, %

Types of events	Share of "Definitely yes" and "Rather yes than no" responses				
	Lower middle income group	Upper middle income group	Middle income group as a whole	Low-income group	High-income group
Rallies and demonstrations advocating for people's economic and social rights	32	26	***30***	30	21
Rallies and demonstrations against the local governments' and authorities' unlawful abuse of power	28	23	***26***	30	23
Rallies and demonstrations advocating for the rights of local communities and against migrants	21	20	***21***	24	15
Rallies and demonstrations advocating for democratic rights and freedoms (freedom of speech, freedom of assembly, freedom of demonstration, etc.)	19	18	***19***	17	12
Rallies and demonstrations in support of local and federal authorities	12	12	***13***	10	11
Rallies and demonstrations in support of opposition parties and movements	7	7	***6***	6	8

To conclude, even though modern Russia does exhibit significant potential for political protests (the highest being in low-income groups), *this potential is barely linked to supporting opposition parties and movements.* It is important to note that, when analyzing Russians' readiness to go to rallies and demonstrations, we are yet to observe the stabilizing role of middle income groups: in most cases, people with mid-level income hover somewhere in between the "revolutionaries" from low-income groups and people with high income, who are least inclined to protest. Interestingly enough, the lower subgroup of the middle income group has turned out to be the most likely to protest when it comes to protecting economic and social rights (32%). Consequently, *even though Russia's middle income groups can hardly be called a wellspring of radicalism, they resemble society's stable anchor even less.*

We shall now draw up our final conclusions on middle income Russians' social and political activity.

1. Russians with mid-level income suffer from a high degree of alienation from the government: only 24% of them believe that they are able to influence municipal policy, and as few as 15% think themselves capable of influencing national policy. The upper subgroup of middle income groups is slightly less alienated, approaching high-income groups, which are the least alienated of all. The lower middle income subgroup, on the other hand, is characterized by the poorest political involvement (which is even lower than among Russians with low income), which may be interpreted as an indirect indicator of this group's widespread protest sentiments.
2. Survey results show that the frequency of contributing to grassroots organizations and various types of communities tends to depend on income level. Consequently, the political involvement of people with mid-level income is also on the middle level: they contribute to organizations/communities more than people with low income (4–9% vs. 3–6%) but less than people with high income (7–12%). This pattern does have certain exceptions, pertaining to organizations with low involvement levels (at around 1 to 3%), such as volunteer movements or veteran associations. Respondents with mid-level income tend to contribute to these more often than respondents with high or low income.
3. Middle income groups are also characterized by mid-level political activism per se: as rule, they are more active politically than low-income groups but less active than high-income groups, or at least as active as them. Furthermore, the differences between the upper and lower middle income subgroup are minimal. The only exception is voting: this type of activity sees the most involvement from low- and middle income groups (33% each) and far less involvement from people representing high-income groups (22%).
4. Just as other social strata, middle income groups mostly get involved in politics while acting out of altruism (wishes to help society and people) or healthy egoism (protecting their own civil rights and ensuring personal development). Very few people in modern Russia become activists due to a desire to make more money or improve their career prospects.

5. In terms of their general interest in politics, which serves as an indicator of political inclusion (and, consequently, of potential readiness to mobilize), middle income groups (with 67% being interested in politics) rank between low-income groups (62%) and high-income groups (30%), approaching the latter. At the same time, the percentage of people who are keenly interested in political updates and follow them closely is the highest among middle income groups.
6. When it comes to potential readiness for political activism in response to violations of their rights, middle income groups barely differ from other social groups and strata, Russian society being highly homogeneous in this respect. We should emphasize that, based on survey data, people with mid-level income are inclined the most to take a lawful course of action by appealing to the authorities with a petition (20%), while the need for armed resistance is justified very rarely (only by 2%).
7. Middle income groups' potential readiness to join rallies and demonstrations for a number of causes (mostly to protect their social and economic rights and to stop the authorities' abuse of power) occupies the middle ground between the more radical low-income groups and high-income groups, which are less inclined towards protesting.

Thus, the analysis of nationwide survey data shows that middle income groups in modern Russia do not fully perform the stabilizing political factor function that is expected of them. Based on the general middle class theory, middle income groups are supposed to be more socially and politically active and invested in achieving constructive goals, such as positive collaboration between civic society and the state and the suppression of radical protests. But in reality, a higher level of actual inclusion into the networks of social collaboration and political involvement, as compared to the rest of the population, is typical of high-income rather than middle income groups of Russians. At the same time, we have seen almost no confirmation of fears arising out of the Olson—Huntington model, which dictates that middle income groups generate radical moods; that said, the lower subgroup of the middle income group does display an occasional inclination towards radicalism. In modern Russia, people with mid-level income tend to rank between the more politically active but more moderate high-income groups, on the one hand, and the least active low-income groups, which, nevertheless, are more prone to radical protests. This intermediate social and political stance, along with rather vague self-identification, proves that the Russian middle class has not yet shaped itself into a unique major social entity, which was stressed multiple times in the previous chapters of this book.

References

Korotaev A, Vaskin I, Bilyuga S (2017) The Olson—Huntington hypothesis on the Bell-Shaped relation between the economic development level and social and political destabilization: quantitative analysis study. Soc Rev 16(1):9–49.

Volkov D, Kolesnikov A (2016) Self-organization of the civic society in Moscow. Motivations, opportunities, and extents of politicization. Carnegie Moscow Center, Moscow, pp 24–25
Yanitsky ON (2013) Social movements: theory, practice, prospects. Novy Khronograf, Moscow (2013), p 76

Yury V. Latov Leading Researcher at the Academy of Management of the Interior Ministry of Russia, Leading Researcher at the Federal Center of Theoretical and Applied Sociology of the Russian Academy of Sciences (former Institute of Sociology, Russian Academy of Sciences) and Professor at Plekhanov Russian University of Economics. He is a sociologist (Ph.D. in Sociology—2008) with a background in economy (Ph.D. in Economy—1993). His research and consulting practice is concentrated on shadow economy, comparative studies, sociology of education, civil society, extremism prevention. Author of over 250 articles and chapters in scientific monographs. His recent publications are chapters "External Political Discourse of Russia and Evaluation in Russians" and "Russians on the Future of the Country: Old Worries and New Hopes" in the monograph "Russian Society and Challenges of the Time. Book Five" Ed. by Gorshkov M.K. 2017; "Russian on its Way Towards a Society with More Justice and Less Corruption: Analyzing Relations Between Citizens and the State" in the monograph "Dreaming an Ideal Society in Russia and China" Ed. by Gorshkov M.K., Li Peilin. 2016 (co-authored with Latova N.V.).

Vladimir V. Petukhov is Head of the Center of the Complex Social Studies at the Federal Center of Theoretical and Applied Sociology of the Russian Academy of Sciences (former Institute of Sociology, Russian Academy of Sciences). V. Petuhov is a famous Russian researcher in the sphere of political science and political sociology. He is the author and the coordinator of several research projects, devoted to a wide range of issues: the problem of the value shifts in Russian society, ideological and political attitudes and values, the phenomena of political participation and civil self-organization, the problems of social mobility and so on. He had taken an active part in many projects conducted by the Institute of Sociology of RAS: "Ten Years of Reforms in the Perceptions of the Russians", "Russia, Europe, Germany in the Focus of the Russian Public Opinion", "Large Russian Business: The Social Role and the Social Responsibility", "Perestroika: 20 Years Later. In the Perception of the Russians", "Rich and Poor in Contemporary Russia", "Bureaucracy and Authority in New Russia", "The Young Generation of New Russia", "The Evolution of the Democratic Values of the Russians", "Russia on a New Turning Point: the Most Common Fears of the Russians", "The Fall of the Berlin Wall: Before and After (the Foreign Policy Priorities of the Russians)". V. Petuhov is the author of more than 150 scientific papers, published either in Russia or abroad. He is the Deputy Chairman of the Scientific Council of VCIOM (Russian Public Opinion Research Center).

Chapter 19
The Rise of the Middle Income Group in China—Take the Megacities Beijing, Shanghai and Guangzhou for Example

Yelin Yao and Haidong Zhang

On one hand, the middle income group is considered the main participants of the consumer market with strong purchasing power. Their sustained expansion shall release their consumption potential and drive the national economic growth. On the other hand, their expansion is critical for the formation of the olive-shaped distribution pattern and the olive-shaped society and it brings a stable society. However, with the gathering speed of economic globalization in recent years, the even aggravated income bipolarization and intensified imbalance of social development have caused the middle income group in the developed countries to begin losing ground. According to Pew Research Center's latest data, the total middle class households in U.S. have fallen below half of all the households, from 61% in 1971 to 49.4% in 2015[1]; According to German Institute for Economic Research (DIW), the share of the middle income group has fallen from 64 to 58% from 1997 to 2013,[2] as those living near the poverty line have raised from 30 to 35% of all the population and the share of high income group has gone up from 14 to 17% of the whole population. Meanwhile, the middle income group in EMs such as China was rising. The data from China Society Survey (CSS 2015) shows that the middle income share of the whole population was 37.4% in 2014 (Peilin et al. 2016).

After more than three decades of high-speed growth, with significant increase in average per capita income, the middle income group has gradually grown into a major force for social development in China. As the most developed areas of economy, society and culture, Beijing, Shanghai and Guangzhou are the places that are most prepared to foster the middle income group. As where the epitomes of the middle income group reside, research of them shall reveal the tendency of their

[1] guancha.cn https://www.guancha.cn/america/2015_12_10_344252.shtml.

[2] Elite Reference: https://qnck.cyol.com/html/2015-10/07/nw.D110000qnck_20151007_1-07.htm

Y. Yao (✉) · H. Zhang
School of Sociology and Political Science, Shanghai University, Shanghai 200444, China

P. Li and M. K. Gorshkov (eds.), *The Middle Income Group in China and Russia*, Research Series on the Chinese Dream and China's Development Path,
https://doi.org/10.1007/978-981-16-1464-4_19

cohorts as in other places in China. Based on the surveys carried out in the above cities, the paper highlights and analyzes the characteristics and forming channel of the middle income-group.

19.1 A Study of the Middle Income Group in Megacities in China

This paper uses data from Survey on Living Conditions of Megacity Residents as carried out in Beijing, Shanghai and Guangzhou by the Shanghai Institute of Social Science Survey of Shanghai University, between November 2014 to October 2015. Two-stage sampling was employed in this survey. The normal random sampling with map was used in the first stage, with which the representative population sampling of all classes and the starting point of the middle-class population was achieved. 50 communities in each city were selected and 20 households were extracted for each community. As 1 adult of each household was chosen, a total of 1,000 samples were extracted from each city. In the second stage, the adaptive cluster sampling was used targeted at the middle class. It aimed at taking the representative middle-class samples, for which a total of 1000 samples were extracted from each city. A total of 6,010 residents has been successfully interviewed in this two-stage survey. As the paper mainly addresses the characteristics of the middle income group in megacities and takes the income as the standard of the group, the individual cases of the students and the income missing cases were eliminated. So, the analysis is finally launched according to the 5,611 samples acquired from Beijing, Shanghai and Guangzhou, of which 2,854 were from the first stage and 2,757 were from the second stage.

19.2 The Definition, Presumption of Scale and the Constitutive Features of the Middle Income Group

(1) The definition of the middle income group

Literally speaking, the concept of middle income group is about the income, in which there is no implication of occupation. To determine middle income individuals, absolute and the relative indexes can be used as two methods. As the absolute index is easier to be deducted and compared, it can hardly reflect the change of the income structure. Building the olive-shaped society means modifying the current income structure, for which the relative index shall be adopted. Li Peilin et al. think that it is relatively proper to use the relative index to measure the middle income individuals, as both the income disparity and their shares and tendency are taken into consideration. In addition, the interference from purchasing power is excluded. So, this index shall help analyze the middle income individuals from both the income level and the percentage of the whole population (Peilin and Di 2015).

The paper also adopts relative index, and the interviewees are hereby divided into four income groups based on their annual income last year: people whose income is below 0.75 times of the median are defined as the low income group, whose income is between 0.75 times and 1.25 times of the median are defined as the lower middle income group, whose income is between 1.25 times and 2 times of the median are the upper middle income group and those whose incomes is above 2 times of the median are the high income group. It is defined herein that the middle income group comprises of the lower middle income group and the upper middle income group.

(2) **The presumption of scale of the middle income group**

It is mentioned above that two-stage sampling was employed in this survey, the normal random sampling with map in the first stage and the adaptive cluster sampling targeted at the middle class in the second stage. So, the presumption of scale of the middle income group was based on the samples from random sampling stage, that is the analysis was carried out based on the 2,854 samples from the first stage. The median of the individual annual income of the interviewee stood at ¥48,000, with which standard we define the four income groups (see Table 19.1). Of which, the interviewees that fell in the middle income group were 1,182 people, which took a share of 41.42%; 1,137 people, 39.84% of all samples fell in the low income group; there were 535 people who had the high income, which took a share of 18.75%.

In terms of the regions, in Beijing, as 435 of the middle income group out of the total of 897 people lived there, the share of the group in Beijing was 48.50%; in Shanghai, as 368 of the middle income group out of the total of 1,011 people lived there, the share of the group in Shanghai was 36.77%; in Guangzhou, as 379 of the middle income group out of the total of 956 people lived there, the share of the group in Guangzhou was 39.65%. It is worth mentioned that there was a relatively higher share of low income group in Shanghai and Guangzhou, around 45%, while the share of the same cohorts in Beijing was below 30%; in addition, Beijing had the highest share of the high income group, which stood as high as 23.85%. Shanghai had the high income share next to Beijing and Guangzhou had the lowest share (Table 19.2).

Table 19.1 Scale of income groups in Beijing, Shanghai and Guangzhou

Category	Standard	Qty. (N)	Share (%)
Low income group	¥36 k and below	1,137	39.84
Lower middle income group	Between ¥36 k and ¥60 k	801	28.07
Upper middle income group	Between ¥60 k and ¥96 k	381	13.35
High income group	Above ¥96 k	535	18.75
Total		2,854	100

Table 19.2 Scale comparison of all income groups in Beijing, Shanghai and Guangzhou

In: N, %

Category	Beijing		Shanghai		Guangzhou	
	N	%	N	%	N	%
Low income group	257	28.65	454	45.35	426	44.56
Lower middle income group	287	32.00	239	23.88	275	28.77
Upper middle income group	148	16.50	129	12.89	104	10.88
High income group	205	22.85	179	17.88	151	15.79
Total	897	100	1,001	100	956	100

(3) The constitutive features of the middle income group

We analyze the constitutive features of the middle income group in megacities in China in terms of gender, age, political status, household registration type, location of the household registration, educational attainment, job status, etc. based on the 5,611 samples acquired from the two-stage survey.

As for gender, males showed the lower share as in the low income group, which was only 33.02%; the shares in the lower middle income and upper middle income were separately 46.28% and 55.83%; males showed the higher share in the high income group, which reached 62.32%. Of the cities Beijing, Shanghai and Guangzhou, the males in Guangzhou showed the highest share as in the middle income group, 52.15%. Beijing came next with 48.66% and Shanghai came the third with 47.31%.

As for age, the low income group showed the highest average age, 46; the lower middle income group had an average age of 43; the upper middle income group had an average of 38; the lowest average age went to the high income group, 36. In general, the general average age of the middle income group was 42. Of the cities Beijing, Shanghai and Guangzhou, Guangzhou showed the lowest average age, 40; Beijing came next with 41 and Shanghai came the third with 44.

As for political status, the CPC member group showed the lowest share as in the low income group, which was only 8.53%; the CPC member group also showed the highest share in the upper middle income group, which reached 19.47%. In addition, the CPC member group' shares in the lower middle-income group (15.99%) and high income-group (17.45%) were both above 15%. The CPC member group had its highest share in Shanghai among the three megacities as in the middle-income group, which stood at 21.04%. Guangzhou came next with 17.09% and Beijing came last with 14.09%.

As for household registration type, the high income group showed the lowest share of non-agricultural household registration holders, which was 84.23% and the highest share of non-agricultural household registration, which was 77.99%. The non-agricultural household registration shares as in the low income group and lower middle income group were separately 79.48 and 80.65%. The non-agricultural household registration share in the middle income group in Shanghai was evidently higher than other two cities, which reached 87.97%. The non-agricultural household registration shares as in the middle income group were separately 78.78% in Beijing and 73.37% in Shanghai.

As for location of the household registration, 22.92% of the low income group hold the non-local one, while the share of non-local household registration holders as in the lower middle income and upper middle income group were separately 23.66% and 27.38%; the highest share of the non-local household registration population was in the high income group, which was 24.68%. The non-local household registration share in the middle income group in Shanghai was the lowest of the three cities, which was 21.04%. Beijing came next with 21.49% and Guangzhou saw the highest number, 32.54%.

As for educational attainment, the share of those who received undergraduate education and above took 57.36% of the high income group, and the corresponding share in the upper middle income and lower-middle income were separately 42.61% and 17.58%; the share of those received undergraduate education and above took only 12.03% of those low income group (see Table 19.3). Of the three megacities, the educational attainment of the middle income group in Shanghai was the highest, reaching a percentage of 27.58% in terms of undergraduate education and above, while the educational attainment share of such in other two cities failed to reach a quarter.

As for job status, above 80% of the interviewees either had fixed employer or salary income. The share of employers in the high income group was evidently higher than other groups, which reached 11.81%, while the percentage dropped to 2% as in the middle income group. The higher percentages as in the low income group were freelancers, contracted labors/labor dispatched workers and errand workers/casual labors (see Table 19.4).

Of the megacities Beijing, Shanghai and Guangdong, above 90% of the interviewees either had fixed employer or salary income as in the middle income group, while the corresponding share in Guangzhou among the middle income group was

Table 19.3 Educational attainment of all income groups in Beijing, Shanghai and Guangzhou

In: N, %

Category	Low income group		Lower middle income group		Upper middle income group		High income group	
Educational attainment	N	%	N	%	N	%	N	%
Below the undergraduate	1,763	87.97	1,186	82.42	392	57.39	629	42.64
Undergraduate and above	241	12.03	253	17.58	291	42.61	846	57.36
Total	2004	100	1,439	100	683	100	1,475	100

Table 19.4 Job status of all income groups in Beijing, Shanghai and Guangzhou

In: N, %

Income group	Low income group		Lower middle income group		Upper middle income group		High income group	
Job status	N	%	N	%	N	%	N	%
Employee with fixed employer	1,404	80.41	1,254	87.39	604	88.43	1,172	80.49
Employer	28	1.6	27	1.88	15	2.2	172	11.81
Self-employed labor	72	4.12	56	3.9	30	4.39	64	4.4
Domestic helper	9	0.52	10	0.7	3	0.44	4	0.27
Freelancer	54	3.09	36	2.51	18	2.64	28	1.92
Contracted labors/labor dispatched workers	40	2.29	22	1.53	5	0.73	2	0.14
Errand workers/casual labors with no fixed employer	72	4.12	16	1.11	2	0.29	1	0.07
Others	67	3.84	14	0.98	6	0.88	13	0.89
Total	1,746	100	1435	100	683	100	1,456	100

77.12%. It is worth noted that the share of self-employed labors, employers, freelancers, contracted labors/labor dispatched workers as in the middle income group was much higher in Guangzhou than that in Beijing and Shanghai (see Table 19.5).

As for the management activity, the share of people that were in the management positions were distinctly higher in the high income group than any other groups, where nearly 60% of the high income group were in the management position, of which, 47.25% managed inferiors and reported to superiors while 11.43% only managed inferior and reported to no superiors (see Table 19.6). In addition, there was disparity despite the lower and upper middle income group were under the same group, as 37.42% of the upper middle income people worked in the management activity, which was 14.1% higher than the lower middle income people. For the management activity, 70.25% of the people only reported to superiors and managed no inferiors, which was a high number than any other income group.

Among the three megacities, Shanghai had the highest share of people in the management activity as in the middle income group, which stood at 35.93%. Guangzhou came next with approximately 30% and Beijing came last with 20.05% (see Table 19.7). Both the shares of the interviewees who "managed inferiors and reported to superiors" and "managed no inferior and reported to no superior" as in the middle income group were higher than those in Beijing and Shanghai. This also explained in a different angle why the self-employed individuals showed a relatively high share in the middle income group in Guangzhou. 70.9% of the people who

Table 19.5 Job status of middle income group in Beijing, Shanghai and Guangzhou

In: N, %

City	Beijing		Shanghai		Guangzhou	
Job status	N	%	N	%	N	%
Employee with fixed employer	754	92.4	585	93	519	77.12
Employer	8	0.98	11	1.75	23	3.42
Self-employed labor	24	2.94	18	2.86	44	6.54
Domestic helper	3	0.37	0	0	10	1.49
Freelancer	17	2.08	6	0.95	31	4.61
Contracted labors/labor dispatched workers	4	0.49	5	0.79	18	2.67
Errand workers/casual labors with no fixed employer	3	0.37	4	0.64	11	1.63
Others	3	0.37	0	0	17	2.53
Total	816	100	629	100	673	100

Table 19.6 Management activity of all income groups in Beijing, Shanghai and Guangzhou

In: N, %

Category	Low income group		Lower middle income group		Upper middle income group		High income group	
	N	%	N	%	N	%	N	%
Manage inferiors and report to no superiors	26	1.5	30	2.1	20	2.92	166	11.43
Manage inferiors and report to superiors	267	15.42	303	21.22	236	34.5	686	47.25
Report to superiors and manage no inferiors	1,216	70.25	939	65.76	351	51.32	477	32.85
Manage no inferiors and report to superiors	222	12.82	156	10.92	77	11.26	123	8.47
Total	1,731	100	1,428	100	684	100	1,452	100

Table 19.7 Management activity of middle income group in Beijing, Shanghai and Guangzhou

In: N, %

City	Beijing		Shanghai		Guangzhou	
Management activity	N	%	N	%	N	%
Manage inferiors and report to no superiors	10	1.22	16	2.54	24	3.61
Manage inferiors and report to superiors	154	18.83	210	33.39	175	26.32
Report to superiors and manage no inferiors	580	70.9	359	57.07	351	52.78
Manage no inferiors and report to superiors	74	9.05	44	7	115	17.29
Total	818	100	629	100	665	100

"reported to superiors and managed no inferiors" as in the middle income group in Beijing, which was apparently higher than Shanghai and Guangzhou.

To sum up, despite the shared general category of middle income group, there are evident disparities between the lower and upper middle income group in each structural characteristic, such as gender, age, educational attainment and management activity. The latter tend to have received higher education, participate in more management activity and take higher position, which is an all-round advantage. On the other hand, the similarity and discrepancy are also demonstrated in the regional comparison of the middle income group in Beijing, Shanghai and Guangzhou. The similarity of the three cities is that the male youth are the main body of the middle income group, of which 80% hold the non-agricultural household registration and around 25% received undergraduate or above education. The discrepancy of the three cities is about the employment category and management activity in the middle income group. As the self-employed individuals in the middle income group in Guangzhou had an evidently higher percentage than that in Beijing and Shanghai, the share of individuals in the middle income group who were in the management position was apparently higher than that in Beijing and Guangzhou.

19.3 The Forming Channel of the Middle Income Group

Marketization is the institutional drive of fostering the middle income group. Within this process, more and more social members have the opportunity to enter the middle income group. This paper discusses how the market has shaped the middle income group by factors such as occupational characteristics, employment sectors, job search channels and housing conditions.

The core occupational characteristic of the middle income group is the employability. Pertinent researches believe that the core characteristic of the middle income group is that they do not own the production materials while rely more on "organizational capital" and "cultural capital" to acquire occupational and social status (Yucheng and Xiaoshuang 2016). The employability of middle income group is mainly presented by the employment category and the source of income. As for the employment category, 87.72% of the middle income group either have fixed employer or salary income; in terms of the income source, almost all (98.05%) of the middle income group has their income mainly from the salary. 80.16% of the groups completely rely on the current employment salary.

The middle income group mainly get employed in the non-state sector, and the non-state-owned sector has become an important channel for fostering the middle income group. There is a critical division in the labor market in China, of which the division between the institutional and non-institutional sectors' labor market is an important part (Zhiguo and Ma 2016). It can be seen that the state power on shaping the middle income group is retreating with process of marketization. Of all the middle income people in Beijing, Shanghai and Guangzhou, 53.06% work in the non-institutional sector, and the rest 46.94% work in the institutional sector. The income in the private business is directly linked with the performance, which brings about the initiative of the labors, is very attractive. The data show that of all the middle income people who are employed outside the institutional sector, more than half (57.02%) work in the private business, in which 3.58% are the private business owners. In addition, 12.24% of the middle income group run individual business, 10.46% work in the collective-owned enterprises and 9.47% work in the foreign-invested enterprises or ventures.

The market channel is the primary channel for the middle income group to seek jobs. With the declining of the work unit system, the unified position allocation era is long gone: pretty small percentage of employment is realized by the planned allocation channel (substitute of parent/relative, national enrollment, organizational job allocation/transfer, etc.) and the market recruitment channel (individual job application, recommendation by employment agency and introduction by a third party) become dominant (see Fig. 19.1).

Zhou Xiaohong believes that with the advancing of marketization, the reform of housing system has driven the expansion of the middle class (Xiaohong and Chenqing 2013). Man Yanyun also agrees that the privatization of real estate has contributed a lot to the emerge and rise of the middle class in China since 1990s (Yanyun 2013). As the frontier of the reform and opening up, the earlier launched reform of housing system in Beijing, Shanghai and Guangzhou has brought a well-developed commercial residential building market. The survey shows that the percentage of the middle income group who own their housing is 63.85%, and the percentage of renting houses is also high, which stands at 27.74%. Of the middle income group who own their private housing, only 3.16% have the self-built housing while most of them (96.74%) have the self-owned housing. The ways to purchase private housing include buying commercial residential housing and buying affordable housing by welfare or institutional factor. The market factor plays an important role in buying private housing for middle income households in Beijing, Shanghai and Guangzhou. According to

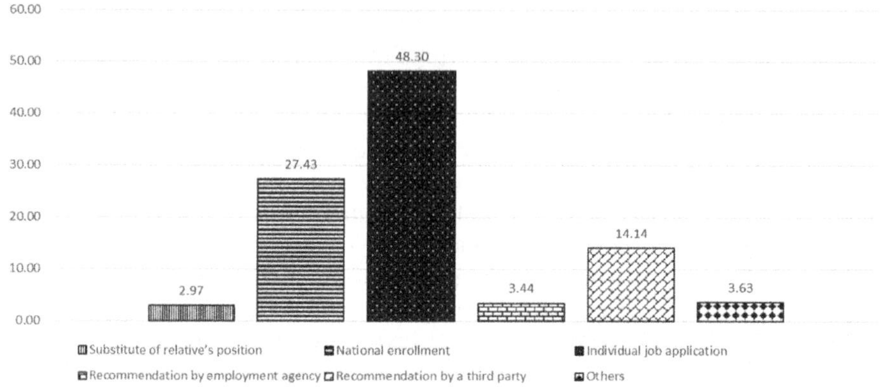

Fig. 19.1 Employment channels of middle income group in Beijing, Shanghai and Guangzhou (%). *Note* This is a multiple-choice question in the questionnaire

the data, 92.99% of them buy their commercial residential housing on the market instead of the affordable housing provided by the government.

In addition, as for individuals, the market capacity is critical for people to enter the middle income group. According to the experience of many countries, the middle income group are mainly formed by the four occupational groups: senior management staff, technicians, clerks and service staff in the commercial sector. The statistics show that the four occupation categories above have taken up more than 80% of all the middle income group in Beijing, Shanghai and Guangzhou. In which, the "core middle income group" (typically those who are in charge of the organizations and enterprises and technicians) have reached 9.75 and 32.32% separately. In the marketization reform, the non-institutional sector recruit employees based on their individual market capacity and promotion and appointment system is also being formed gradually for the institutional sector. So, a reasonable occupation generally requires one to have corresponding market capacity. Those who have higher market capacity can get better occupations and higher social status.

Therefore, we can see that as the frontier of reform and opening up, megacities in China showcase high level of marketization; meanwhile, the industrial agglomeration has attracted massive high quality or high skilled people, i.e., people with high market capacity. Those elements render evident advantages for the cultivation of middle income group in megacities (Haidong 2016).

19.4 Conclusions and Discussions

After the analyses of the structural analysis of the middle income group in Beijing, Shanghai and Guangzhou, we can conclude a general "profile" of the middle income group in megacities: as for the occupation, they are non-labor workers; as for the education, they have high educational attainment; as for the income, they enjoy upper middle income.

The continuous expanding scale of middle income group demonstrates great improvement of our economic and social development, which has positive meanings in more than one way. Strong economic power as such income group feature, their sustained expansion shall significantly drive the consumption and economy. And the tendency shall help China to avoid both polarization of society and the middle income trap, and play a role in navigating the whole society toward an even proper olive-shaped society structure. So, the cultivation and expansion of the middle income group is a critical issue for the current research of the group.

First, we have clearly observed how the market force has shaped the middle income group by factor analyses such as their occupational characteristics, employment sectors, job search channels and housing conditions. Therefore, the decisive role of market in resource allocation shall be given full play so as to comprehensively deepen reform and re-adjust the relation between the government and the market. For example, the comprehensive marketization reform can be implemented to boost the growth of private enterprises and encourage the startup of the individual labors. Recent years, the overheat of the real estate market is witnessed. Fast growing housing prices has set a great impedance to the up flow of the middle income group. Comments such as "housing prices have exterminated too many middle class who were born in 1980s" and "the real estate is the Grim Reaper of the middle class" are wide spread on the social media. Therefore, it requests the authorities to exert function on monitoring market order, take effective measures to safeguard the proper living demand, refrain speculation and stabilize housing prices. In the middle of December 2016, the Central Economic Work Conference clarified the positioning of "housing for living, not for speculation", which demanded the proper house purchase behavior out of living purpose.

Second, in terms of individuals, only improved market capacity can endow one with higher social class entrance. The expansion of the middle income group shall largely rely on the conversion of the low income group to the middle income group. Note that the migrant workers are the main body of the low income group in cities. From the research results, the major factor that affects the income level of the migrant worker is the human capital of them, that is their educational attainment and occupational skills. Therefore, we should improve vocational education and skill training system, with large scale occupation training plan implemented. The migrant workers should be encouraged to improve their income by enhanced production skills. In this way, 80% of the Post-80's Generation migration workers shall enter the middle income group in future (Peilin and Di 2015).

Third, we should also attend to the large low income group when we cast light on the middle income group. The formers show significant distance in terms of life quality when compared to the middle income group. The measures to further expanding the middle income group so that more people can enjoy higher quality life shall be an imminent issue for the further development of the society. The "share" development conception was raised in the fifth plenary session of the 18th CPC central committee. To translate the conception into concrete policies, such as the proper regulation of income distribution and the narrowing down of the gap between the rich and poor shall all be arduous tasks. Only when the "share" conception is transferred into real policies and actions can the expansion of the middle income group be sustained.

However, as the most developed regions in China in terms of society and economy, the scale of the middle income group is simply higher when compared to other regions in China. This is brought by typical economic and social conditions. Despite the typical characteristics of the statistics may represent the tendency of the whole middle-class group in China, we should also realize that it can never represent all the middle-class group reality in China.

References

Haidong Z (2016) The formation of middle income group in megacities and the social structural characteristics. China Soc Sci Today

Peilin L, Guangjin C, Yi Z (eds) (2016) Blue book of China's society: society of China analysis and forecast (2017). Social Sciences Academic Press (China), Beijing

Peilin L, Di Z (2015) Make efforts to develop an olive-shaped distribution pattern: an analysis based on data from the Chinese social survey for 2006–2013. Soc Sci China (1)

Xiaohong Z, Chenqing (2013) Globalization, social transformation and the construction of middle class in China. In: Cheng L (ed), China's emerging middle class. Shanghai Translation Publishing House, Shanghai

Yanyun M (2013) Globalization, reform of housing in China and the rise of the middle class. In: Cheng L (ed), China's emerging middle class. Shanghai Translation Publishing House, Shanghai

Yucheng L, Xiaoshuang J (2016) Research on the occupational characteristics of the middle income group in megacities in China. China Soc Sci Today

Zhiguo L, Ma J (2016) The sector division of labor market and the advantage of institutional employment. Chinese J Popul Sci (4)

Yelin Yao is a Ph.D. candidate in School of Sociology and Political Science, Shanghai University. Her main research area is social stratification and middle class. Her main publications include *Marketization and Market Capacity: The Generation Mechanism of Chinese Middle Class: Examples of Beijing, Shanghai and Guangzhou* (2016), *The Expansion of Middle-Income Groups and the Formation of Olive-Type Society* (2017).

Haidong Zhang is a Professor in School of Sociology and Political Science, Shanghai University. He now serves as the Executive Deputy Director of the Shanghai Institute of Social Science Survey of Shanghai University and Vice Secretary-General of Chinese Association of Sociology. He focuses his research in the fields of social quality and social inequality. His main publications include *Social Quality: theory, Method and Empirical Study* (book) in 2011 and *Social Quality Study on Shanghai (2010–2013)* (book) in 2016, 'The study of Attitudes Toward Social Inequality in Urban China' (Sociological Study, 2004), 'Social Quality Research and Its Recent Development' (Sociological Study, 2012), 'The Alienation of City Residents: Based on data of 2010 Shanghai Survey' (Sociological Study, 2014).

Chapter 20
Middle Income Groups in Russian Metropolitan Cities

P. M. Kozyreva and A. I. Smirnov

The living conditions in a metropolitan city, as in any other large city, are differentiated by many contradictory features. On the one hand are problems that bring hardship to citizens' lives such as overpopulation, poor environment, social isolation, frantic pace of life, enormous information flow, depression and stress. People living in large cities become extremely vulnerable to natural disasters, rampant crime, theft, robberies, murders, terrorist attacks and various emergencies. The vulnerability of people living in such cities is exacerbated by constant crises and pressure imposed by immigrants. On the other hand, there are great opportunities for employment, receiving a prestigious education, an interesting job and specialization, realizing carrier ambitions, solving financial problems, accessing high-quality medical and other services on a paid and free basis, and enjoying various cultural leisure and entertainment options.

These features largely determine the population size and composition, the pace and principal trends of development, and the level and quality of life of the middle income groups in metropolitan and other large cities, i.e. those groups that are actively engaged in business and production, promote production development by being consumers of bulk goods and services, and provide a considerable share of tax revenues to the budget.

[1] Russian Federal State Statistics Service. Assessment of the number of permanent residents as of January 1, 2017 and for 2016 on average. URL: https://www.gks.ru/wps/wcm/connect/rosstat_main/rosstat/ru/statistics/population/demography/ (accessed on: August 24, 2017).

P. M. Kozyreva (✉)
HSE University, Institute of Sociology of FCTAS RAS, Moscow, Russia

A. I. Smirnov
Institute of Sociology of FCTAS RAS, Moscow, Russia

P. Li and M. K. Gorshkov (eds.), *The Middle Income Group in China and Russia*, Research Series on the Chinese Dream and China's Development Path,
https://doi.org/10.1007/978-981-16-1464-4_20

Currently, there are 15 large cities in Russia whose population exceeds 1 million people. Of these, only Moscow and St. Petersburg can be regarded as truly world-class metropolitan cities, with populations of 12.4 and 5.3 million people, respectively.[1] These metropolitan cities are home to practically all federal state management services, the largest scientific, technical and manufacturing centers, and numerous production facilities. They are the main centers of business activity of the country, where over half of tax revenues into the Russian budget are formed. The labor markets of these largest economic centers are rather specific and exceed the labor markets of many European countries by their size.

In this chapter, we tried to determine the size and composition of middle income groups in Russian metropolitan cities and identify the special features of their formation, which would help clarify a number of important problems related to various aspects of everyday life of middle income groups, and also assess their role in society and the prospects for further development. Special attention is given to the study of employment problems, labor market position and consumer opportunities of middle income groups in Russian metropolitan cities. We examine the particulars of the social well-being of citizens from the viewpoint of their adjustment to long-term economic crisis conditions.

The study is based on the 25th wave (December 2016) of the Russia Longitudinal Monitoring Survey of HSE (RLMS-HSE).[2] Based on the purpose and objectives of the study as well as the features of formation of the RMLS-HSE's sample, which was created as representative nationwide, three groups of respondents over 14 years of age were identified: (1) residents of Moscow (N = 1,274); (2) residents of cities whose population exceeds 1 million people—St. Petersburg, Kazan, Krasnoyarsk, Nizhny Novgorod and Chelyabinsk (N = 2,095); (3) residents of other cities (N = 8,153). This approach allowed us to obtain and analyze reliable and comparable empirical data on the features of formation and living conditions of the middle income groups in different types of large cities.

Then, as with the analysis of other problems covered in the preceding chapters of this book, all respondents were divided into four groups according to different income levels: low-income groups (0.75 or less than the median); lower middle income groups (0.75–1.25 times the median); upper middle income groups (1.25–2 times the median); and high-income groups (2 times the median).

According to the RLMS-HSE data analysis, on the one hand, the average income level of the population of Russian metropolitan cities is much higher than in other cities; on other hand, one can clearly identify a more distinct differentiation and a deeper polarization of the population by income level, which increases income and social inequality. In this case, Moscow residents enjoy the highest income level in Russia today. According to Table 20.1, *the middle income groups make up two-thirds of the population of Moscow and almost three quarters of the population of other*

---

[2] Russia Longitudinal Monitoring survey, RLMS-HSE», conducted by National Research University "Higher School of Economics" and OOO "Demoscope" together with Carolina Population Center, University of North Carolina at Chapel Hill and the Institute of Sociology RAS. (RLMS-HSE websites: https://www.hse.ru/rlms, https://www.cpc.unc.edu/projects/rlms).

Table 20.1 Size of income groups in different types of cities, 2016, %

Income group	Moscow	Cities with population over 1 million	Cities with population under 1 million
High-income groups	25.4	10.4	9.2
Upper middle income groups	36.8	30.1	21.7
Lower middle income groups	29.9	42.5	40.4
Low-income groups	7.9	17.0	28.7

million-population cities. While the upper middle income groups predominate in Moscow, in other million-population cities it is the lower middle income groups.

It is noteworthy that in the Russian capital the share of the high-income population is triple the share of the low-income citizens, while in other cities the opposite situation is true. In spite of the growth of some new opportunities amid the emergence and development of market relations in Russia, the risk of poverty both for the most vulnerable groups and for the employed population in mid-size and small cities considerably exceeds opportunities for sustainable growth of well-being, thus impeding the expansion of middle income groups. The situation is made considerably worse by the negative consequences of a deep economic crisis, thus worsening or freezing the material positions of the middle income groups of the population and impeding the reduction of poverty.

The income inequality that becomes particularly deep in the metropolitan cities leads to restricted access for a considerable part of the population to various social and economic resources, including housing and other property, food consumption, the labor market and social services. A high concentration of such restrictions, even if the income level does not officially fall below the poverty line, is very often perceived as poverty and understood as inadequate conditions necessary to ensure consumption in accordance with the standards accepted in society[3]. It is for this reason that many people belonging to lower and upper middle income groups start feeling poor when faced with problems that worsen their lives. At the end of 2016, when defining their positions on the scale of financial well-being that includes 9 steps (from the lowest—"poor" to the highest—"rich"), 46% of representatives of the lower middle income groups and 40.6% of representatives of the upper middle income groups from the adult Moscow population placed themselves in the three lower positions, which correspond to poverty or low income. In particular, 4% and 1.3% saw themselves as poor, i.e. found themselves on the first step of the scale. In other million-population cities, the share of those feeling poor was 51.8% of the lower middle income groups and 36.1% of the upper middle income groups, including those who admit they are poor (5.3 and 1.8%). These conclusions are confirmed by other studies. Thus, in the course of the sociological survey conducted by the Russian Public Opinion Research Center (VCIOM) in May 2017, 39% of Russians admit that they are poor.

[3] Modernization of Russia: Social and Humanitarian Changes/ed. by N. Ya. Petrakov.—Moscow, St. Petersburg: Nestor-Istoriya, 2011. P. 71.

The situation was worse only in 2009 when 41% of respondents declared themselves to be poor.[4]

The position of socially vulnerable groups of the population still remains especially difficult in metropolitan cities, including disabled persons, multi-child families and single parent families, etc. who experience an increased risk of being in the lower income groups. A chronic lack of money leads to a high concentration of various restrictions that impede access to other resources. Under the 2014–2016 economic crisis conditions, there were attempts to mitigate negative implications of declining living conditions and partially make up for the incurred losses. However, such compensation measures related to indexation of salaries, pensions, social benefits and other financial income of the population were implemented too late or were insufficient to cover such losses.

There is still a considerable income gap between men and women in Russia. According to the RLMS-HSE, the average income of Russian women is four times less than that of men. The difference between the income of men and women is observed in practically all industries of the economy and among workers of different specializations. In the metropolitan cities, the income of women and men is higher than in other cities, but unlike other cities, women's income is nearly equal to that of men. This is mainly due to the high level of employment of women in highly paid positions in large cities. According to the analysis, in Moscow women belong to the upper income levels more frequently and to the lower income levels less often than men. But in other million-population cities, such chances for women and men are practically equal. At the same time, in all large cities women less often belong to upper middle income levels, but are more frequently included in the lower middle income levels.

Representatives of the middle income levels are somewhere in the middle in terms of their education level in all types of urban settlements. In this case, *one can clearly observe a trend testifying to the increasing income of citizens belonging to various groups because there are more respondents with higher educations, which leads to higher incomes.* This is well illustrated by the monitoring data provided in Table 20.2. As for secondary vocational education, its impact on the formation of income groups in cities is nearly imperceptible. It is also clear that Moscow residents markedly surpass people living in other cities by their education level in all income groups. At the end of 2016, two-thirds of the respondents from the upper middle income levels from Moscow possessed higher or secondary professional education (41.5 and 24%, respectively) and almost 61% of those in lower middle income groups (34.5 and 26.1% respectively) had such an education.

One of the most notable features of the middle income groups is that they include citizens who are mostly older than other people living in the city. For example, in Moscow the average age of respondents in the lower and upper middle income groups is 50.2 and 49.3 years old, respectively, while respondents from the low-income

[4] Russian Public Opinion Research Center (VCIOM). Consumer Opportunities of Russians: Monitoring. Press Edition No. 3407. URL: https://wciom.ru/index.php?id=236&uid=116289 (accessed on: August 20, 2017).

Table 20.2 Share of respondents with higher and secondary professional education in income groups in different types of cities, 2016, %

Income group	Moscow		Cities with population Over 1 million		Cities with population Under 1 million	
	Higher	Secondary professional	Higher	Secondary professional	Higher	Secondary professional
High-income groups	56.5	24.1	47.4	25.6	47.2	27.7
Upper middle income groups	41.5	24.0	38.6	24.7	35.1	27.4
Lower middle income groups	34.5	26.1	29.5	25.2	26.2	27.6
Low-income groups	21.4	22.4	21.1	25.7	18.5	26.2

Table 20.3 Average age and share of respondents receiving pension, by income group in different types of cities, 2016, %

Income group	Moscow		Cities with population over 1 million		Cities with population under 1 million	
	Average age, years	% receiving pension	Average age, years	% receiving pension	Average age, years	% receiving pension
High-income groups	47.1	35.2	44.3	34.4	43.7	33.8
Upper middle income groups	49.3	40.8	45.9	35.9	46.0	38.4
Lower middle income groups	50.2	47.4	46.7	37.5	47.5	40.6
Low-income groups	41.5	26.5	41.1	27.7	41.8	27.2

groups are only 41.5 years old, and those from the high-income groups are 47.1 years old (Table 20.3). In the lower and upper middle income groups, respondents over 60 years old are much more represented than young people under 30 years old (39.6 and 31.7% versus 20.8 and 18.3%, respectively). In the group of respondents with the lowest income, the share of the older generation was much smaller than the share of young people (19.4 vs. 27.6%), while in the group of people with the highest income the difference between these age cohorts is much reduced (22.2 vs. 25.7%).

In other million-population cities, the average age of surveyed residents in the upper and lower middle income groups was 46.7 and 45.9 years old, respectively, while the average age of the representatives of groups with the lowest and highest income is much smaller—41.1 and 44.3 years old, respectively. It is obvious that in such cities the prevalence of senior respondents over young people under 30 years old in the lower and upper middle income groups is less perceivable than in Moscow (30.8 and 26.3% vs. 22.5 and 23.7%, respectively).

Furthermore, *the middle income groups are to a greater extent than other groups formed by elderly people receiving pensions, most of whom include people receiving an age-based retirement pension.* Table 20.3 shows that both in Moscow and in other million-population cities the share of people receiving pensions in the middle income groups is higher than in the low-income and high-income groups. For most of them their pension is a very important factor ensuring their inclusion in the higher income groups. For example, at the end of 2016 only 5.2% of the surveyed pensioners living in Moscow belonged to the low-income groups while 35.2 and 37.4% belonged to the lower and upper middle income groups, respectively, with 22.2% to the wealthiest ones.

It is worth noting that *newcomers achieve financial success more frequently than those who were born and grew up in metropolitan cities.* Thus, among those people who were born and continue to live in metropolitan cities (in the same city) there are more residents belonging to the low-income groups (15.2 vs. 11.2%) and lower middle income groups (38.8 vs. 36.1%), but fewer residents in the upper middle income groups (30.2 vs. 36.1%) than among other citizens. In addition, in Moscow this trend is less obvious than in other million-population cities.

Employment is an exceptionally important factor determining the characteristics of the formation of groups of various income levels in large cities. Thus, analysis of the RLMS-HSE's data confirms that in metropolitan cities the share of the employed among the upper middle income groups is 1.5–2 times higher and among the high-income groups it is twice as high as people belonging to the low-income groups. In this case, among employed Muscovites the share of people in the low-income and lower middle income levels is much less than among the employed residents of other million-population cities (5.1 and 19.2% vs. 12.9 and 38.2%, respectively), but is considerably higher than those who belong to the upper middle income and high-income groups (40.3 and 35.4% vs. 34.5 and 14.4%, respectively).

The importance of the employment factor when establishing different income groups is determined by the pay level. Wages remain the main source of income for the Russian people, which fully explains the higher income level of Moscow residents. According to official data, the average monthly nominal salary of Moscow employees is approximately 1.5 times higher than such salary in St. Petersburg and other million-population cities.[5]

Like in other cities, in metropolitan cities the salary is differentiated due to inter-industry and intra-industry wage inequality. Because earnings do not always correspond to the level of professional skill and a person's individual contribution, many employees frequently rely not on advanced education and training but on other factors

[5] Russian Federal State Statistics Service. Average monthly nominal salary of employees according to a full range of organizations by subjects of the Russian Federation in 2013–2017. URL: https://www.gks.ru/wps/wcm/connect/rosstat_main/rosstat/ru/statistics/wages/ (accessed on: August 10, 2017).

that can influence their earnings.[6] The conditions of a metropolitan city with its extensive labor market allow one to "search" for a salary that will be higher and easier to obtain, but without achieving it through more diligent and harder work.[7] But if we consider the situation as a whole, we can state than "under the Russian market conditions, the accumulated human capital improves employees' competitive positions many times over and that higher education is valued approximately to the same extent (in relative terms) as it is valued in the labor market of other countries".[8]

It is noteworthy that *distribution of the employed among the groups with different income levels in large cities depends very little on the form of ownership of those enterprises where they are employed.* Though many people living in cities consider work in the private sector to be an opportunity to increase their household income level and a successful model of the social and economic adaptation under market economic conditions, wages at private enterprises are often rather modest. According to the RLMS-HSE, people employed in the private sector do not earn much more than those working at public enterprises. It is only in Moscow that employees of private enterprises belong to the high-income groups (37.5 vs. 29%) more frequently than employees of the public sector, but they are much more rarely included in the upper middle income groups (34.6 vs. 46.7%). According to official statistics, in mid-2017 in Moscow, public sector enterprises, educational institutions and organizations employed nearly 23% of those employed while in the private sector the share is 77%, including the private sector—51%; organizations of mixed form of ownership—12%; public organizations—1%; foreign-invested organizations—13%.[9]

In other million-population cities, no obvious distinctions were identified when distributing the respondents from the employed population by groups with different income levels depending on the enterprise's form of ownership. The lack of high and, most importantly, guaranteed earnings, and the unstable position of private enterprises have become the most important factors preventing an inflow of workers into the private sector. First and foremost, this is relevant for young people who are guided mainly by pragmatism when selecting a profession and future employment. However, a desire for more meaningful and interesting work and self-actualization irrespective of any difficulties in satisfying these needs has not disappeared and is still typical of the younger generation.

According to Table 20.4, *the professional structure of the middle income groups in metropolitan cities is based on professionals and semiprofessionals.* In addition,

---

[6] Russian and Chinese Population in the Era of Changes: Comparative Study in St. Petersburg and Shanghai at the Beginning of the 21th Century / Ed. by E.N. Danilova, V.A. Yadov, Pan Davei.—Moscow Logos, 2012. P. 286.

[7] *V.S. Magun, G.A. Monusova.* Russian Labor Values within the Context of International Comparisons. Report at the 11th International Scientific Conference on Economic and Social Development Problems.—Moscow. Higher School of Economics National Research University, 2010.

[8] Russian Employee: Education, Profession, Qualification / Ed. by V.E. Gimpelson, R.I. Kapelyushnikov.—Moscow. Publishing House of the Higher School of Economics, 2011. P. 71.

[9] Russian Federal State Statistics Service. Average yearly number of employed in the public and private sectors of the economy in Moscow. URL: https://moscow.gks.ru/wps/wcm/connect/rosstat_ts/moscow/ru/statistics/employment/ (accessed on: August 11, 2017).

Table 20.4 Professional structure of different income groups in metropolitan and other cities, 2016, % of employed by group

Professional group	Moscow and other cities with 1+ million population				Cities with population under 1 million			
	High-income groups	Upper middle income groups	Lower middle income groups	Low-income groups	High-income groups	Upper middle income groups	Lower middle income groups	Low-income groups
Top/mid-level executives	8.9	7.8	4.6	3.8	11.5	7.1	4.9	3.2
Specialists with high skill level	28.8	22.5	18.2	11.5	29.3	19.6	14.8	12.9
Specialists with middle skill level	22.9	21.4	19.4	19.1	20.4	20.3	20.9	18.7
Office and customer support employees	5.9	6.6	5.9	7.2	7.1	5.8	5.6	5.5
Service sector workers	11.9	16.7	18.0	21.1	10.4	16.2	19.4	20.3
Skilled workers	7.8	12.0	14.8	15.8	9.4	11.5	15.4	15.9
Operators, adjusters, etc.	9.2	8.6	11.7	14.4	9.5	13.3	12.3	13.7
Unskilled workers	4.6	4.4	7.4	7.1	2.4	6.2	6.7	9.8

the share of high-level professionals among them is much higher than among people representing the middle income groups from the employed in cities with a smaller population. This applies both to the upper and lower middle income groups (22.5 vs. 19.6%, and 18.2 vs. 14.8%, respectively). This is partly due to the professional structure of different types of localities, e.g. in the employment structure of Russian metropolitan cities, a huge share of the employed population (in Moscow, about half) is concentrated in the sphere of business and financial services, including scientific and research developments. It is also obvious that the upper middle income groups in metropolitan cities are formed from skilled and non-skilled workers much less often than in other cities (13 vs. 19.5%).

Analysis of the monitoring data once again demonstrates that under Russian conditions a relationship between workers' professional qualifications and their salary is still discernible, but is far from linear.[10] We can note that both in metropolitan and other cities many specialists of a higher and medium skill level earn no more or even less than skilled workers as well as operators, adjusters, machinists or unqualified workers, so they quite frequently fall into low-income and lower middle income groups. At the same time, despite a huge number of specialists with a high formal level of professional education, there is a widespread shortage of skilled employees. According to experts, the current shortage in qualified specialists to one degree or another is experienced by 87% of Russian enterprises. There is an especially acute shortage of highly specialized engineering and technical professionals.[11] This and many other similar imbalances greatly complicate the modernization of the Russian economy.

Irrespective of the type of urban settlement, people employed with enterprises and organizations hold higher positions in the income provision structure than those working outside the organized employment sector, a significant share of which is related to the informal sector. At the same time, in Moscow and other million-population cities employment outside enterprises and organizations ensures a higher income than in other cities. Among official full-time employees there are considerably more citizens belonging to the upper middle income and high-income groups than among unofficial employees, i.e. those without an employment history, labor agreement, contract, etc. Moscow surpasses all other cities by the share of citizens belonging to the high-income groups among both official and unofficial employees. In particular, in Moscow the share of the upper middle income and high-income groups among those officially employed reaches 40.0 and 35.1%, respectively, while among unofficial employees the figures are 33.2 and 27.8%. In other million-population cities, the share of the upper middle income and high-income groups among those officially employed reaches 34.1 and 14.9%, respectively, while among unofficial employees they are 27.0 and 11.1%.

---

[10] Salary in Russia: Evolution and Differentiation / Ed. by V.E. Gimpelson, R.I. Kapelyushnikov. – Moscow. Higher School of Economics National Research University Publishing House, 2007. Pp. 410–427.

[11] *I. Semin.* Labor Productivity – National Priority // Expert. 2017. Issue 34. Pp. 28–29.

Fig. 20.1 Impact of employment on distribution of pensioners by different income groups, 2016, %

Secondary employment in metropolitan cities, like in other cities, is most frequently associated with the lowest and highest incomes. Thus, in 2016 in metropolitan cities 6.2% of the surveyed employees both from the high-income and low-income groups had both a primary and a secondary job; this was also true for 5.4% of employees from the lower middle income group and only 4.6% of employees of the upper middle income groups. In million-population cities, the share of people having secondary employment out of the surveyed employees in the low-income and high-income groups is 9.8 and 8.3%, respectively, while out of the surveyed employees from the lower and upper middle income groups the figures are just 5.6 and 6.7%, respectively. Any labor relations and labor payment issues arising at the place of secondary employment, irrespective of the settlement type, are more frequently executed based on an oral arrangement. In small and mid-size cities, the group of unskilled or low-skilled workers is the largest group among those people having secondary employment, but in metropolitan cities it is a group that includes specialists possessing high and mid-level skills.

Employment significantly helps increase the income level of Russian pensioners. The data presented in Figure 20.1 show that in Moscow the overwhelming majority of employed pensioners belong to the high-income or upper middle income groups (47.6 and 44%, respectively) while the share among unemployed pensioners is slightly more than half (17.1 and 36.1%, respectively) while 41.3% belong to the lower middle income groups. It is noteworthy that in other million-population cities the employment factor is less important than in Moscow in terms of increasing pensioners' income. However, at the same time in metropolitan cities *pensions allow unemployed pensioners to be included in the middle income groups.* But this does not mean that the problem of "income-based" poverty of pensioners is fully eliminated.

Unemployed pensioners are at risk of poverty even after pension indexation.[12] It has been proven that given the high cost of living, including expensive medicines, solitary unemployed pensioners lacking any support are most at risk of poverty in metropolitan cities.[13]

Unemployment in metropolitan cities, like in Russia as a whole[14], is more frequently associated with low incomes, i.e. it is more common among representatives of low-resource groups: low-income and lower middle income groups. The presence of an unemployed person of working age in the family is a frequent cause of poverty. But the role of unemployment in the formation of different income groups in such large cities is currently very small. This is due the fact that *in Russian metropolitan cities the unemployment level has been very low over the past several years.* According to Fig. 20.2, the last significant surge in unemployment (under the MOT methodology) in Moscow and St. Petersburg was recorded during the 2009 economic crisis. In 2016, the unemployment level (average annual) was only 1.8% in Moscow, only 1.6% in St. Petersburg, and 5.5% in the Russian Federation as a whole. The level of registered unemployment (measured as the relation of the registered unemployed to the labor force) in metropolitan cities has not recently exceeded 0.6%.

In 2017, we have seen further reduction in the number of unemployed in metropolitan cities, which is further convincing proof of greater employment opportunities in large communities. In mid-2017, the level of registered employment both in Moscow and St. Petersburg fell to 0.4% of the labor force. The most important condition for reducing unemployment and optimizing employment in Russian cities is renewed economic growth, which promoted the recovery of jobs whose number had reduced during the economic crisis and the creation of new ones. The extremely low unemployment level in metropolitan cities was another serious factor improving the positions of women and migrants with specialty in-demand skills. As for unskilled labor migration, its relationship with unemployment is rather specific and small due to the establishment in metropolitan and other large cities of separate labor markets for migrants whose salaries are lower than the average salaries in the respective cities.[16]

According to Table 20.5, *the residents of metropolitan cities having greater employment opportunities have a lower level of fear of losing their job and a higher level of certainty than the residents of other cities of the fact that in case of dismissal they will be able to find a new job that will be no worse than their current one.* But in Moscow, employment problems are the main fear of high-income citizens, whereas in other cities this is the case for low-income groups. It is also obvious that Moscow

[12] *Yu.P. Lezhnina.* Salary in Russia: Evolution and Differentiation/Ed. by V.E. Gimpelson, R.I. Kapelyushnikov.—Moscow. Ves Mir, 2014. Pp. 115–116.

[13] *N.E. Tikhonova.* Phenomenon of Urban Poverty in Modern Russia.—Moscow: Letny Sad, 2003. Pp. 83–84.

[14] See Chap. 2.

[16] *A.A. Sobolevskaya. A.K. Popov.* Post-Industrial Revolution in the Labor Sphere.—Moscow: Institute of World Economy and International Relations (IMEMO), 2009, pp. 170–172.

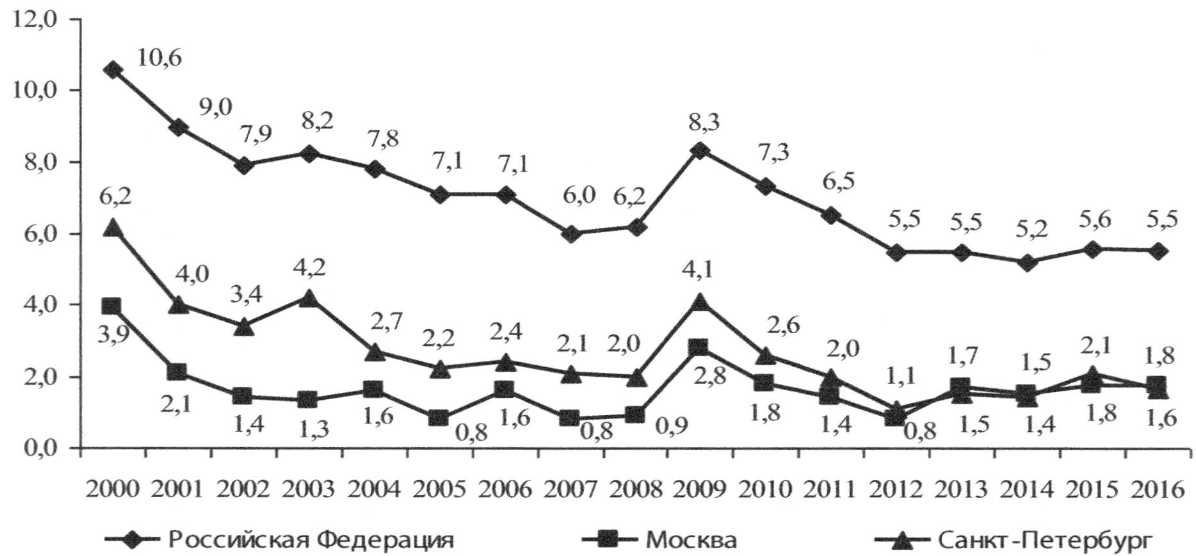

Fig. 20.2 Unemployment level of the population of metropolitan cities and the Russian Federation as a whole, RFSSS, 2000–2016, %[15]

[15] Russian Federal State Statistics Service. Unemployment level of the population by subject of the Russian Federation, average by year. URL: https://www.gks.ru/wps/wcm/connect/rosstat_main/rosstat/ru/statistics/wages/labour_force/# (accessed on: August 8, 2017).

Table 20.5 Attitude to several aspects of employment in metropolitan and other cities, 2006, % of employed by group

Income group	Concern over possible job loss						Certainty of employment opportunities in case of job loss					
	Moscow		Cities with population over 1 million		Cities with population under 1 million		Moscow		Cities with population over 1 million		Cities with population under 1 million	
	Concerned	Not concerned	Concerned	Not concerned	Concerned	Not concerned	Certain	Uncertain	Certain	Uncertain	Certain	Uncertain
High-income groups	59.3	28.0	57.1	32.7	60.1	26.7	43.3	38.3	43.6	36.6	43.1	40.3
Upper middle income groups	55.8	33.0	54.8	28.7	62.4	22.2	44.5	36.4	42.0	36.4	36.3	43.1
Lower middle income groups	53.4	31.3	62.6	22.8	63.8	21.3	60.7	28.6	35.2	40.4	35.2	41.4
Low-income groups	50.1	35.2	58.6	26.8	69.0	17.4	54.5	18.2	44.9	31.6	34.6	40.8

residents from the high-income and upper middle income groups are less certain of the opportunity for successful employment if they lose their job than residents from lower middle income and low-income groups. This is largely explained by the fact that according to research the most sought-after specializations include those that do not require a high level of professional education[17] and, consequently, a high salary.

In metropolitan cities, the level of job satisfaction of employees from the middle income groups is practically the same as in other cities. Thus, at the end of 2016 in Moscow and other million-population cities, 66.1% of employees in the middle income groups were fully or mostly satisfied with their job while 11.0% of them were mostly unsatisfied or completely unsatisfied; among employees belonging to the upper middle income groups, the share of those who are more or less satisfied with their job reached 70.1% while the share of those who are unsatisfied was 11.5%. The most frequent reason for non-satisfaction with one's job is low salary, which is typical of people of all income groups, but to a greater extent for the less affluent and to a lesser extent for the more affluent.

At the same time, in metropolitan cities with their extensive labor markets, employees more frequently desire or are tempted to find a new, more respectable or better paying job. The larger the city is, the more there are of those who wish to find such a job. At the end of 2016, in Moscow their share was 20.1% of employees in the lower middle income groups, and 17.9% of employees in the upper middle income groups (in cities with a population under 1 million people, 15.2 and 15.7% respectively). However, not everyone wishing to find a new job takes real steps to get one. It is also typical that those from the middle income groups wishing to change jobs will take active measures to find a new job much less often than those from the low-income and high-income groups.

The residents of metropolitan cities barely differ from the residents of other cities by the level of satisfaction with their lives. The only exception is Moscow residents, who demonstrate an increased level of positive attitudes. *In all types of cities, the level of satisfaction with one's life generally increases along with the respondents' increased income, while the representatives of the largest middle income groups take an intermediate position according to this indicator.* At the end of 2016 in Moscow, the share of persons who were fully or mostly satisfied with their life in general was 53.1% of respondents in the lower middle income groups, and 55.1% of respondents in the upper middle income groups. In other million-population cities, these figures were 44.2 and 54.3%, respectively, and in cities with a population under 1 million people they were 48.3 and 58.0%, respectively.

A high level of residents' satisfaction with their lives in general was recorded amid increased discontent of city residents with their financial position during the financial crisis. In the Russian capital, the share of people who are not very satisfied or completely unsatisfied with the financial aspect of their lives was 61.2% of the respondents in the lower middle income groups, and 63.3% of the respondents in the upper middle income groups. In other million-population cities, these figures were

---

[17] The Hired Worker in Modern Russia / Edited by Z.T. Golenkova. – Moscow: Novy Khronograf, 2015, p. 112.

70.0% and 51.3%, respectively, while in other cities they were 62.4% and 50.9%. However, in general the residents of metropolitan cities assess their financial position as better than people living in other cities, and therefore, according to the conducted surveys, they are less concerned about the problem of financial well-being and more frequently pay attention to other pressing issues.[18]

At the end of 2016, about half of the respondents of all income groups pointed out the fact that for the last year the financial position of their families had not changed, and over one-third stated that they were living slightly or considerably worse. The population that suffered a considerable, if not the principal, part of the negative implications of the economic crisis had great financial difficulties. The number of Russians who believe they and their families had greatly suffered from the economic crisis increased. The respondents assessed the prospects for their lives very conservatively. Only one in five respondents believed that after 12 months they and their families would live better than today. Two-thirds of the residents of metropolitan and other cities were concerned that they would not be able to provide for themselves and their families during the next year. The representatives of wealthier groups thought that the 2014–2016 crisis hit them much harder than the 2008–2009 crisis, while many citizens from low-income groups expressed concerns that the quality and level of their families' lives would never be the same as during the period of the so-called recovery economic growth in the early 2000s.

The assessments by residents of metropolitan cities of their consumer opportunities look rather contradictory, but only at first glance. Opportunities to improve housing conditions by buying a room, apartment or house as well as making such large purchases as a car, country home, furniture, etc. are assessed by the residents of metropolitan cities approximately in the same way as the residents of other cities (Table 20.6). Of the residents of metropolitan cities representing the upper middle income groups, 8.1 and 25.5% of the respondents assessed these opportunities as positive, while for the representatives of the lower middle income groups these figures were only 5.8 and 13.3%, respectively. It is also noteworthy that among the residents of ordinary cities representing all income groups there are many more people than in metropolitan cities who believe they can pay for their children's tuition at a university or for additional classes, e.g. at a music school, foreign language courses, sports teams, etc. In the cities with a population under 1 million, the share of respondents who can pay for their children's tuition at universities among the upper middle income groups is 51.3% and among the lower middle income groups it is 35.8%. In metropolitan cities, this share is 37.3 and 20.6%, respectively. *The paradox of the assessments is due to the fact that relatively low salaries in small cities, when compared to metropolitan cities, are offset by cheaper goods and services.* However, when it comes to things that are costly to everyone, such as a family vacation abroad, the greater financial opportunities of the residents of metropolitan cities become more obvious.

---

[18] Russian Society and the Challenges of Today. Book Two/M.K. Gorshkov [et al.]; edited by Gorshkov, M. K.; Petukhov, V.V. – Moscow: Ves Mir Publishing Company, 2015, p. 89.

Table 20.6 Assessment of the ability to buy costly goods and services, 2016, %

Able to buy if want to	Moscow and other cities with 1+ million population				Cities with population under 1 million			
	High-income groups	Upper middle income groups	Lower middle income groups	Low-income groups	High-income groups	Upper middle income groups	Lower middle income groups	Low-income groups
Improve their housing conditions	16.2	8.1	5.8	4.7	16.1	12.2	5.3	4.5
Pay for children's extracurricular activities[a]	73.5	70.2	52.5	48.9	81.8	78.1	71.0	56.3
Save up for large purchases	43.2	25.5	13.3	8.5	41.9	29.0	12.5	6.5
Take the whole family on vacation abroad	49.9	27.2	10.3	6.4	42.6	23.9	7.2	2.7
Take the whole family on vacation to a Russian resort	60.1	40.9	23.5	14.7	54.2	42.9	24.3	10.9
Pay for child's college tuition[a]	52.6	37.3	20.6	17.2	63.5	51.3	35.8	19.3

[a]Data provided by those with children of the relevant age

During the 2014–2016 economic crisis, the approaches developed by the urban population to the expenses during the previous crisis were generally maintained. After realizing the long-term and deep character of the last crisis, people began spending their money more wisely. The most popular strategy for rural families to adjust to economic shocks was saving on the consumption of goods and services. Even the high-income groups and especially the upper middle income groups had to seriously economize. However, representatives of the middle income and low-income groups found themselves in the most vulnerable position.

The increasing difficulties of everyday life during the crisis led many city residents to not only start buying less but also taking better care of what they already have. Poor and low-income families started postponing improvements to their property and purchases of durable goods they lacked until better times. In addition, efficient consumer behavior allowed many families to increase their financial security through various items of domestic and cultural use in spite of the general reduction of their true income and standard of living.

But since the beginning of 2017, along with the crisis recovery, Russians' income started to slowly grow, including in real terms. According to experts, the most powerful and promising post-crisis shift was formed in the regions that had already possessed or managed to establish before the start of the economic crisis a framework of more or less modernized industries as well as viable regional development institutions.[19] No wonder that metropolitan cities hold the leading positions among such regions.

Let us conclude the analysis with a summary.

The middle income groups in the Russian metropolitan cities make up the largest but non-homogeneous groups of the population. In Moscow the upper middle income groups predominate, but in other million-population cities the lower middle income groups have greater representation. The representatives of middle income groups differ from other income groups by their higher age and by the fact that they encompass less young people and more senior citizens. The presence of a pension is likely to ensure inclusion of the residents of metropolitan cities into the lower middle income groups while the presence of a pension and any supplemental income helps move them to the upper middle income or high-income groups.

When compared with other Russian cities, metropolitan cities differ by a higher income inequality level that is based on the inter-industry and intra-industry differentiation in terms of wages. While pensions and to a lesser extent other government payments ensure a middle income standard of living for Russian citizens, thus mitigating inequality, a salary is regarded as the most significant differentiating factor.

The basis of the professional structure of middle income groups in metropolitan cities is represented by high-skilled and mid-skilled specialists. A high level of education and professional qualification as well as extensive work experience in extremely low unemployment conditions ensures their stable position in the labor market. At the same time, despite a high level of satisfaction with their jobs in general and its

---

[19] *E. Bezhin, A. Ivanter, O. Inozemtseva, V. Kozlov, D. Tolmachov.* Post-Crisis Puzzle // Expert. 2016. Issue 25, pp. 40–47.

aspects in particular, many employees from the middle income groups try to use the obvious advantages of this position and extensive opportunities of the labor market in metropolitan cities to search for a new job with a higher salary and better labor conditions. This is partially due to the fact that the professional potential of the representatives of the middle income groups is frequently unwanted or is used in an inefficient way, which is related to the lacking number of high-tech and well-paid jobs allowing employees to fully demonstrate their capabilities.

During the 2014–2016 economic crisis, most people in the middle income groups living in metropolitan cities and in other cities had to save money and considerably reduce consumption. Their crisis-related concerns were expressed in a fear of deteriorating personal and family life prospects and being unable to provide for themselves in the near future. However, along with the crisis recovery the signs of reduced anxiety and growing consumer activity among the middle income groups have become more and more obvious, which is especially clearly seen in the largest cities.

Bibliography

Adler N, Stewart J (2007) The MacArthur scale of subjective social status. [Web resource]. The MacArthur Research Network on Socioeconomic Status and Health. https://www.macses.ucsf.edu/research/psychosocial/subjective.php. Accessed 22 Apr 2017

Aleshina MV (2013) Social cohesion: the conceptualization of the notion and the social and cultural realia. A monograph. Variant OJSC Publishers, Moscow

Analitika P (2014) Civic activism: the new social and political actors. Publication date—June 25. https://www.politanalitika.ru/doklad/grazhdanskiy_aktivizm_novye_subekty_obshchestvenno_politicheskogo_deystviya/. Accessed 04 May 2017

Anikin VA, Tikhonova NE (2016) Poverty and inequality in the BRICS nations: the specific case of Russia. Soc Econ 1:78–114

Anikin VA (2013) Motivation to work in Russia: the case of protracted transition from non-competitive to competitive system. J Compar Econ Stud 8:35–60

Atkinson A, Brandolini A (2013) On the identification of the middle class. In: Gornick J, Jäntti M (eds) Income inequality: economic disparities and the middle class in affluent countries. Stanford University Press, Stanford, CA, pp 77–100

Avraamova EM, Maleva TM (2014) The evolution of the Russian middle class: missions and methodology. Soc Sci Contemp Age 4:5–17

Avraamova EM (2008) The middle class in the Putin Era. Soc Sci Contemp Age (1)

Barro R (2000) Inequality and growth in a panel of countries. J Econ Growth 5:5–32; Easterly W (2001) The middle class consensus and economic development. J Econ Growth 6(4):317–335

Baudrillard J (2011) The consumer society: myths and structures (Published in association with Theory, Culture & Society). Nanjing University Press, Translated by Liu Chengfu & Quan Zhigang

Becker GS (1993) Nobel lecture: the economic way of looking at behavior. J Polit Econ 101(3):385–409

Becker GS (1987) A treatise on the family. Huaxia Publishing House, Translated by Peng Songjian

Belanovsky SA, Dmitriev ME, Misikhina SG (2010) Middle class in a rent-oriented economy: why did moscow stop being Russia?—SPERO, Issue 13, fall-winter, pp 69–86

Belyaeva LA (2007) And again on the Russian middle class. Sociol Res (5)

Besstremiannaia GE, Burdiak AI, Zaborovskaia AS et al (2005) Author team led by. Ovcharova TN Income and social services: inequality, vulnerability, poverty.; independent institute for social policy. M: Higher School of Economics National Research University Publishing House

Bezhin A, Ivanter O, Inozemtseva V, Kozlov D, Tolmachov D (2016) Post-Crisis Puzzle. Expert. Issue 25:40–47

Birdsall N, Graham C, Pettinato S (2000) Stuck in tunnel: is globalization muddling the middle? Center on Social and Economic Dynamics Working Paper, vol.1; Cárdenas M, Kharas H, Henao C (2011)

Bourdieu P (2001) Forms of capital. In: Granovetter M, Swedberg R (eds) The Sociol Econ Life 2nd edn. Westview Press, Boulder

Bourdieu P (2015) La distinction: Critique Sociale du Jugement (Le Sens Commun). The Commercial Press, Translated by Liu Hui

Breen R, Jonsson JO (2005) Inequality of opportunity in comparative perspective: recent research on educational attainment and social mobility. Ann Rev Sociol V:223–243

Cao J, Tai L (2015) Measurement of demographic distribution and change of the middle income group in China in a consumption perspective. J Guangdong Univ Bus Stud (6)

Chernikova SA, Cherdantsev VP, Vshivkova GA (2015) Contemporary issues of social security. Fundam Stud (11) (Part 4)

Dai H, Lu H (2001) Consumption culture and consumption revolution. Sociol Study (5)

Danilova EN, Yadov VA, Pan D (eds) (2012) Petersburg and Shanghai at the beginning of the 21th century. Moscow Logos

Decree No. 497 of the Government of the Russian Federation on the Federal Targeted Education Program for 2016–2000 (2015). Dated May 23. https://dokipedia.ru/document/5221854. Accessed 9 Apr 2017

Didenko DV, Dorofeeva ZE (2016) Additional professional education in Russia: the dynamics of scale and economic efficiency (2000–2013). Mir Rossii 4:87–110

DiNardo JE, Pischke J-S (1997) The returns to computer use revisited: have pencils changed the wage structure too? Q J Econ 112(1):291–303

Enterprises Satisfied with Capacities and Sales (2016). Expert, Issue 42

Federal Law «On Education in the Russian Federation» No 273-FZ. 2012. Dated Dec 29. https://www.consultant.ru/document/cons_doc_LAW_140174/. Accessed 04 Apr 2017

Forrier A, Sels L (2003) Temporary employment and employability: training opportunities and efforts of temporary and permanent employees in Belgium. Work Employ Soc 17(4):641–666

Gao Y (2013) Why the downward moving of social status and strata—also on the transformation of the social status and strata identification basis. Chinese J Sociol (4)

General Urban Investigation Group of National Bureau of Statistics (2005) Between RBM 60 Thousand and RMB 50 Thousand: An Exploration of Urban Middle Income Group in China. Data, No 6

Giesecke J, Groß M (2003) Temporary employment: chance or risk? Eur Sociol Rev 19(2):161–177

Gill I, Kharas H (2007) An East Asian Renaissance: Ideas for Economic Growth. World Bank, Washington, DC

Gimpelson VE, Kapelyushnikov RI (2007) Wages in Russia: evolution and differentiation. Publishing House of the State University—Higher School of Economics, Moscow

Gimpelson VE, Kapelyushnikov RI (eds) (2001) Russian employee: education, profession. Publishing House of the Higher School of Economics, Qualification. Moscow

Gofman E (2017) Stigma: notes on the management of spoiled identity. Part 1. Stigma and social identity. [Web resource]. Federal Education Portal. Economics. Sociology. Management. https://ecsocman.hse.ru/text/17687311/. Accessed 22 Apr 2017

Goldthorpe J, Rent H (2000) Class conflict, and class structure: a commentary on Sorensen. Am J Sociol 105(6):1572–1582

Goldthorpe J, Lockwood D (1971) The affluent worker: political attitudes and behaviour. Cambridge University Press, Cambridge

Golenkova ZT (ed) (2015) The hired worker in modern Russia. Novy Khronograf, Moscow

Gorshkov MK, Sheregi FE (2010) The modernization of Russian education: issues and prospects. TsSPiM [Center of Social Forecasting and Marketing], Moscow
Gorshkov MK, Klyucharev GA (2011) Life-Long education in the modernization context. IS RAS, Federal State Research Institution "Center for Social Research", Moscow
Gorshkov MK, Tikhonova NE (eds) (2016) Middle class in modern Russia. Summary of many years' worth of Research. Ves Mir, Moscow
Gorshkov MK et al (2015) Russian society and the challenges of today. In: Gorshkov MK, Petukhov VV (eds) Book two. Ves Mir Publishing Company, Moscow
Gorshkov MK et al (2016) Russian society and the challenges of the time. In: Gorshkov MK, Tikhonova NEM (eds) Book three. Ves Mir
Gorshkov MK, Krumm R, Tikhonova NE (eds) (2009) Alpha-M, Moscow
Gorshkov MK, Krumm R, Tikhonova NE (eds) (2010) Is Russian society ready for modernization? Ves Mir, Moscow
Grabka M, Frick J (2008) The Shrinking German middle class—signs of long-term polarization in disposable income? DIW Berlin Weekly Rep 4(4):21–27
Gurko TA (2011) Institute of family in post-industrial societies. Values Mean 4(13):26–44
Huntington SP, Jorge ID (1996) Political development. Included in hand book of political science (vol II). In: Fred IG, Nelson WP (ed) Translated by Chu Fuyun. The Commercial Press
Huntington S (1989) Political order in chaning societies. Huaxia Publishing House
Ibragimova DK, Akindinova NV, Aukutsionek SP, Bataeva AE (2004) The formation of unemployment expectations and their influence on the economic behavior of the population. In: Social policy: the realities of the 21st century. collection of works by winners of the fourth grant competition. Independent Institute for Social Policy, Moscow
Jenkins SP, Van Kerm P (2009) The measurement of economic inequality. In: Wiermer S, Brian N, Timothy S (eds) The Oxford handbook on economic inequality. Oxford University Press, Oxford
Ji H, Chen Y (2009) Weight and the measurement study of the change of the middle income group. Econ Perspect (6)
Kabashima I (1989) 1989. The Economic Daily Press, Political Participation. Translated by Xie Lili
Kapelyushnikov R, Gimpelson V (2017) Professional structure in the russian labor market. Chief editor: NT Vishnevskaya. Publishing House of National Research University Higher School of Economics
Kapelyushnikov RI (2001) Russian labor market: adaptation without restructuring—M: Higher School of Economics National Research University
Karavai AV (2016) Human capital of Russian workers: condition and factors. Inst Sociol Bull 17:91–112
Kartseva LV (2003) Family model during the transformation of Russian society. Sociol Stud 7:92–100
Kharas H (2010) Latin America's global middle class. Working Paper, Global Economy and Development at Brookings, Washington, DC
Kilpatrick F, Cantril H (1960) Self-anchoring scaling: a measure of individuals' unique reality worlds. J Ind Psychol 16(2):158–173
Kivinen M (2004) Middle class in modern Russia. World of Russia. Sociology. Ethnology 4:143–169
Konstantinovsky DL, Voznesenskaya ED, Cherednichenko GA, Khokhlushkina FA (2011) The education and lifestyle paths of the youth: 1998–2008. TsSPiM [Center of Social Forecasting and Marketing], Moscow
Korotaev A, Vaskin I, Bilyuga S (2017) The Olson—Huntington Hypothesis on the Bell-Shaped Relation between the Economic Development Level and Social and Political Destabilization: Quantitative Analysis Study.] Sociol Rev 16(1):9–49
Kuznetsov VN (2008) Social security. In: Osipov GV, Moskvichev LN (eds) Sociological dictionary. Norma, Moscow, p 48
Latov YV (ed) (2014) Lifelong education as a stimulus for personal development and social and economic inequality factor. TsSPiM [Center of Social Forecasting and Marketing], Moscow

Latova NV (2016) Russians' satisfaction with their life during a crisis: 2015 as the Year of Bifurcation. In: Public Opinion Monitoring: Economic and Social Changes. Issue 3

Lehmann H, Zaiceva A (2015) Redefining informality and measuring its determinants: evidence from the Russian labour market. J Int Dev 27:464–488

Lezhnina YP (2008) Social inequality and social mobility. Social inequality and social policy in modern Russia. Nauka, Moscow

Lezhnina YP (2014) Socio-demographic factors of poverty in modern Russia. In: Gorshkov MK, Tikhonova NE (eds) Poverty and the poor in the modern Russia. Ves Mir, Moscow

Lezhnina YP (2016) Family institution in Russia: on the path of transformation. Sociol Sci Soc Pract (2):70–90

Li C (2003) The construction and ratio of current middle class in China. Chinese J Popul Sci (6)

Li C (2011) Consumption level and consumption method of the middle class. Soc Sci Guangdong (4)

Li C (2014) Education experience and inequality of opportunity for post-80s in China–also comment on Quiet Revolution (Wusheng De Geming, Liang Chen et al). Soc Sci China (4)

Li C (2014) The trending of education inequality 1940–2010—Re-investigation on urban-rural inequality of education opportunities. Sociol Stud (2)

Li L, Guangsu Z (2015) Household loan restrictions. Public Education Expenditures and Social Mobility, China Economic Quarterly, No, p 1

Li L, Zhu B (2015) Current intergenerational mobility and changes in China. Soc Sci China (5)

Li P, Zhang Y (2008) The scale, identification and social attitude of the middle class in China. Society (2)

Li P, Zhang Y (2011) Stratification of consumption: another perspective to initiate economy. Soc Sci China (2)

Li P (2005) Social conflict and class consciousness: a study of current social contradictions in China. Society, No, p 1

Li P (2015) The expansion of middle class and an olive-shaped society. Int Econ Rev (1)

Li T, Ren Y (2011) Reform of Urban Hukou and social integration of floating population. South China Popul (3)

Li W, Wang S (2014) Influence on the weight of the middle income people from the income increment and the income distribution. Stat Res (3)

Li Z, Qiu Z (2016) How will the household background affect children's academic achievement?—Analysis of diversified influence discrepancy from the social and economic status of household in the compulsory education stage. Sociol Stud (4)

Lindemann K (2007) The impact of objective characteristics on subjective social position. Trames 11:54–68. https://www.kirj.ee/public/trames/trames-2007-1-4.pdf. Accessed 04Apr 2017

Liu J, Hu Y (2014) Intergenerational transmission of residents' income based on household wealth and capital. Zhejiang Finan (9)

Liu J (2005) The state, social class and education: sociological study of educational attainment. China Renmin University Press

Liu X (2002) The relative sense of deprivation and the recognition of the strata. Sociol Study (1)

Liu X (2007) The urban strata and the positioning of middle class in China. Sociol Study (6)

Liu Z, Fan Y (2013) Analysis of influencing factors on educational generational mobility. J Educ Sci (1)

Long Y (2012) Dynamic evolution of the scale of the middle income group and the polarization of the income: statistic description and measurement. Financ Trade Res (2)

Long Y (2015) Factor analysis of the weight change of the middle income group—based on the empirical proof of income bipolarization index. Stat Res (2)

López-Calva L, Ortiz-Juarez E (2014) The emerging middle class in developing countries. OECD Development Centre Working Paper, vol 285

Luis FL-C, Eduardo O-J (2014) A vulnerability approach to the definition of the middle class. J Econ Inequal 12(1):23-47. Springer

Lukyanova AL (2010) Return on education: meta-analysis results. High School Econ Econ Mag 14(3)
Magun VS, Monusova GA (2010) Russian labor values within the context of international comparisons. In: Report at the 11th international scientific conference on economic and social development problems. Moscow. Higher School of Economics National Research University.
Maleva TM (ed) (2003) Middle classes in Russia: economic and social strategies. Gandalf Publishers, Moscow
Milanovic B, Yitzhaki S (2002) Decomposing world income distribution: Does the world have a middle class? Review of income and wealth vol. 48 (2), pp 155–178; Kharas H 2010.
Mills C (2002) White collar: the American middle classes. Oxford University Press
Mitrikas A (2004) A. Family as a value: current status and future possibility of value choice in European countries. Sociol Stud 5:65–72
Mozgovaya AV, Shlykova EV (2016) Sociol Ser 16(4)
Nie NH, Sidney V (1996) Participation and political equality. In: Included in hand book of political science (vol II). Fred IG, Nelson WP (eds.) Translated by Chu Fuyun. The Commercial Press
Nikovskaya L, Yakimets V (2015) Shaping and protecting public interests in Russia: from the "Administrative" model to the partnership model. Polit Stud 5:49–64
Peng G, Eunni RV (2011) Computer skills, non-routine tasks, and wage premium: a longitudinal study. J Strateg Inf Syst 20(4):449–460
Petrakov NY (eds) (2011) The modernization of Russia: social and humanitarian aspects. Nestor-Istoriya, St Petersburg , Moscow
Petukhov V, Petukhov R (2015) The democracy of participation: institutional crisis and new prospects. Polit Stud 5:25–49
Pew Research Center (2015a) Are you in the global middle class? https://www.pewresearch.org/fact-tank/2015/07/16/are-you-in-the-global-middle-class-find-out-with-our-income-calculator/
Pew Research Center (2015b) China's middle class surges, while India's lags behind. https://www.pewresearch.org/fact-tank/2015/07/15/china-india-middle-class/
Pew Research Center (2015c). The emerging middle class in developing countries. OECD Development Centre Working Paper, vol 285
Qin G (2011) Intergenerational mobility and discrimination against out-group: an empirical study based on statistics from Chinese general social survey 2005. Chinese J Sociol (4)
Ravallion M (2010) The developing world's bulging (but vulnerable) middle class. World development, vol 38(4), 445–454; Ravallion M, Chen S, Sangraula P (2009) Dollar a day revisited. World Bank Economic Review, vol 23, pp 163–184
Rimskii VL (2013) The market rationality and social arrangement. In: Patrushev SV (ed) The civic and the political in Russian social practices. Russian Political Encyclopedia (ROSSPEN), Moscow
Rose S (2016) The growing size and incomes of the upper middle class. Urban institute. Research report June 2016. https://www.urban.org/sites/default/files/alfresco/publication-pdfs/2000819-The-Growing-Size-and-Incomes-of-the-Upper-Middle-Class.pdf
Russia Economic Report (2014) World Bank. Russian Office. March, Issue 31
Russia in figures (2016) Statistics overview. Federal State Statistics Service. Moscow, 144–148. https://www.gks.ru/free_doc/doc_2016/rusfig/rus16.pdf. Accessed 20 Mar 2017
Russia Longitudinal Monitoring survey (2017) RLMS-HSE», conducted by National Research University "Higher School of Economics" and OOO "Demoscope" together with Carolina Population Center, University of North Carolina at Chapel Hill and the Institute of Sociology RAS. (RLMS-HSE websites: https://www.hse.ru/rlms, https://www.cpc.unc.edu/projects/rlms)
Russian Federal State Statistics Service, Gini (Income Concentration). https://cbsd.gks.ru/. Accessed 17 Mar 2017
Russian Federal State Statistics Service (2017) Distribution of the general volume of the money income and characteristics of the differentiation of the money income of the population. https://www.gks.ru/free_doc/new_site/population/bednost/tabl/1-2-2.doc. Accessed 25 Mar 2017

Russian Federal State Statistics Service (2017) Assessment of the number of permanent residents as of 1 Jan 2017 and for 2016 on average. https://www.gks.ru/wps/wcm/connect/rosstat_main/rosstat/ru/statistics/population/demography/. Accessed 24 Aug 2017
Russian Federal State Statistics Service (2017) Average monthly nominal salary of employees according to a full range of organizations by subjects of the Russian Federation in 2013–2017. https://www.gks.ru/wps/wcm/connect/rosstat_main/rosstat/ru/statistics/wages/. Accessed 10 Aug 2017
Russian Federal State Statistics Service (2017) Average yearly number of employed in the public and private sectors of the economy in Moscow. https://moscow.gks.ru/wps/wcm/connect/rosstat_ts/moscow/ru/statistics/employment/. Accessed 11 Aug 2017
Russian Federal State Statistics Service (2017) Unemployment level of the population by subject of the Russian Federation, average by year. https://www.gks.ru/wps/wcm/connect/rosstat_main/rosstat/ru/statistics/wages/labour_force/#. Accessed 8 Aug 2017
Russian Public Opinion Research Center (VCIOM) (2017) Consumer opportunities of Russians: monitoring. Press Edition No 3407. https://wciom.ru/index.php?id=236&uid=116289. Accessed 20 Aug 2017
Sabirianova Z (2002) The great human capital reallocation: a study of occupational mobility in transitional Russia. J Comp Econ 30:191–217
Samygin SI, Vereshchagina AV, Pechkurov IV (2016) Moscow. Ru-Science
Sedova N (2016) Russians' life goals and strategies in the passion-driven context. Sociol J 2:73–91
Semin I (2017) Labor productivity. Nat Prior Expert (34)
Sobolevskaya AA, Popov AK (2009) Post-Industrial revolution in the labor sphere. Moscow: Institute of World Economy and International Relations (IMEMO)
Solimano A (2008) The middle class and the development process: international evidence. Santiago, Chile: Economic Commission for Latin America and the Caribbean. Mimeographed document
Student-2017 (2017) Eagerness to learn and career prospects VCIOM press-release No 3292. https://wciom.ru/index.php?id=236&uid=116041. Accessed 02 Apr 2017
Tang J (2015) Underprivileged starting line of life—re-discussion of educational inequality in Chinese society. Sociol Stud (3)
The Facets of Russian Education (2015) Center for Social Research, Moscow
Tikhonova NE, Anikin VA (2014) Poverty in Russia compared to other countries. World Russia: Sociol Ethnol 23(4):59–95
Tikhonova NE (2003) Phenomenon of urban poverty in modern Russia. Letny Sad, Moscow
Tikhonova NE (2014) Russia's social structure: theories and reality—Moscow. Institute of Sociology RAS, Novy Khronograf, Moscow
Tikhonova NE (2015) Overt and covert consequences of economic crises for Russians. Sociol Res 12:16–27
Tikhonova NE (2017) Income stratification in Russia as compared to other nations. Soc Sci Contemp Age 3:26–41
Tikhonova NE (2017) Income stratification in Russia: specific features of the model and direction of changes. Soc Sci Contemp Age (2)
Tikhonova NE, Mareeva SV (2009) Middle Classes in Modern Russia. Alfa-M, Moscow
Turner J (1982) Towards a cognitive redefinition of the social group. Cambridge University Press, Social identity and intergroup relations
UNU-WIDER (2017) World income inequality database (WIID3.4). https://www.wider.unu.edu/database/world-income-inequality-database-wiid34 (дата обращения: 25.03.2017 г)
Vakis R, Jamele R, Lucchetti L (2015) Overview: left behind: chronic poverty in Latin America and the Caribbean. Washington, DC: World Bank. License: Creative Commons Attribution CC BY 3.0 и др)
Varlamova SN, Noskova AV, Sedova NN (2006) The place of family and children among Russians' life goals. Sociol Stud 11:61–73
Veblen T (1964) The theory of the leisure class: an economic study of institutions. The Commercial Press, Translated by Cai Shoubai

Volkov D, Kolesnikov A (2016) Self-Organization of the civic society in Moscow. Motivations, opportunities, and extents of politicization. Carnegie Moscow Center.
Wallerstein I (2013) The modern world-system V. 1. Translated by Guo Fang et al The Modern World-System V 1
Wang M, Li Z (2012) Measure of income intergenerational mobility of residents in China—an analysis of the "the second generation" economic phenomenon. J Sun Yatsen Univ Soc Sci Edn (1)
Wang Y, Qian Z (2009) Literature review of measurement bias of income intergenerational flow. Product Res (21)
Wang Y, Xu Q, Xu J (2014) New measurement method and application of the population size of the middle income group. Stat Res (10)
We Y (2009) Study of intergenerational income flow and income inequality. China Financial & Economic Publishing House, Beijing
Wolfson MC (1994) When inequalities diverge. Am Econ Rev 84(2):353–358
World Bank & Development Research Center of the State Council (2013) China 2030: Building a modern. harmonious, and creative high-income society, PRC. China Financial & Economic Publishing House
World Bank (2007) Global economic prospects 2007: managing the next wave of globalization. World Bank, Washington, DC
World Bank (2016) World bank analytical classifications. https://datahelpdesk.worldbank.org/knowledgebase/articles/378834-how-does-the-world-bank-classify-countries
World Bank (2017) GINI index (World Bank estimate). https://data.worldbank.org/indicator/SI.POV.GINI?locations. Accessed 17 Mar 2017
World Bank (2014) Russia economic report. No 31; Meyer M, Sanchez-Paramo C, In focus: economic mobility and middle- class formation. In: Krizis doverija obostrjaet jekonomicheskie problemy Rossii [Confidence Crisis Exposes Economic Weakness]
World Bank (2015) Russia economic report. No 31; Pew Research Center. The American middle class is losing ground: no longer the majority and falling behind financially. Washington, DC: December. https://www.pewsocialtrends.org/files/2015/12/2015-12-09_middle-class_FINAL-report.pdf
World Bank. World Development Indicators. https://databank.worldbank.org/data/reports.aspx?source=world-development-indicators# (дата обращения 29.04.2017 г)
Wright EO (1997) Classes. Verso Book
Wu X (2007) Hukou and intergenerational occupation flow. Sociol Stud (6)
Wu X (2016) Current higher education in China, the formation of elite and the social stratification—primary finds of Beijing College Students Panel Survey (Bcsps). Chinese J Sociol (3)
Wu Y (2013) Education streaming system and education stratification in China. Sociol Stud (4)
Xin K (2016) Urban-rural discrepancy of intergenerational flow of education in China. J Southwest Univ Financ Econ
Xu J, Yi X (2014). Will the increase of public education expenditures mitigate influence from the "second generation" issue?—An analysis of intergenerational income mobility based on the China Health and Nutrition Survey, CHNS. J Financ Econ (11)
Yang Y, Lian Y (2015) A dynamic analysis of social intergenerational mobility in China—Empirical evidence from pooled cross-section data of CGSS (Chinese General Social Survey) and CLDS (China Labor-force Dynamics Survey). Manag World (4)
Yang Z (2016) Is the intergenerational mobility improved by expanded enrollment of higher education? Chinese J Sociol (6)
Yanitsky ON (2013) Social movements: theory, practice, prospects. Novy Khronograf, Moscow
Yastrebov GA (2016) Social mobility in Soviet and Post-Soviet Russia: new quantitative assessment based on the representative survey materials of 1994, 2002, 2006, and 2013. Part I. World of Russia: Sociology, Ethnology, vol 24, No 2, pp 6–36

Yastrebov GA (2016) Social mobility in soviet and Post-Soviet Russia: new quantitative assessment based on the representative survey materials of 1994, 2002, 2006, and 2013. Part I. World of Russia: Sociology, Ethnology, vol 24, No 1, pp 7–36
Yu X (2005) Reproduction of urban-rural dual structure—an analysis of the education policy between 1978 to the End of 1990s. Res Educ Dev (4)
Zhang G, Zhang D, Zhou W (2016) Effects of multi-generational mobility: an evidence from China. Chinese J Sociol (3)
Zhang Y (2004) The attainment of Chinese social status: class succession and intra-generational mobility. Sociol Stud (4)
Zhang Y (2016) Current consumption tendency for all social strata in China—from consumption for survival to consumption for self-cultivation. Sociol Stud (4)
Zhou X (2005) Survey of the Chinese middle classes. Social Sciences Academic Press
Zinchenko NI (2007) The social dimension of security in Russia. Sociol Stud 2:137–140

Polina M. Kozyreva Doctor of Sociology, is First Deputy Director of the Federal Center of Theoretical and Applied Sociology of the Russian Academy of Sciences (former Institute of Sociology, Russian Academy of Sciences). She also serves as Director of the Center for Longitudinal Studies at the Institute of Social Policy of the National Research University Higher School of Economics. She is the Editor-in-Chief of the journal "Sotsiologicheskiy Zhurnal". P. Kozyreva directs one of the largest longitudinal surveys in Russia—"The Russia Longitudinal Monitoring Survey of HSE" (RLMS-HSE), which has been conducted since 1994. Selected publications in English: Ethnicity and Trust: Evidence from Russia// American Political Science Review, 2005 (in co-authorship with D. Bahry, M. Kosolapov and R. Wilson); "Consumption and Lifestyle in Russia" in Handbook on Social Stratification in the BRIC Countries. Change and Perspective/ Editors: Peilin Li (Chinese Academy of Social Sciences, China), M.K. Gorshkov (Russian Academy of Sciences, Russia), Celi Scalon (Brazilian Sociological Society, Brazil), K.L. Sharma (Jaipur National University, India)// World Scientific Publishing Co. Pte. Ltd. 2013 (in co-authorship with A. Smirnov and A. Nizamova); Economic Change in Russia: Twenty Years of the Russian Longitudinal Monitoring Survey// Economics of Transition. 2015. Vol. 23. No. 2. (in co-authorship with Klara Sabirianova Peter); Data Resource Profile: The Russia Longitudinal Monitoring Survey—Higher School of Economics (RLMS-HSE) Phase II: Monitoring the Economic and Health Situation in Russia, 1994–2013// International Journal of Epidemiology. 2016. Vol. 45(2) (in co-authorship with Kosolapov M., Popkin B.)

Alexander I. Smirnov Doctor of Sociology, Senior Researcher at the Federal Center of Theoretical and Applied Sociology of the Russian Academy of Sciences (former Institute of Sociology, Russian Academy of Sciences). His major interests include political sociology, social factors of Russian society consolidation (including institutional changes in army, family, etc.), dynamics of socio-economic conditions of Russian population. His publications are wide range, for example, "Factors forming Trust in Russian Army"// Sociological Studies. 2009, Issue 2, "Labyrinths of Development of Democracy in Russia", 2007 (in co-authorship with Kozyreva P.), "Consumption and Lifestyle in Russia" in Handbook on Social Stratification in the BRIC Countries. Change and Perspective/ Editors: Peilin Li (Chinese Academy of Social Sciences, China), M.K. Gorshkov (Russian Academy of Sciences, Russia), Celi Scalon (Brazilian Sociological Society, Brazil), K.L. Sharma (Jaipur National University, India)// World Scientific Publishing Co. Pte. Ltd. 2013 (in co-authorship with P. Kozyreva and A. Nizamova).

Correction to: The Middle Income Group in China and Russia

Peilin Li and M. K. Gorshkov

Correction to:
P. Li and M. K. Gorshkov (eds.), *The Middle Income Group in China and Russia*, Research Series on the Chinese Dream and China's Development Path, https://doi.org/10.1007/978-981-16-1464-4

The original version of this book was revised. Affiliation of some chapter authors has been updated and author name of chapter 5 has been updated.

Affiliation "HSE University, Institute of Sociology of FCTAS RAS" has been corrected for below listed authors in the respective chapters:

V. A. Anikin
N. Tikhonova
A. V. Karavay
Svetlana V. Mareeva
Y. P. Lezhnina
P. M. Kozyreva

Affiliaiton "Institute of Sociology of FCTAS RAS" has been corrected for below listed authors in the respective chapters:

N. V. Latova
N. N. Sedova
A. I. Smirnov
Yu. V. Latov
V. V. Petukhov

The updated version of the book can be found at
https://doi.org/10.1007/978-981-16-1464-4
https://doi.org/10.1007/978-981-16-1464-4_5

P. Li and M. K. Gorshkov (eds.), *The Middle Income Group in China and Russia*,
Research Series on the Chinese Dream and China's Development Path,
https://doi.org/10.1007/978-981-16-1464-4_21

And author name of chapter 5 has been corrected: Correct chapter author for Chapter 5 has been changed as "Feng Tian" instead of authors "Peng Lu and Xiaoguang Fan".

This has now been amended throughout the book.

The manufacturer's authorised representative in the EU is Springer Nature Customer Service Centre GmbH, Europaplatz 3, 69115 Heidelberg, Germany. If you have any concerns regarding our products, please contact ProductSafety@springernature.com

Printed and bound by CPI Group (UK) Ltd, Croydon, CR0 4YY
30/09/2026
02225289-0011